Pathways from the Periphery

Written under the auspices of the
Center for International Affairs
Harvard University

A volume in the series

Cornell Studies in Political Economy

Edited by Peter J. Katzenstein

A full list of titles in the series appears at the end of the book

Pathways from the Periphery

THE POLITICS OF GROWTH IN THE NEWLY INDUSTRIALIZING COUNTRIES

STEPHAN HAGGARD

CORNELL UNIVERSITY PRESS

Ithaca and London

First published 1990 by Cornell University Press.
First printing, Cornell Paperbacks, 1990.
Fourth printing 1994.

International Standard Book Number (cloth) 0-8014-2499-2
International Standard Book Number (paper) 0-8014-9750-7
Library of Congress Catalog Card Number 90-32300
Printed in the United States of America
Librarians: Library of Congress cataloging information
appears on the last page of the book.

♾ The paper in this book meets the minimum requirements of the American National Standard for Information Sciences—Permanence of Paper for Printed Library Materials, ANSI Z39.48-1984.

For Nancy

It must be considered that there is nothing more difficult to carry out, nor more doubtful of success, nor more dangerous to handle, than to initiate a new order of things. For the reformer has enemies in all those who profit by the old order, and only lukewarm defenders in all those who would profit from the new order, this lukewarmness arising partly from fear of their adversaries, who have the laws in their favour; and partly from the incredulity of mankind, who do not truly believe in anything new until they have had actual experience of it. Thus it arises that on every opportunity for attacking the reformer, his opponents do so with the zeal of partisans, the others only defend him half-heartedly, so that between them he runs great danger.

—Niccolo Machiavelli, *The Prince*, trans. Luigi Ricci, chap. 6

Contents

vii

Acknowledgments

In writing this book, I have accumulated debts to different groups of people.

First, I thank my teachers at the University of California. Ernst Haas was my mentor at Berkeley; perhaps only Ernie's students can fully appreciate how well that term fits. Ernie contributed immensely to my intellectual development and has been a consistent supporter ever since. Others in the political science department, especially Vinod Aggarwal and John Zysman, contributed to my understanding of international and comparative political economy. Robert Price and Ken Jowitt taught me comparative politics, and I have returned on numerous occasions to their insights. My thanks also to Ben Ward and David Collier.

Second, I gratefully acknowledge the various institutions that helped me along the way. I received generous research support from the Brookings Institution, the Institute for the Study of World Politics, the University of California, Berkeley, the Tinker Foundation, and Harvard University. I am particularly indebted to Samuel Huntington and Susan Pharr. As the directors, respectively, of the Center for International Affairs and the U.S.-Japan Program at Harvard, they provided me with support and that most crucial and scarce academic commodity: time.

I have also benefited from working groups sponsored by the Social Science Research Council and the Lehrman Institute, and a collective research project on the political economy of debt funded by the Ford and Rockefeller foundations. Parts of this book have been presented at conferences or seminars sponsored by the Center for U.S.-Mexican Studies at the University of California, San Diego; the Program on Interdependent Political Economy, University of Chicago; the East Asian Institute, Columbia University; the Department of Political Science and the Center for Pacific Rim Studies, University of California, Los Angeles; Duke University; the Institute of International Studies, University of California, Berkeley; the East-West Center, Honolulu, Hawaii; the National University of Singapore; and the Australian National University, Canberra.

My understanding has been deepened by interviews with civil servants, academics, and journalists in Korea, Taiwan, Hong Kong, and Mexico and by visits to research institutes in Singapore and Brazil. These trips resulted in debts to people too numerous to list; some have preferred anonymity. Others who provided key information are named in footnotes. All are thanked for their willingness to entertain the naive questions of an outsider.

For a book of this sort, I have naturally had to depend on the scholarship of country specialists, though I have supplemented their analysis with research in primary sources and interviews. I have made a special effort to single out those scholars who have most influenced my interpretations.

My greatest debt is owed to colleagues who have been struggling with issues similar to those I raise here and who have read and commented on earlier papers and portions of this manuscript or have assisted me in other ways. Chung-in Moon, Tun-jen Cheng, and Robert Kaufman, with whom I have collaborated on several monographs, deserve special mention. Peter Evans and Peter Katzenstein read the entire manuscript and offered constructive criticisms. Roger Haydon edited the manuscript with his usual good judgment and kept me feeling appropriately guilty for missed deadlines.

I extend my deep appreciation to the following people who commented on portions of earlier papers or the final manuscript or who assisted me in my research in other ways: Emanuel Adler, Maria-Helena Alves, Don Babai, Kent Calder, Tom Callaghy, Deborah Cichon, David Cole, Beverly Crawford, Fred Deyo, Jorge Domínguez, Dennis Encarnation, Jeff Frieden, Barbara Geddes, Gary Gereffi, Tom Gold, David Glass, Merilee Grindle, Frances Hagopian, Jeff Hart, Miles Kahler, Robert Keohane, Young-whan Kihl, Byung-Kook Kim, Hagen Koo, David Lane, Kevin Lane, Chung Lee, Stephanie Lenway, Jamie Mackie, Sylvia Maxfield, Helen Milner, Doug Nelson, Joan Nelson, Greg Noble, John Odell, Chien-kuo Pang, Robert Putnam, Eric Ramstetter, John Ravenhill, Deborah Riner, Jeff Sachs, Chi Schive, Michael Shafer, Kathryn Sikkink, Barbara Stallings, Ray Vernon, Ezra Vogel, Robert Wade, Eliza Willis, Edwin Winckler, and Joe Yager. Maura Barry, Amy Englehardt, Tamara Fish, Marie Park, and Lucia Tsai provided first-rate research assistance.

Finally, my thanks go to Nancy Gilson, my wife and companion, to whom this book is dedicated.

STEPHAN HAGGARD

Cambridge, Massachusetts

Pathways from the Periphery

Introduction

The industrialization of the developing world in the postwar period has changed the international division of labor. But the international diffusion of industrial capabilities has been highly uneven. A small group of dynamic, newly industrializing countries (NICs) accounts for the lion's share of total Third World growth in industry and trade.

These countries fall into two broad groups. Several large countries have industrialized through strategies emphasizing self-reliance and import substitution. Brazil, Argentina, Mexico, and India are the most important representatives of this growth path. The East Asian NICs—South Korea, Taiwan, Hong Kong, and Singapore—constitute a second group. Korea and Taiwan promoted industrialization in the 1950s through import substitution; Singapore and Hong Kong were initially commercial entrepôts. Beginning with Hong Kong in the early 1950s, these four countries converged on a path to growth based on manufactured exports, the industrialization strategy known as export-led growth. This book examines the politics of industrialization in the NICs, paying particular attention to the differences between these two growth trajectories, one inward-looking, the other tied closely to world markets.

The newly industrializing countries occupy center stage in a number of controversies in development economics and international political economy. The emergence of new centers of economic power has created problems of political and economic adjustment for the advanced industrial states. The expansion of manufactured exports from the NICs generated protectionist pressures, and the heavy borrowing of large, Latin American debtors threatened the stability of the international financial system in the 1980s. Much of the literature on the NICs is about the international political and economic conflicts associated with their growth.

A second reason for interest in the NICs concerns their successes and failures. The growth of Japan, and then the "Gang of Four," triggered in Europe and the United States an anxious quest for the taproot of East Asia's rapid growth. For development economists, the East Asian NICs vindicated the liberal prescriptions of market-oriented policies and participation in the world economy. Their success in achieving rapid growth with a relatively egalitarian distribution of income made export-led growth a new development orthodoxy in the 1970s, a model that could be exported to other developing countries.

Mired in debt and saddled with staggering problems of poverty and inequality, the Latin American NICs, by contrast, exemplified the costs of the elusive quest for national autonomy through import substitution. Both Mexico and Brazil were once considered development miracles in their own right; now the Latin American NICs are more frequently treated as test cases of policy incoherence, inequality, and dependence.

Surprisingly, there are few cross-regional studies of the NICs. Comparative efforts to analyze the domestic political and institutional bases of alternative paths to industrialization are even rarer. One reason has to do with the dominance of two strands of theoretical thinking, analyzed in Chapter 1. Economists have focused their attention on the effects of policy on development but generally have not examined the determinants of particular policy choices; they treat politics as exogenous. Sociologists, political scientists, and historians working in the world-systems and dependency traditions, on the other hand, have viewed external constraints as determinative of national policies; the result is a similar neglect of domestic political forces and institutions.

A second reason for the paucity of comparative work is its difficulty. The comparison of whole countries over long periods of time raises daunting methodological problems. What can the development of Singapore, a city-state with a population of several millions, possibly have to tell us about a resource-rich, continental country such as Brazil? Compounding problems of comparability are problems of language and of conducting research in closed political systems. Unquestionable evidence for some claims is difficult to find, and some key historical questions, particularly those concerning the perceptions and ideas of decision makers, may never be answered.

If this reads like an apology, it is. No single approach struck me as wholly convincing in establishing the broad historical comparisons I wanted to make. More rigorous and parsimonious theory could be fashioned for particular pieces of the puzzle but only at the cost of abandoning a larger historical context. Nonetheless, it seemed wrongheaded to abandon macro-level comparisons simply because parsimonious theory was lacking.

Eclecticism is highly unsatisfying, though. If induction and comparative historical analysis have a role in the social sciences, they must offer something to the development of theory. Chapter 2 provides a framework for comparative analysis. I advance a typology of growth trajectories in order to identify the variation across cases that I am trying to explain. The key distinction is between countries that industrialized through expansion of manufactured exports and those which sought to build an integrated industrial structure behind protective walls. Three other components of industrial strategy are important: the instruments governments use to achieve their objectives; the balance between local, foreign, and state firms in industrialization; and the overall coherence of policy. The puzzle is to explain why countries adopted the industrial strategies they did, and why they sustained them over time.

To answer these questions, I analyze arguments about the sources of policy change drawn from four different levels of analysis: the international system, domestic coalitions, political institutions, and ideas. I then summarize and attempt to weight the influence of these variables, reaching for some contingent generalizations.

I argue, first, that international shocks and pressures, and the domestic economic crises associated with them, have been the most powerful stimuli for changes of policy. These critical historical junctures shifted the balance of power among sectors in predictable ways and provided incentives to institutional innovation. This book thus confirms the importance of the international context in understanding the policy choices of relatively weak states, though it returns to a set of variables that recent dependency writing has ignored: the role of macroeconomic shocks, country size, and the political influence wielded by great powers.

A weakness of international systemic theory, whether Marxist or realist, is that it cannot explain variations in the behavior of similarly situated states. For this reason we need to examine variables at the domestic level. A second major argument of the book is that theories seeking to predict policy choice from the configuration of social forces—whether conceived in class, interest-group, or sectoral terms—have fundamental empirical and theoretical limitations. The influence of social forces on policy is undeniable, but it is always mediated by institutional setting. In some developing countries political elites have inherited or built organizational structures that significantly constrain the ability of societal actors to achieve their political and economic objectives.

The third argument is that although international pressures may provide the stimulus and domestic social structure broadly constrains choice, policy change is heavily conditioned by the interests of political elites in building and sustaining bases of support. The strategies that states pursue and the fashion in which they are implemented hinge less on broad social-structural forces than on the politically driven choices of state elites; the tactical give-and-take and coalition building characteristic of political life. I see political coalitions not as given by social structure or international constraints but as the constructs of political leadership and organization.

The emphasis I give to politically motivated choice by state actors falls broadly within the realm of rational-choice theorizing, and I have learned from this strand of work. Yet I place great emphasis on the institutional context within which political choice takes place; this is the fourth, and central, argument of this book. "The state" is not only an actor but a set of institutions that exhibit continuity over time; a field of play that provides differential incentives for groups to organize. Because of variations in institutional structure, political elites differ in their organizational capabilities and the instruments they have at their disposal for pursuing their goals. Institutional variation is critical for understanding why some states are capable of pursuing the policies they do. It is at the intersection between choice and institutional constraint that political explanations of economic growth must be constructed.

Part One is theoretical; Part Two is historical. Separate chapters are devoted to the transition to export-led growth in Korea and Taiwan in the 1950s and 1960s. These two countries receive special attention because they are often held up as examples of what other medium-sized developing countries might accomplish. Another chapter is devoted to the development of Hong Kong and Singapore through the late 1960s. Though severely constrained by external environment, the two entrepôts exhibit striking policy differences that underline the significance of domestic politics. Chapter 6 offers a comparative analysis of the responses of the East Asian NICs to the economic turbulence of the 1970s and 1980s, asking how political factors affected their efforts to adjust to new external constraints. Chapter 7 is devoted to a comparison of Mexico and Brazil. While necessarily compressed, the comparison draws out some of the salient differences between East Asian and Latin American growth trajectories.

In Parts One and Two, I attempt to explain state strategies. Part Three makes the case for the importance of state strategy as a causal variable in its own right by reexamining three central controversies in the political economy of development.

Chapter 8 addresses the question of "dependency" by comparing the role of foreign direct investment in the East Asian and the Latin American NICs. I argue that patterns of foreign direct investment and dependency are closely related to phases of NIC growth and to government policies and incentives. Chapter 9 analyzes the effect of development strategy on income distribution. The most powerful determinant of cross-regional variation in income distribution is the distribution of assets, including land and education, but the choice of industrialization strategy has also had important consequences. The strategy pursued by the East Asian NICs was more labor-absorbing and egalitarian than that adopted by the large, Latin American NICs, though this outcome hinged on particular labor-market institutions.

The final chapter addresses a long-standing debate that is of central normative significance: What is the relationship between industrialization strategy and regime type? I find arguments linking authoritarianism with industrial strategy in Latin America to be neither theoretically nor empirically plausible, though the dictates of macroeconomic policy have periodically been important in inclining political, military, and economic elites toward authoritarian solutions. The link between export-led growth and authoritarianism is somewhat more convincing, but I argue that there are no unique institutional solutions to the problems of development. We can expect democratization to create short-term difficulties in the formulation of economic policy, but many of these "difficulties" arise from justified claims for greater social justice and freedom. No doubt there are lessons to be learned from the rapid growth of the East Asian NICs, but it is crucial to remember the political underside to their "success." Authoritarian rule may have given state actors freedom of maneuver in the past, but no ironclad theoretical reasons preclude democratic governments from achieving good economic performance. This fact provides hope for all of the newly industrializing countries discussed here.

Part I

THEORY: THE POLITICAL ECONOMY OF GROWTH

CHAPTER ONE

The Neoclassical and Dependency Perspectives

Two broad paradigms—between which there has been remarkably little communication—have dominated thinking on the economic development of the NICs: the neoclassical view and the dependency perspective. Both suffer from the same weakness—they neglect politics and institutions. Political scientists have turned neoclassical tools to the modeling of politics and institutions, but this work remains confined largely to the study of the United States, where its pluralist political assumptions are plausible. Most empirical writing on the NICs by economists still retains a voluntarist view of policy making. Policy is simply a matter of making the right choices; "incorrect" policy reflects misguided ideas or lack of political "will." This approach poses a profound puzzle for a theory based on rational-actor assumptions: If neoclassical policies are superior, why are they so infrequently adopted? The answer often lies in the political incentives that policy makers face.

The weakness of dependency writing on the NICs stems from an opposite flaw, a tendency to focus on the international- and class-structural determinants of policy. Yet similarly situated states frequently pursue different policies in response to external pressures. In these instances we need theories of how domestic political factors intervene between external constraints and policy choice—again, a theory that addresses the incentives facing political actors.

THE NICS AND THE NEOCLASSICAL REVIVAL

Though the advocacy of import-substituting industrialization (ISI) for latecomers is as old as Hamilton and List, the debate was reopened in the postwar period by Raúl Prebisch's vigorous and influential advocacy of ISI for Latin America. Prebisch combined a skepticism about the benefits of integration into the world economy with infant-industry arguments. Primary producers faced price volatility in the short term and declining terms of trade over the longer run; his prescription was industrialization through protection. It is now frequently forgotten that Prebisch's views corresponded quite closely with those of other pioneers in the field of economic development in the 1950s.[1] Nor were the U.S. and multilateral aid institutions altogether hostile to such a program.

By the mid-1960s these policies had come under attack.[2] Neoclassical critics of ISI argued that many problems of developing countries could be traced not to international systemic factors or to structural rigidities but to misguided government intervention. The argument had three strands. The first stressed the benefits of participation in the international division of labor, the second the costs and distortions of ISI, and the third the performance of countries pursuing market-conforming policies.

Liberal thinking rejects the proposition that trade and investment relations between developed and developing countries are inimical to development. Evidence accumulated contradicting the claim that producers in developing countries faced a secular decline in prices, and short-term market volatility was found to be less disruptive than had been thought.[3] Openness did not preclude LDC industrialization but rather encouraged technological adaptation, learning, and entrepreneurial maturation. Newer theories of trade and investment underscored the net benefits of foreign direct investment as well.[4] Indeed, being a "latecomer" had distinct advantages. Available technology could provide the foundation for new leading sectors, centers of capital accumulation, backward and forward linkages, and, ultimately, exports.[5]

---

1. Raul Prebisch, *The Economic Development of Latin America and Its Principal Problems* (New York: United Nations, 1950). See Prebisch's reflection on his career, "Five Stages in the Development of My Thinking," in Gerald M. Meier and Dudley Seers, eds., *Pioneers in Development* (New York: Oxford University Press, 1984). On the structuralists see Hollis Chenery, "The Structuralist Approach to Development Policy," *American Economic Review* 65 (May 1975): 310–16; Ian M. D. Little, *Economic Development: Theory, Practice, and International Relations* (New York: Basic Books, 1982), pp. 77–85; Albert O. Hirschman, "The Rise and Decline of Development Economics," in *Essays in Trespassing* (New York: Cambridge University Press, 1981), pp. 1–24.

2. See Prebisch, "Five Stages," pp. 180–82.

3. For a review, see Sheila Smith and John Toye, "Three Stories about Trade and Poor Economies," *Journal of Development Studies* 15 (April 1979): 1–18.

4. Raymond Vernon, "International Investment and International Trade in the Product Cycle," *Quarterly Journal of Economics* 80 (May 1966): 190–207.

5. Walt W. Rostow, "Growth Rates at Different Levels of Income and Stages of Growth: Reflections on Why the Poor Get Richer and the Rich Slow Down," in *Why the Poor Get Richer and the Rich Slow Down* (Austin: University of Texas Press, 1980), pp. 259–301.

Contemporary liberals, like their nineteenth-century precursors, tended to ignore the political dimension of the international economy. The fact that asymmetric economic interdependence could generate power relationships between countries did not generally concern them.[6] By contributing to growth, correct economic policies enhanced national power, whereas nationalist prescriptions undermined it. As Harry Johnson, a prolific defender of the market, argued, "No matter whether a country is absolutely strong or absolutely weak, it can maximize the power available to it by concentrating on those activities in which it is relatively more powerful."[7]

Liberals acknowledged the existence of exploitative international economic relations—for example, where monopoly power is used to bias the gains from trade—but treated these relationships as exceptional rather than typical.[8] Even where market imperfections existed, trade intervention was not the optimal policy. The task was not to abandon the market but to undertake reforms to ensure that international and domestic markets would work more efficiently. By contributing to the diffusion of technology and expanding market opportunities, a liberal international order encouraged upward mobility. As Bela Balassa observed in outlining his "stages" approach to comparative advantage:

> [Japan's] comparative advantage has shifted toward highly capital intensive exports. In turn, developing countries with a relatively high human capital endowment, such as Korea and Taiwan, can take Japan's place in exporting relatively human capital–intensive products and countries with relatively high physical capital endowment, such as Brazil and Mexico, can take Japan's place in exporting relatively physical capital–intensive products. Finally, countries at lower levels of development can supplant the middle level countries in exporting unskilled labor–intensive commodities.[9]

A second strand of criticism of nationalist policies focused on their domestic costs.[10] Different writers stressed different distortions, but they

6. Albert Hirschman, *National Power and the Structure of International Trade* (Berkeley: University of California Press, 1945), pp. 13–52.

7. Harry G. Johnson, "Technological Change and Comparative Advantage: An Advanced Country's Viewpoint," *Journal of World Trade Law* 9, 1 (1973): 1. See also Jan Tumlir, *National Interest and International Order* (London: Trade Policy Research Center, 1978).

8. Contrast Richard Cooper, "A New International Economic Order for Mutual Gain," *Foreign Policy* 26 (Spring 1977): 66–120, and Gerald Helleiner, "World Market Imperfections and the Developing Countries," in William Cline, ed., *Policy Alternatives for a New International Economic Order* (New York: Praeger, 1979), pp. 357–89.

9. Bela Balassa, *A Stages Approach to Comparative Advantage*, World Bank Staff Working Paper 256 (Washington, D.C., May 1977), p. 27.

10. On the politics of "associationist" and "dissociationist" strategies see John Gerard Ruggie, ed., *The Antinomies of Interdependence* (New York: Columbia University Press, 1983).

generally treated the interrelated problems of ISI as a syndrome.[11] On the external side the need for raw materials and capital goods to establish import-substituting industries made ISI import-intensive, but the bias against exports contributed to chronic balance-of-payments difficulties. These imbalances were met by a resort to increasing controls over foreign-exchange transactions and damaging stop-go macroeconomic policies. Foreign aid, direct investment, and commercial borrowing were critical mainstays of the strategy, as were earnings from traditional exports of raw materials. Far from reducing external vulnerability, ISI increased it.

External problems were matched by internal distortions. Heavily protected IS industries were oligopolistic in structure and characterized by excess capacity, inefficiency, high mark-up, and low-quality output. These internal distortions naturally had distributional consequences. Trade and exchange-rate policies raised the prices of manufactured goods relative to agricultural products, turning the terms of trade against the countryside where the poor were concentrated. As real resource transfers from the agricultural sector necessarily slowed, the temptation to subsidize industry from the central bank grew, exacerbating inflation. The emphasis on industry at the expense of agriculture limited the expansion of the domestic market, however, and pushed people out of the rural areas. Though ISI had been motivated by a desire to increase employment, the encouragement of capital-intensive production processes constrained the ability of the industrial sector to absorb labor. Dualistic labor markets resulted, in which relatively high-wage employment coexisted with extensive under- and unemployment. Urban marginalization and a skewed distribution of income were the result.

The new neoclassical political economy also underlined a crucial political consequence of ISI: the tendency for state intervention to encourage rent-seeking.[12] The state's control of import licensing and the rationing of foreign exchange invited corruption, smuggling, and black markets as well as inefficiency in the allocation of resources. Ideally, the

11. Influential statements include I. M. D. Little, T. Scitovsky, and M. Scott, *Industry and Trade in Some Developing Countries* (London: Oxford University Press, 1970), and Anne Krueger, *Liberalization Attempts and Consequences* (Cambridge, Mass.: Ballinger for the National Bureau of Economic Research, 1978), both of which summarize multivolume cross-national studies; Bela Belassa, *Policy Reform in Developing Countries* (New York: Pergamon, 1977) and *The Newly Industrializing Countries in the World Economy* (New York: Pergamon, 1981); Carlos Diaz-Alejandro, "Trade Policies and Economic Development," in Peter Kenen, ed., *International Trade and Finance: Frontiers for Research* (New York: Cambridge University Press, 1975), pp. 93–150.

12. Jagdish Bhagwati, *Anatomy and Consequences of Exchange Control Regimes* (Cambridge, Mass.: Ballinger for the National Bureau of Economic Research, 1978).

protection granted to import-substituting industries would be tailored to essential development purposes and ultimately phased out, allowing firms to graduate to competitive status. In fact, high levels of protection persisted. A rational ISI strategy demanded political and administrative capacities beyond the reach of most developing countries. Market-oriented policies, on the other hand, decentralized economic decision making in a context of administrative scarcity and depoliticized policy by discouraging unproductive rent-seeking activities.

The success of the East Asian NICs opened a third line of attack, by providing empirical evidence for neoclassical theoretical claims. Evidence accumulated that the rates of growth achieved through export promotion were superior to those achieved under import-substituting regimes.[13] Despite high levels of dependence on trade, the East Asian NICs significantly outperformed the inward-looking Latin American NICs in the economically turbulent 1970s. In addition, the distribution of income in the East Asian NICs was relatively egalitarian, even by the standards of developed countries. Extensive land reforms in Korea and Taiwan and the absence of low-income agriculture sectors in Singapore and Hong Kong were partly responsible for this outcome, but the labor-absorbing nature of export-led growth made its contribution.

The neoclassical interpretation of East Asia's growth did not go unchallenged. The most telling criticisms came from a theoretically eclectic group of economists, political scientists, and area specialists.[14] The critique followed two lines. The first concerned the role of the state in promoting growth, the second the importance of a particular international context for the success of export-led growth.

Patterns of industrial-structural change in the East Asian NICs, the critics contended, had to be understood, at least in part, as the result of the industrial strategies of developmental states. East Asia did exploit its comparative advantage but not through market-oriented policies alone. Taiwan, Singapore, and Korea supported their industrial planning with

13. See, for example, Bela Balassa, "The Newly-Industrializing Developing Countries after the Oil Crisis," in *The Newly Industrializing Countries in the World Economy* (New York: Pergamon, 1981); James Riedel, "Trade as the Engine of Growth in Developing Countries, Revisited," *Economic Journal* 94 (March 1984): 56–73; Colin I. Bradford, Jr., and William H. Branson, eds., *Trade and Structural Change in Pacific Asia* (Chicago: University of Chicago Press, 1987).

14. Representative works include Gordon White and Robert Wade, eds., *Developmental States in East Asia*, Institute of Development Studies Research Report 16 (Brighton, 1985); Alice H. Amsden, "The State and Taiwan's Economic Development," in Peter B. Evans, Dietrich Rueshemeyer, and Theda Skocpol, eds., *Bringing the State Back In* (New York: Cambridge University Press, 1985), pp. 78–106, and Amsden, *Asia's Next Giant: South Korea and Late Industrialization* (New York: Oxford University Press, 1989); Leroy Jones and Il Sakong, *Government, Business, and Entrepreneurship in Economic Development: The Korean Case* (Cambridge: Harvard University Press, 1980); Chalmers Johnson, *MITI and the Japanese Miracle* (Stanford: Stanford University Press, 1981).

a variety of sector-specific interventions. Financial and fiscal incentives played a role in the development of new sectors, as did protection. The structure of industrial incentives was far from neutral and balanced, and levels of protection in Korea and Taiwan remained high even in those sectors in which a comparative advantage was established. New contributions to the theory of trade offered tentative support to the revisionist view, suggesting that industrial targeting could represent an optimal policy in some markets.[15]

Neoclassical economists offered several responses to these observations. Intervention may have been extensive in the East Asian NICs, they noted, but it has been less extensive than in Africa, South Asia, and Latin America.[16] Moreover, the NICs' efforts at sector-specific steering have either had little effect on overall development or were positively detrimental. Advocates of industrial policy made a leap of faith from the *existence* of a policy having a certain goal to the *achievement* of the intended effects; they neither demonstrated nor theoretically grounded the causal connections. The effect of industrial policy was never measured against the much more substantial influence of consistent and credible macroeconomic policies, the provision of public goods and incentives to private risk taking.[17]

The second major challenge to the neoclassical portrait rested on a revival of export pessimism. The advocacy of export-led growth, skeptics argued, rested on a fallacy of composition.[18] The model worked well when pursued by a small group of states, but if it were generalized, the flood of manufactured exports from the developing world would swamp the political capacity of the advanced industrial states to absorb them. Wolfgang Hager offered the starkest appraisal of the consequences of linking "two worlds," North and South, through free markets for capital, goods, and technology. "One, ours, is characterized by unfree labor markets and still relatively free markets for allocating capital. The other is a world of free labor markets . . . and systems of capital allocation by central plans or strategic consensus by a handful of entrepreneurs and bureaucrats."[19] Availing themselves of existing technology, the NICs

15. See Paul Krugman, ed., *Strategic Trade Policy and the New International Economics* (Cambridge: MIT Press, 1986).

16. Jagdish Bhagwati and Anne Krueger, "Exchange Control, Liberalization, and Economic Development," *American Economic Review* (May 1973): 420.

17. For a critique of the industrial policy literature, see Gary Saxonhouse, "What Is All This about 'Industrial Targeting' in Japan?" *The World Economy* 6 (September 1983): 253–73.

18. William Cline, "Can the East Asian Model of Development Be Generalized?" *World Development* 10 (February 1982): 81–90.

19. Wolfgang Hager, "Protectionism and Autonomy: How to Preserve Free Trade in Europe," *International Affairs* 58 (Summer 1982): 413–28. See also Organization of Economic Cooperation and Development, *The Impact of the Newly Industrializing Countries on*

could achieve levels of productivity comparable to those in the advanced industrial states with substantially lower unit-labor costs. To demand that the industrial worker of Europe or the United States become an object of market forces in the name of "adjustment" was to court the destruction of the postwar welfare state. The only realistic response, according to Hager, is politically to "manage" the trade between these different socioeconomic systems. Slowed growth and increased protectionism in the advanced industrial states appeared to challenge the replicability of export-led growth.[20]

The East Asian NICs did vindicate some important neoclassical prescriptions. Korea and Taiwan did "take off" as the result of policies that allowed them to exploit comparative advantage more fully. These policies included exchange-rate reform and selective import-liberalization. The pattern of incentives under export-promoting policies was far from neutral, but it *was* less skewed than in countries that had pursued ISI. Nor has the new export pessimism been wholly justified. The market for NIC manufactures in industrial countries continued to expand despite growing protectionism.[21] Orderly marketing arrangements, a form of trade restraint based on quotas, allowed the East Asian NICs ample room for maneuver to evade protection.[22] Since such restraints are negotiated, the weak country can bargain for long-term gains, push for ambiguous agreements, form transnational alliances with groups favoring free trade, or simply cheat. In addition, quotas had the perverse effect of forcing the East Asian NICs to upgrade and diversify into new product lines.

A central argument of this book, however, is that the shift to export-led growth was also accompanied by economic, legal, and institutional reforms that the neoclassical interpretation has generally ignored. Even if we accept a modified neoclassical view of the consequences of policy reform, an unremarked puzzle mars the analysis. If export-led growth was a superior strategy, why has policy reform elsewhere proved so infrequent and hesitant? Where reforms have been launched, why have they been accompanied by a range of contradictory interventions? Why, to repeat David Morawetz's question, are the emperor's new clothes not made in Colombia?[23]

Production and Trade in Manufactures (Paris: OECD, 1979), one of the first studies to focus on the NICs.

20. See, for example, Paul Streeten, "A Cool Look at 'Outward-looking' Strategies for Development," *The World Economy* 5 (September 1982): 159–70.

21. Helen Hughes and Jean Waelbroeck, "Can Developing-Country Exports Keep Growing in the 1980s?" *The World Economy* 4 (June 1981): 127–47.

22. David Yoffie, *Power and Protectionism: Strategies of the Newly Industrializing Countries* (New York: Columbia University Press, 1983).

23. David Morawetz, *Why the Emperor's New Clothes Are Not Made in Colombia* (Baltimore: Johns Hopkins for the World Bank, 1981).

Size was frequently cited as a factor, though countries smaller than Korea have pursued import-substituting policies over long periods of time, and the larger NICs vary widely in their openness to the world economy. Economists pointed to the importance of rent-seeking behavior, but this was often a post-hoc observation rather than a theory of policy. Little effort was made to demonstrate the actual importance of rent seeking, and there was no good explanation why rent seeking dominated policy in some instances but was overcome in others.[24]

Explanations for misguided policies tended to cluster around the interrelated factors of nationalism, ideology, and simple irrationality. Robert Bates pointed up the underlying contradiction in these lines of argument: "People are said to display both economic shrewdness and political stupidity."[25] Individuals were assumed to be economically rational and far-sighted in their response to market incentives. All politicians, however, appeared to be myopic champions of inefficiency. This discrepancy demands an explanation.

DEPENDENT DEVELOPMENT

The radical challenge to liberal views of development has come from a diverse group of writers drawing intellectual inspiration from the Marxist tradition of political economy. Dependency theorists, who developed their thinking primarily with reference to the large Latin American NICs, are exemplary of this approach, though they share many basic assumptions with writers on imperialism, proponents of a world-systems perspective, and some structuralist theories of international political economy that are avowedly non-Marxist.[26] Two underlying theoretical assumptions characterize work in the dependency tradition. First, the international economy is conceived as a hierarchically ordered system of dominance. As in a stratified social system, various mechanisms, both political and economic, exist through which inequality is reproduced. Second, the character of the periphery's development has largely been a function of the way in which it was incorporated into the international division of labor. This "postulate of external dominance" holds that external factors are responsible for the distortions that characterize the economies of the developing world.

24. Douglas Nelson, "Endogenous Tariff Theory: A Critical Survey," *American Journal of Political Science* 32 (August 1988): 796–837.

25. Robert H. Bates, *Markets and States in Tropical Africa: The Political Bases of Agricultural Policies* (Berkeley: University of California Press, 1981), p. 2.

26. A useful review of early dependency thinking is Gabriel Palma, "Dependency: A Formal Theory of Underdevelopment or a Methodology for the Analysis of Concrete Situations of Underdevelopment?" *World Development* 6 (November 1978): 881–924.

Early dependency theorists—André Gunder Frank is the favorite target—worked with a highly stylized model in which the extraction of surplus led directly to economic stagnation.[27] Though the debates in North American social science over these initial claims dragged on into the 1980s, the Latin American NICs had already forced reevaluations of the stagnationist hypothesis as early as 1970.[28] Dependency thinking was gradually recast to account for peripheral industrialization, particularly in the large South American NICs.

Following the lead of Fernando Henrique Cardoso, a "new wave" of dependency writing focused on the relationship between the state and foreign and local firms.[29] The "state" was simultaneously a political institution upholding a given social order, the institutional locus of the "state bourgeoisie," and an entrepreneur engaged in production through state-owned enterprises. Foreign and local "capital" were treated both as profit-maximizing firms and as class fractions. The effort to conceptualize the relationship of dependency on foreign firms in both sociological and economic terms produced two subtly different lines of argument. The broader level of explanation was political, accounting for a particular pattern of industrialization on the basis of underlying coalitional interests. The economic consequences of this strategy were explained by a second set of arguments concerning the detrimental effects of integration into the international capitalist system.

The first set of dependency arguments constituted a sociological model of state-society relations that was functionalist in form. The strategy of "dependent development"—essentially the phase of import substitution in which multinationals come to play an expanded role—resulted from a particular transnational class coalition. Peter Evans, for example, saw state elites, foreign firms, and local firms as forming a "triple alliance."[30] Cardoso spoke of an alliance among portions of the

27. See André Gunder Frank, *Capitalism and Underdevelopment in Latin America* (New York: Monthly Review Press, 1967).

28. Fernando Henrique Cardoso and Enzo Faletto, *Dependency and Development in Latin America* (Berkeley: University of California Press, 1979), originally published in 1973.

29. Fernando Henrique Cardoso, "Associated-Dependent Development: Theoretical and Practical Implications," in Alfred Stepan, ed., *Authoritarian Brazil* (New Haven: Yale University Press, 1973). The most important contribution to the "new wave" was Peter Evans, *Dependent Development: The Alliance of Multinational, State, and Local Capital in Brazil* (Princeton: Princeton University Press, 1978). See also Gary Gereffi, *The Pharmaceutical Industry and Dependency in the Third World* (Princeton: Princeton University Press, 1983); Douglas C. Bennett and Kenneth E. Sharpe, *Transnational Corporations versus the State: The Political Economy of the Mexican Automobile Industry* (Princeton: Princeton University Press, 1985), and Richard Newfarmer, ed., *Profits, Poverty, and Progress: Case Studies of International Industries in Latin America* (Notre Dame: University of Notre Dame Press, 1985). For a review, see Stephan Haggard, "The Political Economy of Foreign Direct Investment in Latin America," *Latin American Research Review* 24, 1 (1989): 184–208.

30. Evans, *Dependent Development*.

military, the bourgeoisie, and the middle classes who favored the active participation of foreign capital in national development.[31]

The motives of the partners were, as in any political alliance, a mix of the cooperative and the competitive; the existence of a broader "alliance" by no means precluded continuing negotiations over the precise terms of the relationship. National firms used political access to the government to defend their market position. Bureaucrats and the managers of state-owned enterprises had their own institutional interests, and political elites sought to maximize their objectives by balancing the competing claims of nationalism and economic growth.

Nonetheless, *dependistas* saw foreign firms as the dominant, constraining partner. The power of the multinationals within the triple alliance stemmed from the flexibility inherent in transnational organization, the weight they had in the national economy, particularly in its most dynamic sectors, and the imperfections that characterized the markets in which they operated. Theories of foreign investment emphasizing market imperfections were crucial for the new dependency thinking.[32] Such theories pointed out that the costs of overseas investment deterred firms from going abroad unless offset by firm-specific advantages vis-à-vis local competitors. These advantages included access to finance, technology, product differentiation, marketing capabilities, managerial skills, and economies of scale. These advantages not only gave the MNCs power vis-à-vis local firms in the market; their dominant position within the economy constituted a fundamental constraint on national policy. The result was, as Gary Gereffi notes, a "stunting or restriction of choice among local development options, since these are likely to conflict with global priorities implied by the dependent situation."[33]

Despite recurrent conflicts within the triple alliance, the three partners shared a common interest in rapid accumulation. This in turn dictated a predictable political and sociological configuration, involving authoritarianism and inequality. Evans, for example, made the functionalist argument that the second stage of MNC-dominated import substitution "demanded" the exclusion, even repression, of an already activated urban popular sector; "in the context of dependent development, the need for repression is great while the need for democracy is small."[34] Cardoso argued similarly for Brazil that "the accumulation process required that the instruments of pressure and defense available

---

31. Cardoso, "Associated-Dependent Development."

32. Stephen Hymer, *The International Operations of National Firms: A Study in Foreign Investment,* Monographs in Economics 14 (Cambridge: MIT Press, 1976); Charles Kindelberger, *American Investment Abroad* (New Haven: Yale University Press, 1969).

33. Gereffi, *The Pharmaceutical Industry and Dependency,* p. 61.

34. Evans, *Dependent Development,* p. 48.

to the popular classes be dismantled."[35] Guillermo O'Donnell's model gave a more central role to domestic factors, such as popular sector mobilization, the growth of technocratic roles, and the military's perception of threat, in explaining "bureaucratic-authoritarianism."[36] Nonetheless, his most controversial hypothesis linked military intervention in politics to the "imperatives" of a "deepening" phase of ISI in which foreign firms were crucial players.

These political-sociological arguments were supplemented by a critical approach to the multinational corporation that accounted for the negative economic and sociological consequences of "dependent development." I can review these arguments briefly, since they have been summarized elsewhere.[37] Dependency theorists focused particularly on the generation of inequality and those behaviors of foreign firms detrimental to economic development.

Inequality was generated in different ways.[38] The introduction of capital-intensive production processes by foreign firms contributed to a segmentation of the labor market. While creating a demand for skilled and semiskilled workers, it displaced or neglected traditional labor-absorbing industries. Because industrial dynamism depended on the production of goods such as consumer durables that were beyond the means of most of the population, the mass of the population was excluded as consumers; the state may even compress wages and skew patterns of distribution to create or deepen favored product markets. The economic problems attributed to dependency on foreign firms were numerous: the introduction of inappropriate products, patterns of consumption, technologies, and production processes; industrial concentration; the displacement of local producers; undesirable trade behavior; transfer pricing. It is a testament to the dependency research program that a sophisticated literature emerged to test these propositions and uphold a number of them.[39]

Criticizing dependency theory has become an academic industry of the worst sort. The crudest formulations are attacked with vehemence, the overall contribution and the more sophisticated variants ignored.[40]

---

35. Cardoso, "Associated-Dependent Development," p. 147.

36. Guillermo O'Donnell, *Modernization and Bureaucratic Authoritarianism* (Berkeley: Institute of International Studies, University of California, 1973).

37. See Richard Newfarmer, ed., *Profits, Poverty, and Progress,* and Thomas Biersteker, *Distortion or Development: Contending Perspectives on the Multinational Corporation* (Cambridge: MIT Press, 1978). For more conventional views, see Richard E. Caves, *Multinational Enterprise and Economic Analysis* (New York: Cambridge University Press, 1982).

38. Biersteker, *Distortion or Development,* pp. 1–26.

39. Newfarmer, *Profits, Poverty, and Progress.*

40. For a criticism of cross-national studies of dependency, see Robert W. Jackman, "Dependence on Foreign Investment and Economic Growth in the Third World," *World*

This is particularly curious given the obvious impact changes in the world economy have had on developing countries in the last decade. I limit myself to four observations that are relevant to the subsequent analysis and have been, I believe, overlooked.

First, many of the distortions and distributional consequences that *dependistas* attributed to the operation of the multinational corporation paralleled quite closely the effects neoclassical economists traced to the broader choice of development strategy. Some effects of foreign investment operated independently of national policy.[41] For example, the interest of MNCs in fostering technological dependence holds across import-substituting and export-oriented investments. Yet many of the distortions highlighted by the dependency theorists—neglect of agriculture, inequality, inappropriate production processes and patterns of consumption, to name a few—could be attributed to import substitution and an array of other national policies. It is no coincidence that two of the most influential proponents of the model of dependent development—Cardoso and Evans—were students of Brazil. A comparative analysis that reaches beyond Latin America suggests that the conduct and performance of multinational firms is only an intervening variable between policy choices and economic outcomes. Dependency is as much an effect of national policies as their cause.

A second observation concerns the concept of dependence itself. Dependency analyses of NIC industrialization, including efforts to extend the dependency paradigm to East Asia,[42] have focused on the role of the multinational corporation. This tactic overestimates the importance of foreign direct investment and rests on an extremely restricted view of how the international system constrains state behavior. The main adjustment challenge facing the East Asian NICs in the 1970s involved navigating an increasingly politicized international trading system. By the 1970s commercial borrowing far overshadowed foreign direct investment as a source of external capital in the NICs. Viewed over a longer time frame, supply shocks and global macroeconomic trends have had a more profound effect on developing countries than has the multina-

Politics 34 (January 1982): 187–93; for an economist's view, Sanjaya Lall, "Is 'Dependence' a Useful Concept in Analysing Underdevelopment?" *World Development* 3 (November–December 1975): 799–810; for a sophisticated Marxist critique, Bill Warren, *Imperialism: Pioneer of Capitalism* (London: New Left Books, 1980); for criticisms directed explicitly at the "new wave" dependency theorists, see David G. Becker, *The New Bourgeoisie and the Limits of Dependency* (Princeton: Princeton University Press, 1983), pp. 3–16, 323–42.

41. Richard Newfarmer, "International Industrial Organization and Development: A Survey," in Newfarmer, ed., *Profits, Poverty, and Progress*, pp. 13–62.

42. See Folker Fröbl, Jürgen Heinrichs, and Otto Kreye, *The New International Division of Labor: Structural Unemployment in Industrialized Countries and Industrialization in Developing Countries* (New York: Cambridge University Press, 1980).

tional corporation. These facts do not invalidate the basic dependency insight, but they do suggest the need for a more differentiated conception of international constraints.

Third, the dependency perspective was oddly economistic and apolitical in its view of the international system. Much dependency writing ignores the independent significance of political and military relationships. These, too, have had an important shaping influence on national policy.

The final observation concerns the significance of domestic politics and the wide variation in state responses to similar situations of dependency. The attempt to outline a parsimonious conception of international structure missed the variation in state strategies and capacities. In one formulation, for example, Immanuel Wallerstein included in the semiperiphery not only the socialist states of East Europe but advanced mineral-exporting states such as South Africa and the newly industrializing countries of Latin America and East Asia![43] Much dependency thinking rested on surprisingly crude functional and economistic theories of politics that ignored institutions and processes. Detailed sectoral studies provided some correction, but the focus on external constraints drew attention away from an examination of the political forces shaping national strategies.

Both the liberal and the dependency perspectives share a common disability: the tendency to ignore how domestic political forces constrain economic policy and shape state responses to the external environment. The reasons are worth reiterating. The neoclassical revival has a prescriptive, even proselytizing, thrust. Pareto-optimal policies are used as a normative benchmark to critically assess government-induced distortions, usually with little attention to those distortions which result from underdevelopment itself. With this perspective comes a strong voluntarism, the belief that economic successes can be broadly replicated if only "correct" policy choices are made. Doubtless many LDCs can profit from market-oriented reforms, but it is unlikely that the East Asian model can be exported in toto. The success of the East Asian NICs rested not only on certain discrete *policies* but on the particular political and institutional context that allowed the NICs to adopt those policies in the first place.

The dependency perspective, by contrast, suffers from what might be called the "structuralist paradox." The model was outlined to help identify the international constraints associated with certain development paths in order to overcome them. The determinist strand of dependency

43. Immanuel Wallerstein, "Semi-peripheral Countries and the Contemporary World Crisis," *Theory and Society* 3, 4 (1976): 461–83.

thinking, however, downplays the importance of countervailing state strategies. Behavior disappears. Countries are called "dependent" by virtue of their characteristics and remain so regardless of their actions.[44] Studies of host-firm bargaining suggest that this view is simply inaccurate. The international environment should be seen not as a rigidly determinate structure but rather as a set of shifting constraints within which states can learn and expand their range of maneuver.[45]

If the triple alliance is conceived as a broad sectoral division of labor between the state, local firms, and foreign firms, then *all* developing countries are characterized by *some* form of triple alliance; so, for that matter, are all developed economies. Preoccupation with dependency deflects attention from the central theoretical question. *Under what conditions* will the state supplant foreign investment in strategic sectors, support local capital in doing so, or tighten its regulatory grip? The answer to this question demands a comparative political perspective.

44. Here I follow a similar criticism of theories of imperialism made by Kenneth Waltz, *Theory of International Politics* (Reading, Mass.: Addison Wesley, 1979), pp. 33–37.

45. See, for example, Theodore Moran, *Multinational Corporations and the Politics of Dependence* (Princeton: Princeton University Press, 1974), pp. 153–72.

CHAPTER TWO

Explaining Development Strategies

Political analysis can contribute to the study of development in examining why different development strategies are chosen, persist, and shift. Development strategies are packages of policies aimed at steering economic activity into a particular mixture of ownership and sectors.[1] Choosing development strategies as the object of analysis raises methodological problems, however. First, "strategy" implies a purposiveness of state action that may not exist; imputing a central design requires caution. Strategies emerge by default, trial-and-error, and compromise; take years to crystallize; and are often plagued by internal inconsistency. Second, strategies consist of *packages* of policies. It is useful to disaggregate "strategies" where possible, since different policies involve different political cleavages and conflicts.

One further assumption must be made clear. Development strategies are not unambiguously given by factor endowments; if they were, we would live in the neoclassical world. Natural endowments constrain the universe of possibilities and help explain patterns of trade, but similarly endowed countries have pursued different strategies. If endowments are constraining, a political explanation of policy should be able to account for their importance by tracing the pressures from owners of different factors seeking to maximize their returns.

---

1. See Bela Balassa, "The Process of Industrial Development and Alternative Development Strategies," in Balassa, *The Newly Industrializing Countries in the World Economy* (New York: Pergamon, 1981); and Gustav Ranis, "Challenges and Opportunities Posed by Asia's Superexporters: Implications for Manufactured Exports from Latin America," in Werner Baer and Malcolm Gillis, eds., *Export Diversification and the New Protectionism: The Experiences of Latin America* (Champaign: Bureau of Economic and Business Research and College of Commerce and Business Administration, University of Illinois, 1981). On the concept of development strategy more generally see Albert Hirschman, *The Strategy of Economic Development* (New Haven: Yale University Press, 1958).

STATE STRATEGIES AND DEVELOPMENT TRAJECTORIES

Outlining different development trajectories and phases within them is the first step in isolating the differences between the East Asian and Latin American NICs. Three historical patterns of developing-country growth can be distinguished: an import-substitution trajectory, characteristic of Mexico and Brazil and several other large LDCs; an export-led growth trajectory, of which Korea and Taiwan are the most successful cases; and a related entrepôt path, of which Singapore and Hong Kong are examples (see Table 2.1).

Virtually all developing countries began their contact with the world economy as exporters of primary products, and many remain dependent on commodity exports. In this stage (PPE) the primary sector produces both food for local consumption (the traditional sector) and raw materials and foodstuffs for export (the enclave sector). Exports generate local purchasing power and finance the import of consumer goods, though borrowing may also be important. The nonprimary sector consists mainly of commercial services and craft production; demand generated in the export sector can lead to the development of light manufacturing as well. Policy supported this pattern in the typical colonial economy. Trade was relatively free and exchange-rate policies orthodox.

Variations in the primary-product export phase are politically salient; I mention two here. First, the way the commodity is produced and processed affects social organization. Historically, plantation production is associated with large landholdings, extreme income inequality, and the creation of a rural proletariat. Mining creates a concentrated labor force. The production of some crops, such as rice and cocoa, can be carried out efficiently by independent smallholders. These variations have consequences for the distribution of income and assets and influence the possibilities for collective action.[2] A second variation concerns ownership; export industries and commercial services may be owned locally or by foreigners. Ownership affects the locus of capital accumulation, the strength of local business classes, and the independence of the government from foreign interference.[3]

The first transition is toward import-substituting industrialization. In the first stage of ISI the earnings from primary-product exports and foreign borrowing finance the import of selected producer goods. These

2. See Michael Shafer, "Sectors, States, and Social Forces," unpublished ms.
3. This point is central to Fernando Henrique Cardoso and Enzo Faletto, *Dependency and Development in Latin America* (Berkeley: University of California Press, 1979).

Table 2.1. Three development trajectories

	Economic structure	Core policies
1. Import substitution		
a. Primary-product export phase (PPE). Brazil pre-1930, prerevolutionary Mexico	Raw materials or food exports, traditional agriculture, handicraft production, and limited manufactures	Free trade and foreign investment, gold-standard exchange-rate policy
b. Import substitution Phase 1 (ISI 1). Brazil and Mexico, c. 1935–1955	Growing manufacturing activity, particularly consumer goods	Protection, fiscal and financial supports to industry
c. Import substitution Phase 2 (ISI 2) Brazil and Mexico, c. 1955–1965	Industrial deepening in consumer durables and intermediates	Same as ISI 1, plus new role for state-owned enterprise and multinationals
d. Import substitution Phase 3 (ISI 3) Brazil and Mexico, c. 1965 to present	Continued deepening, including capital goods, increased manufactured exports	Same as ISI 2, plus new incentives to export and increased borrowing
2. Export-led growth		
a. Primary-product export phase Korea and Taiwan, c. 1900–1945	Same as 1a	Colonial administration of economic activity
b. Import substitution Phase 1 (ISI 1) Korea, c. 1945–1964; Taiwan, c. 1945–1960	Same as 1b	Same as 1b
c. Export-led growth Phase 1 (ELG 1) Korea and Taiwan through 1970	Manufacturing growth led by exports of labor-intensive goods	Devaluation, selective liberalization, financial and fiscal supports to export industry
d. Export-led growth Phase 2 (ELG 2) Korea and Taiwan, c. 1970 to the present	Industrial deepening coupled with upgrading of exports	Targeted industrial policies
3. Entrepôt growth		
a. Pure entrepôt phase Singapore pre-1967; Hong Kong, pre-1950	Specialization in commercial and financial services	Free trade and investment
b. Export-led growth Phase 1 (ELG 1) Singapore, 1967–1979; Hong Kong, c. 1950–1970	Manufacturing growth led by labor-intensive goods, continued service growth	Same as 3a
c. Export-led growth Phase 2 (ELG 2) Singapore, 1979–present; Hong Kong, 1975–present	Upgrading in specialized products, expansion of financial and commercial services	Selective industrial policies

imports provide the foundation for local manufacturing, usually beginning with nondurable consumer goods. ISI may occur "naturally," as the result of balance-of-payments problems, supply interruptions associated with wars, or growth of the domestic market.[4] ISI is also advanced, however, by policies designed to manage balance-of-payments crises, particularly trade and exchange controls, and by explicit industrial policies designed to raise the rate of return to manufacturing. These policies typically include multiple exchange-rate regimes, protection, and subsidized credit.

The size of the domestic market is clearly an important variable in explaining the duration of ISI. Countries with larger markets are likely to pursue import substitution over longer periods of time. Production of consumer durables and intermediate and capital goods, sectors in which scale economies are important, will appear economically viable. Promoting these sectors involves a large element of government choice, however, and raises important policy questions about the appropriateness of different leading sectors. In its second phase ISI is still dependent on the export of raw materials and foodstuffs and foreign borrowing, since investment in new industrial capacity increases the demand for imported capital and intermediate goods. The extension of protection to new sectors continues the bias against exports, though it serves as an incentive to new, import-substituting, direct foreign investment.

A final stage of this growth path, seen in the 1970s and 1980s in Latin America, has been to supplement import substitution with the expansion of manufactured exports, usually in response to the chronic balance-of-payments difficulties associated with ISI. The nature of these efforts varies, but export promotion generally includes special incentives designed to compensate for the continuation of inward-oriented policy.

The industrialization of those countries now pursuing export-led growth strategies also began with a period of primary-product export and was similarly followed by a period of import substitution. The limitations of the first phase of ISI were met in part by continued import substitution in selected sectors but primarily by a shift in incentives to favor the export of light, labor-intensive manufactures. This is the strategy known as export-led growth. The transition entailed stabilization, exchange-rate devaluation, selective import liberalization designed to give exporters access to inputs at world prices, and more targeted supports to exporters.

This change in policy to export-led growth led to a structural relation-

4. See Albert Hirschman, "The Political Economy of Import-Substituting Industrialization in Latin America," in Hirschman, *A Bias for Hope* (New Haven: Yale University Press, 1971), pp. 85–123.

ship with the world economy very different from that characteristic of import-substituting growth. Both exports and imports rose rapidly. Foreign investment continued to substitute for imports in certain product lines, but the new incentives encouraged export-oriented investment as well. As under import substitution, the precise weights of foreign, local, and state capital in the industrial sector varied, as did the degree of explicit government steering.

A third economic transition came in the development of more technology- and capital-intensive sectors. Policy could play an important role in this stage as well. Though the government might rely on market signals of changing comparative advantage, it might also anticipate or lead changes in the industrial structure by targeting particular industries for support. This second phase of export-led growth thus bears some resemblance to the third stage of import substitution, though the overall structure of the economy is more open than under ISI.

Entrepôts, finally, develop large service and commercial sectors in line with their function as intermediaries between primary-exporting hinterlands and regional, imperial, and world economies. With no rural sector of their own, they draw both food and labor from the hinterland. The first important transition is a diversification from purely commercial activities into manufacturing. With small domestic markets, trade is free; and though industrialization begins by servicing local demand, its expansion is of necessity tied to world markets. Nonetheless, policy can affect the balance between local and foreign firms. The extent of direct government involvement in production can also vary. The second transition, similar to that in the export-led growth model, moves toward further industrial diversification, but commercial and entrepôt functions continue in importance.

Several endogenous economic forces help explain transitions between different growth phases, among them the accumulation of capital and changing comparative advantage. However, as this stylized portrait already suggests, government policy is also important. Four components of strategy demand explanation. The first is the strategy's *orientation*. The crucial difference between the East Asian and Latin American NICs is the difference between industrialization through exports and import substitution; a central puzzle is to examine the conditions under which the East Asian countries adopted and sustained the policy reforms that produced export-led growth.

But other aspects of strategy vary as well. Even countries pursuing similar strategies exhibit variation in extent of state intervention to promote industry. Hong Kong's laissez-faire stands in sharp contrast to Korea's dirigism. What explains this variation in the choice of policy *instruments?* Strategies are also pursued under the auspices of different

27

agents. To what extent (and why) are local, foreign, or state-owned enterprises given precedence? Finally, we must be concerned with what Barry Posen has called the *integration* of a given strategy.[5] Development frequently suffers because contradictory goals are pursued simultaneously and initial choices are not sustained. We therefore want to know how politics affects the internal coherence of policy and the consistency with which it is pursued over time.

A STRATEGY FOR COMPARATIVE HISTORICAL ANALYSIS

Answering these questions through comparative analysis of a small number of cases raises further methodological difficulties.[6] Theories cannot be tested convincingly, generalizations remain highly contingent, and we risk highlighting favored explanations at the expense of more compelling ones. On the other hand, small-number comparisons make it possible to examine the political process during periods of policy reform more closely and expose more clearly the mechanisms that link variables. The approach employed here uses comparative historical analysis to do three things: weight competing explanations of policy change; generate some contingent generalizations; and develop more convincing explanations of particular cases. I begin by outlining a series of arguments that have been used to explain policy change. These are drawn from four distinct levels of analysis: the international system, domestic coalitions, domestic institutions, and ideology. I explore the logic, strengths, and weaknesses of these arguments and summarize the role each has played in explaining variation across six cases: Korea, Taiwan, Singapore, Hong Kong, Brazil, and Mexico.

Since the argument is complex, I first outline it in a schematic way. International pressures are the most powerful stimulus to policy reform. The strength of different social groups—agricultural interests, labor, and business—can constrain or widen the feasible set of policy reforms, but it is difficult to explain policy outcomes by reference to coalitional interests alone, particularly where social groups are poorly organized, interests are subject to uncertainty, and states are "strong." External shocks do provide a stimulus to reform, and social forces are broadly constraining; nonetheless, explaining the reform process demands we

5. Barry R. Posen, *The Sources of Military Doctrine* (Ithaca: Cornell University Press, 1984), pp. 24–29.

6. On the methodology of comparative analysis I have profited from Theda Skocpol and Margaret Somers, "The Uses of Comparative History in Macrosocial Inquiry," *Comparative Studies in Society and History* 22 (1980): 174–97; Charles Tilly, *Big Structures, Large Processes, Huge Comparisons* (New York: Russell Sage Foundation, 1984); and John Odell, *U.S. International Monetary Policy* (Princeton: Princeton University Press, 1983), pp. 15–78.

pay attention to the interests of politicians, the institutional context in which they operate, and the ideas available to them concerning economic growth.

My argument rests on comparative analysis of both the "method of agreement" and the "method of difference" sort. Countries with similar growth paths should exhibit some crucial similarities. Those which follow alternative paths can be compared on the basis of hypothesized "critical differences." I also explore some variations among countries following a similar trajectory, a method designed to isolate the peculiarities of particular cases.

INTERNATIONAL CONSTRAINTS: SHOCKS, SIZE, AND POWER

The international system can constrain state choice in two ways: through market pressures, and through political pressures. To construct a theoretical explanation of the relationship between external market pressures and policy change, we need to look at how these pressures affect incentives both to new economic activity and to state intervention.[7] One would predict a shift from primary-product exports to the first stage of ISI when commodity-producing countries face price shocks or when international political or economic conditions sever access to markets, supplies, and capital. Price shocks change the relative rates of return between agro-export and import-competing sectors. Incentives to substitute for imports will also occur when foreign-exchange earnings and capital inflows dwindle and needed inputs become scarce.

Policy actions are likely to be supportive of these shifts, however. First, where the price shock is severe, political resistance will oppose adjustment through the market, for example, through large devaluations or changes in domestic wages and prices. States are likely to intervene to counteract such pressures. Second, sharp declines in export prices or volumes or reduced availability of external finance are associated with balance-of-payments crises. Governments respond to such crises by adopting trade and exchange controls that favor domestic producers over imports. This may not begin as a conscious strategy of industrialization, but it will generate its own constituency in the favored sectors. These sectors will gain as a result of their enhanced profitability and will want such policies to continue.[8] Finally, times of economic crisis are

7. See Helen V. Milner, *Resisting Protectionism* (Princeton: Princeton University Press, 1988); Jeffry Frieden, "Classes, Sectors, and Foreign Debt in Latin America," *Comparative Politics* 21 (October 1988): 1–20.

8. See Ronald Rogowski, "Political Cleavages and Changing Exposure to Trade," *American Political Science Review* 81 (December 1987): 1121–38.

conducive to an expansion of executive authority more generally. Thus we would expect external shocks to be met not only with discrete policy changes but with institutional innovations that tend to be centralizing and interventionary.

Similarly, entrepôts will try to diversify out of purely commercial activities when conditions in either the hinterland or the world economy obstruct the entrepôt's role as intermediary. The logic is the same; the returns to commercial activity decline in comparison to the returns on manufacturing, creating new incentives for government to support manufacturing.

The cases support these expectations, though with two critical caveats. One concerns the nature of the shocks, the other the importance of an additional intervening variable: size. The Great Depression was a watershed in the economic history of Latin America. Though responses to the shock varied across the region in ways that must be explained, the 1930s represent a period of policy change and an expansion of government capabilities.

Economic conditions in the world economy are not the only forces affecting patterns of trade and financial flows, however, and may not even effect all states in uniform fashion. The "world" depression of the 1930s did not hit Korea and Taiwan as it did the Latin American countries, because they were incorporated into the Japanese empire. Wars, revolutions, decolonization, and political conflicts with trading partners can also alter patterns of trade and investment and give rise to similar external shocks. The two world wars were important catalysts to industrialization in Latin America. In all of the East Asian cases external political changes played a role in change of strategy. In Korea and Taiwan severe balance-of-payments crises associated with war and reconstruction forced import substitution. In Hong Kong the Chinese Revolution and the strategic embargo associated with the Korean War reoriented traditional trade patterns. In Singapore the breakdown of association with Malaysia launched a new phase in Singapore's economic growth.

It is also important to note that countries of different sizes and resource endowments will respond to external shocks in very different ways. In relatively small, import-substituting countries and in those with few resources the plausibility of continuing import substitution is lower and the need to generate nontraditional exports more pressing. In large or resource-rich economies, by contrast, external shocks and balance-of-payments crises may plausibly be met by "deepening" import-substituting policies, while the country relies on commodity exports for the requisite foreign exchange.

Price shocks and the interruption of trade are likely to force a rethinking of primary-product and entrepôt strategies. But it is not true that expanding world trade will provide sufficient incentive to launch export-oriented policies. The reason has to do with the way domestic firms respond to changes in the international environment under different policy regimes. The strategy of protection, once chosen, will entrench the interests of policy makers and the private sector in the domestic market. Once manufactured export–oriented growth is launched, by contrast, firms acquire a stake in sustaining the policies associated with an outward-looking strategy. This strategic choice also exposes firms to international market signals. As unit labor costs rise, returns to labor-intensive manufacturing will decline. Export-led growth faced predictable problems of adjustment across the 1970s as a result of shifting comparative advantage (see Chapter 6). The *instruments* deployed to respond to these pressures and the *agents* responsible for diversification varied across cases, though. Korea responded with an aggressive, state-directed push into heavy industries; Hong Kong barely budged from its tradition of laissez-faire.

In sum, external economic shocks are likely to have an important influence on outward-oriented policies—whether based on entrepôt activities or the export of primary products or manufactures. They have a differential effect on countries pursuing inward-oriented strategies; much depends on size and the plausibility of "staying the course."

Market constraints are not the only international pressures to affect small states. The international system also acts on state choice through direct political pressures from external political actors. Major powers possess various assets—military capability and aid funds in particular—that give them leverage over smaller states. The difficulties involved in modeling these relationships in a way that avoids post hoc reasoning are well known: power resources are difficult to specify ex ante, they are not easily translated into control over outcomes, and apparently weak states exhibit remarkable powers of resistance.[9]

Nonetheless, it is clear that the greatest influence is exercised by formal empire or military occupation, since under such circumstances the very administrative structures that control the colony's economic activity are in the hands of the metropole. A lesser but still significant degree of influence will be exercised by an alliance leader where the client faces a significant external military threat and/or depends on extensive aid links. In such settings the alliance leader can tie continued military and economic support to policy reform. Transnational networks are also likely to be dense. Finally, the smallest degree of influence

9. On the problems of power analysis see David Baldwin, "Power Analysis and World Politics: New Trends versus Old Tendencies," *World Politics* 31 (January 1979): 161–94.

can be expected where there are asymmetrical economic relations but no direct imperial controls, security link, or extensive governmental aid ties. Though the major power still has potential influence through the manipulation of market access, the conditions for effective exercise of such influence are quite stringent.

This distinction among formal empire, military alliance, and economic hegemony is useful in distinguishing the degree of influence exercised by major powers in East Asia and Latin America and suggests a revisionist view of American influence in the Western hemisphere. There is little doubt that early in this century the United States exercised control over an informal empire in the Caribbean and Central America. But by the 1930s the large Latin American countries had been independent for over one hundred years and frequently adopted policies quite at odds with American policy preferences. Security considerations had some role in economic developments in Mexico and Brazil in the late 1930s and during World War II, but these worked to *increase* freedom of maneuver for these countries, since the United States was more concerned about their stance in the global conflict than the Latin American nations were dependent on the United States for security. Latin America's geographic distance from the "long arc" of U.S. containment policy in the postwar period has meant that the large states have usually not relied militarily on the United States; and when they have, it has been primarily for reasons of domestic "security." Rather than see the extension of a U.S. presence in the region as justified by a legitimate security need, they have resisted it as an unwanted expression of hegemony.

Korea, Taiwan, Hong Kong, and Singapore, by contrast, have all been colonies in this century. The early development of Singapore and the economic policy of Hong Kong to this day have been overseen by the British. The primary-product export phase of Korean and Taiwanese development came under Japanese auspices and was strongly shaped by a military-strategic conception of the imperial division of labor that combined production of raw materials and foodstuffs with investment in infrastructure and industry. By 1950 the divided republics of China and Korea were fully integrated into a U.S. security complex in Asia. In both cases the United States financed import-substitution based on a significant array of state controls. Aid was important not only materially but also because of the political support it rendered to the two new regimes. Given the unusual dependence of both countries on U.S. largesse and the unavailability of commercial borrowing, changes in aid flows could have a powerful influence on policy. The influence of external shocks, size, and great powers on the orientation of economic policy is summarized in Table 2.2.

Table 2.2. The international system and transitions in East Asia and Latin America

1. Import substitution (Mexico and Brazil)	
PPE to ISI 1	Depression and war-related shocks crucial; security conditions favor policy independence
ISI 1 to ISI 2	Size and availability of foreign investment are permissive conditions
ISI 2 to ISI 3	Size and availability of foreign investment, including commercial borrowing, are permissive conditions
2. Export-led growth (Taiwan and Korea)	
PPE to ISI 1	Policy developed initially by Japan as part of economic and military strategy; continued in postwar period following balance-of-payments crises; supported by United States
ISI 1 to ELG 1	Size, U.S. influence, and declining aid crucial; availability of foreign investment and growing world trade are permissive conditions
ELG 1 to ELG 2	Changing comparative advantage and protection in major markets crucial
3. Entrepôt growth (Singapore and Hong Kong)	
Entrepôt to ELG 1	Small size and political and economic rupture with hinterlands crucial; availability of foreign investment and growing world trade are permissive conditions; in Hong Kong, continuing influence of colonial relationship
ELG 1 to ELG 2	Changing comparative advantage and protection in major markets crucial

SOCIETY AS AN EXPLANATION

Societal or interest-based explanations of public policy are common to very disparate traditions of political economy, from Marxism to contemporary neoclassical political economy.[10] A societal, interest-based, or

10. Markos Mamalakis, "The Theory of Sectoral Clashes," *Latin American Research Review* 4, 3 (1969): 9–46, outlines a coalitional approach based on sectors; Robert Kaufman, "Industrial Change and Authoritarian Rule in Latin America: A Concrete Review of the Bureaucratic Authoritarian Model," in David Collier, ed., *The New Authoritarianism in Latin America* (Princeton: Princeton University Press, 1979), pp. 165–254, offers a sophisticated mix of class and sectoral approaches; Peter Gourevitch, *Politics in Hard Times* (Ithaca: Cornell University Press, 1987), adopts a sectoral approach that derives interests from international position; Michael Lipton, *Why Poor People Stay Poor: The Urban Bias in World Development* (Cambridge: Harvard University Press, 1977), sees the crucial cleavage not in class or sector but between countryside and city.

coalitional approach—the terms will be used interchangeably—rests on several simple assumptions. Policies have distributional consequences around which groups will mobilize to advance their interests. Politicians will respond to these pressures to achieve their own personal, political, and ideological aims; policies will be exchanged for support. Policy will therefore "reflect" the interests of "dominant" coalitions, whether seen as ruling parties, sectors, classes, or shifting coalitions of interest groups. The state is conceptualized as an arena through which coalitional battles are waged.

But, it must be noted, there are important theoretical and methodological problems to face in establishing causal connections between coalitions and public policies, particularly in the NICs. The first is identifying the relevant coalition. The easily identifiable electoral and legislative coalitions that determine public policy in the advanced industrial states are not relevant in the authoritarian NICs. Even during democratic periods in Singapore, Korea, and Brazil, the links between electoral politics and economic policy have been tenuous. Once we move outside the legislature, we face the question how the dominant coalition can be identified. Are the relevant cleavages those based on sector, class, factors of production, firms, interest groups?

One strategy is to begin deductively, identifying the groups likely to be favored by a particular strategy.[11] This approach is treacherous, however, because of the temptation to infer that favored groups were, in fact, the "dominant" coalition. Many coalitional arguments mistakenly identify a given social configuration as the source of policy when in fact the configuration may be only weakly related to or even a *consequence*, rather than the cause, of policy choice. A much more stringent criterion for demonstrating societal influence involves showing how groups overcome dilemmas of collective action, gain access to centers of decision making, and exercise influence. This research strategy of the "smoking coalition" underlies much pluralist and instrumental Marxist scholarship. This approach, too, has its drawbacks, the most important being that social structure can operate as a constraint on government action through the "law of anticipated consequences" even in the absence of overt attempts to wield influence.

My approach is to combine both methods. I begin with some simple deductive expectations concerning the interests of different sectors and how their political capabilities might constrain or widen the ability of state actors to pursue certain lines of policy. I do not gauge extent of societal influence simply by policy outcome, however; the process of

---

11. This is the strategy adopted by Frieden, "Classes, Sectors," and Rogowski, "Political Cleavages."

influence must be convincingly traced. The groups I examine are agricultural interests, the industrial working class, and business. These correspond roughly to the factors of land, labor, and capital, though I recognize that none of these constitutes a homogeneous group.

The Legacy of the Countryside

Two somewhat different hypotheses have related the political position of the agricultural sector to strategies for industrialization. One is that import-substituting industrialization is the result of the defeat of rural agricultural interests by rising urban, industrial political forces. The trade and exchange-rate policies supporting ISI are biased against export agriculture, and the cheap food policies favorable to industrialization turn the internal terms of trade against agriculture as well. Conversely, one would expect more balanced trade and exchange-rate policies, such as those associated with export-led growth, where agricultural interests are strong or where political elites have a particular concern about the allegiance of the peasantry.[12]

A second hypothesis has already been suggested; it centers on the existence of a comparative advantage in natural resources.[13] In resource-rich countries devaluation will not advance industrialization but benefit only the agro-export sector. Industrialization will therefore be achieved only through protection and subsidy. Natural resource endowment is fate. Once the government opts for industrialization, natural resource rents can be used to finance it over a long period, if they can be captured for that purpose. Resource-poor countries do not have the option of relying on export income to continue ISI. When the balance-of-payments problems associated with ISI emerge, such countries are more likely to try devaluation and export promotion.

In the cases examined here the pursuit of industrialization has been accompanied by a relative political weakening of agricultural interests, and the existence of a comparative advantage in natural resource exports has constrained policy choice. However, it is difficult to tie industrial policy directly to the outcome of an overt political clash between sectors.

As colonies, Korea and Taiwan were "agricultural appendages" to Japan, though Japan invested heavily in their agricultural modernization. Decolonization was followed by land reform, motivated in Taiwan by the debacle on the mainland and in Korea by the political pressures

---

12. Jeffrey Sachs, "External Debt and Macroeconomic Performance in Latin America and East Asia," *Brookings Papers on Economic Activity* 2 (1985): 523–73.
13. See Ranis, "Challenges and Opportunities."

associated with the division of the peninsula. (Hong Kong and Singapore did not have to contend at all with the thorny problem of agricultural transformation.) Gauging the importance of the land reforms (and the absence of an agricultural sector in the entrepôts) for subsequent industrial strategy demands that we consider some tricky counterfactuals. Such a rural social structure eliminated a potential source of opposition to industrializing initiatives: there was no social force to contest the first moves toward ISI, and the state's freedom of maneuver was correspondingly enhanced. The absence of an export-oriented rural elite might also have mitigated the sectoral conflicts that usually surround devaluation and thus eased the transition to export-led growth. There is no evidence in either case, however, that political concern with the rural sector was an influence in the transition to an outward-oriented strategy.

The redistribution of assets in land had a broadly equalizing effect on development in Korea and Taiwan. (The absence of a rural sector in Singapore and Hong Kong had the same consequence, since agricultural incomes tend to be lower than those in the modern sector.) This, in turn, had political consequences. The reforms in Korea and Taiwan created rural support for both regimes. After the shift to export-led growth, comparative advantage in agriculture declined rapidly. As rural political support remained important to both regimes, policy moved to protect farmers, traversing a path followed by the advanced industrial states.[14]

The shock in the 1930s to the agriculture- and mining-based economies of Latin America strengthened the position of manufacturing interests. The political transition to a national strategy favoring industry showed a wide variation of coalitional patterns, however, and did not necessarily involve the "defeat" of agriculture.[15] In Brazil the transition was accompanied by political compromises with rural elites, and in Mexico new rural elites quickly arose to replace the old. ISI may be disadvantageous to the rural sector *as a whole,* but large landholders benefited from the new course nonetheless. Despite unfavorable pricing policies, the drive to industrialization was accompanied by efforts to modernize agriculture because of its continued, and even heightened, importance in generating foreign exchange. A new stratum of commercial agricultural interests was created through the extension of irrigation, infrastructure, and credit, but at the expense of the peasantry.[16]

14. See Kym Anderson and Yujiro Hayami, *The Political Economy of Agricultural Protection: East Asia in Comparative Perspective* (London: Allen & Unwin, 1988).
15. See Kaufman, "Industrial Change and Authoritarian Rule."
16. Merilee Grindle, *State and Countryside: Development Policy and Agrarian Politics in Latin America* (Baltimore: Johns Hopkins University Press, 1986), p. 15.

There are important variations between Mexico and Brazil. Mexico's social revolution may have cleared the way for a growth strategy based on greater attention to domestic industry, but the revolution also legitimated redistribution of land. This project was pursued under Lázaro Cárdenas in the 1930s but faltered over the decade as a result of a variety of political pressures, including the creation of new landed interests from the "revolutionary family" itself. Despite recurrent pressures for redistribution of land, ownership remains highly skewed. The revolution and the Cárdenas period had an unexpected political consequence: the creation of a party organization that ensured political support from, and control over, the peasantry. In Brazil, Getúlio Vargas's centralizing Estado Novo increased the political independence of the central government from regional forces but did not entail state penetration of the rural sector, which is still characterized by a sharp dualism between latifundio and minifundio.

Overall, the political weakening of rural elites seems only indirectly linked to the transition to ISI. Nor is there evidence that the strength of rural interests was important in the transition to export-led growth, though the elimination of rural elites in Korea and Taiwan and their absence in Hong Kong and Singapore may have expanded the government's freedom to maneuver. The most salient comparison across regions has to do with the distribution of land and the *effects* of industrial policy on the distribution of income. Neither Mexico nor Brazil experienced the equalizing reforms of Korea and Taiwan, through which large landholders were virtually eliminated as a class. The origins of the rural social structure have long historical roots in both Mexico and Brazil, but the pursuit of ISI contributed to extensive rural poverty and a skewed distribution of income.

Labor

The political weakness of the industrial working class is a feature common to all of the NICs. Analysts of Brazilian and Mexican labor have stressed the importance of state- and party-corporatist controls respectively. Although there are differences in the political organization of labor in the East Asian NICs, labor movements have either been weak (Taiwan and Hong Kong) or, where active, drawn under state-corporatist control (Singapore) or repressed (Korea).

The timing of the political mobilization of the urban industrial working class and its relation to the political system do provide a point of contrast between the East Asian and Latin American NICs, however. Because of a longer history of industrialization in Latin America, the organization of labor occurred at a relatively early stage of the region's

37

political development and was tied to the emergence of leftist parties and ideologies. Despite a variety of subsequent controls and struggles between capital, the state, and labor, organized labor was a tacit or explicit political ally in the strategy of import substitution. The longer ISI was pursued, the greater was the constraining weight of its urban political constituency, in which organized labor plays a central role.

Drawing primarily on the Argentine and Brazilian cases, Guillermo O'Donnell has argued that the second phase of ISI demanded new controls on labor.[17] There is no compelling economic reason why this should be so, however, and the argument sits poorly with historical fact. In Mexico the corporatist organization of labor predated the adoption of ISI policies. In Brazil secondary ISI was part of a quasi-populist political project that antedated the military coup of 1964.

Variations in the mobilization and political organization of labor in Brazil and Mexico help explain differences in macroeconomic policy. In Mexico corporatist control over labor allowed the Partido Revolucionário Institucional (PRI) to weather a sharp and painful devaluation in 1954. The pattern of "stabilizing development" that ensued remained more or less intact until the 1970s. In Brazil, by contrast, the competitive bidding for labor and popular sector support associated with a multiparty system contributed to inflationary pressures in the 1950s and early 1960s. Unlike Mexico, Brazil lacked the political institutions to contain these conflicts. The sharp compression of wages and the repression of the labor movement that followed the military coup resulted from political considerations as much as from economic strategy, but the dictates of stabilization did play a role in subsequent political controls. In the late 1970s wage compression in Brazil and Mexico had another source: the effort to adjust to huge external debt burdens.

The hypothesized link between labor control and secondary ISI is questionable. Other political and economic factors were at work, and if anything, labor appears to act as a political force for the continuation of an inward-looking strategy. A plausible connection *can* be said to exist between the pursuit of a strategy based on exports of labor-intensive manufactures and labor weakness, however.[18] The weak form of the argument holds that the absence of a mobilized labor movement facilitated export-led growth by expanding the freedom of maneuver of both government and business. At the political level, weak labor movements help explain the absence of leftist and populist coalitions that might

17. Guillermo O'Donnell, *Modernization and Bureaucratic Authoritarianism* (Berkeley: Institute of International Studies, University of California, 1973); Collier, *The New Authoritarianism.*
18. This point is made in Fred Deyo, *Beneath the Miracle: Labor Subordination in the New Asian Industrialism* (Berkeley: University of California Press, 1989).

have provided political support for nationalist economic policies. Weak labor movements allowed the state to impose relatively free labor markets, thus keeping wage pressures down and increasing profits and managerial flexibility.

A stronger form of the argument asserts that labor was controlled *for the purpose* of pursuing export-led growth. This claim cannot be sustained as a general proposition, but neither can it be wholly rejected. In Singapore, Taiwan, and Korea labor controls initially had political rather than economic-strategic roots, and in Hong Kong a steady stream of refugees and peculiar features of the union structure have kept labor weak. But it is plausible to argue that concerns about labor activism have contributed to maintaining tight labor regimes, and in some cases, including Singapore and Korea, the link has been explicit.

The Interests of Capital

In both East Asia and Latin America the protectionist policies associated with the first stages of ISI benefited local entrepreneurs and came to be championed by them. This observation is quite different from arguing that business power was crucial in explaining the adoption of import-substituting policies. In Taiwan, in particular, it is more accurate to say that protection created the local bourgeoisie than the other way around. In both Mexico and Brazil the adoption of a coherent policy toward industrial development was slow in coming, and while the evidence remains highly controversial, it seems to have resulted as much from state interests and piecemeal adaptation to international shocks as from entrepreneurial influence on decision making.

Explaining the shift to secondary ISI, and particularly to export-led growth, in terms of business interests is particularly difficult. Export-led growth, with its demand for international competitiveness, poses a threat to firms oriented toward the domestic market. In Korea or Taiwan there is no evidence that local industry was the driving force behind export-oriented policies, even though it was to profit from them enormously. In Singapore local manufacturing was actually marginalized by a strategy based on multinationals. In Hong Kong we can make a more plausible case that business influence mattered, but ironically it was not the influence of manufacturing interests that was important. Rather, the large commercial and financial establishment acted as a force for laissez-faire *against* the interests of manufacturing.

Several characteristics of the business class were favorable to the adoption of export-oriented policies in Korea and Taiwan, however. Relatively small internal markets caused the problems of ISI to surface quickly, and surplus capacity in light manufacturing could be turned to production for international markets. Most important, the period of ISI was relatively short and the state was able both to force and to ease the transition to international markets. The ability to shift policy toward a more outward-looking growth strategy did not reflect business interests; rather, it rested on the government's political autonomy from the short-term interests of the private sector.

This does not mean that government was oblivious to business concerns. The high level of risk and uncertainty associated with an export-oriented course helps explain some of the anomalies in the neoclassical interpretation of East Asian industrialization, particularly those concerning the *instruments* deployed to achieve rapid export growth. Prior to the adoption of outward-looking policies, potentially competitive firms are unaware of their advantages. The willingness of firms to invest in new activities can be enhanced, though, by policy and institutional mechanisms that reduce risk, provide information, and enhance the credibility of the government's commitment to a particular policy line. These mechanisms also have the political effect, and motivation, of tying business to the government.

The turn to export-led growth in the larger Asian NICs must therefore be understood as a two-tiered policy reform. At one level the state acted to move the macro-level incentives to industry in a direction more conducive to the exploitation of comparative advantage, a project demanding some insulation from business pressures. The state also intervened on the micro-level—through targeted loans, selective protection, the provision of information, and the organization of business itself—to reduce the risks associated with the transition.

In the large Latin American NICs the longer duration of ISI produced entrenched protectionist interests that constituted an important constraint on the freedom of government maneuver. As protection was extended upstream into new industries (ISI 2), the coalition supporting inward-looking policies was broadened. Domestic end-users of protected intermediates and capital goods were naturally disadvantaged in efforts to penetrate foreign markets. When the Latin American NICs did adopt more outward-oriented policies, as in Brazil after 1964 and in Argentina and Chile in the 1970s, the experiments were conducted under authoritarian regimes that showed significant independence from local manufacturing interests.

Since the power and influence of multinational corporations has been a central topic of debate, it is worthwhile anticipating here an argument I develop in more detail in Chapter 8. The incentives associated with secondary ISI and export-led growth provided new opportunities for multinationals, adding them to the coalitions favoring the new policy course. Two caveats are important, however. First, MNCs seeking to exploit the new incentives, whether export-oriented or import-substituting, entered in quantity *after* the change in policy. It is thus misleading to argue they were responsible, in any more than a permissive sense, for the new course. Second, there are still important variations in the weight of local and foreign capital among countries pursuing *similar* strategies. Explaining this variation demands we pay attention to the opportunities and threats foreign firms pose, the level of development of local firms when MNCs enter, and the political links between the private sector and the government.

In all cases except Singapore, where the local private sector was weak, export-led policies provided opportunities for national firms. Given their external orientation and the rapid growth in world trade, multinationals and local firms could coexist without the threat of denationalization. In Latin America the role of foreign direct investment involved greater potential for political conflict. Though the regimes governing MNCs vary between Mexico and Brazil, the shift to a secondary phase of ISI was accompanied by a wooing of American multinationals, which quickly came to occupy a dominant position in the industrial structures of the two countries. The central social-structural comparisons between the NICs in the two regions, and their relationship to the different development paths, are outlined in Tables 2.3 and 2.4.

Table 2.3. The agricultural sector and transitions in East Asia and Latin America

1. Import substitution (Mexico and Brazil) PPE to ISI 1 and ISI 1 to ISI 2	Relative weakening of agricultural interests, but maintenance of stratified rural social structure. ISI detrimental to rural sector, though natural resource exports finance it
ISI 2 to ISI 3	Increase in incentives to export-oriented agriculture, including foreign agribusiness
2. Export-led growth (Korea and Taiwan) PPE to ISI 1	Land reforms occur simultaneously with turn to ISI, contributing to relative equity in distribution of income and assets
ISI 1 to ELG 1	Absence of natural resource exports a background condition for transition
ELG 1 to ELG 2	Agriculture gradually protected; some efforts to concentrate and modernize production
3. Entrepôt growth (Hong Kong and Singapore)	No significant agricultural sector

Table 2.4. Business, labor, and transitions in East Asia and Latin America

1. Import substitution (Mexico and Brazil)	
PPE to ISI 1	History of labor organization with ties to left parties, though movements are controlled early by party- and state-corporatist organizations. Business and organized labor gain from ISI, but influence over initial policy choice is weak
ISI 1 to ISI 2	Influenced by length of ISI 1 and resultant strength of urban-based ISI coalition; MNCs benefit, but influence over policy weak; regimes governing MNCs differ, as does balance among state, local, and foreign firms
ISI 2 to ISI 3	More incentives to export-oriented firms, both local and foreign; business influence unclear. Some link in Brazil and in Mexico's export-processing zones to wage policy
2. Export-led growth (Korea and Taiwan)	
PPE to ISI 1	Local firms benefit, but influence over policy is weak; labor either weak or controlled
ISI 1 to ELG 1	Weak labor movements conducive to ELG; business ambivalent, but short period of ISI and relative political weakness of ISI coalition ease transition; regimes governing MNCs differ, as does balance among state, local, and foreign firms
ELG 1 to ELG 2	New controls on labor (Korea); countries vary on adjustment strategy
3. Entrepôt growth (Singapore and Hong Kong)	
Entrepôt to ELG 1	Weak labor movements conducive to ELG; dominance of commercial capital influences Hong Kong's laissez-faire, but strong domestic manufacturing sector leads ELG 1; weak domestic manufacturing sector in Singapore means MNC dominance
ELG 1 to ELG 2	Wage policy is tool of adjustment (Singapore); countries vary on adjustment strategy

THE STATE AS ACTOR AND ORGANIZATION

Shifts in policy tend to solidify new coalitions that can constrain state action at some later time; the development of both ISI and exporting coalitions are examples. Changes in policy are not well explained in terms of the expressed interests of societal groups, however. Although I give greater weight to the force of international shocks, I note that adaptation to these shocks is mediated by political processes; some states respond to shocks aggressively, others fall into decline and sclerosis. Social-structural and international constraints are also likely to be of less importance in understanding the coherence of policy and the instruments through which it is pursued. The reasons are important to understand, since they provide the justification for a closer look at the state as both actor and institution.

First, the beneficiaries of policy reforms frequently have ambivalent or conflicting interests and may not be important political players. Their interest in a new policy course may be revealed only over time. Particularly during times of economic crisis, state actors are positioned to act independently—to construct, rather than merely reflect, emergent coalitions. Second, the very power of social forces is a function of the legal and institutional setting in which they operate. This is particularly true in the authoritarian political settings of the NICs. Finally, changes in strategy are generally accompanied by broader institutional changes that are crucial to their success. Interest groups are unlikely to expend resources on such innovations; as Douglass North argues, "institutional innovation will come from rulers rather than constituents since the latter would always face the free rider problem."[19]

A coalitional approach to policy looks at the interests and organizational power of dominant social actors; a statist or institutionalist approach, by contrast, explains policy in terms of the preferences and organizational power of state elites. These may include a rather broad set of political, military, and bureaucratic elites occupying offices in which authoritative allocative decisions are made, but I focus mainly on the role of top political leaders in the executive branch. State elites seek to build coalitions by extending policy favors that enhance the welfare of particular groups, creating and sustaining new bases of support in the process.[20] Their freedom of maneuver depends, however, on institutional setting and the organizational resources they have at their disposal. Three dimensions of the state as an institutional and legal structure bear on the ability of political elites to realize their interests. The first is degree of insulation from societal pressures, which in turn is a function of the institutional arrangements linking state and society. The second is cohesiveness of the decision-making structure itself. The third is instruments that are available to state elites in pursuing their political

19. See Douglass North, *Structure and Change in Economic History* (New York: Norton, 1981), p. 32.
20. See Robert H. Bates, *Markets and States in Tropical Africa: The Political Bases of Agricultural Policies* (Berkeley: University of California Press, 1981), and Barry Ames, *Political Survival: Politicians and Public Policy in Latin America* (Berkeley: University of California Press, 1987).

and substantive goals. Variations in these institutional characteristics influence policy choice and implementation.

Mancur Olson has suggested why the institutional arrangements linking state and society are critical to economic growth. Economic development, he argues, can be viewed as a problem of collective action.[21] Different social groups may benefit in the long run from cooperative sacrifices, but in the short run each has an interest in turning economic policy into a distributive game. If groups are allowed to organize for the purpose of influencing policy, distributional coalitions will result, restricting the range of state choices and the overall flexibility of the economy. Olson notes that wars have been one way such networks have been destroyed. An equally dark conclusion is that "successful" economic development requires institutions that restrain, control, weaken, or encapsulate the independent organizational strength of social forces, thereby insulating decision makers from group pressures and expanding the range of their directive powers.

Autonomy alone is certainly not a sufficient condition for optimal economic policies. Without it, however, state elites would find it difficult to pursue politically sensitive policies associated with shifts in overall strategy: lowering or control of real wages, raising of interest rates, uncompensated devaluation, lifting of subsidies or protection, and intersectoral or intertemporal resource transfers.

Advocates of a coalitional approach would not dispute this argument but would contend that such costs are routinely imposed on politically weaker groups. If adjustment costs are routinely imposed on weak actors, there is a prima facie case for a coalitional approach to policy. Certain growth policies are more likely to be adopted and succeed, however, when politicians have independence from the demands of *dominant*, as well as subordinate, social groups. Indeed, dominant social groups, whether export-oriented agriculture or import-substituting firms, present a greater challenge to policy reform precisely because of their ability to organize effectively.

Much of the literature on state "strength" has failed to specify adequately how we would identify a state as "autonomous" independently of the policy outcomes to be explained.[22] Apparently "authoritarian" re-

---

21. See Mancur Olson, *The Rise and Decline of Nations* (New Haven: Yale University Press, 1982), and Barbara Geddes, *Politician's Dilemma: Building State Capacity in Latin American Democracies*, unpublished ms.

22. On the concept of state "strength" see Peter Katzenstein, "Conclusion: Domestic Structures and Strategies of Foreign Economic Policy," in Katzenstein, ed., *Between Power and Plenty* (Madison: University of Wisconsin Press, 1978), pp. 295–336, and Eric Nordlinger, *On the Autonomy of the Democratic State* (Cambridge: Harvard University Press, 1982); see also the discussion of "soft" and "hard" states in Gunnar Myrdal, *The Challenge of World Poverty* (New York: Vintage, 1970), pp. 208–52.

gimes may be extensively penetrated by social forces and allow significant independent political organization, whereas corporatist structures in democracies have proved successful in extracting restraint from labor and business. Allowing that variations occur within the same regime type, I argue nonetheless that democracies and polities organized on the basis of clientelistic networks are less insulated than corporatist regimes and those authoritarian regimes which limit autonomous political organization and public contestation. As a result, economic policy in liberal-democratic and clientelistic systems is more likely to be explained by coalitional and rent-seeking pressures and less likely to be consistent and internally coherent. Put differently, the power of coalitional arguments is contingent on institutional context.

The cases examined in this book suggest repeatedly that state-society linkages limiting the level of independent organization of interests were crucial in explaining several key transitions, including the move from the primary-product phase to ISI, the move to "stabilizing development" in Mexico after 1954, the move to more market-oriented policies in Brazil after 1964, and above all the adoption by the East Asian NICs of the policies associated with export-led growth.

Internal organizational characteristics of the state, including most important the cohesiveness and centralization of decision making, are the second factor affecting the ability of the state to change course. Governments have greater freedom of maneuver when bureaucrats and political elites have similar priorities or are allied. An internally cohesive state is more likely to pursue consistent and credible policies. "Pieces" of an internally divided state are more likely to seek societal clients and, simply, to pursue their independent visions of the public good. Brazil and Mexico have experienced periods of relatively consistent policy—Mexico from 1954 through 1970 and Brazil following the coup in 1964—that reflect such internal bureaucratic coherence. Korea in the 1950s provides a case study in internal fragmentation. On the whole, however, the larger states of Latin American have had greater difficulty maintaining internal coherence, and though intrabureaucratic conflict is certainly not absent from the East Asian NICs, the period of export-led growth in all four has been characterized by a relatively centralized and concentrated apparatus for economic decision making.

Finally, policy choice is influenced by the range of policy instruments the state commands. In Brazil, Mexico, Korea, and Taiwan the turn to import substitution corresponded with a period of state building and the accretion of new policy instruments. Institutions do, of course, change, but important variations in the instruments of national policy can be traced to this early period of national consolidation. For example, strong and conservative central banks developed early in Mexico and Taiwan but not in Korea and Brazil. Once developed, state actors tend to view solutions to particular problems through the lens of the instruments that are available to them; their options are limited or expanded by the tools they have at hand. This fact is important in explaining the way particular strategies are pursued. The most important example explored here is the way in which the East Asian NICs adjusted to the shocks of the 1970s. The Korean leadership used its control over the financial system to direct a second round of import substitution. Taiwan relied to a greater extent on fiscal measures and state-owned enterprises, and Singapore's strategy hinged on the control of wages. By contrast, Hong Kong, which had developed few instruments of intervention, relied primarily on a market-oriented system of adjustment.

To summarize, policies reflect the effort to build and sustain coalitions, but available organizational resources expand or contract politicians' freedom of maneuver. Characteristics of the state as an institution—the degree of autonomy from social forces, the cohesion of the policy-making apparatus, and the available policy instruments—are crucial in understanding policy reform.

IDEAS: THE TRANSMISSION OF POLICY-RELEVANT KNOWLEDGE

The logic of the argument so far has been broadly structural and involves identifying a set of antecedent conditions—international, coalitional, and institutional—that are conducive to particular outcomes. If these situational constraints and state capacities could be shown to determine unambiguously the policy choices taken, an ideational perspective would be superfluous. The analysis of ideas could at best verify structural explanations by showing how situational constraints operated in the decision-making calculus. Yet in fact, the range of options open during a time of crisis is not entirely given by the setting. If state elites periodically achieve autonomy from societal influences, the economic ideologies available to them might loom large as an explanation of state action. State autonomy may explain the *capacity* to formulate and execute an economic program, but it does not answer the nagging question where state interests come from.

By "economic ideologies" I refer to more or less coherent frameworks of policy-relevant knowledge. Less general than ideology broadly conceived, economic ideologies embody theoretically grounded beliefs about cause-effect relations. Economic ideologies have coalitional implications, but usually they are not generated by particular societal interests, even in the advanced industrial states. These ideas originate among professional economists and policy analysts and are transmitted internationally through international organizations, bilateral aid missions, and the training of professional economists and domestically through universities, research centers, and think tanks.

The structuralism of the United Nations Economic Commission on Latin America and the various forms of dependency thinking that later grew out of it provided a theoretically elaborated rationale for nationalist policies. It is plausible to argue that these ideological currents shaped the direction of economic policy in several Latin American countries; that ideas themselves acted as a kind of constraint. Since size, external shocks, and domestic political interests pushed in the same direction, however, it is difficult to establish the independent role of ideas. The shift to export-oriented growth in East Asia provides a somewhat better testing ground, since the domestic political constraints appear to have been somewhat less binding. Korea and Taiwan both faced declining U.S. aid commitments, but various ideas existed about how to respond. In the mid-1950s more conservative Kuomintang (KMT) members championed a statist adjustment strategy, while in 1962 young colonels in the Korean junta were advocating "self-reliant" policies. In both cases American advisers influenced development thinking. Similarly, Hong Kong's economic orientation has been institutionally entrenched in a succession of powerful financial secretaries for whom laissez-faire constituted a virtual article of faith.

The pattern described suggests one methodological point about disentangling the influence of ideas: the plausibility of ideological arguments for policy choice increases with the degree of autonomy of political elites from societal or international constraints. When these constraints operate, it becomes more difficult to separate ideational and material variables; when political elites are autonomous, their ideological visions and "projects" weigh more heavily on the course of policy. The influence of these political and ideological variables is summarized in Table 2.5.

This chapter outlines a framework for comparative historical analysis. I began by tracing three growth trajectories and identifying the critical transitions within them. Policy played an important role in these transitions. Four components of national strategy are of interest: orientation, instruments, agents, and integration or coherence. I outlined a series of causal variables aimed primarily at explaining and identifying the salient differences between the development paths of Latin America and East Asia. This framework has three purposes. The first is to advance the logic of different theoretical arguments and identify the reasons why some causal factors are likely to operate more powerfully than others. Second, the chapter establishes a set of dimensions along which the cases

Table 2.5. Institutions, ideas, and transitions in East Asia and Latin America

1. Import substitution (Mexico and Brazil)	
PPE to ISI 1	Corresponds with interests of centralizing state elites building new support coalitions; orchestrated under relatively autonomous states
ISI 1 to ISI 2 and ISI 2 to ISI 3	State-initiated strategy changes; diffusion of ISI ideology contributed. In Mexico, party dominance and internal cohesion mean stable growth (1954–1970); greater internal splits within party and state (1970–present). In Brazil, democratic government (1948–1964) means inflationary growth; greater cohesion initially under military; less coherence under pressures for political opening
2. Export-led growth (Korea and Taiwan)	
PPE to ISI 1	Corresponds with interests of centralizing state elites building new support coalitions; single-party dominance in Taiwan means coherent strategy; nominally democratic rule in Korea yields highly inconsistent strategy
ISI 1 to ELG 1	State-led strategy changes, with autonomy, internal cohesiveness, and wide array of instruments assisting the transition; U.S. ideological influence appears important
ELG 1 to ELG 2	Strategies vary depending on prior instruments of intervention
3. Entrepôt growth (Hong Kong and Singapore)	
Entrepôt to ELG 1	State-led change, though under laissez-faire ideological orientation and highly autonomous colonial "state" in Hong Kong; more interventionist state in Singapore tied to deep political conflicts and building of new bases of support
ELG 1 to ELG 2	Strategies vary depending on prior instruments of intervention

may be compared and summarizes some of the empirical findings. Finally, it helps identify puzzles particular to individual cases. In Part Two I undertake a comparative historical analysis of the growth trajectories of the individual NICs, focusing particularly on key points of policy reform and transition.

PART II

HISTORY: INDUSTRIALIZATION
IN COMPARATIVE PERSPECTIVE

CHAPTER THREE

Korea: From Import Substitution to Export-Led Growth

External constraints, including political partition, a loss of major markets, and persistent balance-of-payments problems, were the critical factors pushing Korea and Taiwan toward import-substituting policies immediately after World War II. However, there were important differences between the two countries in instruments of policy, balance between the public and private sectors, and overall coherence of policy. These can be traced to differences in the political institutions of the two countries.

A legacy of Japanese imperialism as much as of American occupation, the Korean state appeared archetypically strong. American support for conservative forces, partition, and war virtually eliminated the left, and land reforms reduced the power of rural elites. Nonetheless, the government proved less insulated than might appear, because of networks of patronage that developed between the Liberal party and its supporters. Adopting a coherent development strategy would have reduced Syngman Rhee's control over aid funds and policy instruments that were crucial to sustaining political support. Despite his high dependence on U.S. aid, Rhee stubbornly resisted American economic advice.

The narrowness of Rhee's base of support, the corruption of the regime, and the lack of a coherent economic strategy produced a general political crisis in 1960. The short-lived Second Republic that followed demonstrated clearly the importance of political institutions for achieving economic goals. Though reformist, the new government had no way of containing the conflicting demands placed on it by newly mobilized social forces. The collapse of this brief democratic interlude set the stage for military intervention, which in turn resulted in a restructuring of the political and administrative systems and a basic change in economic policy.

JAPANESE AND AMERICAN LEGACIES

During the interwar period the Japanese colonial bureaucracy oversaw Korea's position as a rice producer in a regional division of labor, investing heavily in infrastructure and "rationalizing" traditional land relationships through the fixing of property rights.[1] These reforms increased Japan's ability to extract food surpluses from the colony, but they increased tenancy and polarized the countryside. The colonial bureaucracy also fostered industrial expansion. Light manufacturing proliferated in the 1920s, primarily under Japanese auspices, though the beginnings of important Korean business groups can be traced to the period as well.[2] After 1931, and particularly after the Japanese attack on China in 1937, Korea became a supply and production base for Japan's expansion into Manchuria. Heavy industries were established under the auspices of state-designated companies.

On Japan's defeat the left gained wide influence as the political grouping least tarnished by collaboration. Organizations of workers, peasants, and youth emerged throughout the country in a burst of political activity in the fall of 1945. A coalition of predominantly leftist forces proclaimed the aim of a people's republic and a commitment to social as well as political liberation.

Not surprisingly, the American occupation forces did not find the People's Republic to their liking, and "liberated" Korea was subjected to a relatively hostile occupation.[3] The net effect of the policies of the American Military Government (AMG) was to strengthen the right,

1. See Peter Duus, "Economic Dimensions of Meiji Imperialism: The Case of Korea, 1895–1910"; Samuel Pao-San Ho, "Colonialism and Development: Korea, Taiwan, and Kwantung"; and Ramon H. Myers and Yamada Saburo, "Agricultural Development in the Empire," all in Ramon Myers and Mark Peattie, eds., *The Japanese Colonial Empire: 1895–1945* (Princeton: Princeton University Press, 1984); Sang Chul Suh, *Growth and Structural Change in the Korean Economy* (Cambridge: Harvard University Press, 1978); and Bruce Cumings, *The Origins of the Korean War* (Princeton: Princeton University Press, 1981), chaps. 1 and 2.

2. On Korean industry under the Japanese see Carter Eckert, *The Colonial Origins of Korean Capitalism: The Kochang Kims and the Kyongsang Spinning and Weaving Company, 1876–1945* (Seattle: University of Washington Press, 1990); Leroy Jones and Il Sakong, *Government, Business, and Entrepreneurship in Economic Development: The Korean Case* (Cambridge: Harvard University Press, 1980), pp. 27–28; Daniel Sungil Juhn, "Korean Industrial Entrepreneurship, 1924–1940," in Yung-whan Jo, ed., *Korea's Response to the West* (Kalamazoo, Mich.: Korea Research and Publications, 1971); E. B. Schumpeter, *The Industrialization of Japan and Manchukuo, 1930–1940* (New York: Macmillan, 1940); Dalchoong Chang, "Japan's Transnational Corporations and the Political Economy of the Relationship between South Korea and Japan" (Ph.D. diss., University of California, Berkeley, 1982).

3. Cumings, *Origins*, 101–34; Gregory Henderson, *Korea: The Politics of the Vortex* (Cambridge: Harvard University Press, 1968), pp. 113–47.

gathered initially in the Korean Democratic Party (KDP) and later around nationalist leader Syngman Rhee. More important, the AMG bolstered the bureaucracy, police, and new military machinery, which later gave Rhee the organizational tools with which to build support and control opposition.[4] An American effort to build a "third force" between right-wing nationalists and the left floundered. The failure of the UN Joint Commission to solve the problem of unification and the subsequent policy of separately sponsored elections favored the right over both moderates and Communists, who opposed partition. By independence in August 1948 rightist forces were in control of a state apparatus that, despite its nominally democratic form, showed important continuities with the Japanese colonial period.

The left, meanwhile, was excluded from power and gradually saw its base of political support in the countryside and labor movement whittled away. Rural uprisings in the fall of 1946 were suppressed. The power of the rural "people's committees," which had assumed governmental functions in some areas, had largely been broken by the national police prior to that time, though scattered rural-based insurgency continued until the eve of the Korean War.[5]

The autumn uprising of 1946 coincided with the defeat of leftist unions as well.[6] The first national trade union federation, the General Council of Korea Trade Unions (GCKTU), was formed in 1945 and pressed a radical program including workers' participation in management. Supported by employers and right-wing politicians, a small group of anti-Communist workers formed an alternative Federation of Korean Trade Unions (FKTU) in March 1946. In September 1946 a walkout by railway workers organized by the GCKTU led to a wave of strike activity

4. Cumings, *Origins*, pp. 101–34; Henderson, *Korea*, pp. 113–47. On the continuity of the legal system see Gregory Henderson, "Law and Judicial Practice in South Korea: A Korean-American Chance Missed," in Wonmo Dong, ed., *Korean-American Relations at the Crossroads* (Princeton Junction, N.J.: Association of Korean Christian Scholars of North America, 1982), pp. 60–70.

5. On the origins of Korean Communism see Robert Scalapino and Chong-sik Lee, *Communism in Korea*, 2 vols. (Berkeley: University of California Press, 1972). On the rural insurgencies see Cumings, *Origins*, pp. 267–381, and John Merrill, "Internal Warfare in Korea, 1948–1950: The Local Setting of the Korean War," in Bruce Cumings, ed., *Child of Conflict: The Korean-American Relationship, 1943–1953* (Seattle: University of Washington Press, 1983), pp. 133–62.

6. For an analysis of the defeat of the leftist unions, see Stewart Meacham, "Korean Labor Report," prepared for the Secretary of Labor, November 1947, mimeo reproduced by American Friends Service Committee, 1986. Meacham was labor advisor to the commanding general of the United States Armed Forces, Korea. U.S. International Cooperation Administration, Office of Labor Affairs, "Summary of the Labor Situation in South Korea," mimeo, October 1955; Park Young-ki, *Labor and Industrial Relations in Korea* (Seoul: Sogang University Press, 1979); George Ewing Ogle, "Labor Unions in Rapid Economic Development: Case of the Republic of Korea in the 1960s" (Ph.D. diss., University of Wisconsin, 1973), pp. 45–53.

that was broken by the national police with the support of the American Military Government. With the arrest, harassment, and flight of the GCKTU's leaders and the identification of the General Council with the Communists' unpopular support of trusteeship proposals, the confederation declined in membership and was finally outlawed. At both the plant and the national level the pliable FKTU stepped into the breach. Korea thus entered the first phase of its postindependence industrialization with a severely weakened labor movement.

The weakening of the left eliminated the socialist option, but the main determinants of policy were external. The partitioning of the country left the south largely without fertilizer, iron, steel, and other raw materials and intermediates. The departure of the Japanese created a vacuum in external economic relations and domestic management. Between 1944 and the end of 1946 the number of manufacturing establishments dropped by 44 percent, manufacturing employment by nearly 60 percent. Total industrial output in 1948 was one-fifth of the 1940 level, and retail prices almost doubled between 1946 and 1947.[7] Postwar trade dwindled to very low levels, creating severe balance-of-payments difficulties. Protection and exchange controls were not so much chosen as imposed by events.

SYNGMAN RHEE AND THE POLITICAL BASES OF KOREAN ISI

Rhee assumed office against a backdrop of political and economic turmoil, and the police and the bureaucracy became the main bases of his political power. These institutions "were present in all parts of the country, highly centralized, feared by the general population and ready to serve a government which could effectively insulate them from political parties and public opinion."[8] Rhee's creation of the Liberal party in 1951 gave him a quasi-corporatist organization that linked the party with the Korean Youth Corps, the labor union movement, student organizations, and farmers' cooperatives.

Rhee's apparent political autonomy was partly checked by the democratic institutions imposed by the Americans. The biggest force in the National Assembly was the KDP, built around a group of absentee landlords and industrialists. Initially supporters of Rhee, they came to

---

7. Charles R. Frank, Kwang Suk Kim, and Larry Westphal, *Foreign Trade Regimes and Economic Development: South Korea* (New York: Columbia University Press for the National Bureau of Economic Research, 1975), p. 8; Paul W. Kuznets, *Economic Growth and Structure in the Republic of Korea* (New Haven: Yale University Press, 1977), pp. 28–34.

8. Sungjoo Han, *The Failure of Democracy in South Korea* (Berkeley: University of California Press, 1974), p. 17.

oppose his autocratic control of the bureaucracy. The nature of political institutions became the main object of contestation. The KDP sought to institute a cabinet form of government that would increase the Assembly's control over patronage. Through a series of political maneuvers and strong-arm tactics, Rhee forced constitutional amendments in 1952 that weakened the legislature and strengthened the executive.[9]

The political setting was conducive to land reform.[10] Reforms had begun under the AMG with the sale of Japanese properties to tenants, but the American reforms had not touched Korean holdings. Facing elections in 1950 in the wake of significant rural uprisings, carrying the stigma of collaborationism and confronted with sweeping reforms in the north, the KDP had little choice but to support reform, though actual transfers of property did not take place until the Korean War itself. These reforms were not followed by a political and organizational commitment to rural development, however. Once the landlords had been dislodged and problems of rural insurgency solved, the locus of political conflict shifted to the urban centers. As a result, Rhee gave much greater emphasis to industry and the urban areas than did the Kuomintang on Taiwan.

American aid was key to the political economy of import-substitution in the 1950s. The significance of U.S. support for the regime can hardly be overstated. Aid financed nearly 70 percent of total imports between 1953 and 1962 and equaled 75 percent of total fixed capital formation.[11] The United States sought various institutional reforms in an effort to gain greater leverage over Korean economic policy making. These included the formation of a Combined Economic Board, joint control over counterpart funds, and, after 1956, annual stabilization programs. The reforms sought by the Americans cut directly against Rhee's political interests, however. The Americans wanted higher taxes, which would have enhanced the Assembly opposition; decreased government expenditure, which would have reduced the power of the bureaucracy; and a

9. On the weakening of the legislature and the trend to autocracy see Henderson, *Korea*, pp. 162–74.

10. On the reforms see C. Clyde Mitchell, "Land Reform in South Korea," *Pacific Affairs* 22 (June 1949): 144–54; Robert B. Morrow and Kenneth H. Sharper, *Land Reform in South Korea* (Washington: U.S. Agency for International Development, 1970); Hsin-Huang Michael Hsiao, *Government Agricultural Strategies in Taiwan and South Korea* (Nankang, Taipei: Academica Sinica, 1981); Sung Hwan Ban, Pal Yong Moon, and Dwight H. Perkins, *Rural Development*, Studies in the Modernization of the Republic of Korea (Cambridge: Harvard University Press, 1980), pp. 283–97; Cumings, *Origins*, chap. 2.

11. The most succinct summary of the aid relationship is David Cole, "Foreign Assistance and Korean Development," in Cole, Young-il Lim, and Paul Kuznets, *The Korean Economy: Issues of Development*, Korea Research Monograph 1 (Berkeley: Institute of East Asian Studies, University of California, 1980), from which the following data are extracted.

more realistic exchange rate, which would have reduced Rhee's discretionary control over foreign exchange and imports. The United States also sought reductions in defense spending and a curbing of the police, two key bases of Rhee's support.[12] But as long as Rhee could use the country's geostrategic significance to sustain the flow of aid, there was little incentive to institute domestic reform.

The first government-to-government pact, signed in December 1948, outlined the quid pro quo of the aid relationship and implied a lack of trust in the Korean government. The United States expected certain economic reforms: sound fiscal and monetary policies, the privatization of Japanese properties, and the creation of a counterpart fund into which the Korean government would deposit the local currency equivalent of all U.S. aid. The use of these counterpart funds would be determined jointly by the Americans and the Koreans. In 1949 and 1950 aid commitments were cut in order to extract compliance.

The war came to Rhee's rescue, reducing the willingness of the United States to press reform. Rhee exploited his position as "defender of the free world," and he used splits between the UN military command and the UN Korean Reconstruction Agency (UNKRA) to maintain maximum flexibility over the use of aid. Numerous conflicts ensued; the most divisive concerned the exchange rate. The Koreans claimed that local currency advances made to the Americans during the war, rather than government profligacy, were at the root of inflation. Rhee insisted on repayment of the advances at a rate that became increasingly overvalued with wartime inflation.[13]

Aid conflicts also reflected broader differences over development strategy.[14] Advisers to UNKRA wanted Korea to pursue a rationalized program of infrastructural development and import substitution. This program was to be financed by large infusions of development assistance

12. This point is made by Joungwon A. Kim, *Divided Korea: The Politics of Development, 1945–1972* (Cambridge: Harvard University Press, 1975), p. 131.

13. The most detailed discussion of aid conflict is Gene Lyons, *Military Policy and Economic Aid: The Korean Case, 1950–1953* (Columbus: Ohio State University Press, 1961), which covers only the early period. See also U.S. House of Representatives, Committee on Foreign Affairs, Subcommittee for Review of Mutual Security Programs, Staff Survey Team, *Report . . . on Economic Assistance to Korea, Thailand, and Iran* (Washington, D.C.: USGPO, 1960); Sock Kyun Chu, "Why American Aid Failed," *Koreana Quarterly* 4 (Autumn 1962): 81–93, and Stephan Haggard, Byung-Kook Kim, and Chung-in Moon, "The Transition to Export-Led Growth in Korea, 1954–1966," Committee on Research on Social and Political Organization Working Paper, Harvard University, 1989. For evidence of Rhee's personal involvement in the exchange rate controversies, see C. Tyler Wood (chief U.S. aid administrator) to State Department, telegram, Sept. 5, 1953, National Archives, Record Group 59, 895.00/9–553.

14. See John P. Lewis, *Reconstruction and Development in Korea*, Planning Pamphlet 94 (Washington, D.C.: National Planning Association, 1955).

but also by an increased exploitation of Korea's comparative advantage in mineral and agricultural exports and a mobilization of domestic resources. The American-controlled UN Command and U.S. aid agencies emphasized the importance of stabilization for achieving these goals and insisted on using a substantial portion of aid for commodity imports designed to slow inflation.

Rhee certainly cared less than the Americans about inflation. The U.S. strategy seemed to offer a return to the export-oriented economy of the Japanese occupation and called into question U.S. commitment to new productive investments. Rhee's objections were above all political, however. Policies that appeared a complex and confusing patchwork in economic terms can be explained by reference to Rhee's use of the instruments of economic policy—allocation of foreign exchange, bank credit, import licenses—to sustain political support. Between 1953 and 1960 Korea saw a bewildering succession of exchange-rate regimes. None lasted for two full years; all undervalued the dollar.[15] The possession of foreign exchange and aid goods at considerably less than their market value presented an opportunity for pure arbitrage to those favored traders willing to provide kickbacks to the Liberal party.[16] Rhee's control over imported grains and other goods allowed him to distribute largesse directly to government employees and others, protecting them from inflation. Domestic firms profited as well, purchasing raw materials supplied as part of the U.S. aid program at an overvalued official exchange rate and selling finished goods at prices that reflected scarcity values. The selective allocation of loans and the noncompetitive award of government and U.S. military contracts were additional means of favoring supporters. The Liberal party even invested directly in private projects receiving U.S. aid.

The desire to cement a close business-government relationship also helps explain why the state's direct role in production was limited in Korea compared to Taiwan.[17] The Americans wanted to sell off Japa-

15. The most detailed account of changes in the exchange rate regimes of the fifties is in Frank, Kim, and Westphal, *Foreign Trade Regimes*, chap. 3.

16. Evidence on this type of activity is scattered, and the scope of corruption is impossible to measure. See Lyons, *Military Policy and Economic Aid*, p. 91; Jones and Sakong, *Government, Business, and Entrepreneurship*, pp. 270–74; Committee on Foreign Affairs, Staff Survey Team, *Report;* Joungwon A. Kim, *Divided Korea*, p. 152; U.S. General Accounting Office, *Report on Examination of Economic and Technical Assistance Program for Korea, International Cooperation Administration, Department of State, Fiscal Years 1957–1961, Part I* (B–125060), Sept. 21, 1962, pp. 85–91; Kyong-dong Kim, "Political Factors in the Formation of the Entrepreneurial Elite in South Korea," *Asian Survey* 16 (April 1976): 465–71. Korean evidence is reviewed in Haggard, Moon, and Kim, "Transition to Export-Led Growth."

17. E. Grant Meade, *American Military Government in Korea* (New York: Columbia University Press, 1951), pp. 203–12; Jones and Sakong, *Government, Business, and Entrepreneurship*, p. 144.

nese industrial properties, but initially there were few qualified buyers and the properties ended up in government hands. The political pressure on American and Korean property managers from bureaucrats, high-ranking military officers, and prospective entrepreneurs was intense. Despite the maintenance of some state-owned enterprises, substantial privatization took place and contributed to the growth of several industrial groups.

The combination of the effort to maximize aid inflows and the political use of economic instruments resulted in a highly inconsistent economic program summarized neatly by David Cole and Young Woo Nam:

> [Rhee and his followers] rejected the idea of overall planning and were not interested in trying to define the longer-run objectives or an integrated set of policies. This probably reflected a belief on their part that they could retain more flexibility and achieve better results in negotiations with aid donors by proceeding on an ad hoc basis. . . . To have agreed to [an economic plan] would have exposed the government to serious political risks.[18]

The dominance of political considerations in the making of economic policy had institutional correlates, particularly the lack of support given to technocratic reformers.[19] Plans drafted through the prime minister's planning and budget office (1948–54) languished because of conflicts between Rhee and the prime minister. In 1955 Rhee established the Ministry of Reconstruction (MOR) to coordinate overall planning, appointing Song In-sang, a former banker with experience at the World Bank, its first head. In 1958 an Economic Development Council was formed under the auspices of the Ministry of Reconstruction, which made a concerted effort to locate American-trained economists and advance them to positions of authority within the ministry. Through the Combined [i.e., Korean-American] Economic Board, the MOR maintained close working relations with the U.S. Embassy and the United States Operations Mission.

As a new ministry with no set constituency, the Ministry of Reconstruction represented a significant enclave of developmentalist thinking; the Research Department of the Bank of Korea and the Bureau of the Budget in the Ministry of Finance were similar enclaves. No high-level political support was given to these organizationally scattered reformers, however. The Economic Development Council drafted a Three Year Plan by 1959, but it was shelved by a Liberal cabinet besieged

18. David Cole and Young Woo Nam, "The Pattern and Significance of Planning in Korea," in Irma Adelman, ed., *Practical Approaches to Development Planning: Korea's Second Five-Year Plan* (Baltimore: Johns Hopkins University Press, 1969).

19. For details on the administrative reforms, see Haggard, Kim, and Moon, "Transition to Export-Led Growth."

with political difficulties.[20] The Ministry of Reconstruction had to compete with more powerful, politically connected ministries, particularly the ministries of Finance and Agriculture, and with the Liberal party itself.

A standard judgment on the Rhee period holds that inconsistent, politically motivated ISI policies were responsible for slow growth.[21] This assessment, based on a comparison with performance after the shift toward export-led growth, is misleading on two counts. First, it overlooks the rebuilding and expansion of the private sector under Rhee. GDP growth averaged only 3.9 percent from 1953–55 to 1960–62, but this can be traced to the sluggish performance of agriculture and services. Industry grew at 11.2 percent a year.[22] Without the threat of competition or denationalization from foreign firms, with high tariff barriers and with little competition from state-owned enterprises, Korean firms developed rapidly over the 1950s, particularly in construction, textiles, milling, and light consumer goods. By the late 1950s the Korean economy did exhibit symptoms attributed to ISI: an overemphasis on consumer goods, production geared to a limited domestic market, a high dependence on imported intermediates and foreign capital, weak exports, and continuing balance-of-payments problems. But blaming ISI alone overlooks the importance of changes in American aid policy, particularly the annual stabilization programs launched in 1956. These programs had the effect of slowing inflation, but they also slowed private investment. Gross investment declined in real terms in both 1958 and 1959 after having grown rapidly from 1953 to 1957. The GNP growth rate peaked at 8.7 percent in 1957, then declined to 7.0 percent in 1958, 5.2 percent in 1959, and 2.3 percent in 1960.[23]

It is difficult to disentangle the various causes for the weakening of Rhee's political base.[24] Rhee's age and poor health, his autocratic character, and the gradual decline in his charismatic appeal as a nationalist leader no doubt contributed. Nonetheless, it is clear that corruption and the economic slowdown played a role in expanding the opposition. Within the Liberal party a group of hard-liners around the president urged the use of the police to "manage" the opposition; after 1958 such

20. Hahn Been Lee, *Time, Change, Administration* (Honolulu: East-West Center, 1968), p. 91; Quee-Young Kim, *The Fall of Syngman Rhee*, Korea Research Monograph 7 (Berkeley: Institute of East Asian Studies, University of California, 1983), pp. 15–22.

21. See, for example, Anne Krueger, *The Development Role of the Foreign Sector and Aid* (Cambridge: Harvard University Press, 1979).

22. Kuznets, *Economic Development*, p. 51.

23. Economic Planning Board, *Statistical Yearbook 1962* (Seoul: Economic Planning Board, 1962), p. 69.

24. Quee-Young Kim, *The Fall of Syngman Rhee*, provides a detailed analysis of the outlook of the participants in the April 1960 uprising. See also Sunjoo Han, *The Failure of Democracy*.

tactics were employed with greater frequency. Following the dramatic rioting of April 19, 1960, to protest electoral fraud and corruption, in which students played a leading role, Rhee resigned, paving the way for the Second Republic.

Economic development and the elimination of corruption were given priority by the new Chang Myon government.[25] Technocrats gained wider access to top political authorities. The primary interest of party regulars, however, was to gain access to the spoils of office. The *sequencing* of reforms also proved politically costly. The pursuit of a more realistic exchange rate, supported by a U.S. stabilization fund, and the increase in charges for government services reduced popular support for the government and undermined business confidence.[26] But immediate economic issues were not central to the political polarization of the final days of the Chang Myon government: reform of the bureaucracy and military, purge of corrupt officials, and unification with the north ranked as the most salient, and divisive, issues. The main problems facing the government were political and organizational. Lacking any organizational autonomy, even from its own supporters, the reformist government was unable to reconcile the conflicting demands placed on it from left and right. Finally, it proved incapable of maintaining order.

KOREA ISI: A SUMMARY

External constraints, including the severing of economic relations with Japan, chronic balance-of-payments difficulties, and the dislocations of war, appear overwhelmingly important in explaining Korea's adoption of an inward-looking course. The key question concerns the shape that program would take: the balance between state and local firms, the instruments of state intervention, and the coherence of policy.

American influence was no doubt important in shaping Korean ISI, but it varied over time. Prior to independence, it was profound. The U.S. presence and subsequent partition excluded the organized left from power and suppressed radical labor, peasant, and other organizations. This pattern allowed the conservatives to consolidate their hold on a nominally democratic but highly centralized state. The United States

25. See Sunjoo Han, *The Failure of Democracy*, pp. 213–15; Se-jin Kim, *The Politics of Military Revolution in Korea* (Chapel Hill: University of North Carolina Press, 1971); John Kie-chang Oh, *Korea: Democracy on Trial* (Ithaca: Cornell University Press, 1968).

26. Cheryl Payer has argued that the reforms were the proximate cause of the military coup, in "Pushed into the Debt Trap: South Korea's 'Export Miracle,'" *Journal of Contemporary Asia* 5, 2 (1975): 153–64. See also Henderson, *Korea*, p. 181, who attaches some importance to the economic reforms in weakening the government. Contrast both with Sunjoo Han, *The Failure of Democracy*, pp. 207–15.

thus shaped the broad political context within which subsequent policy would unfold. ~~American influence declined~~, however, as the U.S. role shifted ~~from occupying power to economic and military patron~~. U.S. interest in Korean security gave Rhee more leverage than his economic dependence might suggest. As an American adviser to UNKRA noted: "More often than not we have gotten our ears pinned back in these disputes we have not been able to avoid. More than once—over the essentiality of a Republic of Korea anti-inflationary policy, or the pricing of aid goods to be sold on local markets or the underwriting of a non-essential public investment project—we have backed down from 'firm' positions."[27] It should also be noted that U.S. aid ideas adjusted to economic realities. Except on the "tolerable" level of inflation, U.S. advice was not rigid and certainly not liberal. Defending a program aimed at "self-sufficiency," John Lewis argued in 1955 that it "represented no doctrinaire preference for autarky or rejection of the conventional comparative costs doctrines of international trade; it is simply a practical response to the present realities of the international market."[28]

The way Korean ISI was implemented is best explained by reference to the political interests of state elites and the institutional context in which they operated. The executive was "strong" in its coercive capability, its ability to play on external threats, and its relative independence from the legislature. Rural elites and domestic entrepreneurs were politically weak and factionalized. Yet Rhee did have to be concerned with the maintenance of political support given the democratic institutions imposed on him by the Americans, particularly with the growth of political opposition after 1954. The discretionary allocation of aid goods, licenses, vested properties, tax exemptions, and government contracts was a crucial political instrument. Maintaining and deploying these instruments undercut efforts at rational planning. Components of an effective decision-making structure began to appear during the 1950s, but these "islands" of technocratic rationality were largely circumvented in the making of key allocative decisions.

THE POLITICS OF EXPORT-LED GROWTH: PHASE 1

The critical shift in Korea's postwar economic development is the ~~move toward export-led growth in the early 1960s~~. This change can also be traced to external pressures. A ~~new emphasis in the U.S. aid program on achieving "self-sufficiency,"~~ declining ~~aid commitments,~~ and a greater

27. Lewis, *Reconstruction*, p. 44.
28. Ibid., p. 67.

willingness to press policy reforms changed the incentives facing Korean elites. Yet pressures for reform had been applied before, and without success. The transition to export-led growth, and the shape it assumed, must be understood in terms of the conjunction of external pressure with crucial institutional and political changes at the domestic level: the concentration of power in the executive, the rationalization of the economic policy-making machinery, and the development of new instruments for steering industrialization. The new strategy did not go unopposed. The business-government nexus was viewed with suspicion by the opposition, which saw continuities with the corruption of the Rhee period. Only after a political crisis in which martial law was once again invoked did Park Chung Hee consolidate the new course.

Institutional Change and State Power: Executive Dominance

Following the seizure of power by the military in May 1961, all political parties and organizations were banned, over 4,300 politicians barred from political activity, and the press subjected to new controls. These actions were later justified by Park Chung Hee in terms of the trade-off between democracy and development:

> In order to ensure efforts to improve the living conditions of the people in Asia, even undemocratic emergency measures may be necessary. . . . The people of Asia today fear starvation and poverty more than the oppressive duties thrust on them by totalitarianism. . . . The Asian peoples want to obtain economic equality first and build a more equitable political machinery afterward.[29]

The actual consolidation of political authority proved circuitous. In August 1961 Park promised a return to civilian government in May 1963. A national referendum in December 1962 ratified a constitution providing for a strengthened executive. Hoping to capitalize on the opposition's disarray, the junta announced an early election. Park accepted the nomination of the Democratic Republican Party (DRP), which had been organized by Kim Chong-pil, head of the Korean Central Intelligence Agency (KCIA) and a key figure in the coup. Intense factional splits developed within the Supreme Council for National Reconstruction (SCNR), the body of coup leaders. Younger, more radical officers wanted an extension of military rule, in part to carry out the first Five Year Plan. When Park announced he would postpone the elections and hold a referendum on continued military rule, he precipitated

---

29. Park Chung Hee, *Our Nation's Path* (Seoul: Hollym Publications, 1971), pp. 39–40.

a general political crisis and strong protests from Washington. Park relented on the referendum. Even with a fragmented and politically tainted opposition, Park won only a narrow victory amid charges of election fraud.

Despite the return to nominally democratic rule, the executive continued to wield tremendous power. The legislature under Park remained a weak body, dominated in any case by the DRP.[30] Instruments of political control devised under the military also remained in place. The most important was the KCIA, which combined external and internal intelligence-gathering functions, maintained close links with the ruling party, and established a pervasive presence throughout society.[31] The executive's penetration of the countryside also became more effective.[32] Though the coup leaders initially adopted populist measures toward the agricultural sector, such as cancellation of "usurious" debts, a 1962 law provided that all local agricultural cooperative staff should be appointed by the central government rather than elected by members. The cooperatives provided additional means for channeling benefits for political ends, since they were the sole means through which fertilizer and government credit were distributed.

The limiting of labor demands was, it seems, viewed as an integral component of the new industrial course. David Cole, an American adviser, testified that "the choice in the mid-sixties was whether to concentrate on trying to do something about raising wages or expanding employment, and the choice was to expand employment."[33] Real wages in manufacturing hit a peak in 1959 that would not be regained until 1967, when wages began to turn up in response to labor-market pressures. Entrepreneurs thus entered the export-led growth phase with the benefit of a sustained pause in real wage growth.

Labor had been weakened before the turn to outward-looking growth, however. The initial controls on labor under military rule resembled those on other social groups and had no distinctive economic rationale. Following the coup, all unions were disbanded and the Federation of Korean Trade Unions (FKTU) restructured on industrial lines. Candi-

30. On the historical weakness of the Korean legislature see Chong Lim Kim and Seong-Tong Pai, *Legislative Process in Korea* (Seoul: Seoul National University Press, 1981), pp. 3–21.
31. On the KCIA see U.S. House of Representatives, 95th Congress, Hearings before the Committee on International Relations, Subcommittee on International Organizations, *Investigation of Korean-American Relations*, Part 6 (Washington, D.C.: USGPO, 1977), pp. 23–24, 89–113.
32. Vincent Brandt, "Local Government and Rural Development," in Ban, Moon, and Perkins, *Rural Development*, p. 260.
33. House Subcommittee on International Organizations, *Investigation of Korean-American Relations*, Part 6, p. 167.

dates for important positions needed government approval, the organization was subsidized by the government, and a tripartite style of labor committee mediation, conciliation, and arbitration gave the government new leverage. The reorganization also greatly strengthened the central offices over the industrial unions, branches, and chapters, and though this would later facilitate government intervention in the selection of the union leadership, at the time it marked an improvement over the fragmented structure of the 1950s.[34]

The initial pause in wage growth appears, therefore, to have resulted as much from market conditions as from government action. Once the strategy of export-led growth had been launched, and as wages began to turn up in response to tightening labor markets, the government did use its power over labor for explicitly economic ends. In 1969 a study commissioned by the Presidential Secretariat concluded that greater "supervision" and "guidance" over unions was required to allow for more "efficient" resolution of conflicts. The committee's recommendations, including partial decentralization of the union structure and the creation of joint labor-management councils, were embodied in new labor legislation in 1972. Moreover, following a lengthy labor dispute between Korean workers and two American firms in 1968 and 1969, a Special Law on Trade Unions and Mediation of Labor Disputes in Enterprises Invested by Foreigners created extraordinary arbitration committees for foreign enterprises. The Law on the Establishment of the Free Export Zones, also passed in 1970, limited workers' right to strike.

Reform of the Decision-Making Structure

The capabilities of the state were also strengthened through a centralization of economic policy making. Two innovations were crucial. The first was the organization in the presidential mansion, or Blue House, of the presidential secretariats, two dealing with political and two with economic affairs; they allowed Park to monitor economic issues on a daily basis. The second innovation was the creation of the Economic Planning Board (EPB) in June 1961.[35] This key organizational innovation came from reformist technocrats who had languished under Rhee and Chang Myon. Budgetary and planning powers were, drawing on

---

34. This and the following paragraph draw on Ogle, "Labor Unions," pp. 107, 169, 223, 232–42, and an interview with the author. For a personal account of the environment in which labor organizers and the Christian Urban Industrial Mission worked in the sixties, see Ogle, *Liberty to the Captives* (Atlanta, Ga.: John Knox Press, 1977).

35. For a detailed analysis of the formation of the Economic Planning Board, see Haggard, Kim, and Moon, "Transition to Export-Led Growth."

the example of India, combined in the same ministry. The EPB took over planning functions from the Ministry of Reconstruction and budgetary functions from the Bureau of the Budget in the Ministry of Finance. It was also granted control over foreign borrowing and direct investment. The screening of foreign investment applications and the ability to guarantee foreign loans gave it a powerful tool in shaping the sectoral distribution of investment. The EPB also absorbed the Bureau of Statistics, increasing its information-gathering capacity.

The EPB combined and concentrated various enclaves of developmentalist thinking that previously had been scattered and separated. Its centrality in interministerial coordination, and the importance the military gave to economic issues more generally, was signaled by the elevation of its head to the status of deputy prime minister. The EPB's control over the budget and its formal review, planning, and coordinating powers reduced the ability of other ministries to initiate projects independently. Unconstrained by relations with the legislature, the EPB wielded tremendous power over economic decision making.

The Development of New Policy Instruments

State capacities were also enhanced by the creation, or seizure, of new policy instruments for the guidance and support of the private sector. Soon after the military coup the government repossessed privately held shares of the commercial banks, arguing that they constituted illicitly accumulated wealth, and created two new state-owned financial institutions: a Medium Industry Bank and the National Agricultural Cooperatives Federation.[36] The military placed the Bank of Korea under the control of the Ministry of Finance. Operating on the basis of plans advanced through the EPB and the Ministry of Finance, the Bank of Korea could designate specific sectors to receive loans from the commercial banks at preferential rates.

More important than targeted support was the finance extended to exporters.[37] Short-term export loans were granted without limit to firms that had confirmed orders. These loans, which were automatically rediscounted by the Central Bank, covered all phases of production and

36. For a detailed analysis of the Korean financial sector, see David Cole and Yung Chul Park, *Financial Development in Korea, 1945–1978,* Studies in the Modernization of Korea (Cambridge: Harvard University Press, 1983).

37. See Wontack Hong and Yung Chul Park, "The Financing of Export-Oriented Growth in Korea," in Augustine H. H. Tan and Basant Kapur, eds., *Pacific Growth and Financial Interdependence* (Sydney: Allen & Unwin, 1985), pp. 163–82; Yung Whee Rhee, Bruce Ross-Larson, and Garry Pursell, *Korea's Competitive Edge: Managing the Entry into World Markets* (Baltimore: Johns Hopkins University Press for the World Bank, 1984), pp. 9–19.

procurement for export, including imports of needed raw materials and intermediates. An innovative domestic letter of credit system extended financing not only to direct exporters but to their suppliers, and their suppliers in turn. This innovation was extremely complex to administer, since it demanded calculations of the share of value-added coming from each input, but it drew small firms into the export game. Long-term financing and foreign-currency loans were also made available to encourage investment in export industries.

A key issue of debate is the role of trade policy in the expansion of Korean exports, and in Korean industrial policy more generally. Does the Korean case suggest the importance of import liberalization for export expansion? The empirical evidence is far from conclusive.[38] Richard Leudde-Neurath has shown that the empirical studies on which the neoclassical case has rested overestimate the extent of liberalization through the mid-1960s.[39] Under an export-import link system established in 1963, exporters were granted import rights based on their export performance. These rights could be used to import for domestic sale or could be sold at a premium. In conjunction with the exchange-rate reforms, this system allowed exporters to operate on the basis of world-market prices.

In the early stages of export-led growth, however, tariffs remained high on import-competing goods. As Wontack Hong puts it bluntly, "in principle, imports of finished consumption goods have not been allowed." But "finished consumption goods" were prominent among those in which Korea dramatically expanded its exports during the 1960s.[40] If one turns from tariff barriers to quantitative restrictions and nontariff barriers, the story is similar. The neoclassical case generally overlooks a wide range of discretionary controls used to limit "excessive" imports: quantitative restrictions, advance import deposits, "provisional" duties, and the sheer administrative complexity of importing. The neoclassical case also assumes that announced reforms were in fact implemented and overlooks critical issues of timing. Although there was some increase in the number of items "automatically approved" for

38. For the expression of reservations in a basically neoclassical account, see Frank, Kim, and Westphal, *South Korea*, pp. 54–55, and compare with Krueger, *The Foreign Sector and Aid*, pp. 89–94, and Bela Balassa, "Export Incentives and Export Performance in Developing Countries," *Weltwirtschaftliches Archiv* 114 (1978): 24–61.

39. Richard Leudde-Neurath, "State Intervention and Export-Oriented Development in South Korea," in Gordon White and Robert Wade, eds., *Developmental States in East Asia* (New York: St. Martin's, 1988). Leudde-Neurath gives particular attention to the detailed study based on price comparisons done by Larry Westphal and Kim Kwang Suk, "Industrial Policy and Development in Korea," *World Bank Staff Working Paper* 263, 1977.

40. Wontack Hong, *Trade, Distortions, and Employment Growth in Korea* (Seoul: Korea Development Institute, 1979), pp. 100, 107.

import by the Ministry of Commerce and Industry, it was not until 1967 that import liberalization became a major policy goal. An American economist, Ronald McKinnon, was invited to Korea to advise on the tariff reform and recommended that a uniform rate be adopted for those items Korea wanted to develop. Some of McKinnon's suggestions were adopted, but Kwang Suk Kim suggests that "the basic structure of the new tariff rates finally approved by the National Assembly turned out to be not much different from the original one"—a result of lobbying by industrial associations and ministries.[41]

Other policies for guiding the industrial structure and supporting exports, such as tax policies, have been outlined elsewhere and need not be reviewed here.[42] The point to stress is that the initial expansion of exports was achieved through reforms at two levels. Macro-level reforms changed the broad structure of incentives, but at a second, microeconomic level a significant battery of state supports and institutional reforms reduced the risks and transactions costs of shifting into the export business. Exchange-rate and trade policies established a permissive framework for the realization of comparative advantage, and more targeted policies pushed firms to exploit it.

The Road to Reform

The consolidation of political power and the centralization of decision-making authority did not in themselves constitute a coherent strategy: it remains to be explained *why* reforms were undertaken. The military initially viewed the yearly stabilization plans, initiated under Rhee at American insistence, as an undue constraint.[43] Influenced by populist economic advice, the junta expanded public works and investment, granted pay increases to state employees, and guaranteed high and stable prices to farmers. The formation of the National Agricultural Cooperative Federation and the Medium Industry Bank reflected the government's interest in consolidating support among farmers and small and medium-sized industries. The result of the military's decision to act quickly to achieve economic results was inflation.

To the extent that an overall vision existed, it was codified in the first Five Year Plan and the Economic Bluebook of the Korean Military,

---

41. Kwang Suk Kim, "The 1964–65 Exchange Rate Reform, Effective Export Promotion Measures, and Import Liberalization Program," Korean Economic Policy Case Studies 3 (Honolulu: East-West Center, November 1984), pp. 17–19.

42. Kwang Suk Kim, "The 1964–65 Exchange Rate Reform," pp. 54–55.

43. See J. A. Kim, *Divided Korea*, p. 240; the best summary in English of the evidence on the corruption of the military government is House Subcommittee on International Organizations, *Investigation of Korean-American Relations*, pp. 226ff.

prepared by a small group of technocrats in July 1961. The plan included sectoral and aggregate targets that had been boosted artificially in order to distinguish it from its Second Republic predecessor.[44] The plan envisioned a form of "guided capitalism" in which "the principles of free enterprise . . . will be observed but in which government will either directly participate or indirectly render guidance to the basic industries and other important fields."[45] The plan foresaw export expansion in both primary products and manufactures, but exports were to be used primarily to finance "self-reliance" through the development of infrastructure and basic industries.

The early actions of the military government provoked mixed reactions from the new Kennedy administration in Washington.[46] Prior to the coup the White House had begun a reassessment of Korea policy. Government studies found previous aid efforts poorly organized and ineffective; political changes since the fall of Syngman Rhee demanded a new approach. The leverage the United States had through its aid ties should be used to secure economic reforms while encouraging greater participation by foreign investors and multilateral institutions in Korea's development. Reestablishing Korean diplomatic relations with Japan was an important component of the U.S. strategy.

Though impressed by the reformist zeal of the military, the United States was troubled by the government's unwillingness to accept budgetary and monetary discipline. By 1963 inflationary policies had weakened Park's position. Severe food shortages in early 1963, following a bad harvest, were exacerbated by Park's policy of paying high prices to farmers in an effort to gain rural political support. PL 480 aid for 1963 had been lowered from previous allotments in November 1962, but, more important, the director of AID had independently suspended aid disbursements in 1962 in an effort to force the government to bring spending and income into line.[47] Because of the delicacy of the political situation, there were disagreements within the U.S. government over the wisdom of pressing too hard. Nonetheless, the United States used the aid weapon to force policy changes, both through the short-run manipulation of aid to achieve limited goals and through an announced intention to reduce aid commitments over the longer run.[48]

44. Wolf, "Economic Planning in Korea," and interview with Lee Duck Soo, who drafted the Economic Bluebook.

45. *Summary of the First Five-Year Economic Plan, 1962–1966* (Seoul: n.p., 1962), p. 28.

46. Early U.S. views can be found in "Task Force Report on Korea," June 6, 1961, Box 127, National Security Files, John F. Kennedy Library.

47. Interview, AID official, October 1986.

48. For a discussion of leverage, see telegram 838, April 29, 1963, U.S. Embassy, Seoul, to Secretary of State, Record Group 59, National Archives; House Subcommittee on International Organizations, *Investigation of Korean-American Relations,* p. 166; *Far Eastern Economic Review,* July 11 and 18, 1963.

Park attempted to maintain his freedom of maneuver by seeking private commercial credits.[49] Inexperienced in foreign borrowing, the government had not foreseen the high interest rates, front-end fees, short repayment periods, and government guarantees that lenders would seek. By November 1962 the government was forced to curtail imports of machinery and equipment bought with foreign commercial credit. Trade policy became more restrictive in 1963, and the government returned to a multiple exchange-rate system.

Finally, in April 1963, the government negotiated a major stabilization program with the United States, including ceilings on growth of the money supply, the budget deficit, commercial bank credit expansion, and foreign-exchange reserves.[50] The next American target was the exchange rate. Drawing on a study commissioned by AID, the United States pressed devaluation despite strenuous objections from Korean business and government officials.

The period from 1962 through early 1964 was punctuated by periods of acute tension between the United States and Korea. The United States was demanding critical economic reforms just as Park was facing both power struggles within the junta and a transition to democratic rule. The targets of the 1963 stabilization program were not met, but the government's acceptance of the need for reform allowed a gradual reconciliation with the United States. Acceptance of the need to stabilize also marked the culmination of a gradual turn within the junta away from populist ideas and toward greater conservatism and reliance on technocratic advice.

Inflation, balance-of-payments problems, and forced stabilization taught the Park regime important lessons. Economic difficulties forced a reassessment of the inward-looking growth strategy the military had initially favored; they also provided an object lesson in the political costs of aid dependence. Reliance on the Americans made the Korean government extremely vulnerable to changes in aid levels. Political pressure from the Americans pushed Park to adopt policies that would increase his economic independence by creating alternative sources of foreign exchange. As Anne Krueger puts it succinctly, "the export-promotion policies of the government were adopted as a means, not as an end."[51]

The final moves toward an outward-looking strategy evolved during the two years following Park's assumption of the presidency in January 1964. These had their origins in a group of American advisers working closely with mid-level planners in the Economic Planning Board and the

49. *Far Eastern Economic Review*, August 8, 1963.
50. Telegram 690, November 17, 1963, U.S. Embassy, Seoul, to Secretary of State, Record Group 59, National Archives.
51. Krueger, *The Foreign Sector and Aid*, p. 85; *Far Eastern Economic Review*, September 19, 1963.

Ministry of Commerce and Industry. A Joint U.S.-Korean Economic Cooperation Committee, formed in July 1963, became a locus for the discussion of development strategy, including the promotion of exports, the coordination of commercial and investment relations, and fiscal and financial reform.

The reforms moved along two mutually supportive tracks. At one level American economists and their allies in the Korean bureaucracy focused on a set of macro-level reforms in the system of incentives.[52] The devaluation of May 1964, the first of these reforms, was followed by the implementation of a floating unitary exchange rate in March 1965. These exchange-rate measures were taken in conjunction with the first of Korea's standby arrangements with the International Monetary Fund. In return for a credit of $9.3 million to intervene against speculative fluctuations in the market, Korea undertook a further series of reforms: a tight money policy, increases in taxation, higher import duties on nonessential items, limits on international borrowing, and greater export efforts. The devaluation improved the balance of payments, allowing some import liberalization. Domestic interest-rate reform came in the fall of 1965 and was the direct result of recommendations made by three American advisers.

The second level of institutional reform and micro-level interventions has received less attention as a source of Korea's export success.[53] In March 1965 the Joint Export Development Committee was established, consisting of AID officials and representatives from the relevant ministries and from the private sector. This committee was designed to coordinate policy across usually rigid institutional boundaries. Though empowered only to make recommendations, the committee received high-level political support, and a large share of its suggestions were adopted. The core of the export program was a set of credit incentives extended to new export products. This program demanded the capacity to analyze the export potential of products down to the sectoral level. An elaborate network of exporters' associations developed to provide services in the areas of marketing and quality control and maintained close relations with their sectoral counterparts in the Ministry of Commerce and Industry and the newly formed Korean Trade Promotion Corpo-

52. The following account of the macro-level reforms draws on interviews with AID officials involved in these reforms, including David Cole, Roger Ernst, and Gilbert Brown. See also Ronald Mackinnon, *Money and Capital in Economic Development* (Washington, D.C.: Brookings, 1973), pp. 105–11. The early activities of the Joint Committee are described in *Korea Annual 1964* (Seoul: Hapdong, 1965).

53. Exceptions are Rhee, Ross-Larson, and Pursell, *Korea's Competitive Edge;* Amicus Most, *Expanding Exports: A Case Study of the Korean Experience* (Washington, D.C.: USAID, 1969). See also Haggard, Moon, and Kim, "Transition to Export-Led Growth," which provides closer detail on the reform.

ration (KOTRA), modeled on the Japan External Trade Organization (JETRO). Granted special favors, such as the right to allocate quotas among firms, the industrial associations assisted in the setting of sectoral export targets. Initially, such targets were set in command fashion by the military government, but over time the target-setting process, like Korea's planning efforts more broadly, became a means to exchange information and represent interests.[54]

The high level of attention given to this process can be seen after 1965 in the holding of National Export Promotion Meetings of ministers, top bureaucrats, economists, representatives of the trade associations, and the chief executive officers of the largest firms. These meetings were religiously attended by Park himself, who had the power to solve problems by fiat.[55] At a lower level the Export Development Committee worked to coordinate a wide range of supportive measures, from quality control and technical assistance in design and packaging to the coordination of marketing and the arrangement of visits by foreign buyers.[56]

The consolidation of power through both organizational and electoral means allowed the government to sustain the reforms over the protests of various groups.[57] Privileged traders and ISI industries, such as sugar and flour milling, were hurt. Farmers were forced to accept higher fertilizer prices without the type of relief previously extended through budget subsidy. The real interest rate put a severe squeeze on the activities of the underground money market, which had played a crucial role in providing working capital to Korean firms. Some of the most vociferous protests came from elements within the Korean government concerned with the Military Assistance Program. The MAP had been financed out of counterpart funds. The export drive might expand Korea's foreign-exchange earnings, but it would diminish the foreign exchange to which these elements had privileged access.

The most politically difficult issue, however, involved reestablishing the government's relations with the private sector. The military was publicly committed to the elimination of corruption. At the same time, however, Park justified the coup, military rule, and his own candidacy on economic grounds; performance was the key to legitimacy. As Kyongdang Kim writes, "the only viable economic force happened to be the

54. Rhee, Ross-Larson, and Pursell, *Korea's Competitive Edge*, pp. 21–38; David Cole and Young Woo Nam, "The Pattern and Significance of Planning in Korea," in Irma Adelman, ed., *Practical Approaches to Development Planning: Korea's Second Five-Year Plan* (Baltimore: Johns Hopkins University Press, 1969).

55. Rhee, Ross-Larson, and Pursell, *Korea's Competitive Edge*, pp. 29–35.

56. See Most, *Expanding Exports*.

57. David Cole and Princeton Lyman, *Korean Development: The Interplay of Politics and Economics* (Cambridge: Harvard University Press, 1971), pp. 88–89; interviews with David Cole and Gilbert Brown.

target group of leading entrepreneurial talents with their singular advantage of organization, personnel, facilities and capital resources."[58] This political dilemma was resolved through policies and institutions that extended support to privileged portions of the private sector while eliminating opportunities for nonproductive economic activity.

The early actions of the military, including a "clean-up campaign," attacked conspicuous consumption by urban industrialists and purged the bureaucracy of purportedly corrupt and inefficient officeholders. The military also pressed forward a new version of the Chang Myon government's Special Law for Dealing with Illicit Wealth Accumulation. Some of the accused declared bankruptcy and paid fines. Others offered the idea of a business-government partnership, in which the government would extend financial assistance to industry in line with the priorities of the first plan while excusing the accused from criminal prosecution. In the ensuing negotiations an alliance was forged between domestic business and the government, though it was built around a new set of incentives.

The most contentious political battles associated with the new strategy came not over the stabilization, exchange-rate, and credit reforms of 1964 and 1965 but over the normalization of economic relations with Japan.[59] Park recognized that a successful settlement of property claims would provide crucial economic and political resources. In late 1962, with encouragement from the United States, Korea and Japan reached an understanding in which Japan provided a $300 million grant, $200 million in government-to-government aid, and $100 million in commercial credits.

Japanese interests in normalization were spelled out in a joint economic survey published in 1965:

> It is natural that in less developed countries where living standards are low and labor is abundant, the necessity of promoting labor intensive industry is paramount. In this case, it is not unusual for a majority of those labor intensive industries to be from the sector of declining industries of the developed countries or from the process subcontracting sector.[60]

58. Kyong-dong Kim, "Political Factors in the Formation of the Entrepreneurial Elite in South Korea," *Asian Survey* 16 (May 1976): 470.

59. The following draws on Kwan Bong Kim, *The Korea-Japan Treaty Crisis and the Instability of the Korean Political System* (New York: Praeger, 1971), *passim*.

60. *Direction and Background of Japan-Korea Economic Cooperation*, joint economic survey of the Japan Economic Research Council and Korea Productivity Organization, October 1965, quoted in Tsuchi-ya Takeo, "Masan: An Epitome of the Japan-ROK Relation," in *AMPO*, special issue, *Free Trade Zones and Industrialization in Asia* (Tokyo: Pacific-Asia Resources Center, 1977), p. 59.

The chance to recapture traditional markets appealed to Japan's "Korea lobby," which mobilized extensive resources in favor of the treaty. These complementarities were also recognized by the conservative Korean Businessmen's Association, formed in 1961 by the "illicit wealth accumulators." Representing the largest firms in the country, the KBA came to see that it could capture some of the light industry in which Japan was losing its comparative advantage. Normalization would also open the Japanese market and provide a solution to the market saturation that had accompanied the ISI policies of the 1950s. More important, the KBA's members would gain access to capital and technology.[61]

Opponents of the treaty viewed the matter in a political light. As J. A. Kim summarizes, "the primary issue throughout the political crisis [over normalization] in Korea was not opposition to Japan, but opposition to the Korean government, which, it was feared, would use financial resources from Japan to further consolidate its internal control."[62] The close relationship between foreign resources, Korean business, and the maintenance of power by a narrow political elite that had typified the Rhee period was now being replicated under Park. The opposition also stressed the various imbalances associated with export-led growth: attention to exports at the expense of the domestic market, to industry at the expense of agriculture, and to accumulation at the expense of equity.

In March 1964 a broad coalition formed to oppose the treaty, and students demonstrated against the negotiations. In June, Park declared martial law and imposed new restrictions on the press. Though martial law was lifted in July, another round of protests began in 1965, reaching a high point in June when the treaty was signed. In a late-night maneuver subsequently known in Korea as "the snatch,"[63] the bill was passed by an Assembly from which all of the opposition members had resigned. At the same time authority was granted to send troops to Vietnam, an arrangement that garnered substantial foreign exchange for the government from the United States.[64] Park's treaty victory was followed almost immediately by new statutes to encourage direct investment.[65]

Though protests continued, the Park government weathered the

61. Kwan Bong Kim, *The Korea-Japan Treaty Crisis*, chap. 3.
62. J. A. Kim, *Divided Korea*, p. 257.
63. Ibid., p. 262.
64. The most extensive analysis of Korea's involvement in Vietnam is Frank Baldwin's critical "America's Rented Troops: South Koreans in Vietnam," *Bulletin of Concerned Asian Scholars* 7 (October–December 1975): 33–40. See also Princeton Lyman, "Korea's Involvement in Viet Nam," *Orbis* 12 (Summer 1968); and Se Jin Kim, "South Korea's Involvement in Vietnam and Its Economic and Political Impact," *Asian Survey* 10 (June 1970): 519–32.
65. Early efforts to induce foreign investment are reviewed in *Korea Annual, 1965* (Seoul: Hapdong, 1967), pp. 157–59.

storm. In May 1967 Park ran in presidential elections on the basis of successful economic performance, aided by the settlement. Even in urban areas, where opposition to the regime was concentrated, Park improved his standing significantly. Policies and reforms associated with the formulation of the second Five Year Plan sustained and institutionalized the reforms of 1964 and 1965, but by 1966 the export orientation had been definitively established.[66]

THE TRANSITION TO EXPORT-LED GROWTH

External conditions were the most important factor accounting for the change in strategy. The effort to expand exports and increase foreign investment and borrowing came in response to declining aid commitments from the United States. The United States used aid leverage to generate both political and economic reforms, and the longer-term reduction in aid commitments forced the Park government to search for new sources of foreign exchange.

Aid leverage had been attempted against Rhee earlier, though perhaps not with the same determination exhibited by the Kennedy administration. To explain the way the new strategy was implemented, therefore, we must pay attention to the political interests and capacities of the military. The coup leaders justified their intervention in politics on the grounds that they could correct the distortions of the Rhee era. Exploiting their political autonomy, the military undertook wide-ranging economic reforms: the centralization of economic decision-making, the seizure of new instruments of policy, and the creation of new institutional mechanisms linking the state to the private sector. These reforms gave Korea's export orientation its dirigist style.

The economic thinking of the military was vague, however. Embarrassingly, early policies seemed to mirror the Rhee pattern of building support by dispensing largesse. When these expansionist policies began to falter, the technocrats offered an exit. It is at this point that available ideas about the development process contributed to the way in which the new government responded to the foreign-exchange constraint. American advisers and their Korean counterparts had been emphasizing the importance of stabilization, exchange-rate reform, and support for exports for over a decade. Now these reforms promised to reduce the government's vulnerability to external political pressures by generating new sources of government—and party—revenue.

The political opposition was fragmented, labor weak, the countryside,

66. See Adelman, ed., *Practical Approaches.*

as always, poorly organized. Nonetheless, these conditions were partly the result of the government's strategy; the broad powers of the executive, both under the military and after 1964, were important not only in restructuring the government but in controlling opposition. The political position of business was initially quite weak, providing an opportunity for the government to restructure its relations with the private sector. As the resolution of the Treaty Crisis demonstrated, even in a nominally democratic setting the ruling party would not hesitate to use highly irregular tactics to achieve its controversial aims. Korea's turn to export-led growth was "state-led," not only in its dirigism but in reflecting the particular political interests and powers of the Park leadership.

CHAPTER FOUR

Taiwan: From Import Substitution to Export-Led Growth

The external conditions pushing toward import substitution in Taiwan resembled those in Korea. They included political partition, the loss of traditional export markets, and acute foreign-exchange constraints. However, important differences in the two political systems affected the way import substitution was implemented. The Kuomintang (KMT) was committed not to repeat the economic mistakes on which the Communists had capitalized on the mainland: the squelching of productive economic activity, inflationary fiscal and monetary policies, and inattention to the countryside. Possessing few organic connections with Taiwanese society and resembling in organization and strategy a Leninist party, the KMT enjoyed substantial political autonomy and was able to carry through wide-ranging reforms. Unlike in Korea's ISI phase, effective political support was extended to the technocrats at a relatively early stage, allowing a more systematic approach to industrial planning and agricultural policy and a more harmonious aid relationship with the United States.

The most controversial issue was the size of the state sector itself. Conservatives in the KMT, including the military, championed an interventionist state and exhibited a skepticism regarding the growth of private economic power in the hands of the local Taiwanese. This position was weakened by American pressure and, more important, by the successful development of local firms that accompanied ISI policies. Several factors help explain the transition to export-led growth. The resolution of the Taiwan Straits crisis in 1958 allowed the government to focus more squarely on national economic development and enhanced the position of the technocratic reformers. As in Korea, however, so in Taiwan foreign-exchange constraints appear to have impelled reform.

Two Legacies: The Mainland and
the Japanese Colonization

The KMT was formally reorganized along Leninist lines in 1923–24. In actuality, the Nationalist government of the Nanking Decade (1927–37) was quite weak.[1] Despite the much-celebrated Northern Expedition of 1926 that sought to unite the country, the government's territorial reach was limited. The factionalism of the party was exacerbated by the centrifugal pull of regional warlords. Gradually the center of authority shifted away from the party and state toward Chiang Kai-shek and the military. With the militarization of the party, as Lloyd Eastman argues, "the Nationalist regime tended . . . to be neither responsible nor responsive to political groups or institutions outside the government. It became, in effect, its own constituency."[2]

This insulation extended to the Chinese manufacturing class, the most important elements of which were concentrated in Shanghai. Parks Coble shows that relations between the state and Chinese capital were "characterized by government efforts to emasculate politically the urban capitalists and to milk the modern sector of the economy."[3] State control over banking became a means for establishing a favored "state capitalist" sector of competing semigovernmental corporations and agencies, a model that was extended to confiscated Japanese properties on Taiwan when the KMT moved to Taiwan following defeat at the hands of the communists on the mainland. These actions were justified by an ideology favoring extensive state intervention in the economy. Based on Sun Yat-sen's "three principles of the people," KMT ideology combines private ownership of the means of production and central planning in an eclectic mix. The third principle, translated variously as "people's livelihood" and "socialism," guarantees "economic freedom" but also expresses a concern with equity, an aversion to the concentra-

---

1. The following draws on Robert Bedeski, *State-Building in Modern China: The Kuomintang in the Pre-War Period* (Berkeley: Institute of East Asian Studies, Center for Chinese Studies, University of California, 1981); Parks M. Coble, Jr., *The Shanghai Capitalists and the Nationalist Government, 1927–1937* (Cambridge: Harvard University Press, 1980); Lloyd Eastman, *The Abortive Revolution: China under Nationalist Rule, 1927–1937* (Cambridge: Harvard University Press, 1974); Hung-mao Tien, *Government and Politics in Kuomintang China, 1927–1937* (Stanford: Stanford University Press, 1972); C. Martin Wilbur, *The Nationalist Revolution in China, 1923–1928* (New York: Cambridge University Press, 1983); and Thomas Gold, "Origins of Development Strategies: The Nationalist Chinese State on the Mainland and Taiwan," in Gary Gereffi and Don Wyman, eds., *Manufactured Miracles: Development Strategies in Latin America and East Asia* (Princeton: Princeton University Press, 1990).
2. Eastman, *The Abortive Revolution*, p. 286.
3. Coble, *The Shanghai Capitalists*, p. 3.

tion of economic power, and the need to "regulate" and even "restrict" capitalism.[4]

On the mainland programs for industrial and infrastructural development, and monetary, fiscal, and institutional reforms, were pushed by reformers in the bureaucracy who saw economic development and closer cooperation with the private sector as prerequisites for effective political power.[5] This view suffered at the hands of the military, which saw territorial control as the top priority and was engaged in military campaigns over the decade of the 1940s. Nor were the "technocrats" exempt from the pervasive corruption of the KMT's last years on the mainland. With the coming of war and revolution, all possibilities of pursuing a rational economic course were lost. Between 1945 and 1949 the military's claims on the budget were increasingly financed by the printing of money. National finances fell into complete disarray. Following an abortive currency reform in 1948, prices reached hyperinflationary levels, contributing to the KMT's declining political and military fortunes.[6]

On Taiwan, by contrast, economic development under the Japanese had been substantial.[7] As in Korea, Japan's interest in extracting an "export surplus" led to the economic transformation of the rural sector, even if the existing social structure remained intact. Investments in rural infrastructure, expanded agricultural inputs, and the fixing of property rights contributed to the creation of a commercialized agricultural sector producing rice and tropical products linked to processing industries, including sugar. An extension system and a network of farmers' associations assisted the Japanese in rural surveillance but also hastened the adoption of new technologies; these associations were revived and strengthened under KMT rule.

Japanese zaibatsu and locally established Japanese firms dominated the modern enclave. Until 1924 Taiwanese were prohibited from form-

---

4. See Leonard Shihlien Hsu, ed., *Sun Yat-sen: His Political and Social Ideas* (Los Angeles: University of Southern California Press, 1933); Bedeski, *State-Building*, pp. 123–52; Chien-kuo Pang, "The State and Economic Transformation: The Taiwan Case" (Ph.D. diss., Brown University, 1988), pp. 79–82. For an account placing primary emphasis on ideology, see A. James Gregor with Maria Hsia Chang and Andrew Zimmerman, *Ideology and Development: Sun Yat-sen and the Economic History of Taiwan* (Berkeley: Center for Chinese Studies, University of California, 1982).

5. On the debate over the effectiveness of the KMT on the mainland see Albert Feuerwerker, *The Chinese Economy, 1912–1949* (Ann Arbor: Center for Chinese Studies, University of Michigan, 1960), pp. 47–62, and John Chang, *Industrial Development in Pre-Communist China: A Quantitative Analysis* (Chicago: Aldine, 1969).

6. See Shun-Hsin Chou, *The Chinese Inflation* (New York: Columbia University Press, 1963), pp. 15–17.

7. Samuel Ho, *Economic Development of Taiwan, 1895–1970* (New Haven: Yale University Press, 1978), p. 29; and Chang Han-yu and Ramon Myers, "Japanese Colonial Development Policy in Taiwan, 1895–1906," *Journal of Asian Studies* 22, 4 (1963): 433–49.

ing corporations without Japanese participation, and even thereafter Taiwanese were largely restricted to small-scale industry, commerce, and land development. Such restrictions did not prevent a small number of collaborating Taiwanese families from becoming wealthy through land development, banking, and the exploitation of commercial monopolies granted to them by the Japanese.[8] As in Korea, the industrial structure was diversified after the mid-1930s to include war-related heavy manufactures and the development of raw materials needed by Japanese industry. As Japan mobilized the Taiwanese economy for its drive to the south, many Taiwanese concerns were merged with Japanese ones, weakening, but not destroying, the nascent Taiwanese bourgeoisie.

THE CONSOLIDATION OF STATE POWER ON TAIWAN

Key to understanding subsequent economic policy in Taiwan is the concentration of political power in the hands of the KMT and, conversely, the political and organizational weakness of indigenous social forces. This peculiar political outcome was the result of the KMT's defeat in civil war on the mainland and its retreat to Taiwan. According to the Cairo Declaration of 1943, Taiwan was to return to the Republic of China after the war. In September 1945 Chiang Kai-shek appointed a military governor to extend Nationalist administration to the island. The first group of Nationalists established a relatively independent provincial administration. Since most of the modern industry on the island had been developed or taken over by the Japanese, early KMT administrators inherited almost complete control of the island's economy, which they badly mismanaged.[9]

The tasks of reconstruction were daunting. In 1946 industrial and agricultural production stood at less than half their 1937 levels.[10] As it was during the 1930s on the mainland, the relationship between public and private was quickly blurred. New and established public entities were run as private enterprises by officials formed into boards of directors. Capital was siphoned out of going concerns in inflated salaries and dividends and through nepotism, and the tradition of financing unprof-

8. Thomas B. Gold, *State and Society in the Taiwan Miracle* (Armonk, N.Y.: M. E. Sharpe, 1986), pp. 39–40.

9. See George Kerr, *Formosa Betrayed* (Boston: Houghton Mifflin, 1965), chaps. 5 and 6; Gold, *State and Society*, pp. 47–55; Fred Riggs, *Formosa under Chinese Nationalist Rule* (New York: Macmillan, 1952); and the history by Chen-kuo Hsu, "The Political Base of Changing Strategy toward Private Enterprise in Taiwan, 1945–1955" (Ph.D. diss., Ohio State University, 1987), chap. 3.

10. Ching-yuan Lin, *Industrialization in Taiwan, 1946–1972: Trade and Import-Substitution Policies for Developing Countries* (New York: Praeger, 1973), p. 37.

itable public enterprises through money creation continued, contributing to the general economic disruption caused by the war.

The provincial government's mismanagement of the economy went hand in hand with a disregard for the interests of the indigenous Taiwanese.[11] Hoping to participate in the Japanese spoils, the Taiwanese faced competition from a government worse than its predecessor in monopolizing industrial opportunities through control of inputs, credit, and transport. When a small incident over licensing triggered a spontaneous island-wide uprising in February 1947, Taiwanese leaders appeared to be in a position to press the provincial government for greater participation in both politics and the economy. With the arrival of military support from the mainland, however, the governor launched a military counterattack. Key Formosan nationalists were liquidated, driven into exile, or silenced; the number of victims has been estimated at between 10,000 and 20,000.[12]

By 1948 Chiang's military position on the mainland was clearly untenable. In December he dispatched a new governor, Ch'en Ch'eng, to the island, along with his son, Chiang Ching-kuo. The war footing and the aim of ultimately recapturing the mainland provided a rationale for the imposition of martial law and the incarceration and execution of large numbers of Taiwanese and suspect refugees.

Like Korea, Taiwan thus began its postwar history without an organized political left. Unlike Rhee, however, the KMT faced *no* organized political opposition and little pressure from the Americans for political reform. Indeed, given the faction-prone nature of KMT politics, the most complicated task was consolidating power *within* the party itself. Drawing on the loyalty and organization of the military's "Whampoa Clique," Chiang Kai-shek established his dominance over the party through a party reform launched in 1950 that centralized decision making and purged opposition.[13]

11. For example, a statute on the confiscation of Japanese properties allowed joint enterprises with 50 percent or more Taiwanese ownership to be taken over by the Taiwanese; others, however, were either nationalized or sold off. Kerr, *Formosa Betrayed*, p. 122. See also George Kerr, *Formosa: Licensed Revolution and the Home Rule Movement* (Honolulu: University Press of Hawaii, 1974); Douglas Mendel, *The Politics of Formosan Nationalism* (Berkeley: University of California Press, 1970); Gold, *State and Society*, pp. 47–55; Hsu, "The Political Base," pp. 83–93.

12. Kerr, *Formosa Betrayed*, p. 310.

13. Very little is known about the internal workings of the KMT. See Hung-mao Tien, *The Great Transition: Political and Social Change in the Republic of China* (Stanford: Hoover Institution Press, 1989), pp. 64–104; J. Bruce Jacobs, "Paradoxes in the Politics of Taiwan: Lessons for Comparative Politics," *Politics* (Australia) 16, 2 (1978): 239–47; Arthur Lerman, "National Elite and Local Politicians in Taiwan," *American Political Science Review* 71 (December 1977): 1406–22; Pang, "The State and Economic Transformation"; and the important papers of Edwin Winckler, "National, Regional and Local Politics" and "Roles Linking State and Society," in Emily Ahearn and Hill Gates, eds., *The Anthropology of*

The KMT retained a complicated, multilevel governmental structure. The national level was made up of five branches, including a directly elected Legislative Yuan and an indirectly elected Control Yuan that maintained the pretense of governing all of China. An elected Provincial Assembly played an advisory role, and county and municipal governments were opened to electoral contestation after 1950, albeit under close party surveillance. Nonetheless, the KMT was relatively unconstrained by these institutions. The party structure paralleled that of the government at all levels, and all important decisions were taken within the upper councils of the party, if not by Chiang personally. As in Leninist systems, party and state became inextricably intertwined.

Important social groups were incorporated into party organizations. State-controlled youth corps preempted independent student organization. Labor, which had been an important force in undermining the KMT's power on the mainland, was also brought under government control. State-created labor unions, penetrated by KMT cadres, were forced on both private- and public-sector enterprises.[14] A special law promulgated in 1947, "Measures for Handling of Labor Disputes during the Period of National Mobilization for the Suppression of Rebellion," gave priority to the prompt settlement of disputes and was in effect until the political liberalization of the mid-1980s. The law eliminated the right to strike and gave local governments extensive powers in mediation and arbitration.

The KMT was also unconstrained by ties with rural elites; indeed, the most dramatic example of state autonomy can be seen in the extensive land reforms of 1949–53.[15] Landlord-tenant relations on Taiwan were not exactly analogous to those on the mainland, and the rebellion of

---

Taiwanese Society (Stanford: Stanford University Press, 1981), and "Institutionalization and Participation on Taiwan: From Hard to Soft Authoritarianism?" *China Quarterly* 99 (September 1984): 481–99. Insights into the factional conflict of the period immediately following the KMT's move to Taiwan can be found in Memo, Strong to Clubb, Sept. 6, 1950, "Summary of Views on Formosa as of Late 1950," National Archives, Record Group 59, 794A.00/9–650.

14. The following is drawn from T. K. Djang, *Industry and Labor in Taiwan* (Nankang, Taipei: Academica Sinica, 1977). See also *Far Eastern Economic Review*, February 28, 1982, p. 76.

15. On the land reform see Martin M. C. Yang, *Socio-Economic Results of Land Reform in Taiwan* (Honolulu: University Press of Hawaii, 1970); Cheng Chen, *Land Reform in Taiwan* (Taipei: China Publishing Co., 1961); Erik Thorbecke, "Agricultural Development," in Walter Galenson, ed., *Economic Growth and Structural Change in Taiwan* (Ithaca: Cornell University Press, 1979), pp. 132–205; Hsin-Huang Michael Hsiao, *Government Agricultural Policies in Taiwan and South Korea* (Nankang, Taipei: Academica Sinica, 1981); Teng-hui Lee, *Intersectoral Capital Flows in the Economic Development of Taiwan, 1895–1960* (Ithaca: Cornell University Press, 1971); and T. H. Shen, *The Sino-American Joint Committee on Rural Reconstruction* (Ithaca: Cornell University Press, 1970). None of these is particularly informative about the politics of the process.

1947 had been a largely urban phenomenon. Nonetheless, the reform impulse was closely linked to past policy mistakes. In the words of Ch'en Ch'eng, governor of Taiwan at the time of the reforms,

> [Communist infiltration of the villages] was one of the main reasons why the mainland fell into Communist hands. On the eve of the rent reduction in Taiwan, the situation on the Chinese mainland was becoming critical and the villages on the island were showing signs of unrest and instability. It was feared that the Communists might take advantage of the rapidly deteriorating situation.[16]

Support from rural elites had blunted KMT support for land reform on the mainland. No such constraints now operated. When the Provincial Assembly raised objections to the 1952 reform, the KMT attacked the body as a tool of the landlords.[17] The reform proceeded in three steps. First, the rent reduction program of 1949 limited rents to a fixed share of crop yield, improving the position of tenants while reducing land values. The second step was the sale of some public land acquired from the Japanese. The final stage, the Land to the Tiller program, was a sophisticated assault on the rural power of landlords, backed by a well-developed rural administration. The proposals were submitted to both provincial and central government legislatures for ratification, but most of the original regulations drafted by the technocrats remained intact when the program became law in January 1953.[18]

Landlords were compensated by a combination of land bonds (70 percent) and stock shares in four government enterprises (30 percent). While the rural reforms undercut the basis of landlord power in the countryside, "compensation" in the state-controlled industrial sector increased the new industrialists' dependence on the goodwill of the regime. As the landlords recognized, stock ownership was divorced from effective control over the enterprises, since the government retained an interest in the companies. Not only were land prices undervalued, but interest rates on the bonds were low and declined even further in panic selling. As a result, the Land to the Tiller program did not generate a new industrial class.

The KMT's stance toward the countryside is not easily summarized. On the one hand, the new class of smallholders was tied to the regime by the extension of the KMT's organizational presence in the country-

16. Quoted in Yu Hsi Chen, "Rural Transformation in Mainland China and Taiwan: A Comparative Study," *Social Praxis* 5, 1–2 (1978): 131.

17. Embassy Dispatch, Sept. 14, 1953, RG 59, 794A.00/9–1453.

18. Samuel P. S. Ho, "Economics, Economic Bureaucracy, and Taiwan's Economic Development," paper prepared for the Workshop on China's Economic Bureaucracies, East-West Center, Honolulu, July 17–20, 1984.

side.[19] The government monopolized inputs and credit. To meet the needs of a swollen urban population—from 1946 to 1950 more than one million refugees arrived in Taiwan—the government controlled the marketing of rice through a rice-for-fertilizer barter system. Not only were the terms of exchange disadvantageous to farmers, but the Food Bureau was empowered to collect rice as payment for taxes, rents on publicly held land and inputs, and repayments for land sold to farmers. The rice had immediate political uses; about half of it was rationed directly to military personnel, civil servants, teachers, and their dependents.

On the other hand, the government invested heavily in agricultural development and sought to rebuild the rural organizations that had ceased to operate after the war. Credit cooperatives, farmers' associations, and community organizations were consolidated into a Farmers' Association that served as an extension service and a provider of credit and inputs. This reorganization displaced rural moneylenders and served as a channel for the expression of rural interests, as did the opening of municipal elections to electoral contestation. Thus an effort at extraction of resources from the rural sector was coupled with various forms of government investment.

By the end of 1950 crucial features of the KMT system were beginning to crystallize. First, the pretext of constitutional rule had been dropped under the exigencies of civil war. Organizational reforms created a leaderist system in which Chiang Kai-shek headed the army, the political system, and an increasingly centralized party apparatus. Alternative centers of political power—leftist and Formosan nationalist forces, labor, students, and landlords—were crushed, displaced, or drawn into state-controlled organizational networks. The shock of past events on the mainland, however, created within the government a strong political current (of which Ch'en Ch'eng was exemplary) that linked economic reform to the consolidation of political power and legitimacy. It is to the exact shape of that economic program I now turn.

The Political Foundations of ISI

American aid operations on Taiwan were resumed in 1950 in response to the Korean War and the changed conception of East Asia's

19. For accounts stressing the control-oriented aspects of the reform, see Yu Hsi Chen, "Rural Transformation"; Raymond Apthorpe, "The Burden of Land Reform in Taiwan," *World Development* 4 (April–May 1979): 519–30; and Alice Amsden, "The State and Taiwan's Economic Development," in Peter B. Evans, Dietrich Rueschemeyer, and Theda Skocpol, eds., *Bringing the State Back In* (Cambridge: Cambridge University Press, 1985), pp. 78–106.

position in American security that it produced.[20] The dependence of the new regime on aid was roughly equal to Korea's. Of a total current-account deficit of $1.3 billion between 1951 and 1962, aid financed $1.1 billion. Total economic commitments, including PL 480 shipments allocated between 1951 and 1965, were almost $1.5 billion.[21] Proceeds from the sales of these commodities were used to finance budget deficits, with the remainder deposited in a counterpart fund to be used for developmental purposes.

Generally, the economic advice offered by the Americans over the 1950s was more consonant with the regime's own objectives than was the case in Korea.[22] For example, the disastrous political consequences of the great inflation on the mainland had a profoundly conservatizing effect on the KMT's macroeconomic policy. As in Korea, the United States pushed various fiscal reforms and economies: tax increases, reform of the tax structure, and overhaul of the personnel and borrowing policies of the state-owned enterprises.[23] But in Taiwan the legacy of hyperinflation made political elites receptive to ideas that were highly unorthodox at the time. At the urging of a small group of Western-trained Chinese economists, of whom S. C. Tsiang (Tsiang Sho-chieh) and T. C. Liu (Liu Ta-chung) were the most important, an effort was made to curb the expansion of the money supply, control fiscal deficits, and mobilize savings through a policy of high interest rates. Though the budget was to remain an issue of contention throughout the 1950s, a commitment to stabilization would not come in Korea until 1964 and 1965.[24]

20. For the history of the aid debate prior to 1950, see Tang Tsou, *America's Failure in China, 1941–1950* (Chicago: University of Chicago Press, 1963), chaps. 9–12; Ernest May, *The Truman Administration and China, 1945–1949* (New York: Lippincott, 1975); Ralph Clough, *Island China* (Cambridge: Harvard University Press, 1978), pp. 7–10; and the review of scholarship in Dorothy Borg and Waldo Heinrichs, eds., *Uncertain Years: Chinese-American Relations, 1947–1950* (New York: Columbia University Press, 1980). The major published source on the U.S. aid program for Taiwan is Neil Jacoby, *U.S. Aid to Taiwan: A Study of Foreign Aid, Self-Help, and Development* (New York: Praeger, 1966).

21. An additional $2.5 billion came in the form of military equipment grants. U.S. aid allowed the KMT to maintain a large military force, which was politically important since the army continued to be a dominant force within the KMT throughout the 1950s.

22. Though there were also aid conflicts in Taiwan. In a strongly worded letter as early as March 1951 the State Department warned the Chinese that the United States could not underwrite the economy of Taiwan indefinitely and that assistance was contingent on reform. Dean Rusk to Dr. V. K. Wellington Koo, March 13, 1951, RG 59, 794A.5MAP/3–751.

23. U.S. Naval Attaché Taipei Joint Weeka (telegram), Dec. 1953, RG 59, 794.00(W)/12–1153.

24. S. C. Tsiang's views of Taiwan's development are spelled out in "Fashions and Misconceptions in Monetary Theory and Their Influences on Financial and Banking Policies," *Zeitschrift für die Gesamte Staatswissenschaft* 135 (December 1979): 584–604; "Taiwan's Economic Miracle: Lessons in Economic Development," in Arnold C. Harberger,

There was also broad consensus between the Americans and the Chinese on the importance of rural development. Through the Joint Commission on Rural Reconstruction (JCRR), formed in 1948 on the mainland, the United States was a vigorous advocate of rural reform on both economic and political grounds.[25] The combination of the commission's joint (i.e., Chinese–American) structure, the high rank and political independence of the Chinese commissioners, and the concentration of technocratic expertise within its ranks suited the JCRR to formulating and implementing reforms. The joint structure encouraged the formation of an alliance between like-minded Americans and Chinese and permitted a greater element of control than existed in Korea during the 1950s over the allocation of aid funds. The commission was crucial in supporting the land reform effort and in reorganizing farmers' associations to make them more representative.

The Americans concurred with their Chinese counterparts, as they did with the Koreans, on the necessity of an import-substituting strategy. The reasons were largely external. In response to a serious balance-of-payments crisis, strict import controls were imposed in April 1951 along with a multiple exchange-rate system. High tariffs, the requirement of full advance payment for imports, and licensing of all imports established the bias toward import substitution. Though Taiwan proved more successful than Korea in maintaining and expanding agricultural exports in the 1950s, trade barriers obstructed the return to a pattern of primary-product exports. Protected or preferential markets for Taiwan's sugar and tropical products were now closed, China's abruptly, Japan's as a result of its own reconstruction efforts.

Despite these areas of agreement between the Chinese and their American advisers, there were also significant points of conflict. These conflicts reflected political imperatives and cleavages within the KMT over the share of resources to be devoted to the military, the priority

---

ed., *World Economic Growth* (San Francisco: Institute for Contemporary Studies, 1984); and "Exchange Rate, Interest Rate, and Economic Development," in Mark Nerlov, Lawrence Klein, and S. C. Tsiang, eds., *Quantitative Economics and Development* (New York: Academic, 1980). See also Pang, "The State and Economic Transformation," pp. 103–6.

25. On the role of the JCRR see Dennis Fred Simon, "U.S. Assistance, Land Reform, and Taiwan's Political Economy," in Edwin Winckler and Susan Greenhalgh, eds., *Contending Approaches to the Political Economy of Taiwan* (Armonk, N.Y.: M. E. Sharpe, 1988); and the AID Survey Report by John D. Montgomery, Rufus B. Hughes, and Raymond H. Davis, "Rural Improvement and Political Development: The JCRR Model," unpublished ms., 1964. Taiwan's industrialization suggests that the bias against agriculture associated with ISI is not inevitable but depends on other policies as well, and thus on the political interests of state elites. For evidence, see Samuel Ho, "Decentralized Industrialization and Rural Development: Evidence from Taiwan," *Economic Development and Cultural Change* 28 (October 1979): 77–96; and for a dissenting view, Hill Gates, "Dependency and the Part-Time Proletariat on Taiwan," *Modern China* 5, 3 (1979): 381–407.

to be given to economic and to military objectives, and the balance between the public and private sectors. Ultimately, the resolution of these disputes hinged on decisions by the top political leadership. Unlike in Korea, however, Chiang Kai-shek had concentrated substantial decision-making authority and new policy instruments in the hands of technocrats during the ISI period.[26] This heritage gave them a political base as well as a channel for American influence.

The significance of the economic bureaucracy in formulating policy makes it worthwhile outlining its basic structure. The Taiwan Production Board, established in May 1949 as an organ of the provincial government, was the first attempt to centralize government control of economic policy. At the suggestion of the United States, an Economic Stabilization Board was established in March 1951, marking a shift in the control of economic policy back to the central government. Chaired by the finance minister, the ESB also coordinated trade policy, approved all large loans, both domestic and foreign, formulated the budget for the counterpart aid funds, screened all private investment applications, and oversaw the administration of the state-owned enterprises, which in the early 1950s accounted for over half of total industrial production. According to one of its early members, the ESB also acted as a "bridge between the KMT and U.S. officials," who participated in the deliberations of the board as observers.[27]

In addition to the JCRR, a Council on U.S. Aid had also been formed on the mainland in 1948. Like the JCRR, the CUSA functioned outside the regular ministries, selecting and overseeing the implementation of aid-funded projects and coordinating aid imports with project needs, Neil Jacoby emphasizes the importance of this agency's autonomy:

> Being free of the need to obtain legislative approval of its expenditures, the Council was able to act speedily on developmental projects. . . . Whereas the top councils of the Chinese government were preoccupied with political and military problems of security and "return to the mainland," the Council could concentrate upon the development of Taiwan. . . . Had U.S. aid been part of the Chinese government's budget, and administered through the regular departments of government, its developmental effects would have been greatly diminished.[28]

In 1953 the Economic Stabilization Board was reorganized and expanded in scope to develop and implement the first four-year plan. Five

---

26. For a detailed map of the economic bureaucracy, see Pang, "The State and Economic Transformation," pp. 57–72.
27. Interview, K. T. Li; Jacoby, *U.S. Aid to Taiwan*, chap. 5.
28. Jacoby, *U.S. Aid to Taiwan*, p. 61.

subcommittees were established to cover specific areas of policy, including agriculture, military spending and the budget, and industry. A Foreign Exchange and Trade Control Commission was also established, which dealt with exchange rates, the allocation of foreign exchange, and aid money.

In general, these ad hoc cabinet boards and commissions, including particularly the Council for U.S. Aid, gave technocrats a base and machinery for operating amid the confusion created by the preservation of duplicated ministries and departments at central and provincial levels. Unlike Korea in the 1950s, Taiwan possessed not only a strong political leadership but an economic policy apparatus staffed with reformist technocrats who maintained good working relations with their American counterparts.

Substantive differences did exist within the economic planning apparatus over the direction of policy, however; they reflected broader political, institutional, and ideological differences. The exact nature of the bureaucratic cleavages over policy remains somewhat obscure and probably did not follow rigid organizational lines.[29] Nonetheless, the Bank of Taiwan, provincial political authorities, managers of the state-owned enterprises, and some members of the FETCC backed a more statist approach to development. They were supported by conservative elements within the party who gave priority to recapturing the mainland and for whom the main "economic" priority was guaranteeing the military's share of the budget. This group accepted the need for monetary stability and a balanced budget but was reluctant to use financial instruments for the purpose of expanding the private sector, which it viewed with some suspicion.

Devaluation was opposed on the grounds that it would be inflationary, though no doubt the opportunities for rent-seeking provided by the FETCC's control over the allocation of foreign exchange were also important.[30] Devaluation was also opposed on grounds of export pessimism. S. C. Tsiang recalls a debate in 1954 with a "well-informed" minister. The minister argued that exports of Taiwan's two major commodities, sugar and rice, were fixed by international agreement and bilateral negotiations with Japan respectively, and as a result were independent of the exchange rate. Tsiang, in turn, argued that devaluation would reveal those firms whose comparative advantage was hidden by an overvalued rate, an argument similar to that made by American advisers in

29. Pang, "The State and Economic Transformation," pp. 115, 117–19.

30. On the rent-seeking nature of Taiwan's ISI see Allan Cole's impressionistic account "The Political Roles of Taiwanese Entrepreneurs," *Asian Survey* 7 (September 1967): 645–54.

Korea. K. T. Li (Li Kwoh-ting), a prominent technocrat, remembers a similar "heated debate" in 1955 before the Economic Stabilization Board. Arguing that Taiwan should seek to exploit its comparative advantage by exporting textiles, he met the argument that the textile industry could not compete successfully with Japanese manufacturers.[31]

A central component of the conservative line was support for a strong state-owned sector. U.S. aid officials first became embroiled in this issue in connection with the compensation program of the land reform. In 1953 a "Statute for Transferring Public Corporations to Private Owner-ship" was passed, but the United States feared that without adequate government support, the goal of turning landlords into capitalists would not be realized.[32] Although the conservatives admitted that state busi-nesses had been inefficient in the past, such businesses were not neces-sarily so. Given the weakness of indigenous entrepreneurial talent, the state should be prepared to take a direct role in production by creating new enterprises and forming joint ventures with the private sector.[33] In the formulation of the second four-year plan in 1956, for example, an ambitious proposal for a steel mill using Philippine ore was elaborated, only to be shelved as a result of U.S. objections.

Underneath support for the state's control of the commanding heights of the economy was an unspoken political issue: Taiwan-mainlander relations. Private-sector growth would inevitably strengthen the native Taiwanese, who then might use their economic power for political ends. The United States, on the other hand, saw the strengthening of the private sector as contributing to longer-run political stability by coopting the Taiwanese into the system.[34]

The industrializing reformers were headed politically by Ch'en Ch'eng, but their moving spirit was K. Y. Yin (Yin Chung-jung), head of the Industrial Development Commission from 1953 through 1955. The IDC was responsible for industrial planning and for developing the

31. S. C. Tsiang, "Exchange Rate, Interest Rate," p. 322, which contains numerous insights into the debates of the 1950s, and K. T. Li, "A First Hand Story about Economic Planning," in *The Experience of Dynamic Economic Growth on Taiwan* (Taipei: Mei Ya Publica-tions, 1976), for this and other anecdotes.

32. T. K. Chang, the minister of economic affairs, was willing to turn all of the five corporations over to the landlords and to let them fail in order to prove the point that private enterprise could not function without state support and guidance. See Simon, "U.S. Assistance, Land Reform."

33. Some of this debate is reprinted in *Industry of Free China* 1, 5 (1954), including particularly Shih-cheng Liu, "On the Development of Taiwan's Industry"; Chang Fong, "An Intermediate Course between Private Enterprise and Government Control," and K. Y. Yin, "A Discussion of Industrial Policy in Taiwan." See also Hsu, "Political Bases," pp. 156–59.

34. The goal of politically strengthening the Taiwanese was implicit in the JCRR's work. See Montgomery, Hughes, and Davis, "Rural Improvement." For a succinct summary of the ethnic issue, see Hung-mao Tien, *The Great Transition*, pp. 35–42.

island's industrial capacity; it was split into sections, the most important of which was the General Industry Section. The IDC believed in a strengthening of the productive elements of the private sector and maintained close relations with refugee capitalists from Shanghai and some of the larger Taiwanese capitalists. Through these direct connections, it sought to encourage investment in designated sectors, including plastics, glass, plywood, and, most important, textiles.

The textile industry illustrates the difference between the self-conscious policy of ISI that characterized the 1950s in Taiwan and the chaotic economic policy generated in Korea by the Rhee regime. As early as 1950 sectoral plans had been launched for the Taiwanese textile industry, with technical assistance from an American engineering firm, imported power looms from Japan, and U.S. aid in the form of raw cotton. CUSA's textile subcommittee, cooperating later with the IDC, acted directly to promote linkages between different segments of the industry by allocating raw cotton and yarn through industry associations. Through the state-owned Central Trust of China, the government also intervened in the weaving stage. The Central Trust engaged in advance purchases and distributed yarn through a quota system to the Textile Guilds and their member mills, guaranteeing its repurchase. Loans were available for plant expansion through CUSA. Applications were evaluated by an American consulting firm, J. G. White, operating as an arm of the aid mission and cooperating closely with the IDC in project evaluation during the 1950s.[35] Beginning in 1953 some price controls were cautiously withdrawn. As K. Y. Yin explained, "while desiring to restore the free market for textiles, [the subcommittee] has not overlooked the possibility of such a free market being taken advantage of by speculators and profiteers."[36]

The comment is suggestive. Though Yin was a reformer, he was by no means in favor of laissez-faire. Like many technocrats who played an important role in Taiwan's industrialization, Yin had an engineering background. He combined arguments for liberalizing measures with a defense of a significant role for the state in planning and allocating resources. The ultimate aim of industrialization, he argued, was to reduce dependence on American aid and develop an "independent and self-sustaining economy," a goal not articulated in Korea until after the military coup.[37] This vision required a careful designation of those

35. See Thomas Gold, "Dependent Development in Taiwan" (Ph.D. diss., Harvard University, 1980), pp. 96ff., which contains information not included in his *State and Society;* Hsu, "Political Bases," 159–69.

36. K. Y. Yin, "The Development of the Textile Industry in Taiwan," *Industry of Free China* 1, 1 (1954): 26.

37. K. Y. Yin, "A Discussion."

industries which were viable and in which Taiwan had a comparative advantage. Yin argued for protection from "the menace of unfair competition from abroad," government rationing of credit, foreign exchange, and raw materials, and licensing control over the investment decision-making process itself.

THE POLITICS OF EXPORT-LED GROWTH: PHASE 1

Through the mid-1950s the two policy lines coexisted. Intermediate-goods industries developed by the Japanese, among them fertilizers and chemicals, continued to be run by the government, and public-sector enterprises expanded, though not at the rate of overall economic growth. A significant battery of controls on trade, the allocation of foreign exchange, and the licensing of industrial activity remained in place. On the other hand, high rates of substitution were achieved by private consumer-goods manufacturers. The ISI regime and the IDC's efforts at industrial promotion were bearing fruit in the growth, in both absolute and relative terms, of the private sector.

By the mid-1950s the economy was experiencing several problems typically attributed to import substitution. The first was market saturation and slowed growth. GNP growth rates dropped every year from 1952 through 1956. Per capita consumption did not increase at all in 1956 and only marginally in 1957; investment was sluggish through 1957. The slowdown gave domestic business an interest in some kind of policy reform, but the reforms they advocated had little to do with an expansion of exports. In 1957 the Provincial Assembly of Industries appealed to the Ministry of Economic Affairs to permit firms to organize on a cartel basis to limit competition. According to K. T. Li, the government was "pestered" by business with "requests to restrict the construction of new plants in their fields on the grounds that production had already saturated domestic markets."[38] There was a search for new secondary import-substituting industries, including chemicals, rayon fiber, urea, plastics, even autos. Expansion through secondary ISI was championed in particular by those favoring the state-run enterprises.[39]

A second problem was corruption, which, unlike in Korea, was recognized as a drag on growth. The overvaluation of the exchange rate encouraged arbitrage at the expense of productive activity. In 1954 Yin was already complaining about the "profiteers" who "in the name of factories they have founded with negligible capital and symbolic or

38. Li, "A First Hand Story," p. 99; Lin, *Industrialization*, pp. 74–75.
39. Gustav Ranis, "Industrial Development," in Galenson, *Economic Growth*, p. 219.

make-believe equipment, scramble for the privilege of obtaining foreign currency allocation or import quota."[40] The planners were ahead of the private sector. Larger projects included in government plans had to be postponed because private capital would not come forward.[41] As in Korea after the transition to export-led growth, state objectives in Taiwan did not always move in tandem with those of the private sector, even if they favored its long-term development.

The third and most persistent problem was the balance of payments. Though traditional export activity did make an important contribution in earning foreign exchange, the expansion of industrial exports was hampered by the trade and exchange-rate regime. T. C. Liu and S. C. Tsiang's 1954 IMF mission to Taiwan had as a principal objective an increase in exports. They made a sweeping set of proposals, including the institution of an exchange-surrender certificate system that would have allowed an equilibrium exchange rate to emerge through trade in the certificates and the replacement of quantitative restrictions on imports with tariffs.[42] Some steps were taken in 1955 to reverse the bias against exports through a small devaluation and the rebating of import duties and certain taxes for exporters, but these reforms were not integrated into a larger plan and did not have the full backing of the government.

In 1958, in connection with the onset of the Taiwan Straits crisis, O. K. Yui (Yui Hung-chun), an early opponent of devaluation, was replaced by Ch'en Ch'eng as premier. The assignment reflected Chiang's confidence in and support of Ch'en Ch'eng as a manager of the economy, as well as a new political strategy that focused explicitly on building the island's economy as the foundation from which other political objectives might be realized.[43] The post of premier carried with it the chairmanship of the Council on U.S. Aid, a body long insulated from the influence of the regular ministries. Ch'en Ch'eng proceeded to install his people in key posts. By far the most important assignments went to K. Y. Yin. Forced out of the government by conservative forces in 1955, Yin at

40. K. Y. Yin, "Adverse Trend [*sic*] in Taiwan's Industrial Development," *Industry of Free China* 2 (August 1954): 1–5.

41. K. T. Li describes how PVC and rayon plants could not find investors until U.S. aid authorities offered loans and the government offered assistance in project engineering and plant operation. Not only did these industries become among the fastest-growing in Taiwan over the 1960s, but the group undertaking the PVC operation subsequently became the largest industrial group in Taiwan. Li, "A First Hand Story," p. 99.

42. See Tsiang, "Exchange Rate, Interest Rate."

43. The following draws on Li, "A First Hand Story"; Pang, "The State and Economic Transformation," pp. 113–15; Winckler, "State Struggle and Class Conflict in Taiwan"; and interviews with Tsiang, Li, Paul Tsai, a lawyer involved in the legal reforms, Wan-an Yeh, a member of the IDC in the fifties, and Joe Yager, deputy chief of mission, American Embassy.

one time held the positions of secretary-general of the ESB, head of the Foreign Exchange and Trade Control Commission, chairman of the board of the Bank of Taiwan, and vice-chairman of CUSA. In August the ESB was disbanded after an Administrative Reform Committee found that it was too powerful and overlapped with the functions of the regular ministries. Its most important functions were absorbed by CUSA and a newly formed Industrial Coordinating and Planning Group. The chairman of CUSA was Ch'en Ch'eng; its secretary-general, K. T. Li, a protégé of K. Y. Yin's. These changes were crucial, since they effectively combined in the hands of the reformers influence over the budget, planning, aid allocation, finance, and trade and exchange-rate policy, an organizational pattern parallel to that in Korea.

The first reform package of April 1958 drew on the work of the economists Tsiang and Liu. In late 1957 foreign-exchange problems had worsened, and Chiang Kai-shek formed a nine-man group to address the problem. Arguing that the trade and exchange-rate regime created corruption and inefficiency, as well as contributing to balance-of-payments difficulties, K. Y. Yin argued for liberalization.[44] This reform simplified the multiple exchange-rate system, relaxed some import restrictions, rationalized the system of allocating imports of raw materials, and initiated new measures to promote exports. Tsiang sold the crucial reform, a devaluation from 25 to 36 New Taiwan dollars to the U.S. dollar, to the political leadership when he convinced them it would not prove inflationary.

In the same year the Americans began to play a more active role in the reform process. With American help, Taiwan had weathered a second confrontation with the People's Republic of China over the offshore islands of Quemoy and Matsu, though the United States had stated clearly that reunification by force was unacceptable and renewed its call for economic reform. Aid was used in the short run, through both threats and promises, for the purpose of extracting, but also supporting, reforms. The process of influence is described by Jacoby: "In Taiwan, the U.S. AID Mission often played the role of 'whipping boy' for the development-minded officials of the Joint Commission and the Council. These officials could argue for economic reforms within the Chinese government on the grounds that they were under pressure by the U.S. government."[45]

Following a visit by Under Secretary of State C. Douglas Dillon in 1959, AID proposed an eight-point program including liberalized ex-

---

44. K. Y. Yin, "A Review of Existing Foreign Exchange and Control Policy and Technique," *Industry of Free China* 12 (November 1959): 2–21; interview, Wan-an Yeh.
45. Jacoby, *U.S. Aid to Taiwan*, p. 131.

change controls, the sale of more government enterprises and more effective management of those retained, and noninflationary monetary and fiscal policies. One goal of the program was to reduce military spending. Chinese reformers seized the opportunity to expand the agenda into a Nineteen-Point Program of Economic and Financial Reform, including additional domestic measures aimed at increasing savings and private investment, reducing consumption, removing subsidies, and raising utility rates. In return the United States offered to extend a $30 million program loan. Though $10 million of this loan was ultimately cancelled for failure to comply with suggested limits on military spending, the passing of the Straits crisis returned the government to a more conservative fiscal stance.

The Institutional Foundations of the New Course

The neoclassical interpretation of Taiwan's export success has focused largely on the liberalization of imports and the exchange-rate reform.[46] As in Korea, the reforms in Taiwan were preceded by a set of institutional changes that centralized decision-making power and reduced the influence of contending conceptions of policy. In Korea, this set of changes took place only after a change in regime. In Taiwan the process was more incremental, evolving out of existing "strong" state structures. As a result, between the 1950s and the 1960s there are greater continuities than is often recognized in the nature of state intervention in the economy. As in Korea, various interventions served to reduce the risk of shifting into the export business by providing various premiums and reducing information and transactions costs. They also suggest the actions of a dirigist state intent on steering the industrial structure in a desired direction.

Taiwan has generally not used the financial system as an instrument of industrial policy to the same extent that Korea has.[47] Dominated by state-owned banks, Taiwan's financial system is relatively undeveloped. Interest rates are set by the government. Banks are extremely conserva-

---

46. The neoclassical interpretation is contained in Bela Balassa, *Development Strategies in Semi-Industrial Economies* (Baltimore: Johns Hopkins University Press for the World Bank, 1982), chap. 10; J. Fei, G. Ranis, and S. Kuo, *Growth with Equity: The Taiwan Case* (New York: Oxford University Press, 1979); G. Ranis, "Equity with Growth in Taiwan: How 'Special' is the 'Special Case'?" *World Development* 6, 3 (1978); M. H. Hsing, John H. Power, and Gerardo Sicat, *Taiwan and the Philippines: Industrialization and Trade Policies* (New York: Oxford University Press, 1971).

47. On Taiwan's financial system see Robert Wade, "East Asian Financial Systems as a Challenge to Economics: Lessons from Taiwan," *California Management Review* 27 (Summer 1985): 106–27; C. Liang and M. Skully, "Financial Institutions and Markets in Taiwan," in Skully, ed., *Financial Institutions and Markets in the Far East: A Study of China, Hong Kong, Japan, South Korea, and Taiwan* (London: Macmillan, 1982).

tive. Reliance on collateral is typical, and the ability of bankers to judge risk and to make loans on a cash-flow basis notoriously low. A public-sector bias also operated in the 1950s; through 1957 public enterprises accounted for over one-half of the outstanding loans and discounts by all banks. In July 1957, however, the Bank of Taiwan launched an export-loan program under which short-term loans were extended to exporters to cover the whole chain of their export operations. Firms were granted credit lines on the basis of past export performance and future plans. The effective subsidy could be substantial. Loans repayable in foreign currencies carried a 6 percent interest rate, those in local currencies 12 percent. By contrast, loans available through the financial system to private-sector borrowers ranged between 20 percent and 22 percent.

The close relationship that developed between the government and private-sector associations in Korea is not to be found in Taiwan, nor has the Taiwanese government acted to promote industrial concentration. Nonetheless, several important sectoral associations performed functions supportive of export activity, effectively cartelizing trade in some sectors.[48] From their members these groups collected dues to be placed into a cooperative fund, out of which bonuses were paid to exporters. Firms were allocated export targets and paid penalties for falling short. In the case of the cotton textile industry, only 40 percent of total output could be sold on the home market, with excess sales subject to penalties. These arrangements were overseen by government agencies and covered significant sectors of Taiwan's export industry during the 1960s, including cotton and woolen textiles, steel, and rubber products. In 1970 the government established a China External Trade Development Council, similar to Korea's KOTRA, to promote exports and conduct market research for exporters.

Even neoclassical accounts of the country's growth express reservations about the extent of import liberalization.[49] The tariff system coupled high rates with various offsetting packages.[50] The ratio of customs

48. Lin, *Industrialization*, pp. 108–9.
49. Studies of import-liberalization include T. H. Lee, K. S. Liang, Chi Schive, and R. S. Yeh, "The Structure of Effective Protection and Subsidy in Taiwan," *Economic Essays* (Taipei) 6 (November 1975); Lee and Liang, "Taiwan," in Bela Balassa, ed., *Development Strategies in Semi-Industrial Economies;* and Lin, *Industrialization*, pp. 110–15, all of which find redundant and high tariffs, particularly in the "import-competing" category. Maurice Scott, "Foreign Trade," in Galenson, *Economic Growth*, finds that the ratio of net customs revenues to imports drops from what he admits are unusually high rates (25–31 percent) in the mid-1950s to 17 percent in 1959–60, but there is very little change in this ratio until after 1969–70. See Wade's review of these studies in "State Intervention in Outward-Looking Development: Neoclassical Theory and Taiwanese Practice," in Wade and Gordon White, eds., *Developmental States in East Asia* (New York: St. Martin's, 1988).
50. Tein-Chen Chou, "The Pattern and Strategy of Industrialization in Taiwan: Specialization and Offsetting Policy," *The Developing Economies* 23 (June 1985): 138–57.

revenues to imports ranked 24th among the ratios of 82 countries as late as 1977; import liberalization became a divisive political issue only in the late 1970s and early 1980s.[51] To be able to offer reduced duties on those raw materials and intermediate goods required by exporters, it was necessary to *increase* the rates on finished goods, since the government relied heavily upon customs duties as a source of revenue. An additional offsetting package is the rebate of both customs duties and commodity taxes on imported raw materials, without which the export of many categories of products would not be possible. Exporters were also allowed to use a portion of their foreign-exchange earnings to import raw materials for sale to other end-users, in effect granting local monopoly rents as a reward for export performance. Though this premium declined over the 1960s and was finally abolished under IMF pressure in 1970, it provided additional windfalls to the early exporters. Tein-chen Chou refers to this administratively complex system as one of "import tariffs-cum-export rebates" or "domestic sales subsidizing export sales," a system in which the domestic consumer bears the ultimate cost and the government exercises significant discretion.[52]

The removal of quantitative restrictions was not dramatic, either. Luxury goods and those produced by state monopolies and affecting national security could be restricted. Domestic producers could also apply to limit the import of other items. These items had to meet the following criteria: first, local producers must be capable of satisfying domestic demand; second, quality must be reasonable; and third, the price, inclusive of tariffs, must not be over a certain margin above the price of comparable imports. In 1960 this margin was 25 percent, lowered to 15 percent in 1964, 10 percent in 1968, and 5 percent in 1973.[53]

Domestic-content legislation was an additional way of reserving the local market for national firms; the theory of backward linkages is explicitly invoked by planners as justification for special inducements to industry.[54] Surveillance over these items rested with the Industrial Development Bureau of the Ministry of Economic Affairs, the bureau responsible for industrial policy and with the closest links to the private sector. The share of tradable items on the "permissible" list, an indicator used to show the level of liberalization, is also misleading since some imports are limited by country of origin. Would-be importers may also be asked to supply evidence that they cannot secure comparable imports

51. Ibid., p. 151.
52. Ibid.
53. Kuo-shu Liang and Ching-ing Hou Liang, "Incentive Policies for Import Substitution and Export Expansion in the Republic of China," *Economic Review* (International Commercial Bank of China, Taipei), November/December 1978.
54. Scott, "Foreign Trade," p. 333, and interviews with officials in the Industrial Development Bureau.

domestically, for example, by obtaining a written statement from the relevant producer association.[55]

Perhaps the major instrument for guiding investment has been the Statute for the Encouragement of Investment, a piece of omnibus legislation promulgated in July 1960 and conceived as an important correlate to the Nineteen-Point Program. The legislation was formulated by CUSA at Ch'en Ch'eng's direction precisely to circumvent interministerial conflicts and permit a coordinated approach.[56] The statute, frequently revised and updated, governs investment by foreign nationals, overseas Chinese, and local investors. Relying on tax incentives to steer investment, the statute reduces the discretionary power of the government to select specific firms for support and thus has probably contributed to a level of industrial concentration lower than in Korea. Two sorts of industries qualify for preferential treatment: "productive enterprises," an extremely broad range of investments, and a more select group of "encouraged enterprises." This second group appears on a list called the "Categories and Criteria for Special Encouragement of Important Productive Enterprises," which is under constant revision. Signaling the priorities of government planners, the list is open to change on the basis of recommendations by interested foreign and domestic investors. The list has become more elaborate and discriminating over time. In addition, the granting of incentives often depends on various conditions, including minimum scale of production, product standards, and local-content requirements. The statute has come under continual attack. Liberals have argued that the incentives serve only to compensate for the difficulties created by restrictive regulations, and that if regulations were removed, they would be unnecessary.[57] Nonetheless, the revisions of the statute constitute a virtual history of Taiwan's industrial policy.

Finally, the government has made extensive use of the state-owned enterprise to realize industrial aims, particularly in the substitution of intermediate and capital goods. Over the course of its postwar development, Taiwan has had one of the largest state-owned sectors in the developing world. Contrary to neoclassical accounts, its relative size has fallen only very gradually and even increased in importance in the early 1970s. In a range of heavy industries, including petrochemicals, nonferrous metals, and shipbuilding, state initiatives date to the heyday of export-led growth in the late 1960s. The turn to world markets was thus coupled with anticipatory actions aimed at deepening Taiwan's base in intermediate and capital-intensive industries.

55. See Robert Wade, "Sweet and Sour Capitalism," unpublished ms., chap. 5.
56. Pang, "The State and Economic Transformation," p. 128.
57. On these debates see *Taiwan Economic News* (Taipei), August 4 and September 29, 1980.

KOREA AND TAIWAN COMPARED

The origins of an import-substituting strategy in Korea and Taiwan are quite similar. Both faced severe problems of war reconstruction and a severing of traditional market ties; external shocks are the most important factor in their inward orientation over the 1950s. Both were tightly integrated into the American security orbit as a result of the Korean War. Both became dependent, to roughly equal degrees, on aid for the financing of ISI. Despite a tendency to belittle the ISI phase of their development, both countries witnessed a rapid growth of the private manufacturing sector in the 1950s.

At a general level, there are also some interesting similarities in the configuration of social forces in the two countries—similarities that have a bearing on their strategies of economic growth. In both countries the power of rural elites was broken early; there was no rural counterweight to the government's interest in industrialization, no sectoral conflict such as that seen in many Latin American countries. Partly because of their external political situations—divided countries facing Communist adversaries—little ideological or organizational space was allowed for socialist, leftist, or populist forces, nor was labor allowed an independent voice. ISI in the two larger East Asian NICs was not a child of cross-class alliances, as it was to some extent in Latin America. When the transition to export-led growth took place, both systems had labor movements that were weak, either because they were effectively organized by the government, as in Taiwan, or because more independent alternatives were circumscribed, as in Korea. Labor markets were not subject to union "interference," wage levels responded to the dictates of supply and demand, and the government guaranteed labor peace.

There are, however, important differences between the two countries in state structure and political history that date to the period of decolonization. These differences account for differences in the instruments, agents, and coherence of policy. The most obvious is the nominally democratic character of the Korean system imposed by the Americans as compared to the one-party structure in Taiwan. Syngman Rhee's need to build political support during the 1950s led to an inconsistent economic program. Those technocratic resources available were scattered and lacked firm political support. Efforts to develop a planning capacity were overridden or neglected by central political authorities. On Taiwan, by contrast, political control was much more effective and the administrative ability to sustain difficult policy measures greater. An impressive planning apparatus developed in the 1950s, though it was initially split between different policy lines. The key issue was not the desirability of import substitution or the role of planning; on this there was consensus. The issue of contention was the degree of emphasis given to strengthening the private sector.

These differences in political structure affected the ability of the United States to exercise policy leverage. In Taiwan close working relationships were established between the Americans and Chinese in a set of relatively insulated policy forums. In Korea, by contrast, influence over policy was jealously guarded at the top.

What factors influenced the shift toward a more outward-looking strategy? Several explanations can be dismissed. Though a slowdown in growth was certainly important, the organized political pressure of the private sector does not appear to have shaped the design of government policy. In Korea, Park Chung Hee struck a more or less explicit deal to support the private sector, but on the government's terms. The private sector grew rapidly in the 1950s in Taiwan, providing new opportunities for the Taiwanese. But politically the private sector was weak. To the extent the private sector advocated a shift in policy to respond to the problems of ISI, it was toward cartelization of the domestic market and further government support for import substitution. The argument can be stated more strongly. Not only was the shift in policy designed in isolation of private-sector interests, it *demanded* such isolation to be effective. In both cases the heart of the reform was a rewriting of the rules of the game to eliminate or reduce the opportunities for rent seeking and arbitrage that characterized ISI in both countries. Nor were foreign firms important; foreign capital followed, rather than led, the shift toward export-led growth.

External constraints were crucial in providing incentives to reform. In both countries, balance-of-payments difficulties preceded the reform effort; in both countries, the United States exploited them. The extent of Korea's and Taiwan's dependence on American aid is virtually unprecedented. But only when the United States began to link aid giving to policy reform, both in the short run through the manipulation of disbursements and through an announced intention to withdraw over time, was leverage effective. In Korea, Park initially attempted to resist by vigorously pursuing other channels of funding, including the settlement with Japan and commercial borrowing. In Taiwan the transition was smoother. Yet in both cases the reforms were ultimately sold to the political leadership as leading to a degree of political independence. Ironically, a strategy depending heavily on world markets was sold on grounds of self-reliance.

But leverage to what end? Why not seek to continue the ISI course, balancing trade at lower rather than higher levels of exports? The transmission of policy-relevant knowledge must be taken into account as a component of U.S. influence. In both cases the transition was worked out through a close alliance between American and local technocrats, though in Taiwan the weight of domestic expertise was undoubtedly heavier. This transnational alliance advanced a set of ideas that, while varying on fine points, represented a broad orthodoxy: stabilization, devaluation, strengthening of the private sector, support for exports, foreign investment, trade liberalization, and market-oriented reforms.

Yet the late years of the Syngman Rhee regime demonstrate that leverage and a clear program are not enough. Pressured to change course, facing annual stabilization programs and declining growth, Rhee failed to respond. The implementation of reform also hinged on distinct political interests and institutional capabilities. In both Korea and Taiwan the transition was preceded by centralizing reforms that signaled new developmental alliances between executives and reforming technocrats. In Korea these reforms were possible only in the wake of a change in regime; in Taiwan they emerged more gradually. Institutional and political change allowed for swift and flexible policy action by permitting technocrats to both coordinate and override the advice of competing ministries. In both cases these measures took place in political contexts that were highly managed; broader public opinion, including that of business and labor, played a marginal role.

Political change allowed the transition to export-led growth to take place, but it also modified its nature in a statist direction. Changes in incentives were important, particularly the difficult tasks of devaluation and stabilization. At the same time both governments manipulated an array of instruments that had the effect of reducing risk for firms embarking on the new and uncertain business of operating in international markets. In Korea these instruments served the political function of securing support from, as well as control over, the domestic private sector. "Liberalization" in the two larger Asian NICs thus came to have a distinctly mercantilist cast.

CHAPTER FIVE

Singapore and Hong Kong:
The Transition to Export-Led Growth

The growth trajectories of the entrepôts differ from those of Korea and Taiwan. Strategically located to act as service centers for vast hinter-lands, Singapore and Hong Kong have been outward-looking from the beginning. As a result they have been particularly vulnerable to external shocks. Political events interrupting trade with the hinterland were the key factor pushing the two entrepôts toward externally oriented indus-trialization.

Several political factors contributed to the success of this transition and provide the basis for some comparison between the city-states and the larger East Asian NICs. Neither of the city-states had to contend with traditional rural-based elites or the modernization of agriculture. The institutions governing labor relations in the two city-states are different, yet in both cases they were conducive to the relatively free operation of labor markets. Finally, the city-states possess political systems bearing important similarities to the larger East Asian NICs. Hong Kong has been a colony administered by the British, whereas Singapore is an independent and nominally democratic nation-state. Yet both possess strong and independent executives, weak, subordinate legislatures, and economic technocrats who are operationally autonomous. These politi-cal factors contributed to the coherence of policy in the two city-states.

There are important differences between Hong Kong and Singapore, however. Even for the economically open and vulnerable city-states, the cases where international shocks should have the greatest explanatory power, we required a close attention to domestic politics to explain variations in the instruments and agents associated with export-led growth. Singapore's economic policy has been highly interventionist. The government has extended fiscal and financial incentives, established its own enterprises, and intervened extensively in the labor market. Hong Kong, by contrast, has pursued an almost completely laissez-faire course. Another contrast involves the role played by multinational corporations. Singapore has relied on foreign investment to a much greater extent than Korea, Taiwan, or Hong Kong, where local firms spearheaded industrialization.

Two factors help explain these differences. The first is the economic capability of the local manufacturing sector. In addition to a long-standing commercial establishment, Hong Kong inherited a group of manufacturers that developed under Nationalist auspices, particularly in Shanghai. In effect, Hong Kong experienced a phase of "disguised" import substitution, on the mainland, and laissez-faire worked there because of the large pool of entrepreneurial capability. In Singapore, by contrast, the domestic private sector was weak, concentrated primarily in services. Inducing foreign capital and establishing state-owned enterprises substituted for local entrepreneurial weakness.

The second crucial difference between the two concerns the way political authority was constituted. In Singapore the People's Action party came to power only after a concerted political struggle with the left. As in Korea, the instruments of economic policy were used to woo voters and consolidate political control; state intervention in Singapore reflects a history of deep-seated social conflict. By contrast, colonial political authority was never seriously contested in Hong Kong, no electoral constraints operated, and economic policy was concentrated in the hands of a powerful financial secretary. Social expenditures increased over time, partly in response to political pressure from below, but the government made no fundamental compromises with laissez-faire.

INDUSTRIALIZATION IN SINGAPORE

Founded in 1819, Singapore initially served as a transshipment point for trade with East Asia.[1] It became a regional entrepôt with the extension of British control over the Malay peninsula and the growth of the rubber and tin industries in the late nineteenth century. Working through a network of Chinese intermediaries, a European commercial

1. On Singapore's early role as an entrepôt see Wong Lin Ken, "Singapore: Its Growth as an Entrepôt Port, 1819–1941," *Journal of Southeast Asian Studies* 9, 1 (1978): 50–84; Helen Hughes, "From Entrepôt Trade to Manufacturing," in Hughes and You Poh Seng, eds., *Foreign Investment and Industrialization in Singapore* (Canberra: Australian National University Press, 1969); D. J. M. Tate, *The Making of Modern Southeast Asia*, vol. 2: *Economic and Social Change* (Kuala Lumpur: Oxford University Press, 1979), pp. 149–81, 231–60.

establishment in Singapore oversaw the two-way movement of goods throughout the region. The larger "agency houses" invested directly in tin mining and the rubber plantations and dominated Singapore's entrepôt trade.

The Depression and the accompanying slump in commodity prices generated concern over Singapore's future as an entrepôt. In 1931, and again in 1934, Straits governor Cecil Clementi offered proposals for a customs union with Malaya; both went down before strong opposition from commercial interests. The Depression produced the Imperial Preference Scheme and textile quotas, the main target of which was Japan.[2] Responses to the IPS and textile quotas revealed the conflicts of interest between Britain, its entrepôt, and the hinterland. The Federation of Malay States applied the preference scheme to a wide range of goods, but in the Straits Settlements, including Singapore, opposition from laissez-faire commercial interests was strong.[3]

Despite the absence of protection, industries linked to trade developed in Singapore: tin and rubber processing, maintenance and repair connected with shipping, and those local consumer goods which could undersell imports because of lower transport costs. These manufacturing industries, primarily under Chinese control, were given a boost by World War I and the Depression. Nonetheless, in 1960 manufacturing accounted for only 11.9 percent of GNP, and 94 percent of Singapore's exports were reexports. With several exceptions, those manufacturing enterprises which did exist tended to be small, capital-poor, family workshops with close links to the retail trade.[4]

Dependency arguments have explained this economic structure by reference to the dominance of foreign capital. Foreign investors were interested primarily in resource extraction and commerce and thus had few incentives to engage in other economic activities. Nonetheless, they preempted possibilities for indigenous capital accumulation.[5] However, it seems more accurate to attribute economic structure to the dominance of commercial activities rather than to foreign ownership per se, since Chinese were also engaged in commerce and banking. In any case,

2. For an account of the drift to bilateralism in the region, see Osamu Ishii, *Cotton Textile Diplomacy: Japan, Great Britain, and the United States, 1930–1936* (New York: Arno, 1981).

3. Tate, *Southeast Asia*, p. 251.

4. Cheng Siok Hwa, "Economic Change in Singapore, 1945–1977," *Southeast Asian Journal of Social Science* 7, 1–2 (1979): 96; Theodore and Frances M. Geiger, *Tales of Two City States: The Development Progress of Hong Kong and Singapore* (Washington, D.C.: National Planning Association, 1973), p. 175; Robert Gamer, *The Politics of Urban Development in Singapore* (Ithaca: Cornell University Press, 1972).

5. See for example James Puthecheary, *Ownership and Control in the Malayan Economy* (Singapore: Eastern University Press, 1960); Jan Pluvier, *South-East Asia from Colonialism to Independence* (Kuala Lumpur: Oxford University Press, 1974).

Singapore entered the postwar period still very much an entrepôt, with a weak manufacturing sector.

Independence and the Consolidation of PAP Power

Taiwan and Korea had nationalist movements, but independence there came through war settlements and the new regimes were shaped by occupying powers as much as by indigenous political forces. Decolonization in Singapore followed a pattern that confirms Tony Smith's observation: "Civil war lurks in the heart of every movement for national liberation."[6] While the left was tamed early in Taiwan and Korea, it remained a major contender for political power in Singapore through the early 1960s. This pattern of political development helps explain the role of the state in the Singapore economy.

Initially the pace of decolonization moved more slowly in Malaya than in Singapore.[7] In 1955, however, an alliance of conservative communal parties led by Tengku Abdul Rahman, won victory in the first legislative elections, forcing the British to promise full independence for Malaya in 1957. In elections for the Legislative Assembly in Singapore in 1955, two conservative parties fielded the largest number of candidates: the Progressive party, which maintained close links to the mercantile establishment and was favored by the British; and the Democratic party, sponsored by the Chinese Chamber of Commerce. In a dramatic upset the conservative parties were soundly defeated by left parties, which exploited nationalist themes and called for speedy and complete decolonization.

A coalition government was formed by David Marshall of the Labour Front, a party ideologically akin to the British Labour party, but the key to the political situation during the 1950s lay on the left.[8] In the immediate postwar period the British dismantled Communist-controlled

6. Tony Smith, *The Pattern of Imperialism* (New York: Cambridge University Press, 1981), p. 121.

7. See J. A. C. Mackie, *Konfrontasi: The Indonesia-Malaysia Dispute, 1963–66* (Kuala Lumpur: Oxford University Press, 1974), pp. 36–55; C. M. Turnbull, *A History of Singapore, 1819–1975* (Kuala Lumpur: Oxford University Press, 1977), pp. 257–334; and the excellent work by Chan Heng Chee, *A Sensation of Independence: A Political Biography of David Marshall* (Singapore: Oxford University Press, 1984), pp. 89–111.

8. The politics of this period, and particularly the PAP's relations with the Communists, remains highly controversial. See Chan Heng Chee, *Sensation of Independence*, pp. 89–111; C. Paul Bradley, "Leftist Fissures in Singapore Politics," *Western Political Quarterly* 18, 2 (1965): 292–308; Yeo Kim Wah, *Political Development in Singapore, 1945–1955* (Singapore: Singapore University Press, 1973), *passim;* Gary Rodan, "The Political Economy of Singapore's Industrialization: State Policy and International Capital Movement" (Ph.D. thesis, Murdoch University, Australia, 1986), chap. 3. Lee Kuan Yew told his side of the story in a remarkable series of radio broadcasts in September and October 1961, reprinted as *The Battle for Merger* (Singapore: Government Printing Office, 1961).

unions. In 1948 the Malayan Communist Party (MCP) adopted a strategy of armed struggle. This, in turn, was met with a sophisticated program of political controls and counterinsurgency. Stymied in the jungles, the MCP moved toward a united front strategy after 1951, focusing organizing efforts among Chinese immigrants in the cities. In Singapore the labor movement and students in Chinese secondary schools received particular attention.

After the elections of 1955 the People's Action Party (PAP) became the main opposition force to the Labour Front government. Formed in 1954, the party was split between a moderate nationalist leadership, centered on Lee Kuan Yew and other English-educated middle-class professionals, and a left wing sympathetic to, if not infiltrated by, the banned Communist party. A liberalized political atmosphere created new opportunities for the left to rebuild through labor organizing, united front tactics, and an emphasis on nationalism and decolonization. In 1955 and 1956 the left organized confrontations between labor and students and the self-rule government in the hope that Marshall would adopt unpopular positions on internal security. Lee Kuan Yew had qualms about the tactics of the left wing but was engaged in a united front strategy of his own, since the organizational links between the PAP left, students, and workers were indispensable. In 1957 the left came close to seizing control of the party, but the moderates were saved by government detention of leading PAP activists.

Thereafter the moderates moved along two fronts to consolidate power, one within the party itself, the other through the electoral arena. Within the party Lee introduced a hierarchy of membership that distinguished between ordinary and "cadre" members and allowed the moderate leadership to perpetuate itself. In the name of resisting Communist penetration, the PAP was transformed into "a cadre party in mass party guise."[9]

In the broader political arena the PAP leadership advanced a popular nationalist platform that included the provision of social services, economic development, and merger with Malaya (which would take place in 1963). In 1959 the PAP won 53.4 percent of the total vote and took 43 of 51 legislative seats. But electoral victory by no means settled the intraparty struggle for power. The left challenged the moderates over the constitutional settlement but finally broke away over the merger issue to form the Barisan Socialis party in July 1961.[10] The PAP leadership

9. Chan Heng Chee, "Political Parties," in Jon S. T. Quah, Chan Heng Chee, and Seah Chee Meow, eds., *Government and Politics in Singapore* (Singapore: Oxford University Press, 1985), p. 159.

10. The following draws on Chan Heng Chee, *Singapore: The Politics of Survival, 1965–1967* (Kuala Lumpur: Oxford University Press, 1971); Lee Kuan Yew, *The Battle for Merger;* Mackie, *Konfrontasi,* pp. 36–55; Chan Heng Chee, *Sensation of Independence,* pp. 205–7.

defended merger as an economic necessity, on the grounds that an independent Malaya would gradually seek to handle its own trade. Outside a Malaysian federation, Singapore was not a viable economic entity; incorporated into it, Singapore would become the center of the peninsula's import-substitution efforts.

Lee's motives were also political. Inclusion in the more conservative federation would restrain the left. Under the PAP's merger plan, the federal government would have a large say in internal security matters whereas Singapore would retain autonomy in labor and educational affairs—policy areas the PAP could use to consolidate political support. The apparent leftward drift of Singapore politics in early 1961 made the merger proposal attractive to the federation government as well. A marriage of convenience was consummated between the PAP and the conservative Tengku Abdul Rahman, who saw the inclusion of Singapore as preferable to its independent, and possibly leftist, development.

The PAP's merger proposal put the Barisan Socialis in an awkward position. Since the economic arguments for merger were compelling, the Barisan Socialis was reduced to denouncing the specifics of the PAP's plan. Controlling the referendum, the PAP made its own proposals most attractive, winning the vote of confidence handily. The referendum marked the beginning of a gradual consolidation of political power in the hands of the PAP and a decline in the fortunes of the left.[11] Lee did not hesitate to invoke national security as a justification for repressive measures, and PAP leaders were surprisingly frank in their defense of the secret police, detention without trial, and curbs on press freedom.[12] In February 1963 the Internal Security Council launched "Operation Cold Store," involving the arrest of several Barisan Socialis leaders; and in September and October, immediately following the elections, further steps were taken against "extremists." As in Korea, divisions within the opposition and the inability to offer a credible alternative to the PAP were also important in weakening the left.

The crucial factors in the evolution of PAP power, however, were the strategic use of state resources to build bases of support and the incorporation and control of potential opposition. This task became crucial following the breakaway of the Barisan Socialis, since the left had oc-

11. Thomas Bellows, *The People's Action Party: The Emergence of a Dominant Party System,* Southeast Asia Studies Monograph 14 (New Haven: Yale University Press, 1970), and Chan Heng Chee, *The Dynamics of One Party Dominance: The PAP at the Grass Roots* (Singapore: Singapore University Press, 1978), stress the organizational capabilities of the government, while Rodan, "Political Economy," and Frederic C. Deyo, *Dependent Development and Industrial Order: An Asian Case Study* (New York: Praeger, 1981), give greater weight to coercion and manipulation.

12. See for example Goh Keng Swee, *The Economics of Modernization* (Singapore: Asia Pacific Press, 1972), pp. 230–35.

cupied key positions in the middle and lower ranks of the party hierarchy and in the labor movement. One of the first acts of Lee's government was to disband the City Council and centralize the functions of the urban government at the national level, allowing the PAP to control the provision of services, particularly housing. Chan Heng Chee describes the intertwining of state and party at the grass roots:

> It would seem almost inapt to speak of PAP "dominance" . . . but for the fact that there is an increasing merger of Government and party at the local constituency. So, where party activity levels off, newly created governmental institutions such as the Citizens' Consultative Committees and the community centres replace the party's organizational roles and functions, and the ubiquitous presence of the party is felt through these three institutions in combination—one party and two non-party.[13]

An important element of this control structure pertained to labor. With the defection of prominent labor leaders to the Barisan Socialis, the Singapore Trade Union Congress divided into a PAP-aligned National Trade Union Congress and a socialist Singapore Association of Trade Unions. Industrial conflict became a component of the larger political struggle. Nearly half of those arrested in Operation Cold Store were SATU officials, and additional union leaders were arrested following the September 1963 elections. Deregistration of dissident unions followed, and by 1966 the NTUC had established its authority over affiliate unions on virtually all questions of policy. The NTUC, in turn, was financially dependent on the government, and its leaders were chosen by the PAP.[14]

The PAP also had to overcome resistance to its political strategy from within the bureaucracy. The civil service was largely localized by 1957, but many English-educated civil servants were hostile to the socialist rhetoric of the PAP and its effort to use the bureaucracy to political ends. The PAP launched a subtle purge, eliminating cost-of-living allowances for higher-ranking civil servants and introducing new disciplinary procedures. Lee Kuan Yew's speech in 1959, at the opening of a political studies center established to train civil servants, is a revealing summary of his political briefs:

> The mass of the people are not concerned with legal and constitutional forms and niceties. They are not interested in the theory of the separation of powers and the purpose and function of a politically neutral civil service

13. Chan Heng Chee, *The Dynamics of One Party Dominance*, p. 133.
14. On labor issues see Deyo, *Dependent Development;* W. E. Chalmers, *Critical Issues in Industrial Relations in Singapore* (Singapore: Donald Moore Press, 1969).

under such a constitution. . . . If the future is not better, either because of the stupidities of elected ministers or the inadequacies of the civil service, then at the end of the five-year term the people are hardly likely to believe either in the political party that they have elected or the political system that they have inherited.[15]

The government also created parastatal bodies outside normal bureaucratic channels in order to implement its programs. Some of the most important of these "statutory boards" date to the early years of PAP rule and reflect the political strategy of the new government: the Public Utilities Board (1959), the Housing and Urban Development Board (1960), and the Economic Development Board (1961).

By 1963, though Singapore was formally still part of Malaysia, the outlines of the new politics were clear. Political power was concentrated in Lee Kuan Yew and the executive. The legislature, once the site of thrilling debates between Marshall, Lee, and other first-generation nationalist leaders, declined in importance. Even the PAP itself became less important than the government it nominally controlled. The left gradually weakened, as much through the astute political and electoral tactics of the PAP as through direct repression. The left's political base was gradually drawn into the PAP's orbit through a restructured union movement and a dense network of local government and services.

It should be underlined that the private sector, including businesses with ties to British capital, was also politically weak. This weakness stemmed from its cautious attitude toward independence and the stigma attaching to the comprador, but even more from the political mobilization that swept the Labour Front and later the PAP to power. With the defeat of the left, the PAP moved in a decidedly conservative direction. As in both Korea and Taiwan, however, the government developed a degree of independence from both left and right.

Toward a New Economic Strategy: Merger and the Failure of ISI

External constraints played a major role in the reorientation of Singapore's industrial strategy and structure, as they had in Korea and Taiwan. After 1963 Singapore's main political and economic problems turned on its relationship with Malaya. Federation implied an economic course very different from independence as a city-state. Only with the

15. Lee Kuan Yew, "Speech at the Opening of the Civil Service Study Centre," August 15, 1959, Singapore Govt. Press Statement TTS/INFS.AU/64/59. See also Seah Chee Meow, "The Civil Service," in John S. T. Quah, Chan Heng Chee, and Seah Chee Meow, eds., *Government and Politics of Singapore* (Singapore: Oxford University Press, 1985), pp. 92–119.

failure of merger in 1965 and the shock of independence would Singapore develop into an export-oriented manufacturing center.

Uncertainty over the future of the entrepôt trade is a leitmotif of Singapore's economic history, but international fluctuations did not present a political problem until the postwar period. Before the 1940s the employment level was self-regulating; immigration declined during periods of recession and emigration rose. After the war the population became more settled, and political barriers limited the free movement of labor. Given the rapid rate of population growth during the 1950s, 4.5 percent annually, maintaining real incomes and employment became a major political and economic challenge.

Prior to 1959 two important studies of the economy had urged industrialization as a way out.[16] On coming to power, the PAP arranged for a World Bank mission to survey the city's industrial potential. The study was conducted in two phases, in late 1960 and in early 1961. Known as the Winsemius Report, the study is candid concerning the link between politics and economic strategy.[17] It begins by noting the worsening of already high levels of unemployment during the industrial downturn of 1957–59 and underlines the political causes: uncertainty concerning the elections of 1959, the confrontational nature of industrial relations, investor concerns over political stability. Yet there was no alternative to industrialization. Entrepôt activity had grown at only 1 percent a year from 1956 through 1960 and was likely to continue sluggish as Indonesia and Malaya sought to control their own trade. Raw materials processing fared even more poorly, declining 21 percent from 1958 to 1960.

The report argued that Singapore could be made a viable manufacturing center on its own, though at the time only one-quarter of total domestic demand was being met through local production. In this the report was far ahead of PAP thinking. The report advocated industrial licensing, antidumping legislation, and the use of government procurement to foster local firms. Though arguing against state participation in industry, it defended increased financial assistance to industry and the formation of an Industrial Bank. The report also argued for a concerted export drive but noted that this tactic would impose constraints. "The

16. International Bank for Reconstruction and Development, *The Economic Development of Malaya* (Washington, D.C.: IBRD, 1955). A 1959 report conducted under the Colombo Plan by Canadian consultant F. J. Lyle resulted in several policy innovations, including tax and import duty exemptions for designated "pioneer industries," later to be a central piece of Singapore's industrial strategy under the PAP. See Cheng, "Economic Change in Singapore," pp. 86–87.

17. United Nations Industrial Survey Mission, *A Proposed Industrialization Scheme for Singapore* (New York: UN Commission for Technical Assistance, Dept. of Economic and Social Affairs, Sept. 1963 [submitted June 13, 1961]).

international consumer is only interested in price and quality, only in what he gets for his money. If Singapore tries to get more than the international market thinks her services are worth, she will outprice herself."[18]

Particular emphasis was therefore placed on industrial relations. Unsatisfactory industrial relations resulted in stoppages, low productivity, and irrational wage demands; and they acted as a deterrent to the foreign investment the city needed to industrialize. Wage increases should be granted only in line with productivity gains, unions should desist from strike activity, and greater managerial flexibility should be allowed in hiring and firing.

Two factors dictated a set of priorities different from those outlined in the Winsemius Report. The first was a matter of making good on electoral promises. Discussing the period in a later budget address, Minister of Finance Goh Keng Swee argued that "while the creation of new industries, by its nature requiring a substantial lead time, could not show quick results, government action in improving the social services [would result in] swift and tangible benefits."[19] The benefits were, of course, more political than economic. This emphasis on social investment between 1960 and 1967 was probably one reason for Singapore's relatively *poor* economic performance. Housing and education accounted for nearly 30 percent of public investment under the 1961–64 State Development Plan, and housing alone absorbed 22 percent of fixed capital formation.[20]

The second reason for delay in adopting the Winsemius recommendations was merger with Malaya, proclaimed on September 16, 1963. The federation ran into trouble almost immediately. The absorption of Chinese-dominated Singapore raised delicate ethnic issues, and the new federation's ruling Alliance party resisted the PAP's efforts to participate actively in electoral politics. The central problems were economic, however.[21] PAP leaders saw merger as a means of industrializing through access to a large, duty-free market. Yet by 1958 Malaya had already launched its own ISI efforts with various industrial incentives. A specter haunted Singapore: the unemployed would gravitate to the city's higher wages while technically skilled workers migrated to the peninsula.[22]

18. Ibid., p. xxiii.

19. Goh Keng Swee, Budget Statement, *Parliamentary Debates of Singapore*, 29, 8 (March 9, 1970): 470–554.

20. Iain Buchanan, *Singapore in Southeast Asia* (London: G. Bell, 1972), pp. 65–69.

21. The following draws on Chan Heng Chee, *Singapore: The Politics of Survival*, and Nancy M. Fletcher, *The Separation of Singapore from Malaysia*, Data Paper 73 (Ithaca: Southeast Asia Program, Cornell University, 1969).

22. Lee Soo Ann, *Industrialization in Singapore* (Camberwell, Australia: Longman, 1973), p. 17.

Until separation Malaysian goods entered Singapore duty-free, even though the federation continued to apply tariffs to Singapore's exports. The merger agreement promised that a common market would be established, but little progress was made. Rather than establish the political basis for industrial complementarity, merger exacerbated industrial competition.

From Merger to Export-Led Growth

The federation lasted less than two years. When it ended, the newly independent city-state faced a powerful set of external constraints. Singapore could not depend on the entrepôt trade to generate adequate employment. Separation also dimmed the prospects for industrial integration with Malaysia and led to new conflicts over commercial policy. Trade tensions eased over time, but hopes for a common market and joint currency area faded quickly. Finally, the PAP faced an unanticipated shock in 1966 when the British Labour government announced its intention to withdraw all military forces from Singapore by 1971. The British bases employed, directly and indirectly, approximately 40,000 workers. The period from the end of merger through 1968 saw intense debate as Singapore groped toward an economic strategy. Two interrelated policy actions ushered in the new course: an effort to attract export-oriented foreign capital, and an intensification of controls on the labor movement.

With Singapore cut off from Malaysian markets, import substitution was not a viable strategy. Given the problems of industrial integration with its neighbors, any drive to industrialize through exports had to look beyond the region to the advanced industrial states. But local investment was heavily concentrated in services, real estate, and domestic trade. With little experience in manufacturing, local firms seemed unlikely to spearhead industrialization. Capital per se was not the problem. The difficulty was the poor technological and marketing capability of local firms, a weakness recognized by Lee Kuan Yew who had little confidence in the local private sector.[23]

A politically and economically weak entrepreneurial class meant that the state and foreign firms would have to play a central role in Singapore's industrialization.[24] In Korea and Taiwan the investment regime

23. See Chia Siow Yue, "The Role of Foreign Trade and Investment in the Development of Singapore," in Walter Galenson, ed., *Foreign Trade and Investment: Economic Development in the Newly Industrializing Countries* (Madison: University of Wisconsin Press, 1985), p. 281.

24. See Goh Keng Swee, *The Practice of Economic Development* (Singapore: Federal Publications, 1977), p. 22.

favored local firms. In Hong Kong it remained scrupulously neutral. In Singapore investment policy was biased in favor of foreign firms. The advantages Singapore offered sprang in part from its entrepôt status. Singapore had no exchange controls or restrictions on the repatriation of capital and remittance of profits, dividends, and interest. Nor were there restrictions on the import of goods and services. Tariffs were low. No rules restricted foreign equity participation. In addition, however, new incentives sought to attract export-oriented foreign investment. In 1967 earlier investment ordinances were replaced by a comprehensive Economic Expansion Act that accelerated depreciation and allowed duty-free import of required equipment and inputs. The key innovation was that profits from the export of approved manufactures were to be taxed at only 4 percent instead of the usual 40 percent corporate tax rate. Given the limited capabilities of local firms, these incentives favored foreign over local investment.

The need for an attractive business climate was dictated by the pressing problems of unemployment and by a competition for investment that weakened Singapore's bargaining hand. As Finance Minister Lim Kim San argued in his 1967 budget speech, "international investors . . . have more or less *free choice* in selecting their plant location. . . . This means that our fiscal incentives must be as attractive as, if not more than, those offered by other countries."[25]

An equally important precondition for the new strategy was the *political* climate and a predictable and stable pattern of industrial relations. The PAP's efficacy in achieving this aim can be seen in the reduction in the number of work stoppages from a high of 161 in 1961 to none in 1969.[26] New labor legislation limited direct and indirect labor costs, expanded managerial autonomy, and weakened the independence and power of the union movement. The PAP had already forged a close relationship with the NTUC in the battles with the left.[27] Beginning in 1965 government control intensified and increasingly took on a de-

25. *Parliamentary Debates of Singapore*, 25, 7 (December 5, 1966), col. 456.
26. The most detailed review of the labor market in Singapore is Linda Lim and Pang Eng Fong, *Trade, Employment, and Industry in Singapore*, World Employment Programme Research Working Paper (Geneva: International Labor Organization, 1982). Data cited are from p. 116.
27. See, for example, Goh Keng Swee, *Some Problems of Industrialization* (Singapore: Government Printing Office, 1963), pp. 14–17. C. V. Devan Nair, a trade union leader critical in garnering labor support for the PAP presents a coherent statement of the PAP's ideology vis-à-vis labor in "Trade Unions in Singapore," in Nair, ed., *Socialism That Works . . . the Singapore Way* (Singapore: Federal Publications, 1978). See also his speeches and writings, *Not by Bread Alone* (Singapore: Singapore National Trade Union Congress, 1982), and Singapore National Trade Union Congress, *Why Labour Must Go Modern* (Singapore: NTUC, 1970), which spell out the logic of collaborative unionism under the PAP.

velopmental rationale. The NTUC was called on to commit itself to a tripartite "Charter for Industrial Progress" based on "cooperative" labor-management relations. A Trade Unions Bill, passed in August, required any strike action to be supported by a secret ballot vote of union members and extended the government's power to register union officials.

Labor representatives were quick to grasp the implications of the export-oriented strategy. Speaking in the debate over the 1967 budget speech, one parliamentarian argued that Singapore should not encourage "those enterprises . . . who would be only interested in exploiting labour and accumulating profits on the basis of sweated labor."[28] Until 1968 the unions still acted independently, and collective bargaining was more important than legislation, administrative action, or the decisions of national arbitration courts in determining employment relations.[29] That changed in 1968. In January of that year the British decided to accelerate the withdrawal of their bases. Citing the need to respond to the new crisis, the 1968 elections were called seven months early. Winning a stunning mandate—all of the fifty-eight legislative seats, fifty-one of them uncontested—the party immediately moved to introduce a new round of labor legislation.

The Employment Act affected working conditions and terms of remuneration. The standard work week was lengthened, the number of holidays reduced, and various restrictions placed on the payment of retirement benefits, paid leave, overtime, and bonuses. Some of the bill's provisions were altered as a result of objections voiced in Parliament, but the basic intent of the legislation was not challenged.[30] In introducing the Industrial Relations (Amendment) Bill, the minister for labor offered a clear developmental rationale: "This Bill, like the Employment Bill, is an attempt to rationalise employer-employee relationship [sic] with a view to attracting new investments and increasing the efficiency of our trading and industrial enterprises."[31] The bill limited the ability of unions to represent managerial or executive employees, exempted promotions, transfers, firings, and work assignments from collective bargaining, and lengthened the minimum and maximum duration of labor contracts.

Singapore thus presents the clearest case of a link between export-led growth and labor control. The PAP's interest in restructuring the union movement in a corporatist direction was initially driven by the political struggle against the left. PAP aims were not fully realized until after

28. *Parliamentary Debates of Singapore*, 25, 9 (December 14, 1966), col. 643.
29. Deyo, *Dependent Development*, p. 47.
30. *Parliamentary Debates of Singapore*, 27, 9–13 (July 10–12, 15, and 31, 1968).
31. *Parliamentary Debates of Singapore*, 27, 13 (July 31, 1968), col. 733.

1968, however, when the government used an external crisis to impose both a new development strategy and a new level of labor discipline.

State and Economy: Institutions and the Instruments of Policy

As in Korea and Taiwan, so in Singapore the successful launching of export-led growth was preceded by institutional reforms that concentrated economic decision making and expanded the economic instruments in the hands of the government. After 1968 a key function of the new institutional machinery was to ease the entry of foreign firms and to forge links between local investors and multinational corporations. Nonetheless, the broad similarities to Korea and Taiwan are noteworthy, particularly the concentration of decision-making authority and the pattern of intervention accompanying a nominally "market-oriented" strategy.[32]

The central policy institution was the Economic Development Board, formed in 1961 and patterned on the Indian Industrial Finance Corporation. The EDB was not accountable to Parliament, enjoyed a high level of operational independence, and concentrated a range of policy instruments in one entity. The Projects Division was the "nerve centre" of the EDB, its most "intellectually active division," and one that revealed a belief in an active state role in industrial guidance.[33] Applications for "pioneer industry" status were analyzed on the basis of whether they would adversely affect other industries, meet minimum criteria for value-added, fill a gap in the industrial structure, or generate linkages with other industries. On the basis of these and other criteria, the division kept and periodically updated a list of desirable industries.

The Investment Promotion Division sought to enhance the image of Singapore as an investment site. The structure of this division paralled the trade promotion organizations established in Korea and Taiwan in the early 1960s, with a network of foreign branch offices. Whereas the Korean and Taiwanese organizations served primarily to establish commercial connections, the Investment Promotion Division had as its primary task the attraction of foreign investment, particularly after 1968.

The exact extent of the government's *direct* involvement in economic

32. Neoclassical accounts include Chia Siow Yue, "The Role of Foreign Trade and Investment in the Development of Singapore"; Helen Hughes, "From Entrepôt to Manufacturing," in Hughes and You Poh Seng, eds., *Foreign Investment and Industrialization in Singapore* (Madison: University of Wisconsin Press, 1969). Contrast these analyses to the indictment of laissez-faire by a leading planner, Goh Keng Swee, *The Practice of Economic Growth* (Singapore: Federal Publications, 1977), p. 104.

33. Lee Soo Ann, *Industrialization*, p. 48. The following also draws on Philip Nalliah Pillai, *State Enterprise in Singapore: Legal Importation and Development* (Singapore: Singapore University Press, 1983), pp. 128–206.

activity through state-owned enterprises is difficult to gauge; detailed data are collected on ownership patterns, but no distinction is made between public and private domestic investment. However, as Linda Lim summarizes, "the government is . . . the major actor in the capital market, given its large participation in the financial sector. Its Central Provident Fund and Post Office Savings Bank hold a majority of national savings. . . . More than half of domestic income passes through government hands in one way or another—through the 42% share of earned income which goes to the Central Provident Fund . . . indirect taxes and the tariffs charged and incomes earned by the various statutory boards and state enterprises."[34] As will be seen in Chapter 6, the extent of state intervention became a political issue in the 1980s.

Singapore in Comparative Perspective

Pressures for Singapore to industrialize came largely from changes in its external environment. Cyclical fluctuations, changes in raw materials markets, and the independence of Singapore's neighbors raised questions about the ability of the entrepôt economy to absorb an expanding work force. A new round of external shocks hit the country in the mid-1960s: the failure of merger, trade conflicts with Malaysia, and the withdrawal of the British. Development options were dramatically narrowed. Industrialization was needed to create employment, but Singapore's small market precluded import substitution. In addition, local capital was weak. The result was an outward-oriented industrialization in which MNCs played a central role.

The *instruments* through which the government pursued export-led growth and the balance between local, state, and foreign firms can be explained only by reference to the political interests and capacities of the PAP elite. Upon assuming power, the government moved in a decidedly interventionist direction, using a combination of economic policy and political organization to further its political objectives and preempt the opposition. PAP ideology stressed the need for "guidance" of the industrial structure: targeted fiscal and financial incentives, state-owned enterprises, an activist economic bureaucracy. Given the political and economic weakness of local capital, MNCs quickly came to play a central role in the new strategy. Their importance reinforced the government's control-oriented stance toward labor. Pursued initially for political ends, labor control became a tool of economic policy. Singapore thus falls

34. Linda Y. C. Lim, "Singapore's Success: The Myth of the Free Market Economy," *Asian Survey* 23 (June 1983): 755.

squarely within the East Asian mold, with a relatively autonomous state, a highly centralized and interventionist economic policy-making apparatus, a weakened left, and a tamed labor movement.

INDUSTRIALIZATION IN HONG KONG

Though external shocks also played an important role in Hong Kong's industrialization, government policy did not change. The colonial government remained as wedded to the norm of laissez-faire after the mid-1950s, when manufactured exports began to take off, as it had been before. Hong Kong thus offers an important challenge to the proposition that successful export-led growth demands state intervention.

Several factors help account for the Hong Kong anomaly. Unlike Singapore, Hong Kong inherited a relatively developed manufacturing sector from China. At the same time market conditions, characteristics of the industrial structure, and political divisions kept labor weak. Important functions that were carried out by the state in the other NICs were undertaken in Hong Kong by the highly developed commercial and banking establishments. These included long-term lending and assistance in marketing and even in product design.

Such observations still beg the question why external shocks failed to generate a more concerted government response. The vulnerability of the entrepôt runs throughout Hong Kong's history as it does through Singapore's, yet crises have been met in the former with a cautious, even fatalistic, response. The reason must be sought in the nature of political authority and ruling ideologies. The PAP lived in the shadow of the social and partisan conflicts of the mid-1950s and operated under electoral constraints; these help explain its interventionist course. In Hong Kong an administrative state faced little organized political pressure to intervene.

It may be argued that laissez-faire simply suited the interests of the dominant commercial and financial establishment of the colony and thus can be explained in purely coalitional terms. Indeed, this convergence of interests makes it difficult to argue convincingly for the importance of political structure and ideology. I attempt to show that the power of the British financial secretary in imposing the market has been no less impressive than the PAP's. The colonial government maintained its independence from the interests of local manufacturers even *after* they had become the dominant economic force in the colony (not to mention maintaining its political distance from labor). Thus although Hong Kong's *economic policy* may constitute an anomaly, its *political struc-*

ture shows surprising parallels to the East Asian pattern: a highly insulated state, limited representation, and a concentrated and internally cohesive economic decision-making structure.

Hong Kong as Entrepôt

After Hong Kong island was ceded to the British in 1842,[35] its commercial role developed quickly; first in opium and illicit trade with the mainland, then as an entrepôt for British exports, for the Chinese coastal trade, and for the great overseas Chinese emigration. Merchant houses such as Jardine Matheson established headquarters in the colony, and banking, insurance, and accounting services developed. By 1900 some local industries had developed, particularly those related to shipping. World War I gave a push to local manufacturing, and by 1934 the amount of capital invested in Chinese concerns equaled that invested in companies owned and managed by Europeans.[36] The British Imperial Preference System provided an incentive for Hong Kong manufactures to enter world markets. Nonetheless, the core of the economy remained the entrepôt trade. In 1880 Hong Kong had handled 21 percent of China's export trade and 37 percent of its import trade; in 1900 these figures increased to 40 percent and 42 percent respectively.[37]

The interwar period was one of mercantilist rivalry, depression, and new concern over Hong Kong's entrepôt status. The most worrisome developments concerned Hong Kong's relationship with China. Anti-imperialism and opposition to the "unequal treaties" became central issues in Chinese politics, with consequences for Hong Kong's trade. In 1925 antiforeign boycotts swept the China coast. China did not achieve an end to extraterritoriality until 1943, but it did achieve tariff autonomy by 1928. Tariffs were raised in 1931, primarily for revenue reasons but also to promote industry.

Hong Kong thus faced problems with its hinterland similar to those confronting Singapore. During the 1930s suggestions were made for tariff negotiations with the Chinese, support for export-oriented man-

35. The territory ceded under the Treaty of Nanking consisted of Hong Kong Island only. Portions of the Kowloon Peninsula opposite Hong Kong and Stonecutter's Island were ceded at the end of the Second Opium War in 1860, and the New Territories were leased in 1898. Peter Wesley-Smith, *Unequal Treaty, 1898–1997: China, Great Britain, and Hong Kong's New Territories* (Hong Kong: Oxford University Press, 1983); G. B. Endacott, *A History of Hong Kong* (Hong Kong: Oxford University Press, 1973).

36. See the "Report of the Commission Appointed . . . to Enquire into the Causes and Effects of the Present Trade Depression in Hong Kong . . . ," Hong Kong, Legislative Council, *Sessional Papers 1935* (Hong Kong: Government Printers, 1935), pp. 87–88, cited hereafter as "Depression Report." See also Frank Leeming, "The Earlier Industrialization of Hong Kong," *Modern Asian Studies* 9, 3 (1975): 337–42.

37. Endacott, *History*, pp. 194 and 253.

ufacturing, and even for a portion of the colony to be placed behind the Chinese tariff barrier. Overall, however, the prevailing government view was that little could be done. A 1935 report is worth quoting for its resigned support of laissez-faire:

> There is little scope in a Colony like Hong Kong, having no natural raw products and but a small domestic consumption, for the ambitious schemes of economic reconstruction or national planning which have become the modern fashion. . . . Unless therefore the entrepot trade can develop sufficiently, or alternative markets be found to compensate for the loss of entry into South China of local products, the Colony's rate of growth must slow down. . . . These matters are entirely beyond local control and, therefore, need not be further discussed here.[38]

External Shocks and Export-Oriented Manufacturing

Rebuilding after Japanese occupation involved the government in the economy in new ways.[39] After the war a range of controls on prices, foreign exchange, and imports and exports were introduced to guarantee supplies of essential commodities.[40] Except for the new attention given to housing and infrastructure, this departure from laissez-faire was temporary and partial. Unlike in Korea and Taiwan, external controls were seen not as serving any developmental function but rather as a means of alleviating distress.

Trade revived rapidly, but two external events changed the economic life of the colony.[41] First, the Chinese Revolution produced a huge influx of migrants, which changed the nature of the entrepreneurial class and had profound consequences for the labor movement. The second shock was the United Nations embargo on trade with China, which provided the stimulus to export-oriented manufacturing.

Flight capital began to enter Hong Kong in substantial amounts following the outbreak of hostilities on the mainland in 1937 and con-

38. "Depression Report," pp. 113–14.
39. Henry J. Lethbridge argues that reconstruction brought Chinese and British elites together in the immediate postwar period. "Hong Kong under Japanese Occupation," in I. C. Jarvie, ed., *Hong Kong: A Society in Transition* (London: Routledge & Kegan Paul, 1969). On the role of the banking community in reconstruction see Y. C. Yao, "Financing Hong Kong's Early Postwar Industrialization: The Role of the Hong Kong and Shanghai Banking Corporation," in Frank H. H. King, ed., *Eastern Banking: Essays in the History of the Hong Kong and Shanghai Banking Corporation* (London: Athlone, 1983), p. 566; G. B. Endacott, *Hong Kong Eclipse* (Hong Kong: Oxford University Press, 1978), pp. 307–8.
40. See Alan Birch, "The Control of Prices and Commodities in Hong Kong," *Hong Kong Law Journal* 4, 2 (1974): 133–50.
41. Gary Catron, "China and Hong Kong, 1945–1967" (Ph.D. diss., Harvard University, 1971), p. 60.

tinued to do so until 1941.[42] Some of this new capital went into the manufacture of light military equipment, giving Hong Kong industry a boost. The Japanese occupation brought business to a halt and reduced the population of the city from about 1.5 million to 500,000. In 1946 the population flow reversed, quickened after 1947 by China's civil war. The great inflation of 1948 and 1949 on the mainland provided an incentive for those with liquid assets to exchange Chinese currency for American or Hong Kong dollars or pounds, using them to import machinery and manufactured goods or holding the new assets in accounts in Hong Kong. Between 1947 and 1955 the annual injection of foreign capital and the net balance on invisibles made up 40 percent of Hong Kong's national income. In 1949–50 the proportion reached 65 percent. Approximately two-thirds of investment from 1947 through 1955, the period of Hong Kong's industrial take-off, was financed from abroad.[43]

The amounts of capital flowing into the colony were arguably less important than the entrepreneurial cadre that brought them. Riding a crest of high profitability in 1946 and 1947, the Shanghai textile capitalists imported machinery that was the most modern in Asia. When Communist victory appeared certain, equipment and raw materials were diverted to Hong Kong. By one estimate, 17 percent of all flight capital was committed to the cotton-spinning industry up through 1951.[44] Existing commercial enterprises assisted the spinners and later served as a bridge to the banking establishment. There is some debate about the relative importance of bank finance and reinvested earnings in Hong Kong's early postwar industrialization.[45] There can be little doubt, however, that the banking community departed from conservative British banking practices in assisting the expansion of the "second generation" of light industries developed by local entrepreneurs after the mid-1950s, including plastics, toys, electronics, watches and clocks, and, above all, apparel.

This assistance and the benefits of an existing commercial establishment reduced the risks of new manufacturing investment, particularly as the government had limited its role in advancing industry. The private sector's expectations vis-à-vis the colonial administration in the late

42. This draws on ibid.; Wong Po-Shang, *The Influx of Chinese Capital into Hong Kong since 1937* (Hong Kong: Kai Ming Press, 1958); and Siu-Lin Wong, "Industrial Entrepreneurship and Ethnicity: A Study of the Shanghaiese Cotton Spinners in Hong Kong" (Ph.D. thesis, University of Oxford, 1979).

43. Edward F. Szczepanik, *The Economic Growth of Hong Kong* (London: Oxford University Press, 1958), pp. 142–43 and Table 5.1, p. 183.

44. Wong, "Industrial Entrepreneurship," p. 126.

45. Ibid., pp. 134ff., disputes Yao's claim of the importance of bank lending during the early postwar period.

1940s are reflected in a publication of the Hong Kong Spinners Association:

> It was moreover apparent that there was scant prospect of government bestowing any special protectionist favours, there being little domestic market to protect in any case. Nor was there any hope that government would take seriously any suggestion to abandon its traditional and basic laissez-faire economic policy just to encourage and nurture infant industries or shore up a tottering enterprise. . . . Any industry would thus have to stand on its own in regard to the severe international competition it was bound to encounter.[46]

The Chinese Revolution had a profound effect not only on capital in Hong Kong but also on labor.[47] Several factors contribute to the weakness of Hong Kong's labor movement, ranging from the small size of manufacturing establishments to the political influence of business on government policy. Two factors appear central, however. By the mid-1920s Hong Kong's trade union movement had gelled into a dualistic structure: "A multiplicity of associations in the crafts and traditional industries of the Colony each heavily influenced by guild traditions of exclusiveness combined with mutual aid for members; and . . . a group of large unions organized on an industrial basis . . . motivated by political ideals of nationalism and anti-imperialism."[48] In 1927 Chiang Kai-shek moved against the Communists in Canton and Shanghai, killing hundreds of labor leaders and bringing the unions under government control. To this day the union movement in Hong Kong reflects fissures in Chinese politics. "Left-wing" unions loyal to the Chinese Communist party and affiliated with the Federation of Trade Unions compete with "right-wing" unions associated with the KMT and the Trade Union Council, though a "neutral" grouping between the two has grown over time.

A more compelling reason for labor weakness is the effect of immigration on conditions in the labor market itself. The high prices and rents caused by shortages and the growth of the city's population had as their corollary a lag in real wage growth. The Chinese Revolution heightened competition between left and right unions, contributing to a period of la-

---

46. Hong Kong Cotton Spinners Association, *Twenty-Five Years of the Hong Kong Cotton Spinners Association* (Hong Kong, 1973), p. 49.

47. This draws on Joe England and John Rear, *Industrial Relations and Law in Hong Kong* (Hong Kong: Oxford University Press, 1981), and H. A. Turner et al., *The Last Colony: But Whose? A Study of the Labour Movement, Labour Market, and Labour Relations in Hong Kong* (Cambridge: Cambridge University Press, 1980).

48. England and Rear, *Industrial Relations*, pp. 128–29.

bor activism that peaked in 1948.[49] Underlying labor-market conditions were slack, however, despite efforts to control immigration through quotas. By 1950 the industrial structure began to change. Small establishments mushroomed, drawing on the large pool of inexpensive labor and weakening the control of organized labor, the large firms, and the government over the labor market. The result was a system of industrial relations in which the market played a central role and collective bargaining was relatively unimportant.[50]

The Hong Kong government did not intervene in the labor market, but government policy reinforced the tendency toward decentralized industrial relations.[51] Unions were recognized by the Trade Unions Ordinance of 1948, but the range of union action was limited by the prohibition of any strike that went beyond a "trade dispute within the trade or industry in which the strikers are engaged . . . and is designed to coerce the Government." The expenditure of union funds for political activities was prohibited in 1961, and, more important, union membership was limited to those persons "habitually engaged or employed in the relevant industry." General unions joining workers in several industries were thus banned. Through 1968 labor legislation could be described as minimalist, limited to the most basic provisions of health and safety.[52]

In December 1950 Hong Kong faced its most serious economic crisis in the postwar period when the United States placed a virtually complete embargo on China.[53] Hong Kong and Macao, seen as weak links in the effort to build an effective quarantine, were treated as parts of China, though negotiations with the United States eased the ban somewhat. In May 1951 the United Nations passed its resolution banning the export of strategic goods to China. In 1951 Hong Kong's exports totaled HK$ 4.4 billion, 36.2 percent of which went to China. In 1955 exports had dropped to HK$ 2.5 billion, with only 7.2 percent going to China.[54]

49. For data on strikes, see ibid., p. 312.
50. Turner, *The Last Colony*, p. 20.
51. This draws on Joe England, "Industrial Relations in Hong Kong," in Keith Hopkins, ed., *Hong Kong: The Industrial Colony* (Hong Kong: Oxford University Press, 1971), pp. 218–19.
52. In 1966 a small increase in ferry fares sparked three days of riots, known as the "Kowloon disturbances." In 1967 the Chinese Cultural Revolution spilled over into the colony in the form of politically motivated strikes organized by "left-wing" unions. This "Confrontation" left over fifty dead. See John Cooper, *Colony in Conflict* (Hong Kong: Swindon Book Co., 1970). Thereafter, greater attention was paid to social welfare. England and Rear, *Industrial Relations*, pp. 360–82.
53. The normally upbeat *Hong Kong Annual Report* claimed that "the Korean War and world events following it have put Hong Kong in an economically impossible position." *Hong Kong Annual Report, 1951* (London: HMSO, 1951), p. 9.
54. E. F. Szczepanik, "The Embargo Effect on China's Trade with Hong Kong," in

These trends in Hong Kong's trade with China were reinforced by the reorientation in China's trade toward the Soviet Union. Had it not been for a concurrent expansion of manufacturing, the loss of the entrepôt trade would have reduced the colony's national income by roughly one-third.[55]

The large, internationally diversified trading companies were crucial for Hong Kong's ability to adjust to the loss of the entrepôt trade, performing functions taken on by the government in other NICs. The embargo provided an incentive for commercial enterprises to establish closer relations with manufacturing. These included not simply arms-length purchases but the provision of credit, raw materials, and designs. Subcontracting and the putting-out system created a virtuous cycle fostering the growth of large and small manufacturing enterprises, a pattern not seen in Singapore. A survey of industry in 1962 noted that "Hong Kong's industry is manufacturing goods to designs and specifications dictated by the purchaser, and, where it is not, the initiative in any transaction comes more frequently from outside than from with the producing firm. . . . At least three-quarters and perhaps more of the manufactures exported are thought to be handled by the export houses."[56]

The Political and Institutional Foundations of Laissez-Faire

Several studies purport to show that the Hong Kong government is not as laissez-faire as it seems, but they suffer from several analytic flaws.[57] They take it as evidence of a revisionist view that the government does, in fact, intervene in the economy in various ways. Yet many of these interventions, such as provision of infrastructure and financial regulation, constitute public goods that have always been accepted as necessary to the functioning of a market economy. These studies also lack comparative perspective. Hong Kong may fall short of an abstract model of the pure market economy, but it remains by far the most laissez-faire economy in the world.

The components of Hong Kong's economic policy can be spelled out quite succinctly.[58] Laissez-faire at the macroeconomic level is defended

E. Stuart Kirby, ed., *Contemporary China II, 1956–7* (Hong Kong: Hong Kong University Press, 1958), p. 85.

55. Szczepanik, *Economic Growth,* p. 48.

56. Economist Intelligence Unit for the Federation of Hong Kong Industries, *Industry in Hong Kong* (Hong Kong: South China Morning Post, 1962), p. 8. A survey of small firms found that this structure remained surprisingly constant; V. F. S. Sit et al., *Small Scale Industry in a Laissez-Faire Economy* (Hong Kong: University of Hong Kong, 1979).

57. A. J. Youngson, *Hong Kong: Economic Growth and Policy* (Hong Kong: Oxford University Press, 1982), pp. 119–60, is a good example.

58. The theory of macroeconomic self-regulation is detailed in Edward K. Y. Chen,

on the grounds that Hong Kong is a self-regulating economy. There are no trade restrictions. There is no central bank. In the absence of foreign-exchange controls, the existence of a developed money market, and control over liquidity creation by foreign banks, an independent monetary policy is difficult if not impossible. Fiscal policy is extremely conservative, and taxes are correspondingly low. Though several analysts have noted countercyclical expenditure—surpluses during periods of rapid growth, deficits during periods of slack—these Keynesian trends are probably not the result of conscious policy.[59]

At the microeconomic level there have been no efforts to steer industry through government loans, protection, or subsidies. The government offers no targeted fiscal incentives; taxes are raised for revenue purposes only. No distinctions are drawn between local and foreign firms, no special incentives either woo the latter or protect the former. Though the government has gradually extended its oversight of labor and financial markets, the regulatory environment is minimalist. Government ownership is confined to the most basic of services—water, the postal system, airport services. Even some of these—electricity, gas, public transport, and communications—are in private hands, though subject to regulation as natural monopolies. The extremes of laissez-faire were reached in 1970 when the financial secretary, Sir John Cowperthwaite, made a spirited argument before the Legislative Council that the government should not collect GNP data. Not only would such an exercise prove costly and time-consuming but "the availability of such figures might lead . . . to policies designed to have a direct effect on the economy."[60]

The most important exception to laissez-faire rule is land policy. Virtually all land in the colony belongs to the Crown, which publicly auctions long-term leases. The government can therefore stabilize the market by expanding or reducing supply unilaterally, and in the 1970s it used its control over land to achieve particular industrial goals.

The political foundations of the colony's economic policy are the subject of some controversy. In Korea, Taiwan, and Singapore the formulation of economic policy operated under broad political constraints

"The Economic Setting," in David G. Lethbridge, ed., *The Business Environment in Hong Kong* (Hong Kong: Oxford University Press, 1984). See also Cheng Tong Yung, *The Economy of Hong Kong* (Hong Kong: Far East Publications, 1977), and the celebratory Alvin Rabushka, *Hong Kong: A Study in Economic Freedom* (Chicago: University of Chicago Press, 1979).

59. See A. S. B. Oliver, "A Keynesian Ghost?" *Far Eastern Economic Review*, March 19, 1970, p. 76.

60. *Hong Kong Hansard, 1969/70* (Hong Kong: Government Printer, 1970), pp. 495–96. The Hansard is the record of Legco sessions.

but took place in decision-making arenas that were relatively insulated from the direct influences of organized social groups. Several studies of Hong Kong, on the other hand, have documented the dominance of commercial and business elites within official government bodies, including the Legislative Council (Legco) and various consultative committees.[61] Poor working conditions, the weakness of the social safety net, and the generally probusiness tenor of public policy have been cited as evidence for class domination.[62]

An alternative explanation emphasizes the ideology of government elites and a governmental structure that allows them to implement it. All formal governmental authority is in the hands of civil servants who are primarily responsible, through the appointed governor, to the United Kingdom and are unconstrained by any accountable electoral politics. Before political changes in the latter 1980s connected with the forthcoming transfer of Hong Kong to China, the governmental structure was a multilayered system of representation with limited elective components. Yet the "unofficial" (i.e., private-sector) representatives on the Executive and Legislative Councils, the most important decision-making bodies, are appointed, as are the members of consultative committees.

These formal characteristics of governance cannot, of course, be taken for indicators of power; government decision making has pluralistic components.[63] But the colonial government retains the power to formulate the underlying agenda. In the realm of economic policy that power has been centralized in the hands of the financial secretary. In the words of one unofficial member of Legco, "it is only the Financial Secretary who can initiate proposals for financial expenditures and he determines the priorities of projects. What comes from the Finance Committee has been carefully vetted by him and the Finance Branch and unofficial members have only the negative power to refuse to approve an expenditure."[64]

Since there are few substantive disagreements between the public and private sectors, ideology and interests push in the same direction. Yet several sorts of evidence point to the importance of government structure and ideas. The first is the evolution of government support for

61. Stephen Tang, "The Power Structure in Colonial Society: A Sociological Study of the Legislative Council in Hong Kong, 1948–1971," unpublished ms., Chinese University of Hong Kong, 1973; and the extension of Tang's work by S. N. G. Davies, "One Brand of Politics Rekindled," *Hong Kong Law Journal* 7, 1 (1977): 44–89.

62. An example is Joe England, *Hong Kong: A Case to Answer* (Nottingham: Spokesman, 1974).

63. For example, despite its title, see Peter Harris, *Hong Kong: A Study in Bureaucratic Politics* (Hong Kong: Heinemann Asia, 1978).

64. Quoted in Alvin Rabushka, *The Changing Face of Hong Kong* (Washington, D.C.: American Enterprise Institute, 1973), pp. 52–53.

industry. The government has always drawn a sharp, if implicit, line between *general* supports that resemble pure public goods and *sectoral* guidance. In the former category the government went so far as to assist in overcoming the free-rider problems associated with business organization by helping form the Federation of Hong Kong Industries in the 1950s; prior to that time "business" did not even represent an organized group.[65] In response to concerns over protectionism and the need for both product and market diversification in the 1960s, the government expanded its promotional and support facilities for industry, established a Trade Development Council (1966) to promote exports, a Productivity Council and Centre (1967) to provide training and consultancy, and an Export Credit Insurance Company (1966) for risks not commercially insurable.

The government's resistance to business requests for targeted sectoral policies can be seen in the recurrent debate over government financing of industry. In 1958 an unofficial member of Legco suggested the formation of a development corporation that would "act as a bridge between Government and private enterprise." The corporation would assist firms by offering medium- and long-term loans that, it was claimed, were difficult for industry to obtain. A committee formed to investigate the idea found no validity to the claim that working capital was unavailable or that interest rates were too high.[66] Interest rates reflect risk and therefore could not be "high." Even if an industrial bank were to be formed, its rates would have to conform to the market. Moreover, "if . . . the available supply of money can find profitable investment in enterprises which require comparatively little capital in relation to employment . . . there would appear to be no advantage in . . . diverting capital to industries which require a relatively heavier capital investment and a correspondingly longer redemption period."[67] Further calls for government finance and assistance were raised by unofficial members in Legco debates in 1962 and again in 1968. The proposals were shunted aside as costly and impractical, on the grounds that "Hong Kong's entrepreneurs . . . are and will continue to be more alert and alive to the practical realities of a changing world than any group of economic mandarins."[68]

---

65. *Report of the Advisory Committee on the Proposed Federation of Industries* (Hong Kong: Government Printer, 1958).

66. *Hong Kong Hansard, 1958*, pp. 119–20, 142.

67. *Report of the Industrial Bank Committee* (Hong Kong: Government Printer, 1960), p. 12.

68. Director of Commerce and Industry Terence Dare Sorby, *Hong Kong Hansard, 1968*, p. 162, in response to a call for the establishment of a new development body empowered to establish industrial priorities. In 1960 Financial Secretary Arthur Clarke seemed to endorse the idea of an activist industrial policy, *Hong Kong Hansard, 1960*, pp. 62–63, but was repudiated by his powerful and articulate successor, Sir John Cowperthwaite, in a

SINGAPORE AND HONG KONG COMPARED

More convincing than these ideological statements is the insight that can be gained through a comparison of Hong Kong with Singapore. Before 1959 the British colonial government maintained an approach to economic policy in Singapore similar to that in Hong Kong, even in the face of substantial social unrest and a domestic private sector that exhibited obvious limitations in absorbing an expanding work force. The move toward a more interventionist stance in Singapore came following the political ascendence of the PAP. Responding to social conflict and electoral pressures, the PAP developed an interventionist style as a means of consolidating support.

In Hong Kong laissez-faire endured despite economic crises more severe than those faced by Singapore and appeals from a well-organized industrial sector that by the mid-1960s equaled in economic importance, if it did not overshadow, the commercial and financial sectors. The ideology guiding Hong Kong's development clearly differs from that in the other NICs, but the political capacity of the government to implement its preferences places Hong Kong squarely in the East Asian pattern.

---

systematic review of the failings of government intervention (*Hong Kong Hansard, 1962,* pp. 138–41). Business appeals for greater government support can be found in the Federation of Hong Kong Industries *Forum,* for example, Fung Hon Chu, "How Should We Diversify?" *Forum* 3 (Spring 1963).

CHAPTER SIX

The East Asian NICs in the 1970s and 1980s: The Politics of Adjustment

The adoption of an export-oriented growth strategy exposed the East Asian NICs to new external constraints. The oil shock of the early 1970s ushered in a period of slowed growth and macroeconomic instability in the NICs' major markets. Quotas on textiles and apparel exports had started in the 1960s, but protection tightened and spread to other sectors. Technological breakthroughs seemed to threaten the NIC advantage in labor-intensive manufacturing. Though the threat was slow to materialize, the NICs also anticipated competition from a "second tier" of exporters of labor-intensive manufactures and competed with one another. Despite various controls on labor organization and activity, all of the NICs were experiencing tightening labor markets and rising real wages by the early 1970s, signaling a gradual shift in their comparative advantage away from low labor costs alone.

Broad similarities in the policy responses of the NICs can be explained by these common external constraints. All of the NICs made efforts to upgrade traditional industries and diversify into new product lines. All renewed efforts to lure foreign investment and launched new initiatives for improving local technological capabilities. All diversified the geographical range of their trade and investment relations, developing new ties with the Third World, Western Europe, and the socialist countries.

The NICs' responses to external constraints varied in ways that reflected their different economic structures. In Korea a relatively large domestic market made plausible a deepening strategy. Taiwan's smaller market and greater dependence on trade pushed it in a more liberal direction. With no domestic market option, Singapore and Hong Kong concentrated on finding new manufacturing niches and expanding their role as international commercial and financial centers. The instruments of intervention and the balance between local and foreign firms also varied with the characteristics of the industries targeted for support. Intermediate and capital goods production, and some high-technology sectors, are characterized by higher capital requirements and greater risk than the light, labor-intensive industries that initiated the NICs' export push. These factors invited increased state intervention and an increased multinational presence.

I argue that institutionalized patterns of policy making, government intervention, and business-government relations also shaped the process of industrial adjustment. In Korea a highly centralized leadership style, the government's use of the state-owned financial sector as an instrument of industrial policy, and close relations between the executive and the large industrial groups produced a dirigist approach to industrial upgrading. In Taiwan, by contrast, technocrats enjoyed greater influence, and the political relationship between government and the private sector was less close. As a result, the government used state-owned enterprises to develop selected industries rather than create national champions and relied on arms-length fiscal and trade instruments and infrastructural investment to support the private sector.

The responses of Singapore and Hong Kong also illustrate the importance of institutional structure. As it had in the past, the PAP relied on its control over the labor market to force adjustment on foreign firms and targeted specific sectors for support. In Hong Kong by contrast, the government staunchly defended laissez-faire, even in the face of industry lobbying, and failed to develop any significant new instruments of intervention. These differences in the objectives, instruments, and agents of industrial policy are summarized in Table 6.1.

A new cycle of policy debate began in the East Asian NICs in the late 1970s and early 1980s. The pressures to reform had both internal and external roots. A second generation of younger, foreign-trained technocrats argued that serious distortions had resulted from state intervention. Reforms naturally favored some sectors over others (see Table 6.2), but the growing maturity and internationalization of NIC firms provided a base of support for some liberalizing measures. Again, external forces were an important source of pressure on governments. High interest rates and the second oil shock cast a shadow over capital- and energy-intensive projects in Korea and Taiwan. Large bilateral trade deficits with the United States brought economic policy in all of the NICs under closer scrutiny. The NICs were pressed to "graduate," to assume the same responsibilities as the advanced industrial states in the international trade and monetary regimes. The mix of prescriptions varied by country but included the liberalization of trade in goods and services and the easing of rules governing foreign investment. After the mid-

Table 6.1. Strategies of industrial adjustment in the East Asian NICs

Country	Policy objectives	Primary instruments	Agents
Korea	Combine ISI "deepening" with an upgrading of exports in a "big push"	Financial system and foreign borrowing; protection	National champions, selective stance to FDI, SOEs
Taiwan	Selective ISI, upgrade exports	Fiscal incentives; technological and infrastructure support	Local and foreign firms, SOEs
Singapore	Upgrade exports, expand financial and commercial role	Labor-market policy	Foreign firms
Hong Kong	Upgrade exports, expand financial and commercial role	Market and infrastructure support	Government neutrality

Source: adapted from Yun-han Chu, "State Structure and Economic Adjustment of the East Asian Newly Industrializing Countries," *International Organization* 43 (Autumn 1989): 652.

1980s exchange-rate policy became a central issue of contention as well. The NICs were pressured by the United States to allow their currencies to appreciate and, in Korea and Taiwan, to liberalize their financial systems so that exchange rates would be market-determined. Currency appreciation itself forced adjustment on export-oriented firms and confronted the government with new conflicts over industrial restructuring and wage policy.

The reform process cannot be understood solely by reference to sectoral and international pressures; we have to consider the broader political and institutional context. In Korea and Taiwan, where state intervention had been greatest, reforms were initially launched under the aegis of governments that retained substantial autonomy from social pressures. In Korea, in particular, autonomy contributed to the government's ability to liberalize and restructure economic policy. By the end of the 1980s, the political context had changed. With political liberalization, interest groups and opposition parties mobilized around economic policy, and governments became more responsive to societal demands, including those from such previously excluded groups as labor. In all of the NICs, however, these new democratic pressures were largely offset by fundamental political and institutional continuities.

By the end of the 1980s political change was most advanced in Korea, where a transition to democracy occurred in 1987. The contest over economic policy was also most sharply defined there, though under a

Table 6.2. Policy cleavages and coalitions

Policy	Favored interests	Threatened interests
Trade liberalization	Trading companies Trading partners Consumers Purchasers of protected capital goods and intermediates	Import-substituting industries, both local and foreign Labor in ISI sectors Agriculture (Korea and Taiwan)
Liberalization of direct foreign investment and technology transfer	Foreign firms Potential joint-venture partners	Previously protected sectors (consumer services, consumer goods producers)
Financial-market reforms Privatization	Large financial and industrial groups	State-owned banks
Liberalization and elimination of targeted and preferential finance	Savers Borrowers without access to subsidized credit	Informal financial institutions (curb market) Borrowers with access to cheap credit
Internationalization	Foreign banks and investors Consumers and savers Industrial borrowers	Domestic financial institutions
Privatization of state-owned enterprises (SOEs)	Large domestic and foreign firms and investors Consumers of SOE goods and services where monopolized Competitive private-sector firms	Workers and management of SOEs Privileged suppliers of goods and services to the SOEs Consumers of SOE goods and services where subsidized

Source: Tun-jen Cheng and Stephan Haggard, *Newly Industrializing Asia in Transition* (Berkeley: Institute of International Studies, University of California, 1987), p. 71.

conservative government in which the executive still wielded tremendous power. From 1986 the KMT on Taiwan faced an organized political opposition and was forced to respond to criticisms of its economic policy as well. At the end of the decade the KMT still dominated the political system, however, and was likely to do so through the 1990s. In Singapore a second generation of PAP leaders confronted eroding support in the 1980s, but the opposition remained scattered and the regime showed little interest in opening the political system. The planned reversion of Hong Kong to China in 1997 forced a wide-ranging debate on the colony's future political structure, opened the door to a more vibrant electoral politics, and raised the question of business confidence in Hong Kong's delicate political and legal structure. A conservative alliance between business in Hong Kong and the government in Beijing appeared successful in its efforts to maintain the administrative status quo.

KOREA

Authoritarianism and the Heavy Industry Drive

Korea, the most aggressive of the NICs in pushing into heavy industries in the 1970s, ultimately faced the most pressing need to stabilize and adjust.[1] It also experienced the most turbulent political history of the four East Asian NICs. In 1970 serious economic problems emerged: a growing reliance on external borrowing, weakening financial structures among leading firms, and balance-of-payments difficulties associated with an expansionist macroeconomic policy. Despite Korea's relatively egalitarian distribution of income, the neglect of the rural sector, inflationary pressures on real wages, government corruption, and regional inequalities provided openings for the opposition, including a newly politicized labor movement and a growing student movement.[2] In 1969 Park Chung Hee won a controversial national referendum that allowed him to stand for a third term. In 1971 Park only narrowly defeated Kim Dae Jung, who made a strong showing by exploiting economic and political grievances.

The causes of the transformation of the Korean political system toward overt authoritarianism in 1972 are the topic of on-going debate.[3] Though Park justified the declaration of a state of emergency on December 6, 1971, by reference to military threats from the north, his speech belied political and economic concerns.[4] Placing "top priority on national security" meant that no "social unrest" could be tolerated. The Special Measures Law that accompanied the declaration tightened na-

1. For an early assessment, see Parvez Hasan, *Korea: Problems and Issues in a Rapidly Growing Economy* (Baltimore: Johns Hopkins University Press for the World Bank, 1976).

2. See David Valence, "Opposition in South Korea," *New Left Review* 77 (January–February 1973): 77–89; Sung-joo Han, "Student Activism: A Comparison between the 1960 Uprising and the 1971 Protest Movement," in Chong Lim Kim, ed., *Political Participation in Korea: Democracy, Mobilization, Stability* (Santa Barbara, Calif.: Clio, 1980); Chae-jin Lee, "South Korea: Political Competition and Government Adaptation," *Asian Survey* 12 (January 1972): 38–45.

3. See Han Sang-jin, "Bureaucratic Authoritarianism and Economic Development in Korea during the Yushin Period," paper presented at the International Conference on Dependency Theory, Seoul, June 6–8, 1985; Sung-joo Han, "South Korea: Politics in Transition," in Larry Diamond, Juan J. Linz, and Seymour Martin Lipset, eds., *Democracy in Developing Countries: Asia* (Boulder, Colo.: Lynne Rienner, 1989), pp. 272–79; Hyug Bae Im, "The Rise of Bureaucratic Authoritarianism in South Korea," *World Politics* 39 (January 1987): 231–57.

4. On the emergency decree see *Far Eastern Economic Review* (hereafter cited as *FEER*), December 11, 1971, pp. 6–7; December 25, 1971, pp. 11–12; January 8, 1972, pp. 20–22.

tional labor laws. Park took advantage of new emergency powers to address economic problems as well. The Emergency Economic Decree of August 3, 1972, instituted price controls, froze curb-market lending, launched wide-ranging reforms in financial markets, and provided preferential credit and administrative privileges to highly leveraged firms.[5]

On October 17, 1972, martial law was declared, the constitution suspended, the National Assembly dissolved, the universities closed, and all political parties banned. The Yusin or "revitalizing" constitution gave Park the power to dissolve the National Assembly and to appoint one-third of its members. Election of the president was made indirect. Executive autonomy reached its peak.

The Heavy and Chemical Industry Plan (HCIP), announced publicly in early 1973, was the direct result of executive initiative.[6] Prepared by a tightly insulated group around Park and the industry-oriented Ministry of Commerce and Industry, the plan bypassed the more liberal Economic Planning Board. Korea was heavily dependent on imports of machinery, chemicals, and transport equipment, and opportunities thus appeared to exist for import substitution. Exports would follow, guaranteeing the efficiency of heavy industries and permitting scale economies. The decisive influence favoring the heavy-industry push was military as much as economic, however. The American rapprochement with China, Richard Nixon's Guam Doctrine, and the defeat of South Vietnam all raised Korean anxieties concerning security. These were only reinforced by Jimmy Carter's announced intention to withdraw American forces from the peninsula. Important components of the plan were devoted to the development of an independent military industrial complex capable of self-sufficiency in a number of weapons systems.[7]

Forms of state guidance and participation varied across the designated "heavy and chemical" sectors. Direct state ownership was the model in upstream petrochemicals and steel, as it was in Taiwan and the large Latin American NICs. In the electronics and machinery sectors industrial estates were built to house private-sector ventures. Specific

5. On the August 28 measures see Leroy Jones and Il Sakong, *Government, Business, and Entrepreneurship in Economic Development: The Korean Case* (Cambridge: Harvard University Press, 1980), pp. 106–8.

6. On the genesis of the heavy industry plan see Byung-Kook Kim, "Managing International Trade and Industrialization: State Capacity and Response in Korea and Mexico, 1954–1982" (Ph.D. diss., Harvard University, 1987), pp. 214–18. A justification of the HCIP can be found in Korean Development Institute, *Long Term Prospects for Economic and Social Development* (Seoul: KDI, 1978), and a critique in Bela Balassa, "Korea's Development Strategy for the Fourth Five Year Plan Period," in *Policy Reform in Developing Countries* (New York: Pergamon, 1977), pp. 119–37.

7. On the question of defense self-sufficiency see *Investigation of Korean-American Relations*, Report of the Subcommittee on International Organizations of the House Committee on International Relations, 95th Congress, 2d sess. (Washington, 1978), pp. 76–88.

projects were negotiated with the large industrial groups, usually acting with minority foreign-equity partners or under license. Protection and fiscal incentives were extended to the new industries. Localization requirements encouraged purchase of Korean capital goods, and government procurement provided guaranteed sales. Finance was the key policy instrument.[8] A massive National Investment Fund, managed by the state-owned banks, mobilized public employee pensions and a fixed portion of all bank deposits, channeling them into designated projects and sectors at highly preferential rates.

A central component of the new strategy was the development of national champions.[9] Investment priorities naturally favored the larger and more technologically sophisticated firms, but restrictive rules toward foreign investors and the creation of General Trading Companies modeled on the Japanese *sogo shosha* suggested an explicit policy of promoting industrial concentration. The GTCs would counter Japanese control of Korean trade, serve as "windows" to international markets for small and medium-sized Korean firms, and ultimately provide conduits for the import of raw materials and technology. Qualifying as a GTC led to numerous financial privileges, but the government demanded a quid pro quo: steadily rising capital and export requirements that limited the GTC club to the largest ten to twelve Korean firms.

State Power, Stabilization, and Adjustment

Though the plan had some successes, such as the highly efficient state-owned Pohang Iron and Steel Company, it also had serious problems that suggest the constraints on state-led adjustment strategies in small, trade-dependent economies. These problems generated a wide-ranging critique of Korea's economic management from a group of market-oriented technocrats. The ability of the government to undertake the liberalizing reforms advocated by these reformers can be traced to continuity in its authoritarian powers.[10]

The HCIP spurred a dramatic investment boom in the late 1970s. The rapid expansion of credit from the state-owned banking sector was supported by an accommodative monetary policy, aggravated by large

8. See Bank of Korea, *The Financial System in Korea* (Seoul: Bank of Korea, 1978).

9. Suk Chae Lee calls the Korean strategy "financial repression cum concentration" in *Growth Strategy and Income Distribution: Analysis of the Korean Experience* (Seoul: Korean Development Institute, 1981).

10. For a more detailed analysis, see Stephan Haggard and Chung-in Moon, "Institutions and Economic Policy: Theory and a Korean Case Study," *World Politics* 42 (January 1990): 210–37; Paul W. Kuznets, "The Dramatic Reversal of 1979–80: Contemporary Economic Developments in Korea," *Journal of Northeast Asian Studies* 1 (September 1982): 71–87.

capital inflows from Middle East construction projects and workers' remittances as well as continued export success. The plan's demand for skilled labor put pressure on labor markets. Real wages increased sharply from 1976 to 1978, outstripping productivity gains and contributing to an erosion of Korea's competitiveness.

From the beginning there was some confusion in the HCIP regarding the goals of industrial deepening and upgrading exports. The plan sought to push Korea into an emerging niche for standardized capital and intermediate goods, thus accomplishing the goals of import substitution and export diversification simultaneously.[11] The generosity of government incentives encouraged rapid corporate expansion, and the reliance on debt, both domestic and foreign, weakened companies' financial structures. The bias toward heavy industries drained investment resources from the light manufacturing sector that remained central to exports and employment.

As the economy overheated in 1978, the reformist cause gained strength within the bureaucracy.[12] Inflation, the squeeze on smaller businesses, and attendant labor problems contributed to the political difficulties Park faced in maintaining the Yusin system. A stabilization plan was finally announced in April 1979, and new investments were scaled back. Implementation of the plan was interrupted by Park's assassination in October, but the new line received strong support from the government of Chun Doo Hwan that came to power in May 1980 through a coup d'état.

Chun Doo Hwan initially attempted to develop a populist image. Through a social development plan,[13] he sought to distance his government from the political and economic failures of the Park era and divert attention from the bloody intervention against the popular insurrection in Kwangju in May 1980. With political routinization and continuing problems with inflation, the emphasis on stabilization once again gained ground.

Korea proved remarkably successful in achieving its stabilization goals. The consumer price index dropped from an average annual

11. On the financial problems and poor planning see Kuznets, "Dramatic Reversal"; Korea Exchange Bank, *Monthly Review*, December 1980, pp. 1–26.

12. The following discussion of the reform effort draws on Haggard and Moon, "Institutions and Economic Policy"; Economic Planning Board, *Economic Survey: Annual Report of the Korean Economy in 1979* (Seoul: EPB, 1980), pp. 119–40; Tony Michell, "What Happens to Economic Growth When Neo-Classical Policy Replaces Keynesianism?" *IDS Bulletin* 13 (December 1981): 60–67; Bijan Aghevli and Jorge Marquez-Ruarte, *A Case of Successful Adjustment: Korea's Experience during 1980–1984*, International Monetary Fund Occasional Paper 39 (Washington, D.C., 1985).

13. Economic Planning Board, *A Summary Draft of the Fifth Five Year Social and Economic Development Plan* (Seoul: EPB, 1981), Part 6. Previous plans had not included "social" in the title.

growth rate of 14.1 percent from 1979 to 1982, a period representing the first stage of the stabilization effort, to a mere 2.9 percent in 1983–84. The capacity to stabilize rested on the quasi-revolutionary powers of the interim military government and the continuation under the constitution of the Fifth Republic (1980) of an authoritarian executive. Fiscal constraint was achieved by targeting politically sensitive programs for elimination or reduction. These included the Grain Management and Fertilizer Funds that Park had used to buttress his support in the countryside by subsidizing prices. In a move unthinkable in most developing countries, a wage freeze was imposed on public-sector employees, promotions delayed, positions downgraded, and hirings frozen. Under the guise of a "social purification" campaign, a large number of government employees were purged outright. Despite strong protests from big business, the government also attempted to curtail credit to the largest firms, though their financial weakness made this reform more difficult.

Government power was also manifest in actions directed against the labor movement. Technocrats attributed Korea's declining competitiveness to the rapid wage increases of the late 1970s; they instituted a wage policy in 1981. A broader set of actions restructured the labor movement itself, though the motivation was political more than economic.[14] Amendments to the Trade Union Law dissolved regional branches and decentralized the union movement to the company level, breaking the links between national unions and their local branches. A new Labor Dispute Law increased the government's power in the mediation of disputes, subjected collective action to prior government approval, and prohibited the involvement of outside groups, including grass-roots church organizations and students, in labor disputes. Some of the "impure elements" rounded up during the social purification campaign and placed in "re-education" camps were labor organizers and other political dissidents.

The long-term program of the reformers was not limited to stabilization. More fundamental was an effort to realign the state's role in the economy by rationalizing various incentive schemes and pursuing a more market-oriented style of economic management. The first priority was the restructuring of the heavy and chemical industry sector itself. The interim military government issued sweeping orders for the reorganization of six problem sectors characterized by surplus capacity.[15] This consolidation of industry did not mean an end to all industrial targeting.

---

14. See Michael Launius, "The State and Labor in South Korea," *Bulletin of Concerned Asian Scholars* 16 (October–December 1984): 2–10; *Monthly Review of Korean Affairs* (June 1984): 1–8; *FEER*, April 3, 1986.

15. Korea Heavy Industries is now a subsidiary of the state-owned Korea Electric Power Co. See *FEER*, June 2, 1983, pp. 65–70.

Lending priorities and tax laws were shifted to give greater emphasis to small and medium-sized firms, a political priority of Chun's, and to designated high-technology industries.[16] Nonetheless, some special industry funds were dismantled.

Import liberalization and the easing of restrictions on foreign investment were seen by the reformers as one way of rationalizing the chaotic system of incentives that had developed during the 1970s and disciplining big business. External pressure from the United States was a key factor in trade policy.[17] Korean statistics on the pace of liberalization are suggestive of the broad range of controls that existed. As late as 1979 Korea's "import liberalization ratio" was less than 68 percent (this is the share of product categories subject to automatic approval; it does not measure the share of total imports liberalized nor rates of protection). In 1983, after heated interministerial battles between the liberals in EPB and functionaries in the more industry-oriented Ministry of Trade and Industry, a five-year advance notice import liberalization scheme was instituted; it would raise the import liberalization ratio to 95 percent by 1988. A tariff reform was launched the next year. Under pressure from the United States, these plans were accelerated. Though the exercise of discretion remained an important component of the trade policy system, most of these liberalizing measures were implemented.

Political Constraints

Despite the government's initial success, the stabilization and reform efforts generated new political constraints. Some of these resulted from a changed relationship with the highly concentrated big-business sector. Control over finance had long been a means of both political control and industrial guidance.[18] In 1983 the government relinquished its holdings in all of the five major commercial banks, though it retained important oversight and regulatory powers, including limitations on the largest

16. See for example Joseph S. Chung, "Korea," in Francis W. Rushing and Carole Ganz Brown, eds., *National Development Policies for Developing High Technology Industries* (Boulder, Colo.: Westview, 1986); United States Trade Representative, *Annual Report on National Trade Estimates, 1985* (Washington, n.d.), p. 136.

17. The following data were supplied by the Economic Planning Board. The definitive study of the bureaucratic politics of the reform is Byung-sun Choi, "Strategic Management: The Institution of a Liberal Economic Order in Korea" (Ph.D. diss., Harvard University, Kennedy School of Government, 1987).

18. On the financial reforms from a comparative perspective see David C. Cole and Hugh T. Patrick, "Financial Development in the Pacific Basin Market Economies," in Augustine H. H. Tan and Basant Kapur, eds., *Pacific Growth and Financial Interdependence* (Sydney: Allen & Unwin, 1986), pp. 39–67; Yoon Je Cho and David Cole, "The Role of the Financial Sector in Korea's Structural Adjustment," unpublished ms., Harvard Institute for International Development, 1986.

groups' holdings in, and borrowings from, the banks. Stymied in their efforts to gain control over commercial banks, the large groups moved aggressively into the unregulated, nonbank financial sector. Several of the largest firms were overextended, however, as a result of following government directives. The result was an erosion of the portfolios of the state-owned banks. Lending created commitments to the largest *chaebol*, and these links were not easily cut. The efforts to privatize and liberalize the state-owned financial sector, and redirect credit away from the largest firms were partly undermined by the very weakness of big business.[19] The government was forced to ease its tight money policy and in 1983 created a massive Central Bank fund to avoid bank failures and bankruptcies.

The larger political problem was the authoritarian nature of the political system. The nature of the transition to the Fifth Republic made it difficult for Chun to distance himself from the Park era. Park's assassination was followed by a wide-ranging debate on constitutional reform and the expectation that authoritarian rule would end. Following the May 1980 coup and the Kwangju uprising, the new government promised a gradual democratization, but the political system remained similar to its Yusin predecessor. Despite some new checks on presidential power and an increase in the autonomy of the legislature, the president was elected indirectly and the executive retained broad powers.[20] Chun ran for president under the new system in February 1981 and, with the best-known politicians in the country jailed or banned from political activity, won over 90 percent of the electoral vote.

Political reform naturally dominated the opposition agenda, but Chun's economic program became a target for attack as well. Import liberalization, the internationalization of the financial sector, and the freeing of regulations on direct investment were portrayed as toadying to foreign pressure. Legislators from the ruling party sided with the opposition in the National Assembly to denounce the United States as hypocritical, protectionist, and unappreciative of Korea's status as a reliable military ally. Debt provided a particular focus for nationalist fears. The claim that foreign funds had been diverted to political ends gained plausibility with a series of financial scandals in which Chun's family was involved.[21] Students began to articulate a more radical and far-reaching critique of the Korean economy and made efforts to estab-

19. See Haggard and Moon, "Institutions and Economic Policy."
20. For a succinct overview of the Constitution of the Fifth Republic, see Edward J. Baker, "The New South Korean Constitution," in Wonmo Dong, ed., *Korean-American Relations at the Crossroads* (Princeton Junction, N.J.: Liberty Press for the Association of Korean Christian Scholars, 1982).
21. See for example *FEER*, October 20, November 10, 1983.

lish organizational links with other disaffected social groups, seeking to penetrate the union movement, for example, to urge a more radical line. Anti-Americanism entered the student lexicon.[22] Grass-roots farmer and workers organizations, supported by the Catholic and Protestant churches, focused attention on rural and urban marginals.[23]

Stabilization placed the Chun government in a more immediate political bind. The stabilization effort cut at virtually every base of support that Park had assiduously cultivated: farmers, civil servants, large and small business. Once committed to some form of democratic transition, the government was forced to devise a political strategy to build and maintain support for the ruling party. The executive came under increasing pressure from its own party to make concessions on a range of economic issues, particularly following the setback in the National Assembly elections of February 1985 in which the newly formed and poorly organized opposition New Korea Democratic Party (NKDP) showed surprising electoral strength, particularly in the cities.[24]

Campus activism and opposition activity increased markedly after 1985, focused on a constitutional amendment that would allow direct election of the president. In the face of extensive protests and the example of the Philippines, Chun turned away from the advice of the hardliners on the Blue House staff. In June 1987 Chun's chosen successor, Roh Tae Woo, announced direct presidential elections and constitutional reforms. Roh won the December 1987 presidential election with a plurality as the two major opposition candidates, Kim Young Sam and Kim Dae Jung, split the opposition vote; but the opposition parties captured a majority of National Assembly seats the following April.

The transition process immediately brought new pressures on economic policy. Roh's announcement of constitutional reform unleashed an unprecedented wave of labor organization and strike activity. Within the legislature, rice-pricing policy, social welfare expenditure, trade policy, and even defense expenditures became politicized. Underlying these debates were political cleavages generated by Korea's massive trade surpluses. While the United States was pressing for more rapid appreciation, labor continued to push for a greater share of national income. The resultant squeeze on export-oriented business produced

22. Timothy Shorrock, "The Struggle for Democracy in South Korea in the 1980s and the Rise of Anti-Americanism," *Third World Quarterly* 8 (October 1986): 1195–1218; *FEER*, October 24, 1985, p. 61.

23. Examples of work in English are studies by the Christian Institute for the Study of Justice and Development, including *The Economic Plight of Korean Farmers* (Seoul: CISJD, 1981); *Realities of Korean Economy* (Seoul: CISJD, 1981); *The Power of TNCs in Korea* (Seoul: CISJD, 1981).

24. See C. I. Eugene Kim, "South Korea in 1985: An Eventful Year amidst Uncertainty," *Asian Survey* 26 (January 1986): 66–77.

confrontations between labor and capital, including threats to move investment offshore. A second axis of conflict centered on the adjustment to be borne through liberalization by the long-protected agricultural sector. Most broadly, Korea's new international position raised the question whether exports were going to continue to lead growth or whether greater attention would be paid to domestic demand.[25] Roh's conservative coalition, control of a centralized state apparatus, and the international orientation of Korea's conglomerates made any sharp break with an outward-oriented strategy unlikely. But the insulation of economic policy making from domestic social forces had clearly declined, generating new distributional pressures on the state.

TAIWAN

Contrasts with Korea

Historically Taiwan has pursued a fiscal and monetary policy more conservative than Korea's. This conservatism could be seen in the two countries' adjustment to the first oil shock. Korea devalued and borrowed heavily to sustain imports, domestic demand, and investment. Taiwan, by contrast, maintained a fixed exchange rate against the dollar and adjusted through domestic recession and a restrained growth of imports.[26]

Industrial policy also exhibits interesting contrasts. Taiwan shunned the use of the financial system to target industries, relying primarily on tax benefits. Following the reforms of 1958 to 1963, manufacturers continued to enjoy a protected domestic market, but between 1970 and 1972 a large number of controlled goods were decontrolled, licenses for many goods were eliminated, and a tariff reform was promulgated.[27] Taiwan was also more open than Korea to foreign direct investment. On the other hand, the size of the state-owned sector shrank only gradually in relative importance following the shift to export-led growth, and it grew in absolute size in the early 1970s as a new generation of enterprises were created in the capital and intermediate goods sectors.

Taiwan's external economic position is one factor explaining this more

25. For a discussion of the emergence of a more inward orientation, see "The Asian NICs: Wrestling with Success," *World Financial Markets* (April 17, 1989), pp. 2–4.

26. Han Sheng Cheng, "Alternative Balance of Payments Adjustment Experiences: Korea and Taiwan, 1973–77," Federal Reserve Bank of San Francisco, *Economic Review,* Summer 1978.

27. Council for International Economic Cooperation and Development, *Fifth Four Year Plan for Economic Development of Taiwan* (Taipei: CIECD, 1969); Maurice Scott, "Foreign Trade," in Walter Galenson, ed., *Economic Growth and Structural Change in Taiwan* (Ithaca: Cornell University Press, 1979), p. 334.

liberal course. Liberal trade policies in Taiwan were eased by favorable current-account balances from 1970 to 1973, after 1976, and particularly in the 1980s, when Taiwan's structural surpluses soared. Overall, Taiwan's smaller size and greater dependence on trade made a "big push" strategy more risky and also created an export-oriented coalition heavily dependent on world markets.

Taiwan's international political position also affected economic policy. Nixon's reassessment of the strategic importance of the mainland did not immediately lead to derecognition by the United States, but Japan quickly normalized relations with the People's Republic of China.[28] The long-term effect of Japan's derecognition on foreign investment proved slight. Foreign investment dropped 50 percent in 1971, and another 50 percent in 1972, but increased more than sixfold to a postwar high in 1973. Japanese investors circumvented Chinese restrictions by establishing dummy corporations to carry out business on Taiwan, and the government maintained diplomatic ties through "private" liaison organizations that fulfilled embassy functions. An even milder effect followed the December 15, 1978, announcement of U.S. derecognition. Equity and foreign-exchange markets panicked temporarily, but the passage of the Taiwan Relations Act in 1979 effectively "re-recognized" Taiwan and adopted the Japanese model of unofficial missions.

Viewed in retrospect, the economic consequences of derecognition appear slight; at the time they constituted a major political challenge. Overall, political vulnerability reinforced liberal policy biases, first, because of the need to maintain and foster international economic ties as a surrogate for political ones; second, because Taiwan's "high" political vulnerability made it particularly sensitive to "low" political pressures to liberalize. During the 1970s the government launched a sustained diplomatic effort to keep trade and investment channels open even where political ties were severed. Business testimony to the U.S. Congress on the Taiwan Relations Act showed clearly how foreign investors could provide a transnational political base for continuity in commercial relations.[29]

---

28. On the evolution of the "Taiwan question" see Robert Barnett, "China and Taiwan: The Economic Issues," *Foreign Affairs* 50 (April 1972): 444–58; Ralph Clough, *Island China* (Cambridge: Harvard University Press, 1978), pp. 202–27; *Taiwan: One Year after United States–China Normalization,* workshop sponsored by the U.S. Senate Foreign Relations Committee and Congressional Research Service (Washington, 1980); Leonard Unger, "Derecognition Worked," *Foreign Policy* 36 (Fall 1979): 105–21. Data provided by the Council on Economic Planning and Development.

29. U.S. Senate, Foreign Relations Committee, *Hearings on S. 245 . . .* (Washington, 1979). This point is made by Dennis Fred Simon, "Taiwan, Technology Transfer, and Transnationalism: The Political Management of Dependency" (Ph.D. diss., University of California, Berkeley, 1980).

Industrial Upgrading

The government did combine market-based adjustment with the selective promotion of certain sectors; Taiwan was by no means laissez-faire.[30] As early as 1969 the government identified the need to transform "the current simple labor-intensive processing industry into one that is more demanding of skills and capital." Government investment in intermediates began even earlier.[31]

Unlike in Korea, however, there was no "big push." The reasons reside not only in differences in international position but in decision-making structure and style. Park's personal involvement in the Heavy and Chemical Industry Plan and the link drawn to military objectives resulted in a reduction in the power of market-oriented technocrats. The concentration of powerful allocative instruments, the close relationship between government and the largest firms, and the use of economic levers to counter an ever-present opposition help explain the dirigist nature of Korea's industrial policy and its emphasis on creating national champions.

Though final decision-making authority rested at the apex of the KMT party in Taiwan, the degree of political interference in economic policy making and the control of discretionary instruments was much less potent. Chiang Ching-kuo did not become vice-premier until 1969. Only then did he gain greater control over the economic ministries, through his chairmanship of the Council for International Economic Cooperation and Development, and even then the Central Bank remained a powerfully independent institution, in contrast to the Bank of Korea. Unlike Park, Chiang pretended no particular competence in economic affairs and relied heavily on the economic bureaucracy. A sharper division of labor existed in Taiwan between the political and economic sides of governance than was the case in Korea. Partly because of ethnic differences, business-government relations were more distant. With no history of independent party or interest-group organization, Taiwanese society wielded weaker political pressures on economic pol-

---

30. Robert Wade, "Sweet and Sour Capitalism: Industrial Policy Taiwan Style," unpublished ms., chap. 5; Tein-Chen Chou, "The Pattern and Strategy of Industrialization in Taiwan: Specialization and Offsetting Policy," *The Developing Economies* 23 (June 1985): 151–55.

31. *Fifth Plan*, p. 110. Insights into industrial policy can be gathered by examining the sectoral emphases of successive plans. The sixth Four Year Plan was scrapped following the oil crisis and a new six-year planning cycle initiated with the Economic Planning Council, *Six-Year Plan for Economic Development of Taiwan, 1976–1981* (Taipei: EPC, 1975). This plan showed a greater emphasis on deepening than any that had come before. It was also revised in 1978–79. In 1979 a *Ten Year Economic Development Plan for Taiwan* (Taipei: EPC, 1979) was published. These revealing documents, and the planning process, are generally ignored in neoclassical analyses.

icy. To adopt Chalmers Johnson's felicitous distinction regarding Japan, the KMT reigned while the economic bureaucracy ruled.[32]

The result was a more incremental approach to planning, what might be called an "engineering" approach. A series of studies by Arthur D. Little in 1971 argued that Taiwan should take advantage of rising wages in the more developed countries by moving into skilled labor–based export industries. This strategy demanded government support, however. "It will be necessary to attract both foreign and domestic industrial investment into specific, previously identified projects . . . it will be necessary to help [local firms] achieve higher productivity and economies of scale through mergers, acquisitions [and] better cooperation . . . linked with financing and technical assistance programs."[33] The government could not shy away from more direct involvement where it was required. "The government may find it necessary to own and operate a significant proportion of the new heavy basic industry, primarily because of large capital needs, shortages in the private sector of available entrepreneurial and management talent experienced in such industry and the business risks involved in some of the priority projects."[34]

Excellent case studies have explored variations in state involvement across sectors.[35] In those industries particularly demanding of capital or representing "natural" monopolies, such as steel and upstream petrochemicals, the government undertook production directly through state-owned enterprises. Unlike in Korea, state-owned companies also undertook shipbuilding and heavy machinery projects, since private investment was not forthcoming. The government backed large expansions of state-owned enterprises in nonferrous metals and heavy machinery, but these plans were effectively scaled back in the face of adverse economic signals.[36]

Partly overlapping with this phase of industrial deepening were efforts to expand Taiwan's presence in high-technology industries.[37] Scrapping

32. See Hung-mao Tien, *The Great Transition: Political and Social Change in the Republic of China* (Stanford: Hoover Institution Press, 1989), pp. 125–29; Chalmers Johnson, *MITI and the Japanese Miracle* (Stanford: Stanford University Press, 1982), pp. 17–34.

33. Arthur D. Little, *A National Industrial Development Overview: Guidelines and Strategy for Taiwan,* reprinted by the Industrial Development and Investment Center (Taipei, 1973), p. 2.

34. Ibid., p. 4.

35. See Simon, "Taiwan, Technology Transfer, and Transnationalism"; Thomas Gold, "Dependent Development on Taiwan" (Ph.D. diss., Harvard University, 1981); Greg Noble, "Contending Forces in Taiwan's Economic Policymaking: The Case of Hua Tung Heavy Trucks," *Asian Survey* 27 (June 1987): 683–704.

36. On the rationale for state-owned enterprises see K. T. Li, "The Growth of Private Industry in the Republic of China," in Li, *The Experience of Dynamic Economic Growth on Taiwan* (Taipei: Mei Ya Publications, 1976). On evaluations of the state-owned sector see *FEER,* April 30, 1982, pp. 49–56.

37. Gold, "Dependent Development," pp. 125–50, on the electronics industry; Dennis

the sixth Four Year Plan in the wake of the oil shock, the EPC issued for 1976–81 a Six-Year Plan that stressed both capital- and technology-intensive industries. After the creation of a cabinet-level Council for Economic Planning and Development in 1977, an even greater emphasis can be seen on technological upgrading and the development of an indigenous scientific, engineering, and research base. The second oil shock hastened the trend. Plans unveiled in 1980 (Ten Year Plan) and in 1982 (Four Year Plan) reflected a turn away from energy and capital-intensive sectors.

Policy instruments included special tax incentives to local research and development, the formation of joint ventures between the government and foreign firms in selected sectors, and targeted government procurement, particularly of computers.[38] During the 1970s the government also created specialized nonprofit organizations to conduct R&D and to assist in its dissemination to the private sector, and in 1980 the government opened a science-based industrial park at Hsinchu. Entrants were required to perform at least some local engineering, and the underlying assumption held that the advantages of local research facilities and the potential for linkages among residents of the park would spill over to indigenous R&D and effective technology transfer. Such efforts are visible in Korea as well, but they are overwhelmed in significance by the targeted development of the heavy-industry sector.

The contrast in government styles can also be seen in the particular attention given to infrastructure in Taiwan. If there is a "big push" in Taiwan, it is the Ten Major Development Projects, which accounted for almost 20 percent of total investment in 1975 and 1976.[39] These projects no doubt had a political rationale, bolstering the position of the new de facto leader, Chiang Ching-kuo, and providing employment and contracting opportunities for retiring military personnel. They included expansion of the steel industry, shipbuilding, and petrochemicals, but the bulk of spending went to railroad expansion and electrification, highway building, and harbor and airport construction. The government did attempt to steer industry in a particular direction, but in contrast to Korea the process was more incremental and relied to a greater extent on general incentives, the provision of infrastructure, and

Fred Simon and Chi Schive, "Taiwan," in Rushing and Brown, eds., *National Development Policies.*

38. See the U.S. International Trade Commission, *Foreign Industrial Targeting and Its Effects on U.S. Industries, Phase III: Brazil, Canada, the Republic of Korea, Mexico, and Taiwan* (Washington, 1985).

39. On the Ten Major Projects see Thomas Gold, *State and Society* (Armonk, N.Y.: M. E. Sharpe, 1986), p. 101. I have also profited from discussion with Greg Noble on these points.

institutional supports. This contrast reflected differences in economic structure, particularly the economy's greater openness, but also institutional and political differences: greater distance between government and business, a more independent technocracy, and a narrower range of industrial policy instruments.

The Liberal Critique

Despite a more market-oriented approach than that seen in Korea, state intervention in Taiwan also met with criticisms from several directions. A persistent group of neoclassical economists questioned the wisdom of any sector-specific interventions.[40] The increased cost of inputs associated with industrial policy was also a consistent source of controversy, pitting protected or monopolized upstream industries against downstream exporters. For example, the synthetic fiber industry resisted the import protection given to upstream petrochemical production.[41] A series of financial scandals in 1985 revealed a variety of structural weaknesses in the banking sector and led to the formation of an Economic Revitalization Committee that proposed an array of liberalizing measures.[42]

Once again external constraints played a powerful role in pushing the government toward policy change. By 1988 Taiwan was running trade surpluses consistently equal to 20 percent of its GNP and had accumulated $75 billion of reserves, giving the country the dubious status of a capital-exporting developing country.[43] Taiwan sought to offset surpluses with the United States through well-publicized buying missions, but despite their large size—several resulting in contracts for over $1 billion—these efforts failed to put a serious dent in the trade imbalance. Bilateral negotiations with the United States cut the average effective rate of protection almost in half in the early 1980s. The Revitalization Committee urged that nominal tariff rates be reduced from the 26.5 percent average level in 1986 to between 15 percent and 20 percent by

40. Perhaps the most persistent liberal critic is S. C. Tsiang. His interpretation of Taiwan's growth is spelled out in "Taiwan's Economic Miracle: Lessons in Economic Development," in Arnold C. Harberger, ed., *World Economic Growth* (San Francisco: Institute for Contemporary Studies, 1984). For his view on industrial policy, see *Taiwan Economic News* (Taipei), August 4 and September 29, 1980.

41. See Gold, "Dependent Development," pp. 269–91.

42. On the Economic Revitalization Committee see Tun-jen Cheng and Stephan Haggard, *Newly Industrializing Asia in Transition* (Berkeley: Institute for International Studies, University of California, 1987), chap. 3.

43. Chi Schive, "Trade Patterns and Trends on Taiwan," in Colin I. Bradford and William H. Branson, eds., *Trade and Structural Change in Pacific Asia* (Chicago: University of Chicago Press, 1986), pp. 307–22.

1991 and 10 percent by 2001. As in Korea, these schedules were accelerated under pressure from the United States.[44] The United States also successfully pressed the liberalization of services, including banking, insurance, motion pictures, leasing, and fast-food chains. By mid-1986 the locus of U.S. pressure had shifted to exchange-rate policy. As it did with Korea, the U.S. Treasury argued that the New Taiwan dollar should be allowed to strengthen and, more generally, that exchange rates should be determined by market forces. In early 1989 the government responded with a wide-ranging liberalization of the exchange-rate regime and an opening of the capital account.[45]

Emerging Political Constraints

During the 1980s broader political forces began to impinge on economic policy. After the KMT consolidated its power following party reform in 1950, politics stagnated under a highly institutionalized, single-party state. Rapid economic growth produced an educated, reformist middle class seeking input into the political system. As Chiang Ching-kuo took over from the elder Chiang, the government coopted the new Taiwanese elite into government service, but without any fundamental change in political structure.[46] As the KMT moved to open electoral politics at the national level, a new political opposition emerged, the *dangwai*, literally "outside the party."[47] Preoccupied with issues of political reform, legally limited in its capacity to organize, harassed by the government, and riven by internal factionalism, the *dangwai* initially proved unable to garner significant support.

Nonetheless, popular discontent with KMT rule gradually surfaced, beginning with the dramatic Chung-li incident in November 1977. Frustrated by government efforts to rig a county election, ten thousand

44. A review of recent actions is Vincent C. Siew, "R.O.C.–U.S. Trade: R.O.C.'s Efforts and Accomplishments in Liberalizing Trade and Improving Market Access," mimeo, Board of Foreign Trade, 1987.

45. For a review of Taiwan's exchange-rate reforms, see Department of the Treasury, "Report to the Congress on International Economic and Exchange Rate Policy," April 1989, mimeo, pp. 18–19.

46. On the political cooptation of the Taiwanese see Hung-mao Tien, "Taiwan in Transition," *China Quarterly* 64 (December 1975): 615–34; Hung-mao Tien, *The Great Transition*, pp. 35–42.

47. On the origins of the opposition and the KMT's response see Mab Huang, *Intellectual Ferment for Political Reforms in Taiwan, 1971–1973* (Ann Arbor: Center for Chinese Studies, University of Michigan, 1976), and Jurgen Domes, "Political Differentiation in Taiwan: Group Formation within the Ruling Party and the Opposition Circles, 1979–1980," *Asian Survey* 21 (October 1981): 1011–28; E. A. Winckler, "Institutionalization and Participation in Taiwan: From Hard to Soft Authoritarianism?" *China Quarterly* 99 (September 1984): 481–527; Tun-jen Cheng and Stephan Haggard, eds., "Political Change in Taiwan," manuscript.

citizens went on a spontaneous rampage. A protest organized in Kaohsiung by the radical *Formosa* magazine faction of the *dangwai* in 1979 ended in rioting. The trial and incarceration of the Kaohsiung defendents focused international attention on the unseemly side of Taiwan's political system, though in Taiwan itself the incident discredited the confrontational approach of the radicals. Within two years elections were restored, and the KMT performed well.[48]

The political context changed dramatically in 1986 when the opposition developed a more coordinated strategy. First, a policy study institution was formed to provide an organizational structure to the opposition. In September 1986, 135 opposition politicians announced the formation of a new political party, the Democratic Progressive Party (DPP).[49] This dramatic gesture posed a challenge to the KMT, but the new party was tolerated, ran in December legislative elections, and received an unexpectedly high 23 percent of the popular vote. After a thoroughgoing review of political issues, the government announced its intention to lift martial law, replacing it with a new security law to mollify the concerns of the conservatives. The new law placed three conditions on political activity: that it not violate the Constitution, support Communism, or advocate political independence or separate statehood for Taiwan. By the end of the 1980s Taiwan was still not fully democratic, but the KMT had successfully managed the problem of succession following the death of Chiang Ching-kuo and opened the space for opposition activity.[50]

The opposition lacked a coherent economic alternative and focused its efforts on establishing its political legitimacy and appealing to native Taiwanese sentiment through the independence issue. Nonetheless, independent and opposition legislators also used the power of interpellation to put the KMT on the defensive on economic questions. Unemployment, financial scandals, the slowdown in investment, the use of the country's surpluses, and consumer and environmental issues were used to cast doubt on government competence. By the end of the decade the long-quiescent labor movement began to stir, placing new pressures on labor-intensive sectors, and in December 1989 elections for a variety of local and provincial offices, the DPP once again increased its share at the popular vote.

The growing complexity and openness of the economy and direct pressure from trading partners lent support to arguments for a market-

---

48. On the 1979 incident see Hung-mao Tien, "Uncertain Future: Politics in Taiwan," in *China Briefing 1982* (Boulder, Colo.: Westview, 1983).

49. See *FEER*, October 9, November 20, December 18, 1986; January 22, 1987; *Wall Street Journal*, October 27, 1986.

50. See Cheng and Haggard, "Political Change in Taiwan."

oriented strategy. Because of Taiwan's political isolation and the continued threat from the mainland, international economic ties had a crucial political function, serving as a surrogate for formal political relationships. The KMT continued to enjoy substantial political power and support and could thus commit itself to liberalization even in the face of protest. The opening of the political structure provided new incentives for KMT politicians to be responsive to societal demands, however, and was likely to moderate both the scope and the pace of liberalization, particularly in the agricultural sector.

SINGAPORE

The Second Industrial Revolution

Though the last of the East Asian NICs to turn to export-oriented growth, Singapore was the first to develop a policy for upgrading its exports.[51] To do so, the government relied on the policy instrument that had been central to its strategy from the beginning: control over labor. By 1970 the problem of unemployment, which had been central to Singapore's political history, was solved and labor shortages developed. In 1971 a tripartite National Wages Council was formed to steer future wage increases. In 1973 wages were allowed to rise at an accelerated pace in order to force firms to create more skilled positions and to adopt more capital- and technology-intensive production processes. This experiment in industrial restructuring was interrupted by the world recession of 1974, and from 1975 through 1978 the government reinstituted wage restraint. In June 1979, as part of a policy called the "Second Industrial Revolution" (SIR), the National Wages Council recommended an average 20 percent increase in wages.

In the 1981 budget the various components of the SIR were integrated into a Ten Year Economic Development Plan, under which Singapore would build a modern industrial economy around science, technology, and an upgrading of skills.[52] Despite the fact that services had been a leading sector in the growth of the 1970s, the goal of the plan

51. The Second Industrial Revolution is described in Lim Chong-Yah, *Economic Restructuring in Singapore* (Singapore: Federal Publications, 1984); Wong Kum Poh, *Essays on the Singapore Economy* (Singapore: Federal Publications, 1982); Linda Lim and Pang Eng Fong, *Trade, Employment, and Industry in Singapore*, World Employment Programme Research Working Paper (Geneva: International Labour Organisation, 1982); Peter S. J. Chen, *Singapore: Development Policies and Trends* (Singapore: Oxford University Press, 1983); Chung Ming Wong, "Trends and Patterns of Singapore's Trade in Manufactures," in Bradford and Branson, *Trade and Structural Change*, pp. 379–434.

52. For the text of the budget statement by Minister for Trade and Industry Goh Chok Tong outlining the Ten Year Plan, see *Straits Times*, March 7, 1981.

was to increase the share of the manufacturing sector in GNP. The measures that followed demonstrated the continuing dirigist bent of Singapore's economic bureaucracy. The wage policy naturally had the effect of discouraging foreign investments in labor-intensive industries. More explicit measures were also used to restructure the activities of foreign firms, however. As early as 1970 pioneer status was withdrawn from pure assembly operations in electronics. The government targeted carefully defined manufacturing segments for special support, using tax incentives to encourage R&D, automation, mechanization, and computerization. Industrial estates were expanded and greater attention given to matching government-financed training to the labor market through specialized training institutes.

The basic pattern of business-government relations remained intact. The new wage policy met resistance from smaller, domestic firms, but as in the past they were politically weak. Domestic entrepreneurs, grouped in the Chinese Chamber of Commerce, had always seen the government's strategy as biased in favor of foreign firms and the government and against local capital.[53] With its emphasis on higher wages and technological capabilities, the SIR only confirmed the dominance of the multinationals.

Downturn and the Adjustment Debate

Through 1984 the growth targets of the plan were met, but the boom in construction and related industries, many of them government-owned, and the expansion of international services disguised continuing weaknesses in the manufacturing sector. Overall cost competitiveness deteriorated, particularly in relation to the other NICs.[54] In 1985 the economy contracted by 1.7 percent. The domestic work force was partly shielded from the recession by the guest worker program. Though 90,000 jobs were lost during the year, only a third of them belonged to Singaporeans. Nonetheless, unemployment reached 6 percent.

In elections held in December 1984 the lone opposition member of Parliament, J. B. Jeyaretnam, was returned and a second opposition candidate, Chiam See Tong, was also seated.[55] Two opposition MPs

53. See for example *Straits Times*, October 10, 1984. Various measures for assisting local industry are outlined in Economic Development Board, *Annual Report 1983/4* (Singapore: EDB, 1984).

54. These developments are outlined in Ministry of Trade and Industry, *The Singapore Economy: New Directions* (Singapore, 1986), which is the report of the economic committee.

55. On the elections and their aftermath see Lee Boon Hiok, "Singapore in 1984: A Time for Reflection and a Time for Change," *Southeast Asian Affairs 1985* (Singapore: Institute for Southeast Asian Studies, 1985).

from different parties in a national assembly of seventy-nine seats hardly appear as a threat to the government, particularly as thirty of the seventy-nine were returned unopposed. But several factors gave the electoral outcome greater significance. First, overall support for the PAP showed a sharp deterioration. The PAP secured only 65 percent of the total vote, down from 78 percent in 1980. The election also highlighted problems of political succession within the PAP. Since the mid-1970s Lee Kuan Yew and the first generation of PAP leaders had been grooming a second generation of new leaders from academia, the bureaucracy, and the private sector. With virtually no political experience, this second generation epitomized the technocratic cast of PAP rule.[56] It tried to project a progressive image to a younger and more affluent electorate; nonetheless, the results must be read as a referendum on the PAP's continuing paternalism.

In March 1985, just as evidence of the downturn appeared, the government formed a blue-ribbon panel to review the economy, headed by Lee Kuan Yew's son, Brig.-Gen. Lee Hsien Loong. The formation of the committee had a variety of political motives, including advancing Lee Hsien Loong's visibility and projecting an image of responsiveness to the recession. The formation of the committee also reflected a growing debate about the role of government in steering the economy. In the eyes of critics the benefit of the SIR had accrued to the government through a combination of higher taxes and fees. Private investment was less robust, and the economy had maintained its momentum only through public-sector construction projects.

The interim report of the committee, published in 1985, argued that Singapore's problems could be traced largely to the high-wage policy.[57] As in the past, the government turned to its control over the labor markets as a central instrument of adjustment.[58] In September the government called for wage restraint and reduced the wage-setting powers of the National Wages Council, thereby moving to a more decentralized process of wage determination. The final report, issued in February 1986, argued for a reduction of the wage bill by cutting employer contributions to the Central Provident Fund from 25 percent to 15 percent and freezing wages for two years, a highly regressive move since workers were not subject to a similar reduction in their contribu-

56. On the selection of the second generation and for interesting insights into the elitist and meritocratic nature of the PAP see Carolyn Choo, *Singapore: The PAP and the Problem of Political Succession* (Selangor: Pelanduk Publications, n.d. [1984?]).

57. Ministry of Trade and Industry, "The Economic Committee: An Interim Report," mimeo, July 1985.

58. Fred Deyo, *Beneath the Miracle: Labor Subordination in the New Asian Industrialism* (Berkeley: University of California Press, 1989), p. 142.

tions to the fund. Broader changes in the government's posture toward labor had actually preceded the formation of the economic committee. From 1979 the government acted to decentralize the labor movement. In 1982 the two largest umbrella unions were broken into smaller, industry-based ones, designed to encourage worker loyalty but also increasing employer leverage.

The final report offered a critique of economic management that was more comprehensive than an attack on excessive wage gains.[59] The explanation of Singapore's downturn focused not only on the changed international environment and short-term factors, such as a contractionary fiscal policy and the collapse of the construction boom, but also on the government's management of the economy and the balance of power between the public sector and foreign and local firms. Though the final report made little mention of the issue, representatives of the private sector in the consultative subcommittees vigorously protested the role the government played in the economy. The subcommittee report on local industry noted that the statutory boards had accumulated surpluses beyond their own operating and capital needs and that prices for services could thus be cut. In 1977 the Chinese Chamber of Commerce and Industry submitted a list of over one hundred state-owned enterprises that competed directly with the private sector. The subcommittee report noted that "local businessmen are being squeezed on both sides. On the one hand, the Economic Development Board is concentrating most of its efforts in promoting huge foreign MNC's. On the other, local businesses have to operate in direct competition with government companies."[60] The subcommittee on the service sector found, similarly, that state-owned enterprises and MNCs had preempted opportunities for private-sector growth.[61]

In 1984 the Ministry of Finance conducted a review of the state-owned sector and in March 1985 announced that the government would start up new industries only where private entrepreneurs had neither "the will [n]or the money to undertake projects on their own or where it is essential for government to provide the entrepreneurship."[62] This caveat was similar to those issued in the past and allowed substantial leeway for continued intervention. The ministry also decided to establish clear rules for the participation of state-owned enterprises in public-

59. Ministry of Trade and Industry, *The Singapore Economy: New Directions.*
60. "Report of the Subcommittee on Local Industry," mimeo, p. 18, and the Singapore Chinese Chamber of Commerce and Industry, "The Roles of the Public and Private Sectors in the Economic Development of Singapore," attached as Annex VIII to the Local Industry Subcommittee Report.
61. "Report of the Subcommittee on the Service Sector," mimeo, p. 31.
62. *FEER,* July 25, 1985, p. 68.

sector projects, an admission that the growth of the public sector may have preempted private-sector opportunities. Privatization also became a government goal, and the ultimate test of its real intentions, though as elsewhere the process faced institutional resistance and proved slower than planned.[63]

The process of structural adjustment in Singapore posed several political issues. The first tension involved relations with the private sector. The subcommittee report on entrepreneurship development noted that "government regulations are often passed without adequate consultation with the business sector. Where there is consultation, such measures are seen to be cosmetic rather than a sincere desire to solicit private sector opinion."[64] Despite the formation of a joint business-government Enterprise Committee to review regulations, the second generation of PAP leaders appeared no more responsive to the local private sector and no more genuinely committed to a diminished state role. Several members of the new elite were drawn from the private sector, but the second generation was also socialized into a PAP ideology emphasizing government leadership and operated in the institutional context of a highly interventionist state. Moreover, several important members of the second generation, including Lee Hsien Loong, came from the military.

The second problem concerned the labor movement. The NTUC has been an important source of PAP support, and to date there is no evidence of an independent labor union movement or of any significant ties between labor and the tiny political opposition. Controls on labor have been accompanied by a genuine commitment to education and training from which workers have benefited. However, a reshuffling of the NTUC structure in the mid-1980s showed a disregard for old-guard unionists who occupied middle-level positions. This stratum has consistently been denied promotion to leadership positions; the PAP has appointed leaders from the outside. Some government actions, such as the decentralization of the labor movement and the call for wage restraint, produced divisions *within* the union movement between leadership and rank and file.[65]

Singapore's adjustment strategy demonstrated the PAP's continuing insulation from both local business and labor. Unlike the Chun regime in Korea, the PAP was still capable of garnering substantial, if declining, electoral support. Continued government strength has been paralleled by a fragmented opposition that showed little ability to offer a coherent

63. See *Report of the Public Sector Divestment Committee* (Singapore: n.p., February 1987).
64. "Report of the Subcommittee on Entrepreneurship Development," mimeo, p. 4.
65. For evidence of splits in the labor movement, see Linda Y. C. Lim, "Export-Led Industrialization, Labour Welfare, and International Labour Standards in Singapore," paper prepared for the Overseas Development Institute, July 1986.

policy or political alternative. Censorship of the foreign press and the arrest of a small number of purported radicals in 1987 revealed that Singapore's political system has changed less than those of Korea and Taiwan and was moving in a less liberal direction. Economic policy, therefore, was likely to continue to reflect the PAP's preferences: a large state sector, an interventionist state, and a skewed triple alliance in which multinationals played the dominant role.

Hong Kong

"Positive Non-Interventionism" and "Diversification"

In 1976 Financial Secretary Philip Haddon-Cave developed a rationale for colonial economic policy that comes as close to a programmatic statement as any Hong Kong pronouncement of the postwar period. His defense of laissez-faire demonstrated clearly the ideological continuity within the government in general and the office of the financial secretary in particular.[66] Coining the term "positive non-interventionism," Haddon-Cave limited state intervention to four areas. First, though Hong Kong comes close to a pure market model of money creation, control of monetary policy and the foreign-exchange markets was justified. Second, regulation of the financial sector was also called for. Third, the government was justified in extending basic social services. These services have not included social security or unemployment relief, but education, medical services, and the provision of public housing became as central to the Hong Kong model as they were in Singapore. Finally, it was appropriate for the government to sponsor industrial and economic advisory boards to maintain a dialog with the private sector over economic policy.

The adequacy of what Haddon-Cave called positive noninterventionism has been a recurrent source of controversy in Hong Kong. Industry's share of GNP dropped during the 1970s and 1980s as the service sector expanded. More than that of the other NICs, Hong Kong's industry was concentrated in sectors vulnerable to protection, particularly textiles and apparel. Hong Kong lagged behind the other NICs in technologically sophisticated product lines.

Under increasing economic and political pressures, the government began in the late 1970s to reexamine its role in the economy.[67] Land

66. Haddon-Cave's speech is in the Hong Kong *Hansard 1976–77*, pp. 827–30. See also R. G. Scurfield, "An Evaluation of Hong Kong Government's Policy of 'Positive Non-intervention' in the Economic Sphere," *East Asia* 3 (Frankfurt: Suhrkamp, 1985).

67. Tzong Biau Lin and Ying Ping Ho, "Export-Oriented Growth and Industrial Diversification in Hong Kong," in Wontack Hong and Lawrence B. Krause, eds., *Trade and*

policy was the first sign of a new direction. The government formally owns all land in Hong Kong, and the auctioning of long-term leases has been the largest single source of government revenue, accounting for 35 percent of government income. A nonprofit corporation was established in 1977 to develop industrial estates, granting leases at substantial discounts to qualified industrial firms.[68]

A second initiative was the establishment of an advisory commission for diversification in late 1977, initiated primarily in response to the growth of protectionism against the textile and apparel industries. The commission's report contained several recommendations, but in its basic thrust it was remarkably similar to a report on the effects of the world depression on Hong Kong's trade written almost fifty years earlier.[69] The report admitted that government needed to assist industry to cope with external shocks, trade restrictions, cyclical fluctuations, and shifting consumer tastes. But it also held that violating the laws of comparative advantage was a hazard equal to, if not greater than, overspecialization. The commission noted several industries as "appropriate" to Hong Kong's future development, including light engineering, electronics, and precision machinery, but it eschewed any explicit sectoral intervention.

The report emphasized the need for improved consultative machinery and broadly supportive measures, and it agreed to establish the Industrial Development Board as a standing body to monitor, plan, and advise on Hong Kong's industry. But unlike in Korea and Taiwan, where industry-oriented ministries carried bureaucratic clout, the IDB was headed by the financial secretary, the standard bearer of the minimalist state. Disagreements surfaced immediately over studies of the electronics and machinery industries commissioned by the IDB, conflicts that are revealing of the institutional, political, and ideological barriers to deeper government involvement in industrial promotion.

Both government and industry recognized that light engineering and electronics were particularly suitable for Hong Kong because they use a modest amount of capital and land. Yet the electronics industry in Hong Kong faced severe structural problems in the late 1970s.[70] These prob-

---

Growth of the Advanced Developing Countries of the Pacific Basin (Seoul: Korean Development Institute, 1981); Edward Chen, "Foreign Trade and Economic Growth in Hong Kong: Experience and Prospects," in Bradford and Branson, *Trade and Structural Change*, pp. 333–78.

68. Mee-kau Nyaw and Chan-leong Chan, "Structure and Development Strategies of the Manufacturing Industries in Singapore and Hong Kong: A Comparative Study," *Asian Survey* 22 (May 1982): 465.

69. See *Report of the Advisory Committee on Diversification 1979* (Hong Kong: Government Printer, 1979).

70. See *Study of the Hong Kong Electronics Industry* (Hong Kong: Hong Kong Productivity Centre, 1982). On the strengths and weaknesses of small industries in Hong Kong see

lems included a reduction in average firm size, a low level of technology, and weak supporting parts and components segments. Small firms had the advantages of flexibility and adaptability, but as subcontractors they possessed limited technological capabilities and lacked the capital required to upgrade production. Unlike in the other East Asian NICs, the technological infrastructure, including domestic R&D, was weak, and the absence of upstream industries made small Hong Kong firms vulnerable to concentrated foreign suppliers.

To develop the industry, several leading firms run by engineers-turned-entrepreneurs called for a levy on electronics exports to support a common research and product development facility, a modest request compared to the direct and indirect support that other NICs give the electronics industry. The government viewed the proposal as an unhealthy precedent and killed it.[71] The report prepared by outside consultants on the industry met with an equally cold reception. That study argued forcefully that the government should take a strategic view of the industry and support the development of a more integrated electronics industry. Such support would have demanded an analytic capability that the government lacked and was unwilling to develop. Instead, the government developed programs based on existing institutions: more funding for manpower training and vocational education, sponsorship of a testing and standards laboratory, and R&D programs in postsecondary schools.

The growth of Hong Kong as a financial center and the revival of entrepôt trade with China following the economic reforms of the 1980s—neither of which demanded government support—appeared to justify the government's reliance on a market-based strategy of adjustment. Hong Kong's development as a financial center was attributable primarily to location: the rapid economic development of the region, the inconvenience of using London, and the demand for an international financial center in an East Asian time zone.[72] The financial and entrepôt sectors were given new life by the mainland's economic reforms, including experimentation with "special economic zones" modeled on the export-processing zones in Taiwan and Korea. The special economic

Victor F. S. Sit, "Dynamism in Small Industries: The Case of Hong Kong," *Asian Survey* 22 (April 1982): 399–409, and Ambrose Y. C. King and Peter J. L. Man, "Small Factory in Economic Development: The Case of Hong Kong," in T. B. Lin et al., *Hong Kong: Social and Political Studies in Development* (Armonk, N.Y.: M. E. Sharpe, 1979).

71. See Y. W. Sung, "The Role of Government in the Future Industrial Development of Hong Kong," paper presented at the conference on Hong Kong and 1997, Center for Asian Studies, University of Hong Kong, December 1984.

72. William F. Beazer, *The Commercial Future of Hong Kong* (New York: Praeger, 1978); Y. C. Jao, "Hong Kong as a Regional Financial Centre: Evolution and Prospects," in Chi-keung Leung et al., eds., *Hong Kong: Dilemmas of Growth* (Canberra: Australian National University, Center for Asian Studies, 1980).

zones provided new investment opportunities for traditional industries in Hong Kong that were facing cost pressures, including rising wages. Textile and apparel manufacturers had already sought to circumvent quota restrictions and rising wages by investing in Southeast Asia and elsewhere. New opportunities were now provided by the PRC. A division of labor evolved, with more capital-intensive portions of the production process performed in Hong Kong, more labor-intensive ones in the zones.

The Political Environment: Dominance of the External

In Hong Kong external and internal political constraints on economic policy have been closely intertwined. The signing of the Sino-British agreement in 1984 guaranteed the continuity of the capitalist system for half a century after sovereignty reverted to China in 1997. The Chinese had strong incentives to be "reasonable," both on economic grounds and because of an interest in establishing an opening to Taiwan. Yet Hong Kong's vulnerability to external political events remained high, and was revealed starkly in the crisis of 1983 and again following the massacre of demonstrators in Beijing's Tiananmen Square in June 1989.

Before Sino-British talks on the colony's future opened, several factors had already weakened the financial system, among them an overexpansion of local deposit-taking companies (DTCs) and investment in a highly speculative property market. Externally, interest rates in the United States rose faster than those in Hong Kong, which remained under the control of a bank cartel that proved slow to respond to changing market signals. As balance-of-payments deficits emerged in the late 1970s, the Hong Kong dollar lost value. The Sino-British talks on 1997 created a crisis of confidence, reflected in a massive exodus from the Hong Kong dollar, uninhibited by foreign-exchange controls.[73] The Hong Kong dollar depreciated at the rate of 28 percent a year during 1982–83, compared to depreciation of a mere 4.1 percent annually from 1977 to 1982. To prevent collapse, the government was forced to underline its commitment to financial stability by pegging the currency to the United States dollar, establishing an administered exchange-rate system, and bailing out financial institutions that faced liquidity crises.

These currency and financial crises were accompanied by a fiscal

---

73. On the inherent fragility of Hong Kong's financial system see Y. C. Jao, "Financial Structure and Monetary Policy in Hong Kong," in S. Y. Lee and Y. C. Jao, *Financial Structure and Monetary Policies in Southeast Asia* (New York: St Martin's, 1982); Y. C. Jao, "The 1997 Crisis and Hong Kong's Financial Crisis," *Journal of Chinese Studies* 2 (April 1985): 113–53.

crisis. Economic slowdown and a depressed property market resulted in government deficits. Financing the debt was not a serious problem, given accumulated surpluses, low tax rates, and the absence of foreign debt and outstanding government bonds. The ability to cut the expenditure side of the budget was not tested, however. Cutting modest social welfare programs could easily produce a politics common to other large urban areas in the developing world: mobilization of community political action groups around service-oriented grievances. Local-level community boards designed to provide citizen input into government had already seen an upsurge in these types of demands and a resulting increase in politicization on the boards themselves.

In addition to the colony's short-term vulnerability to political events in China, Hong Kong also faced questions about how it would be structurally integrated with the Chinese economy. In the 1980s trade and investment relations grew dramatically. The PRC replaced Japan as the largest source of Hong Kong's imports in 1984, and overall trade with China surpassed Hong Kong's trade with the United States in 1985. Hong Kong investment accounted for over half of the total foreign capital the PRC had attracted through the mid-1980s, and the PRC's investment in Hong Kong also increased rapidly.

Hong Kong could become a center for the manufacture of consumer goods for the Chinese market, but this option had obvious limitations since the PRC is likely to prefer to use scarce foreign exchange to import capital and intermediate goods rather than consumer "luxuries." A second option would be to use the labor in the special economic zones to manufacture for the world market while specializing in financial services and upscale production. By the end of the 1980s about 90 percent of Hong Kong manufacturing sourced some or all of its production needs in Guangdong.[74] For industries subject to quota restrictions, this strategy posed difficulties. In 1985 the U.S. government adopted a stringent interpretation of rules of origin, a move aimed directly at Hong Kong textile and garment manufacturers operating in the zones.

The main source of economic uncertainty remained the question of Hong Kong's relationship with China, a question inseparable from Hong Kong's internal political structure. The Sino-British talks, which resulted in the Joint Declaration between China and Britain on Hong Kong, allowed for no formal representation by the government of Hong Kong. Nonetheless, for a combination of ideological and practical rea-

---

74. *FEER*, June 29, 1989, p. 52; John C. Hsu, "Hong Kong in China's Foreign Trade: A Changing Role"; and Joseph Chai, "Industrial Co-operation between China and Hong Kong," in A. J. Youngson, ed., *China and Hong Kong: The Economic Nexus* (Hong Kong: Oxford University Press, 1983).

sons, the British appeared intent on introducing some measures of political democratization prior to "decolonization." In 1984 a wide-ranging debate began over the political reforms that would allow the indirect election of twenty-four unofficial (i.e., non–civil service) members to the Legislative Council, or Legco.[75] Unofficial members had previously been appointed. The British plan was to phase out the appointment system altogether by 1997, shifting power from the Executive Council to a fully elected Legco. These developments did not seem to contradict the stated goals of the Chinese. The Joint Declaration stipulated that the Hong Kong Special Administrative Region would be vested with executive, legislative, and judicial powers; only foreign and defense affairs would remain in Beijing's hands. The chief executive of the new region would be selected by elections or through "consultations" held locally, though he or she was ultimately to be appointed by Beijing. The executive authorities were to be "accountable" to the legislature, a term that seemed to allow for political opposition and even the formation of parties.

Indirect election for an enlarged legislative council breathed new life into consultative district boards, established in 1982. The balance under the new system between administrative and electoral politics, between the executive and the legislature, became a central issue of discussion. Previously politics had operated through a system of appointed and functional representation within a framework tightly controlled by the colonial administration.[76] After 1985 there was open discussion on the possible formation of political parties, either out of the so-called pressure groups formed by professionals to air social and political grievances or from existing factions within the Legislative Council or administrative and district boards.

These developments were viewed with concern by portions of the local private sector that enjoyed access to the colonial administration, and they expressed their interest in insulating the economic system from mass or party politics.[77] The result was a curious marriage of convenience between portions of Hong Kong's economic elite and the PRC in defense of the administrative state. Beijing gradually became more

75. On the background to more recent political developments see Chalmers Johnson, "The Mousetrapping of Hong Kong: A Game in Which Nobody Wins," in *Issues and Studies* (Taipei) 20 (August 1984): 26–50. For a simulation of interest-group politics during decolonization, see Bruce Bueno de Mesquita et al., *Forecasting Political Events: The Future of Hong Kong* (New Haven: Yale University Press, 1985).

76. For an early collection of the views of the "pressure groups," see *Pressure Points: A Social Critique by the Hong Kong Observers* (Hong Kong: Summerson, 1981).

77. Shiu-hing Lo, "Colonial Policy-makers, Capitalist Class, and China: Determinants of Electoral Reform in Hong Kong's and Macau's Legislatures," *Pacific Affairs* 62 (Summer 1989): 204–18.

forceful in spelling out its political views, seeking to head off developments that would reduce its freedom of maneuver after 1997. These amounted to a surprising continuity in political form, but with Beijing taking over London's role. These clarifications of China's views have surfaced since the first meeting of the Basic Law Drafting Committee in July 1985, the joint Hong Kong–Chinese group given responsibility for drafting the "constitution" that will govern Hong Kong after 1997. The Chinese notion of accountability differed, not surprisingly, from liberal democratic norms but found strong support among the conservative businessmen who made up the bulk of the Hong Kong delegation to the committee. The Chinese opposed a system of explicit checks and balances and the formation of political parties, though they indicated a willingness to allow some electoral accountability if the power of the executive were left intact. When the first draft of the Basic Law was circulated, it resembled the colonial system. Functional representation guaranteed conservative legislative majorities, and the issue of direct elections for the entire legislature and for the chief executive would not even be raised until 2011.[78]

The course of political development was jolted by the events of June 1989 on the mainland. Despite the absence of democratic forms, Hong Kong has been a liberal *society,* with freedom to associate, criticize, and persuade. Hong Kong residents provided critical support for the Chinese democracy movement. Following the Beijing crackdown, it became painfully apparent that maintaining economic confidence demanded political autonomy from Chinese interference. Guaranteeing such non-interference, however, rested on revisions in the Draft Basic Law, including the institutionalization of a more representative politics than the Chinese wanted. The dilemma was unresolved at the end of the 1980s, and the Hong Kong economy remained painfully vulnerable to capital flight and immigration.

The Comparative Politics of Economic Adjustment

Shifting comparative advantage and dependence on trade posed a common challenge to the East Asian NICs in the 1970s and generated a similar policy interest in upgrading export industries. Market size was one factor determining the range of industrial possibilities. Korea and Taiwan could entertain a "deepening" of the industrial base through

78. The first draft of the Basic Law revealed to the public was "Draft Basic Law of HKSAR [Hong Kong Special Administrative Region], PRC," *Beijing Review,* May 9–15, 1988, pp. 19–47.

integration into intermediate and capital goods, whereas the city-states could not. Sectoral choices, in turn, influenced the mode of state intervention. In capital-intensive industries or in natural monopolies Korea, Taiwan, and Singapore formed or expanded state-owned enterprises. In other sectors where private investors were capable of organizing production, the state's role was to reduce risk by subsidizing credit, extending infrastructural and technical support, and providing market information.

But the nature of state intervention was not simply a function of market size and sectoral imperatives; it also depended on previous institutional history and patterns of state-society relations. The Korean political system was dominated by an executive that maintained direct ties with large firms that dominated a highly concentrated industrial structure. The Heavy and Chemical Industry Plan reflected both the advantages and the defects of such a system: a tremendous directive power and the ability to act swiftly, but also a high level of discretion and the absence of checks on executive action. In Taiwan, by contrast, the political leadership left economic policy largely in the hands of the technocrats. Though there are differences between "engineers" and "economists" in Taiwan, the government lacked the instruments held by the Korean bureaucracy and was more cautious in guiding the investment process. This caution was reinforced by the country's greater openness to the world economy, its peculiar political status, and a less concentrated industrial structure.

The contrast between Singapore and Hong Kong also shows the importance of domestic structures and ideologies in shaping national responses to external exigencies. Singapore took an aggressive posture toward industrial adjustment, even in the face of an industrial structure dominated by foreign firms. The state fell back on the instrument it had used to launch the first phase of export-led growth, control of the labor market. For better or worse, Hong Kong's policy also exhibited continuities with the past. The government showed reluctance to interfere in the market and relied on neutral supportive measures.

If an emerging third phase of export-led growth can be identified, it is also appearing in reaction to a new round of external pressures. By the end of the 1980s it was too early to gauge the outcome of these exercises in liberalization, though the very openness of the NICs and their dependence on trade appeared to push them toward greater deregulation and integration with world markets. Liberalizing reforms faced three sorts of domestic political constraints, however, and none was insubstantial. The first, within the state itself, came from those portions of the bureaucracy which, for reasons of either vision or interest, believed in government activism. The second source of pressure was the private sector. State intervention was a source of private-sector ambivalence in the NICs. On the one hand, the governments of Korea, Taiwan, and Singapore have been broadly supportive; on the other hand, such support borders on "unnecessary" direction, discretionary power, and interference in managerial autonomy. The private sector's attitude toward reform thus varied by policy issue: supportive of those reforms which expand business autonomy, but critical of those which remove previous privileges.

Finally, the speed and direction of adjustment will be affected, as I have argued, by the expanding scope and level of political participation. In all four cases economic growth has benefited from strong states that have effectively insulated economic decision making from political pressures. Technocrats have been given fairly wide leeway in managing the economy, and political elites have engineered "growth coalitions" of favored sectors while controlling or paying off the losers.

The ruling parties in Korea, Taiwan, and Singapore have varied in their capacity to mobilize political support (see Table 6.3). Korean political elites have had the most difficult time developing a legitimating formula, relying to the greatest extent on coercive means to sustain political power. Taiwan and Singapore have been much more successful in constructing stable political systems, though both the PAP and the KMT witnessed an erosion of support in the 1980s. These differences help account for a politicization of economic issues higher in Korea than

Table 6.3. Electoral support for ruling parties in the East Asian NICs, 1980–89 (percentage share of popular vote in legislative elections)

Year	Korea	Taiwan	Singapore
1980		72.0	77.7
1981	35.6		
1982			
1983		68.0	
1984			64.8
1985	35.3		
1986		63.0	
1987			
1988	34.0		63.1
1989		60.4	

Sources: C. I. Eugene Kim, "South Korea in 1985," *Asian Survey* 26 (January 1986): 69; James Cotton, "From Authoritarianism to Democracy in South Korea," *Political Studies* 37 (June 1989): 256; *Central Daily News* (in Chinese), December 5, 1983, and December 7, 1989; *New York Times*, December 8, 1986; Thomas Bellows, "Singapore 1988: The Transition Moves Forward," *Asian Survey* 29 (February 1989): 145.

in Taiwan and Singapore. Political liberalization produced sharp confrontations over the authoritarian legacies of the Park and Chun eras.

Even in Taiwan, Singapore, and Hong Kong the old structure has become more difficult to maintain. Political liberalization, the emergence of attentive middle-class publics, and the increasing organizational capacities of societal actors have expanded the number of relevant players and placed new demands on the state. Incumbent elites are forced to pursue economic policies with short-term political considerations in mind. The very process of political liberalization offers new opportunities and organizational channels for threatened interests to air opposition, among them the legislature and the press. Costs are less easily imposed.

To date, the political oppositions in the East Asian NICs have not provided coherent alternatives for economic policy. Their basic struggles have centered on political issues and the effort to gain legitimacy and recognition. Moreover, despite political liberalization, oppositions faced entrenched governments and bureaucracies in all of the NICs. Opposition chances of gaining power in the 1990s are remote outside Korea. Nonetheless, oppositions can play the role of critic, articulating the grievances of threatened sectors. In Korea and Taiwan they are likely to be more cautious about participation in the international economy, more hostile to the penetration of transnational actors, more oriented toward the domestic market. In all cases they are likely to stress the distributional and ecological consequences of growth, particularly for previously excluded groups such as labor. These concerns do not necessarily cut against liberalizing reforms; disentangling the state from the economy may be one way of providing greater political opportunities to oppositions over the long run. In general, however, greater politicization will reduce the coherence of policy and the speed with which adjustments can be undertaken.

CHAPTER SEVEN

Mexico and Brazil in Comparative Perspective: Two Import-Substituting Trajectories

The Asian NICs have cultures, colonial histories, resource endowments, and international positions that differ hugely from those of their Latin American counterparts. Such wide variations cloud comparison by limiting the number of variables that can be controlled; outcomes are overdetermined. These methodological problems cannot be resolved fully, but several critical political differences can be isolated to help explain the continuity of ISI in Brazil and Mexico.

I begin with the 1930s and 1940s, when economic policy was affected by the twin shocks of depression and war. Sociopolitical changes are difficult to date, and the timing of phenomena such as the political mobilization of labor varies across countries. In general, though, it is reasonable to suggest that the continuing expansion of industry was accompanied by a relative decline in the power of rural elites at the political center, growing organization on the part of manufacturers, and an expansion of urban labor movements. The causal links between these social changes and the policy experiments favoring industry are permissive at best. Rather, I emphasize the relationship between external shocks, political consolidation, and policy change. Responding to crisis conditions, political elites expanded their power vis-à-vis social forces and increased national administrative capabilities. Groping responses to the Depression and war may not be considered "strategies" when compared with the conscious industrial policies of the postwar period, but they marked a new level of government activism and set the stage for subsequent interventions.

External shocks, interacting with the effects of size and resource endowment, also help explain the development of secondary ISI. By the early 1950s the first phases of ISI were reasonably advanced in Brazil and Mexico. Balance-of-payments problems, aggravated by the end of the Korean War boom, provided an incentive to push ISI farther. The size of the domestic market and the ability to finance industry through exports of natural resource, foreign direct investment, and borrowing made secondary ISI a plausible goal.

"Self-reliance" appealed to political elites on Taiwan and Korea as well. Was it only market size and resource endowment that precluded their adoption of ISI? If so, why did other, smaller Latin American countries, such as Costa Rica and Uruguay, also pursue ISI? By the 1950s political elites in Mexico and Brazil were more constrained by the urban political forces spawned by industrialization than were leaders in Korea and Taiwan, where labor was politically irrelevant during their experimentation with ISI. By contrast, appeals to the "popular sector" influenced economic policy in Brazil during the period of democratic politics from 1945 through 1964, and broad political constraints resurfaced during the political liberalization of the 1970s. Mexico's populist interlude was followed by the incorporation of labor into government-dominated unions, but the ruling party also relied on urban popular-sector support and was constrained by electoral politics, a revolutionary mystique, and in the late 1960s and 1970s the mobilization of new opposition groups.

In both countries a large, protected domestic market shaped the political demands of the domestic private sector, which displayed greater political independence than its counterparts in Taiwan, Singapore, and Korea. The evidence regarding business influence over economic policy remains mixed and appears to have been more institutionalized in Mexico than in Brazil. Nonetheless, it is incontrovertible that as the deepening process advanced, the business coalition supporting ISI widened.

These societal constraints help explain the maintenance of ISI policies once in place, but explaining policy innovation demands attention to the incentives facing state actors. Intervention in support of industry had a strong appeal to politicians, who exploited policy instruments to centralize political power and construct political alliances. But the program of secondary ISI also had a broader intellectual rationale.. In the 1950s structuralism began to influence significant segments of the growing economic bureaucracies in the larger Latin American countries. The ideas of the United Nations Economic Commission on Latin America provided a crucial lens for interpreting economic events; they also appealed to politicians and received a surprising degree of support from external agencies. The continuity of structuralist thinking in the Brazilian bureaucracy, and the strengthening of these ideas in the 1970s in Mexico, provides a point of contrast with the East Asian NICs.

In Korea and Taiwan the relative independence of the state and the weakness of social forces permitted a sharp break with ISI policies that were of short duration. In Mexico and Brazil external shocks and market size pushed policy toward ISI. Economic ideology influenced state responses, and political factors strengthened the commitment over time.

By the 1970s both countries had attempted to supplement ISI with the promotion of nontraditional exports. The Brazilian military's efforts in this direction after 1964 provide interesting similarities with those of the East Asian NICs. Access to Euromarket credit, foreign direct investment, and (in Mexico) an oil boom provided continuing financing for inward-looking policies, however, and not until the debt crisis of the 1980s did ISI come under serious stress.

This chapter follows the stages of the import-substituting trajectory, beginning with a discussion of the primary-product phase of growth and the acceleration of primary ISI during the Depression and World War II. I then examine the turn to a second, more self-conscious phase of import substitution in the mid-1950s before reviewing briefly the third phase, the "debt-led ISI" of the 1970s.

THE PRIMARY-PRODUCT GROWTH PHASE IN MEXICO AND BRAZIL

Brazil and Mexico began their contact with the international economy as exporters of primary products. In Brazil a coffee-support program and investment in infrastructure expanded the central government's role in the economy during the federal First Republic (1889–1930). Despite these signs of change in the state's role and the beginnings of industrialization, the economic liberalism favored by the agro-export sector held powerful ideological sway.[1] Political power was dominated by the "politics of the governors" in which the states of São Paulo, the center of the coffee boom, Minas Gerais, and Rio Grande do Sul were the key players.[2] The larger states even controlled many of the instruments of economic policy and resisted federal incursions on their autonomy. Political power at the state level rested, in turn, on a decentralized hierarchy of rural-based *coroneis* (colonels) who dominated local clientage systems.

Mexico's modern economic development can be traced to the Porfiriato (1877–1911), which exhibits both similarities and contrasts with

1. On the origins of Brazilian industrialization in the nineteenth century see Wilson Suzigan, *Indústria brasileira: Origem e desenvolvimento* (São Paulo: Editora Brasilense, 1986). On government policy see Steven Topik, "State Intervention in a Liberal Regime: Brazil, 1889–1930," *Hispanic American Historical Review* 60, 4 (1980): 593–616.

2. On the politics of the states in the Republic see, for example, John Wirth, *Minas Gereis in the Brazilian Federation, 1889–1937* (Stanford: Stanford University Press, 1977).

Brazil.[3] Porfirio Díaz's rule rested on the cooptation of local and regional *caciques* and a liberal economic strategy based on the promotion of exports and a particular openness to foreign direct investment. Mexico was not as dependent on a single crop as Brazil, and an independent national manufacturing class can be traced to the late nineteenth century in Monterey, Puebla, and elsewhere. But foreigners' domination of mining, petroleum, banking, and utilities was more pronounced than in Brazil (see Chapter 8). Mexico's dependence on the United States was also extremely high.[4] During the American recession of 1907 exports and land values fell, and the financial system experienced severe distress. These shocks exacerbated a variety of rural social cleavages, providing material for revolutionary leaders such as Emilio Zapata and Pancho Villa. New anti-Diaz and antiforeign political forces in the cities protested the crises to which Porfirian liberalism had subjected the country.[5] Through 1930 Brazil managed to accommodate social change within a decentralized, patrimonial political framework. By contrast, the exclusionary and foreign-dominated growth of the Porfirian period contributed to social revolution in Mexico.[6]

Despite these differences between Mexico and Brazil, several factors distinguish the two countries from Taiwan and Korea during the primary-product phase of their development. Mexico and Brazil were politically independent, possessed more diversified economies, and were characterized by a greater decentralization of political power. Government elites (to the extent they can be differentiated from societal elites) confronted entrenched regional and rural interests, fledgling business and working classes, and, in Mexico, foreign investors with concentrated economic assets. Efforts to promote industrialization therefore became intertwined with more fundamental processes of centralizing political authority and state building. The balance of power between the Japanese colonial bureaucracy and domestic social forces was different in the larger East Asian NICs. Korea and Taiwan remained agrarian societies through the 1950s, but the landowning elite had been displaced, enhancing the state's autonomy. Postindependence politicians controlled powerful and independent bureaucracies inherited from the colonial period.

3. On the economic history of the Porfiriato see Fernando Rosenzweig et al., *Historia moderna de México. El porfiriato: La vida económica* (Mexico: Editorial Hermes, 1965).

4. On the socioeconomic origins of the Revolution see John Womack, *Zapata and the Mexican Revolution* (New York: Vintage, 1968).

5. On anti-Diaz forces in the cities see James Cockroft, *Intellectual Precursors to the Mexican Revolution, 1900–1913* (Austin: University of Texas Press, 1968).

6. Douglas Graham, "Mexican and Brazilian Economic Development: Legacies, Patterns, and Performance," in Sylvia Ann Hewlett and Richard S. Weinert, eds., *Brazil and Mexico: Patterns in Late Development* (Philadelphia: Institute for the Study of Human Issues, 1982), pp. 2–55.

EXTERNAL SHOCKS, POLITICAL CONSOLIDATION,
AND THE ORIGINS OF ISI

Brazil

Brazil experienced substantial industrial growth in the 1920s and even earlier, but the twin shocks of war and Depression were crucial stimuli to policy experimentation. With the Depression and the sharp decline in its terms of trade, the government expanded its coffee-defense program by purchasing and destroying coffee. The federal government deficits and expansive monetary policy that accompanied the coffee-defense program accelerated industrial growth. Trade and exchange controls, used to manage the balance-of-payments crisis, had the effect of protecting the manufacturing sector.[7]

External shocks alone are not enough to explain policy, though. Why wasn't the initial, passive response to the crisis sustained? And why did Brazil respond more aggressively than Mexico to the Depression? The answers lie in the political realm. In 1930 a military coup deposed the last president of the Republic and installed Getúlio Vargas. The proximate cause of this change in government was tension among the states over the presidency, but the costs of sustaining liberal policies also fostered opposition. A dramatic political consolidation followed Vargas's ascent. The federal government put down regional resistance, expanded its power vis-à-vis the states, and crushed political movements on both the left and the right. The culmination of this process of centralization, in which the military played a key role, was the declaration of the Estado Novo by Vargas in 1937. The authoritarian Estado Novo is usually associated with the creation of state-corporatist labor structures, but an equally profound change was the triumph of the federal center over the states.[8]

Continued support for coffee during the Depression has been interpreted as indicating underlying continuity between the Republic and the Vargas years. Most accounts date self-conscious ISI policies at the earliest to the Estado Novo, others to the war or even later.[9] The full

7. See Flavio Rabelo Versiani, "Before the Depression: Brazilian Industry in the 1920s," in Rosemary Thorp, ed., *Latin America in the 1930s: The Role of the Periphery in World Crisis* (New York: St. Martin's, 1984). Celso Furtado's initial statement on the link between the coffee defense program and recovery is in *The Economic Growth of Brazil* (Berkeley: University of California Press, 1965), pp. 193–239.

8. For the politics of the 1930s and the emergence of the Estado Novo, see Thomas Skidmore, *Politics in Brazil, 1930–1964* (New York: Oxford University Press, 1967); Peter Flynn, *Brazil: A Political Analysis* (Boulder, Colo.: Westview, 1978), pp. 59–131; John Dulles, *Vargas of Brazil: A Political Biography* (Austin: University of Texas Press, 1967).

9. On the timing of ISI see Warren Dean, *The Industrialization of São Paulo, 1880–1945* (Austin: University of Texas Press, 1969); John D. Wirth, *The Politics of Brazilian Development, 1930–1945* (Stanford: Stanford University Press, 1970).

effects of Brazil's proto-Keynesianism were not fully anticipated, but there was a broad recognition, including within the manufacturing sector, that the health of the economy was tied to coffee, that support for coffee did not mean neglect of industry, and that a passive stance by the government was unacceptable.[10] If we consider an industrialization strategy only as a consistent package of policies backed by a clear theoretical rationale, then ISI came late, perhaps not until the mid-1950s. If we relax the criteria to include an activist response to external shocks, then 1930 is a turning point for Brazil. Import and exchange controls were used to manage foreign-exchange constraints, and the federal stance toward foreign creditors became more aggressive. Exemptions were extended to imported intermediates and capital, but import restrictions on goods "similar" to those manufactured in Brazil were maintained. Such policies were parallel to later ISI policies.[11]

To what extent can these changes be explained by social forces. Did the 1930 revolution or the Estado Novo signal the political ascendence of the bourgeoisie?[12] The end of the Republic marked a *relative* decline in the political power of the coffee planters, if only because new groups increased their voice in the political process. During the 1930s industrial organizations grew. Vargas was not adverse to consulting them, and some representatives of the private sector articulated a nationalist project calling for state support for industry.[13] But the private sector feared that state-corporatist structures would become instruments of control and unwanted intervention, and São Paulo business allied itself with the opposition. In addition, the central policy innovations of the period were a response to the interests of coffee, not manufacturing.

This "bourgeois ascendence" interpretation overlooks the fact that industrialization had other backers, including political and military elites. Nationalist ideologies, including those advanced by the military, equated modernization with industrial growth but overlapped only partially with private-sector views, particularly in the emphasis they placed

10. Stanley Hilton, "Vargas and Brazilian Economic Development, 1930–1945: A Reappraisal of His Attitude toward Industrialization and Planning," *Journal of Economic History* 35 (December 1975): 754–78; Eugene W. Ridings, "Class Sector Unity in an Export Economy: The Case of Nineteenth Century Brazil," *Hispanic American Historical Review* 58, 3 (1978): 432–50.

11. Annibal V. Villela and Wilson Suzigan, *Government Policy and the Economic Growth of Brazil: 1889–1945* (Rio de Janeiro: Instituto de Planejamento Econômico e Social/ Instituto de Pesquisas, 1977), p. 287; Hilton, "Vargas," p. 761.

12. See Flynn, *Brazil*, p. 88.

13. See Eli Diniz, *Empresário, estado, e capitalismo no Brasil: 1930–1945* (Rio de Janeiro: Paz e Terra, 1978); Eli Diniz and Renato Raul Boschi, *Empresariado nacional e estado no Brasil* (Rio de Janeiro: Forense-Universitária, 1978); M. Antonietta P. Leopoldi, "Industrial Associations and Politics in Contemporary Brazil" (D.Phil. diss., St. Anthony's College, Oxford, 1984), chap. 2.

on planning.[14] Among the institutional innovations that expanded state power were a federal council on foreign trade, a precursor to later planning agencies, an agricultural and industrial credit department at the Bank of Brazil, new ministries of labor and industry and commerce, and a department for the administration of public services. Vargas also launched wide-ranging reforms of the bureaucracy and redefined tax jurisdictions at the expense of state and municipal governments.[15] Not all of these innovations were successful, but they expanded the ability of state actors to define and act on an independent policy agenda.

Contrary to the argument that supply interruptions necessarily promote manufacturing growth, industrial production from 1940 through 1945 grew at only half the rate from 1933 through 1939.[16] War-related shortages and the national security concerns of the military pushed Vargas to support industrialization, however. Brazil's first planning efforts had their origins among a cadre of technicians located in the newly formed Administrative Department of Public Services. The United States encouraged these efforts with technical missions, on the grounds that they would free resources for the war; collaborative efforts deepened over the late 1940s and early 1950s.[17] At the army's instigation, the government also became directly involved in production for the first time, building the first integrated steel mill in Latin America.[18]

Mexico

In Mexico the Depression compounded much more fundamental problems of reconstruction. The disruption of the Revolution was not ubiquitous, but the damage to the country's infrastructure was substantial.[19] Agricultural and manufacturing production fell sharply, and the financial system was in complete disarray. Though exports diversified during the 1920s and import substitution advanced, Clark Reynolds nonetheless argues that "the Revolution which had been partly a reac-

14. Stanley Hilton, "Military Influence on Brazilian Economic Policy, 1930–1945: A Different View," *Hispanic American Historical Review* 53 (February 1973): 71–94.

15. For a review of early administrative reforms, see Barbara Geddes, "Building 'State' Autonomy in Brazil, 1930–1964," *Comparative Politics* (forthcoming 1990).

16. Villela and Suzigan, *Government Policy*, p. 139.

17. For a comprehensive review of Brazilian planning efforts, see Roberto de Oliveira Campos, "A Retrospect over Brazilian Development Plans," in Howard S. Ellis, ed., *The Economy of Brazil* (Berkeley: University of California Press, 1969), pp. 317–44; Joint Brazil–United States Economic Development Commission, *The Development of Brazil* (Washington, D.C.: Institute of Inter-American Affairs, 1954).

18. On the initiation of state-owned enterprise in Brazil see Wirth, *Politics.*

19. On the unevenness of the economic effects of the revolution see John Womack, "The Mexican Economy during the Revolution, 1910–1920: Historiography and Analysis," *Marxist Perspectives* 1 (Winter 1978): 80–123.

tion against increasing dualism . . . resulted in an even more dualistic structure of trade and production than before."[20]

As in Brazil, the Depression kindled a debate on economic policy. Orthodoxy was ultimately jettisoned. In 1932 a new economic team abandoned defense of the exchange rate and pursued expansionary monetary and fiscal policies. Tariff changes in 1936–37 protected industry. The dramatic nationalization of foreign oil companies in 1938 redefined the state's role in production.[21] These changes cannot be adequately explained simply as responses to the external shock. Contractionary forces were felt in Mexico as early as 1925, but the government initially followed American advice, maintaining the official gold parity and a balanced budget.[22] By the mid-1930s recovery was already under way, but policy became more interventionist.

Economic policy must be viewed, rather, as a by-product of political consolidation.[23] After the revolution central power was weak, consisting largely of personalistic ties among key military leaders. Not until the ascendence of the "Sonoran dynasty" in 1920 did the central government gain power vis-à-vis regional *caciques* and other organized social groups. The executive exploited political crises, including armed rebellions in 1920, 1923, 1927, and 1929, to form a national army. The creation of a national political party and an independent party bureaucracy further enhanced presidential power.

Before the gradual forging of a new political order, the capacity of the Mexican government to intervene in the economy was extremely limited; institutional change was a crucial prerequisite for policy change, indeed, for any "policy" at all. The first step, during the 1920s, was the reconstruction of the financial system, a task closely linked to the renegotiation of Mexico's external debt.[24] The founding of the Central Bank institutionalized close cooperation between the Ministry of Finance and the private banks and formed the basis for a conservative

20. Clark Reynolds, *The Mexican Economy: Twentieth-Century Structure and Growth* (New Haven: Yale University Press, 1970), p. 205; E. V. K. Fitzgerald, "Restructuring through the Depression: The State and Capital Accumulation in Mexico, 1925–1940," in Thorp, *Latin America in the 1930s*, pp. 242–78.

21. Enrique Cárdenas, "The Great Depression and Industrialisation: The Case of Mexico," in Thorp, *Latin America in the 1930s*, p. 225; Robert Freeman Smith, "The Morrow Mission and the International Commission of Bankers on Mexico," *Journal of Latin American Studies* 1 (November 1969): 149–66.

22. On the expropriation of the oil companies see Lorenzo Meyer, *Mexico and the United States in the Oil Controversy, 1917–1942* (Austin: University of Texas Press, 1977).

23. On the processes of political consolidation in the 1920s and early 1930s see Lorenzo Meyer, *El conflicto social y los gobiernos del Maximato*, Historia de la Revolución Mexicana, vol. 13 (Mexico City: El Colegio de México, 1978).

24. Smith, "The Morrow Mission."

"policy current" within the government.[25] The reform also provided a crucial instrument through which the government could manage the economy. The reorganization of the ministries of Finance and Economy and the centralization of the taxation system had a similar effect.

The social costs of the Depression helped reverse the conservative policy trend of the late 1920s, as in Brazil, but the pattern and extent of social mobilization in Mexico differed from that in Brazil.[26] In seeking to build an independent political base against the conservative Sonorans, Lazaro Cárdenas turned to organized labor, the peasantry, and a revolutionary legacy for support. Cárdenas mobilized peasants and workers into new organizations that were, in turn, integrated into a restructured political party. He endorsed a populist and nationalist program that included increased land distribution, expanded rights for labor, and expropriation of foreign investment in natural resources. Despite continual battles between organized business and the government, business organization and participation in government grew under Cárdenas, and new institutions, such as the Nacional Financiera (1933), extended assistance to manufacturing. Cárdenas's rural-oriented philosophy was not compatible with a sustained commitment to industry, however, and did much to antagonize it.[27]

The reversal of Cárdenas's nationalist-populist experiment under his successor, Manuel Avila Camacho (1940–46), was a crucial turning point in Mexico's economic policy.[28] Cárdenismo represented an assault on the privileges of powerful groups. Small landowners feared the newly mobilized peasantry as much as the latifundistas did. Support for labor, inflationary fiscal and monetary policies, devaluation, an excess-profits tax, expropriations, and price controls alienated foreign and local business, which could easily move money across the border into the United States. After 1938 economic performance sagged, and the reform momentum slowed. A coalition of conservative politicians, backed finally by the labor leadership and the highly manipulable peasant unions, supported Avila Camacho's compromise candidacy against Cár-

25. Sylvia Maxfield, *Governing Capital: International Finance and Mexican Politics* (Ithaca: Cornell University Press, 1990).

26. Ruth Berins Collier, "Popular Sector Incorporation and Political Supremacy: Regime Evolution in Brazil and Mexico," in Hewlett and Weinert, *Brazil and Mexico*, pp. 82–83.

27. Stanley Mosk, *Industrial Revolution in Mexico* (Berkeley: University of California Press, 1950), pp. 21–31.

28. See Ariel Jose Contreras, *México 1940: Industrialización y crisis política* (Mexico City: Siglo XXI, 1977); Nora Hamilton, *The Limits of State Autonomy* (Princeton: Princeton University Press, 1982); Albert L. Michaels, "The Crisis of Cardenismo," *Journal of Latin American Studies* 2, 1 (1970): 51–80.

denas's chosen successor. Segments of the private sector remained wary of the government and even backed an independent candidate, but the end of Cárdenismo opened the way for a new business-state alliance in support of industrialization.[29] Subsequent economic programs were also influenced by large landowners who had gained access to land through their "revolutionary" connections.[30]

The war played an important role in cementing this alliance, providing an additional rationale for intervention and creating a "New Group" of industrialists in the region around Mexico City.[31] Unlike the more established and politically independent regionally based groups, the New Group of import-substituting manufacturers lacked close ties with the private banking system, accepted a conciliatory posture toward labor, showed skepticism about foreign investment, and sought an activist state to promote and protect industry. In response to wartime shortages of consumer goods, these firms were granted special customs and tax exemptions under the 1941 Law of Industries—a turning point in Mexican industrial policy.[32] In 1942 they formed a new business association, known as CANACINTRA. In 1944 an import-licensing system was established, launching a "buy Mexican" campaign. Additional supports were extended under a revised Industry Law in 1945 designed to protect industries developed during the war from foreign competition.

Under Avila Camacho, earlier institutional developments took on a completely new meaning. The government could use its control over labor to advance industrialization. Following purges of leftists within the official union structure, a more tractable labor leadership adopted a new tactical path: unity of the working class with industry in the name of "national development." State mediation of labor-management disputes, the imposition of labor leaders from above, and direct repression dramatically reduced labor's power.[33]

---

29. For a lucid analysis of the factions surrounding the 1940 election, see Albert Michaels, "The Mexican Election of 1940," Council on International Studies, State University of New York at Buffalo, Special Studies 5 (September 1971).

30. Cynthia Hewitt de Alcantra, *Modernizing Mexican Agriculture* (Geneva: United Nations Institute for Social Development, 1976).

31. Mosk, *Industrial Revolution*, pp. 21–31.

32. On the evolution of planning efforts see Leopoldo Solis, *Planes de desarrollo económico y social en México* (Mexico City: SepSetentas, 1975).

33. On the evolution of ideas within the government see Ruben Vargas Austin, "The Development of Economic Policy in Mexico with Special Reference to Economic Doctrines" (Ph.D. diss., University of Iowa, 1958). Austin shows the emergence in the 1930s of a new group of economists influenced by Keynes and Haberler, and by Argentina's countercyclical policies.

Institutions and the Origins of ISI

Routes to the consolidation of political power were quite different in Brazil and Mexico, and this difference had some effect on economic policy. In Brazil during the Estado Novo, landed interests were accommodated within an authoritarian-corporatist political structure. The state's penetration of the countryside was minimal, but the military played an important role in advancing interventionist industrial policies. In Mexico, Cárdenas led a rural-populist experiment that resulted in significant redistribution of land and relied on labor support to carry out an ambitious nationalization of firms in the petroleum sector. Cárdenas's commitment to industry was much less marked than Vargas's, however.

These differences should not overshadow some broad similarities. The economic effects of the Depression are subject to some debate, but it is clear that the external constraints imposed by the Depression and World War II pushed both Brazilian and Mexican political elites toward policy experimentation. The 1930s and the war years were a period of institutional change. Centralization of political authority, the creation of new economic instruments, and a strengthening of economic bureaucracies were crucial prerequisites for an expanded state role in guiding the next phase of industrialization.

Toward Secondary ISI

By the early 1950s substitution in light manufactures was relatively far advanced in Brazil and Mexico. Rather than simply extend protection and assistance to existing industries, further import substitution demanded the identification of investment opportunities in new sectors, such as consumer durables, intermediates, and capital goods. The role of the state grew. Planning functions expanded, state-owned enterprises and banks increased their role, and the government became more active in soliciting foreign capital.

What accounts for this shift in orientation? One argument holds that the existence of comparative advantage in agriculture and raw materials production was a crucial constraint. Given such an endowment, outward-oriented policies such as devaluation and trade liberalization would favor the agro-export sector over manufacturing. Industrialization could come about only through protectionist policies.[34]

34. I was alerted to this argument by Albert Fishlow. See Marcelo Diamand, "Overcoming Argentina's Stop-and-Go Cycles," in Jonathan Hartlyn and Samuel A. Morley, eds., *Latin American Political Economy* (Boulder, Colo.: Westview, 1986), pp. 129–64.

This argument has some merit, but it begs the question why industrialization was a political goal in the first place. Local manufacturers, segments of the labor movement and middle classes, and foreign firms certainly had an interest in continuing an inward-looking industrial course. Yet these groups were not the originators of *new* industrial policy initiatives, and they greeted some measures, such as an expanded role for the state, the entry of foreign firms, and protection for intermediates and capital goods, with ambivalence.

Political elites and technocrats are equally if not more important in formulating deepening initiatives and constructing new political coalitions around them. Once again, external constraints and economic ideologies play a role in explaining behavior. The late 1940s and early 1950s saw new balance-of-payments problems in Brazil and Mexico. New intellectual frameworks in both countries identified the challenges as structural, demanding strategic action by the state.

Brazil

The end of the war made the Estado Novo politically anachronistic, but it took the military to dislodge Vargas and reintroduce democracy.[35] General Enrico Gaspar Dutra won the presidency with the support of a broad coalition that included some landowners and industrialists, Estado Novo politicians, and portions of the working class coopted by new welfare benefits. The breadth of this coalition revealed several features of Brazil's new democracy: the nonprogrammatic nature of political alliances, the weakness of political parties, and the importance of clientelistic politics.[36] Over the protests of industry, however, Dutra initially steered a liberal economic course, dismantling the system of wartime controls, liberalizing imports, and stabilizing the economy. Minister of Finance Pedro Luís Correia e Castro defended the strategy of international specialization by arguing that "the essence of the Latin American economy . . . is a certain concentration of effort in the export of primary products and foodstuffs."[37]

These policies did not last. Imports surged, and by 1947 the reserves accumulated during the war were exhausted. Forced to choose domestic contraction, devaluation, or controls on trade and exchange, Dutra opted for the last, maintaining an overvalued exchange rate. Opposition to the first option is predictable, but unwillingness to devalue bears

---

35. On the military's continuing veto power see Alfred Stepan, *The Military in Politics: Changing Patterns in Brazil* (Princeton: Princeton University Press, 1971), pp. 253–71.

36. On these characteristics of the Brazilian political system see Philippe Schmitter, *Interest Conflict and Political Change in Brazil* (Stanford: Stanford University Press, 1971).

37. Quoted in Wirth, *Politics of Brazilian Development*, p. 70.

examination. The reason for it lies in part with the peculiar position of coffee in the Brazilian economy and of Brazil within the world coffee market. The price inelasticity of foreign demand and Brazil's position as a dominant supplier meant devaluation could actually lower coffee prices. The choice of controls and the maintenance of an overvalued rate therefore cannot be taken as a political victory for industry. Nonetheless, as in the 1930s and 1940s, policy experimentation in response to external shocks favored local manufacturing.[38]

The election of 1950 marked a shift in Brazilian political life and economic policy. Rural-based elites still constituted an important bloc within Congress, but industrialization had increased the political weight of urban interests—labor; the professional, managerial, and bureaucratic middle class; and the manufacturing sector. Weaving together a coalition of these disparate groups was the essence of the second Vargas (1950–1954) and Kubitschek (1955–1959) administrations.

However, developmentalist economic policies led, as much as followed, the interests of this new coalition. Labor's interests were vaguely defined and partly manipulable because of the state-corporatist structures inherited from the Estado Novo. Portions of the middle class were skeptical of an expansion of the state's role in the economy, because the practical implication was an increased clientelism. Drawing on professional middle-class support, the anti-Vargas National Democratic Union (UDN) favored sound fiscal and monetary policies, openness to foreign capital, and relative freedom of trade and capital movements.

The question of business influence on economic policy has been the source of on-going controversy.[39] Business organizations certainly supported an industrializing project and were brought into the government in new ways during the second Vargas and Kubitschek administrations, but business strongly opposed some policies central to the new strategy, such as granting preferential treatment to foreign firms. The search for business influence, as in the literature on the Estado Novo ignores other factors affecting policy, including external shocks, the analytic frameworks of technocrats, and the interests of politicians.

38. Nathaniel Leff, *Economic Policy-Making and Development in Brazil, 1947–1964* (New York: John Wiley, 1968), pp. 14–15; Leopoldi, "Industrial Associations," chap. 2. A crucial early debate over planning appears in Eugenio Gudin and Roberto C. Simonsen, *A controversía do planejamento na econômia brasiliera* (Rio de Janeiro: Instituto de Planejamento Econômico e Social/Instituto de Pesquisas, 1978).

39. Leff, *Economic Policy-Making,* and Flynn, *Brazil,* stake out opposing positions on business influence, with Leff arguing the case for state autonomy from business interests. New evidence has been provided by Leopoldi, "Industrial Associations," chap. 6, and Kathryn Sikkink, "Developmentalism and Democracy: Ideas, Institutions, and Economic Policy Making in Brazil and Argentina (1955–1962)" (Ph.D. diss., Columbia University, 1988), pp. 247–50.

Vargas's own propensity toward statism was visible in plans for investment in basic industries and infrastructure, the creation of the Banco Nacional de Desenvolvimento Económico (BNDE) in 1952, nationalizations in the oil and electricity sectors, and the centralization of economic decision making. Each of these actions served specific political ends,[40] but all addressed new economic problems. During the first two years of the second Vargas regime, export earnings declined. Events reached a crisis by mid-1953. Brazil ultimately attained a small current-account surplus in 1953 and again in 1956, but the combination of rapid, inflationary growth, expanding imports, and stagnation of the export sector, caused in part by the end of the Korean War boom, produced payments deficits. The initial government response to these constraints was far from coherent. Efforts to woo foreign investors were undermined by major nationalizations, and stabilization plans routinely failed. Nonetheless, the external crisis led to a multiple exchange-rate regime that protected the domestic market for import-substituting firms while guaranteeing access to needed imports of intermediate and capital goods.

The Kubitschek regime was a milestone in the evolution of Brazilian import-substitution because of the integrated way in which it approached the task. Immediately on taking office, Juscelino Kubitschek established a National Development Council to oversee the "Targets Program," which accorded priority to vertical integration and investment in the social capital to support it.[41] The actual investment plans were the work of a group of technical experts at the BNDE, who built on previous work by the Joint Brazil–United States Economic Development Commission, a BNDE-ECLA study group, and structuralist ideas.[42] This set of intellectual influences may seem contradictory, but a surprising convergence existed between the earlier work of the Joint Commission and the structuralists on several points, including the need to "rationalize" economic decision making and to provide infrastructural support and incentives to foster import substitution.

Realizing the plan's goals demanded an expansion of the state's role in the economy. The government's share in gross fixed capital formation, excluding the state-owned enterprise sector, rose from 25 percent from 1953–56 to 37 percent at the end of the decade. New policies also served to channel resources to the private sector. Provisions were made to

---

40. On the SALTE Plan and the formation of the BNDE see Eliza Willis, "The State as Banker: The Expansion of the Public Sector in Brazil" (Ph.D. diss., University of Texas, 1986), pp. 138–80; on the nationalizations see Wirth, *Politics*, pp. 93–100; on the centralization of decision making see Leopoldi, "Industrial Associations," chap. 2.

41. "Fifteen Years of Economic Policy in Brazil," *Economic Bulletin for Latin America* 9 (November 1964): 159.

42. Sikkink, "Developmentalism and Democracy," pp. 59–74; Willis, "State as Banker," pp. 59–63.

expand the availability of foreign capital to domestic entrepreneurs through the state-owned BNDE. The tariff reform of 1957 established a tariff council composed of business, labor, and government representatives. The council consolidated the Law of Similars, which restricted import of goods similar to those manufactured in Brazil, and expanded exemptions for inputs and capital goods. Government-business relations were also strengthened through the Grupos Executivos, which determined the scale and scope of sectoral programs for leading or "impulse" sectors.[43]

Realizing plan objectives also demanded a courting of foreign aid and a revision in the government's posture toward foreign investment.[44] Technological and organizational considerations were important in this step, since targeted sectors such as automobiles were not viable without substantial foreign participation. Balance-of-payments considerations were also a pressing factor. In 1955 Instruction 113 empowered the government to grant preferential exchange rates for profit remittances and amortization of direct investment, a move domestic firms protested as discriminatory.[45] This legislation reflected a pattern that would become even more pronounced under the post–1964 military government: a role for foreign and state enterprises relatively larger than in Mexico (see chapter 8).

Mexico

The major political change permitting greater support for industry in Mexico, as argued above, was the reversal of Cárdenas's reformism. The new policy was also pushed along by external constraints and the close relationship forged between government and segments of business during the war.[46] A protectionist Industry Law in 1945 countered foreign

43. On the relationship between the state and the private sector under Kubitschek see Leopoldi, "Industrial Associations," chap. 6, and Sikkink, "Developmentalism and Democracy," pp. 255–57. On the Grupos Executivos see Celso Lafer, "The Planning Process and the Political System in Brazil: A Study of Kubitschek's Target Plan, 1956–1960" (Ph.D. diss., Cornell University, 1970).

44. The role of foreign direct investment in the deepening strategy is the theme of Peter Evans, *Dependent Development: The Alliance of Multinational, State, and Foreign Capital in Brazil* (Princeton: Princeton University Press, 1978).

45. Leff, *Economic Policy-Making*, pp. 59–66.

46. On business-government relations in Mexico see Robert J. Shafer, *Mexican Business Organizations: History and Analysis* (Syracuse: Syracuse University Press, 1973); Sylvia Maxfield and Ricardo Anzaldua Montoya, eds., *Government and Private Sector in Contemporary Mexico* (La Jolla: Center for U.S.-Mexican Studies, University of California, San Diego, 1987). For a guide to the factions of national capital, see Elvira Conchiero, Antonio Guitierrez, and Juan Manual Fragoso, *El poder de la gran burguesia* (Mexico City: Ediciones de Cultura Popular, 1979). For examples of business demands during this period, see Raymond Vernon, *The Dilemma of Mexico's Development* (Cambridge: Harvard University Press, 1965), p. 162.

competition and a deteriorating balance of payments. The government of Avila Camacho's successor, Miguel Alemán (1946–52), accelerated the retreat from Cárdenismo. During his election campaign Alemán actively solicited business opinion and vowed to continue protection and subsidies for industry. Alemán continued the purge of PRI-affiliated unions and the consolidation of a conservative union leadership. Despite periodic labor eruptions—following a devaluation in 1954 and from teachers and railway workers in 1958–59—this structure played a role in containing labor demands and helps explain why ISI in Mexico occurred with greater price stability than in Brazil.

Despite control over labor, the creation of the conservative Bank of Mexico in 1925, and the relatively prominent position of the Ministry of Finance in decision making, development policies in the immediate postwar period were as inflationary as Brazil's. As in Brazil, the demand for imports exhausted wartime reserves. Unlike Brazil, however, Mexico devalued in 1948, perhaps because of its greater vulnerability to capital flight. The Korean War boom again accelerated inflation; the end of the boom and a decline in exports threatened a recurrent cycle of inflation, capital flight, and devaluations.

Inflation generated strong political concerns. One reason was the existence of a substantial private financial sector and the ease of capital flight. The deterioration of real wages also played a role in policy calculations because of the centrality of organized labor within the PRI structure.[47] With his political tenure secure, President Ruíz Cortines (1952–58) could afford to give top priority to slowing inflation following his election. He dramatically increased the authority of the Bank of Mexico and the Ministry of Finance in the formulation of economic policy.[48] The government took the unpopular measure of reversing the loose fiscal policy of the Alemán administration and, over substantial protest, undertook an anticipatory devaluation in 1954. Orthodox macroeconomic policies were maintained: Central Bank authority to raise reserve requirements expanded in order to finance public-sector deficits.

If macroeconomic policy was orthodox, industrial policies were increasingly activist. External factors help explain why. "Técnicos" within the economic bureaucracy interpreted the balance-of-payments problems of the late 1940s and early 1950s, and the deterioration in 1953 in

47. On the concerns of the Ruíz Cortines administration in supporting devaluation see Olga Pellicer de Brody and Esteban L. Mancilla, *El entendimiento con los Estados Unidos y la gestación del desarrollo establizador*, Historia de la Revolución Mexicana, vol. 23 (Mexico City: El Colegio de México, 1978), pp. 117–36.
48. On the influence of the "tecnicos" on economic policy see Vernon, *Dilemmas*, pp. 125–53.

particular, as structural rather than cyclical. As in Brazil, such analysis provided the rationale for the development of a more comprehensive strategy of import substitution.[49] The ideas of the U.N. Economic Commission are visible in important analyses of the economy done by Mexican economists, though there was also a surprising degree of support from external actors. The report of a Combined Working Party of World Bank and Mexican economists, for example, complained about the inefficiency of Mexican policy but not about its basic thrust. Over the long term, the report concluded, Mexican industry could not rely on either existing domestic markets or exports, only "on the expansion of the domestic market and on the possibilities of substituting domestic for imported manufactures."[50]

The year 1954 was a turning point. Fiscal policy, in addition to the devaluation, became more active in support of industry through a series of tax exemptions. Protection was broadened in the same year.[51] In 1955 the Law of New and Necessary Industries was promulgated, formalizing administrative procedures on import restrictions, easing the import of capital goods, and granting new fiscal incentives. As the name of law suggests, it aimed at creating new industries rather than simply granting protection to existing ones, and it provided for consultation between government and private sector. Despite initial signs of a populist orientation, the López Mateos administration (1958–64) exhibited continuity with its predecessors in seeking to extend the ISI process. The government began to elaborate lists of goods deemed feasible for substitution and pressed importers for commitments on domestic production. Import licenses were granted only on the condition that production programs lead to at least 60 percent local content. The promotion of industry was aided by the state's role as financier.[52] From 1947 Nacional Financiera (NAFIN) devoted increasing attention to heavy-industry and public-sector investments. By 1960, 50 percent of NAFIN's outstanding

49. Structuralist ideas were articulated in Mexico as early as 1949 by J. Noyola. See his later "El desarrollo económico y la inflación en México y otros paises Latinoamericanos," *Investigación Económica* 16, 4 (1956); the joint World Bank–Mexican study by Ortiz Mena, Victor Urquidi, Albert Wasterston, and Jonas Horalz, *El desarrollo económico de Mexico y su capacidad para absorber capital del exterior* (Mexico City: Fondo de Cultura Económico, 1953); and the early work of CEPAL's Mexico office, headed by Urquidi, described in Rene Villareal, *El disequilibro externo en la industrialización de México, 1929–1975* (Mexico City: Fondo de Cultura Económico, 1976), pp. 58–67.

50. See *The Economic Development of Mexico: Report of the Combined Mexican Working Party* (Baltimore: Johns Hopkins University Press for the World Bank, 1953), pp. 80, 82.

51. On the range of actions undertaken see Villareal, *El disequilibro*, pp. 58–67; Timothy King, *Mexico: Trade and Industrial Policies since 1940* (London: Oxford University Press, 1970), chap. 5.

52. On NAFIN's role see Nacional Financiera and CEPAL, *La política industrial en la desarrollo económico de México* (Mexico City: NAFINSA, 1971).

credits and securities were in ten firms that had NAFIN as a majority shareholder; another 20 percent was in three state-owned firms.

The new policies encouraged the formation of large, diversified economic groups, usually centered on banks.[53] These groups were in the forefront of forming joint ventures with foreign investors lured by the new industrial policies. The turn to foreign investment in the mid-1950s was, as in Brazil, a self-conscious component of secondary ISI. Private savings, it was believed, had reached a stable limit, but increased government savings through tax reforms were deemed unlikely because of business resistance. Between 1953 and 1957 the desirability of foreign investment was hotly debated by business groups that had a more institutionalized relationship with the state than any in Brazil.[54] CANACINTRA lobbied for restrictive provisions, but the Ruíz Cortines administration saw foreign investment as crucial, the older industrial chambers were strongly supportive, and CANACINTRA itself gradually became less strident on the issue.[55] Adolfo López Mateos nationalized two remaining foreign-owned power companies and restricted foreign access in the mining sector, but foreign investment in manufacturing was welcomed.

A final similarity with Brazil concerns the expansion of the state's direct role in production. Between 1940 and 1970 state enterprises established a presence in metals, transport equipment, chemicals, and fertilizers, all industries deemed basic to the ISI drive. By 1965, thirteen of the largest one hundred industrial firms were parastatal, and all but one had been formed between 1940 and 1960. The state also expanded its role through selective expropriations, including the expropriation of foreign-based electric utilities in 1960. In general, state investment complemented private capital, flowing into sectors linked with domestic firms but having lower rates of return, a pattern visible in Korea, Taiwan, and Singapore as well.

The Transition to Secondary ISI

Coalition factors were propitious to the change of strategy in Brazil and Mexico. The influence of agro-export elites over economic policy had undergone a steady decline, even if their rural bases of power

53. See Salvadero Cordero, "Concentración y poder económico en México," Cuadernos del Centro de Estudios Sociologicos 18 (Mexico City: Colegio de México, 1977), and the debates over which fraction of capital—financial or industrial—was "dominant." J. F. Leal, La burguesia y el estado mexicano (Mexico City: El Caballito, 1972).

54. On the debates over foreign direct investment see Pellicer de Brody and Mancilla, El entendimiento con los Estados Unidos, pp. 117–36.

55. On the conversion of CANACINTRA to support for foreign investment see Dale Story, "Industrial Elites in Mexico: Political Ideology and Influence," Journal of Interamerican Studies and World Affairs 25 (August 1983): 351–76.

remained firm. Manufacturing capital and the urban working class had grown in size and political importance, and both groups had been integrated into ruling political coalitions, albeit in different ways: in Brazil through a cross-class electoral alliance, in Mexico through the organizational efforts of a dominant party. These political differences help explain variations in macroeconomic policy in the two countries: the interest in stabilizing and ability to stabilize in Mexico, and the greater tolerance of inflation in Brazil.

Given the new "correlation of forces," it is not surprising that political elites had an interest in the new ISI project and used it for their own coalition-building purposes. The new emphasis on industry promised rapid growth and had broad nationalist appeal. Yet the formulation of the new policies grew out of sophisticated structuralist analyses that began to appear by the late 1940s and early 1950s, largely in response to growing external constraints. These analyses exercised particular influence among "técnicos" but found a surprising degree of support within the international development policy community as well. The new developmentalism provided a framework for understanding external constraints and provided support for an industrializing project that shaped, as well as responded to, coalitional interests.

THE THIRD PHASE OF ISI:
DEBT-LED GROWTH AND EXPORT PROMOTION

The final period of ISI, from the mid-1960s in Brazil and the early 1970s in Mexico to the debt crises of the 1980s, was a long and eventful one. Both countries faced new balance-of-payments constraints, which stemmed in part from the oil shocks but also from vulnerabilities associated with the import-substitution strategy itself. In response both governments sought to expand nontraditional exports, in Brazil's case with substantial success. Efforts to promote exports were frequently at odds with macroeconomic, exchange-rate, and tariff policy, however, and neither country departed fundamentally from its commitment to ISI. The reasons can be found in the continuing force of ISI interests and ideologies, not only in the private sector but in the government itself. Despite their authoritarian structures, both governments faced strong political pressures to maintain high levels of economic growth. In Brazil these pressures resulted from an extended transition to democratic rule; in Mexico, from electoral pressures and the emergence of new opposition forces. The commitment to an expansionist ISI program had consequences that included an expanded role for the state in the economy and a dramatic increase in external indebtedness.

Bureaucratic Authoritarianism in Brazil

In *Modernization and Bureaucratic Authoritarianism,* Guillermo O'Donnell argued that the 1964 military coup in Brazil resulted in part from the dictates of a new "deepening" strategy.[56] I have argued that deepening had its origins in the mid-1950s and combined populist appeals with developmentalist ideas. If economic factors contributed to military intervention—and this point remains debatable (see Chapter 10)—the culprit was inflation. Inflation aggravated distributional conflicts, weakened business confidence, and activated labor to defend real wages.[57] Similarly, if military intervention was functional for a set of economic policies, it was not for deepening but stabilization.[58] As in other Southern Cone bureaucratic-authoritarian regimes, a new team of technocrats was initially given the freedom to impose austerity by freezing wages, cutting government expenditures, raising taxes, and restricting credit.

For the technocrats, the stabilization exercise was a wedge to begin wide-ranging reforms that would alter the institutional and political arrangements held responsible for misguided policy in the first place.[59] The Ministry of Planning increased its power over the budget process, and a newly created Central Bank imposed a global monetary budget. Financial markets were liberalized. Dependency theorists have emphasized that this new course had an important external dimension, in the new opening to foreign direct investment.[60] The wooing of foreign investment was not new, though, and by the early 1970s the importance of foreign direct investment was dwarfed by the growth of foreign borrowing. Nonetheless, it is true that João Goulart's populist politics did deter foreign investors in the early 1960s. The new government quickly repealed a restrictive 1962 law on profit remittances and actively advertised a changed investment climate. The new policy course also smoothed relations with the United States and the multilateral agencies.[61]

In Brazil, as in the East Asian NICs, such policy reforms rested on

56. Guillermo O'Donnell, *Modernization and Bureaucratic Authoritarianism* (Berkeley: Institute of International Studies, University of California, 1973), pp. 60–69. For a review of the debate, see David Collier, ed., *The New Authoritarianism in Latin America* (Princeton: Princeton University Press, 1979).

57. Michael Wallerstein, "The Collapse of Democracy in Brazil," *Latin American Research Review* 15, 3 (1980): 3–40.

58. Albert Fishlow, "Some Reflections on Post-1964 Brazilian Economic Policy," in Alfred Stepan, ed., *Authoritarian Brazil* (New Haven: Yale University Press, 1973), pp. 84–97.

59. Campos, "A Retrospect," pp. 317–44.

60. Fernando Henrique Cardoso, "Associated-Dependent Development: Theoretical and Practical Implications," in Stepan, *Authoritarian Brazil,* pp. 142–78.

61. On American foreign policy toward Brazil during the coup period see Phyllis Parker, *Brazil: The Quiet Intervention* (Austin: University of Texas, 1979).

substantial political autonomy. Through the early 1970s the "hardliners" within the military dominated the government's political strategy, which became increasingly repressive. The government subjected organized labor to repression and controls reminiscent of the Estado Novo. Populist political leaders were banned from politics. The Second Institutional Act of 1965 abolished political parties, suspended basic political rights, concentrated authority in the hands of the president, and made his election indirect. Some reforms demanded autonomy not only from the working class, which bore the costs of stabilization, but from the private sector as well. Local industry expressed concerns about credit restrictions, the greater openness to foreign investors, and the intention to reduce protection and subsidization of industry.

In 1967 the emphasis on stabilization was abandoned, both because objectives had been achieved and because the military needed to revive support among the domestic private sector and middle classes.[62] The new team concurred with its orthodox predecessors on the importance of "rationalizing" and depoliticizing economic policy making but showed basic continuity with earlier structuralist thinking in the tolerance for inflation and the emphasis it placed on state intervention in support of industry.

The period from 1968 through 1973 is considered the "Brazilian miracle," but a fundamental continuity in policy runs throughout the 1970s.[63] Neoclassical accounts have emphasized reforms designed to nudge Brazil in a more outward-looking direction: new export subsidies, a reduction of protection, and a policy of minidevaluations. These export-promoting measures had some success, but the history of import substitution had created an industrial structure and political interests that limited the range of reform and influenced the instruments the government could use to achieve its objectives. Export promotion, ac-

62. On the links between the private sector and the state under the military see Sergio Abranches, "The Divided Leviathan: State and Economic Policy Formation in Authoritarian Brazil" (Ph.D. diss., Cornell University, 1978).

63. For competing interpretations of the "miracle," see Edmar Bacha, "Issues and Evidence on Recent Brazilian Economic Growth," *World Development* 5, 1/2 (1977): 46–67; Werner Baer, *Industrialization and Economic Development in Brazil* (New Haven: Yale University Press, 1975); Bela Balassa, "Incentive Policies in Brazil," *World Development* 7 (1979): 1023–42; José Roberto Mendonça de Barros and Douglas Graham, "The Brazilian Economic Miracle Revisited: Private and Public Sector Initiative in a Market Economy," *Latin American Research Review* 13, 2 (1978): 5–38; Celso Furtado, *Analise do modelo brasileiro* (Rio de Janeiro: Civilização Brasileira, 1972). Albert Fishlow shows the continuity of policy through the 1970s, in "A Tale of Two Presidents: The Political Economy of Crisis Management," in Alfred Stepan, ed., *Democratizing Brazil* (New York: Oxford University Press, 1989), pp. 83–119, while Antonio Barros de Castro and Francisco Eduardo Pires de Souza defend the "big push," in *A economia brasileira em marcha forçada* (Rio de Janeiro: Paz e Terra, 1985).

cording to Bela Balassa, "involved superimposing a system of export incentives on the system of import protection." Import protection continued at relatively high levels, and the large dispersion in protection among different product categories necessitated a battery of subsidies to offset adverse affects on exports.[64]

The effort to promote exports may not have constituted an abandonment of ISI as a broad strategy, but changes did occur in the sectoral emphasis of industrial policy, the role of the state, and relations with international financial markets. The military government initially emphasized the production of consumer durables, an approach harshly criticized by opponents for its reliance on a narrowly "middle-class" market.[65] Gradually this focus was supplemented by the promotion of intermediate and capital goods. This sectoral emphasis entailed an expansion of the state-owned enterprise sector. Between 1968 and 1974 state participation in industry grew from 37 to 45 percent of total invested capital and from 60 percent to about 75 percent of the total net worth of the one hundred largest firms.[66] Reforms in the financial market transformed the private banking sector into a much more significant political force than it had been in the past, but the state's role in financial intermediation also grew.[67]

The expansion of the state sector was directly linked to a third key feature of Brazil's strategy: foreign borrowing. By 1981 the country's nonfinancial state enterprises accounted for nearly half of the country's foreign debt. Incentives to private borrowing included exemptions from some financial taxes and credit controls and favorable exchange-rate and interest-rate policies.[68]

External shocks, political developments, and the availability of foreign capital all served to reinforce the basic thrust of industrial policy over the 1970s.[69] In response to the first oil shock the government briefly attempted stabilization, though in combination with higher tariffs, quantitative restrictions, and outright import prohibitions that underlined the continuity with past policies. The Second National Development Plan (1975–79) was squarely within the structuralist policy tradition, calling for massive new investments in energy, pulp and paper, petro-

64. Balassa, "Incentive Policies," p. 1028.
65. For the structuralist critique of ISI, see Furtado, *Analise do modelo brasileiro.*
66. See Bacha, "Issues and Evidence"; Baer, *Industrialization and Economic Development.*
67. Jeffry Frieden, "The Brazilian Borrowing Experience: From Miracle to Debacle and Back," *Latin American Research Review* 22, 2 (1988): 109–12.
68. Frieden, "Brazilian Borrowing," p. 102.
69. Frieden, "Brazilian Borrowing," p. 103.

chemicals, fertilizers, steel, and nonferrous metals—many of which demanded a direct government role in production.

Political developments also played a role in the rejection of an orthodox response to the oil crisis and the pursuit of an expansionist macroeconomic policy. By the mid-1970s splits within the military and an unexpected setback at the polls in November 1974 had produced a new political strategy of gradual liberalization. To control the process, the military sought to build allies in civil society through greater attention to social development, lifting the lid on wages, but above all through an aggressive emphasis on growth.[70] This political context made stabilization policies anathema, particularly as business was already protesting the expansion of the state's role in the economy. At current levels of national savings, the government could reconcile its economic and political objectives only by borrowing. In 1974 Brazil's external debt totaled $18.5 billion; by 1984, when commercial credit had dried up, Brazil's debt neared $100 billion.

The entry of the military is frequently interpreted as marking a fundamentally new era in Brazil's political economy. Certainly there were important discontinuities with the preceding period. Dismantling of the populist coalition allowed the government to impose steep costs on labor and pursue an elitist development model that widened income disparities (see Chapter 10). The state's new political autonomy allowed it to introduce market-oriented reforms that would have been unlikely under democratic-populist auspices. The role of the state and foreign firms expanded relative to that of national capital, and the promotion of exports received new attention.

However, many features of this "new" model were foreshadowed in the turn to secondary ISI in the mid-1950s: the importance of foreign direct investment, an expanded role for the state in both planning and production, and high levels of protection and subsidy for industry. Politics even exhibited some surprising continuities.[71] At several key decision points the military was constrained by the social and economic weight of ISI interests and ideologies, both in the private sector and within the economic bureaucracy itself. The very effort to control the transition to democracy tempted the military to maintain rates of growth that could be sustained only by extensive borrowing.

---

70. Alfred Stepan, *Rethinking Military Politics* (Princeton: Princeton University Press, 1988).

71. For evidence that economic policy remains highly politicized under the military, see Willis,"State as Banker"; Abranches, "Divided Leviathan"; Frances Hagopian, "The Politics of Oligarchy: The Persistence of Traditional Elites in Contemporary Brazil" (Ph.D. diss., Massachusetts Institute of Technology, 1986).

Mexico in the 1970s: The End of "Stabilizing Development"

In the late 1960s dissident economists and intellectuals elaborated a wide-ranging critique of Mexican ISI.[72] Alternative models of development stressed the need to widen the domestic market, give greater attention to income distribution and rural poverty, and curb increasing business concentration and political power. Labor militancy and land seizures increased, and the country experienced a brief period of urban guerrilla activity. The repressive underside of the Mexican political system was revealed in 1968 when police attacks on a student demonstration in the capital city left fifty dead and over five hundred wounded.

On his election in 1970 Luís Echeverría sought to respond to these increasing social and political tensions through a reorientation of economic policy. Characterizing Echeverría's program runs the risk of lending it a coherence his six-year term (*sexénio*) lacked. Two sets of priorities coexisted. The first, neopopulist strand addressed political pressures from the left and the "popular sectors" with redistributive measures, a change from "stabilizing development" to a strategy Echeverría labeled "shared development." The new government slated education and social welfare for increased expenditure, revised labor laws to allow for more frequent wage adjustments, and extended subsidies to basic foodstuffs. Nationalist legislation also increased the government's control over foreign direct investment and technology transfer.

The second challenge, however, was the need to address the growing economic problems associated with ISI: a relative neglect of agriculture and the decline of agricultural exports, increasing balance-of-payments constraints; and a slowdown in the growth rates of leading import-substituting sectors. The initial industrial policy statements of the Echeverría administration stressed the need to rationalize the industrial structure and promote nontraditional exports.[73] As early as 1971, it became clear that the weight of import-substituting firms in the economy limited the political opportunities to use trade policy reform as a means of doing so.[74] Rather, tax rebates, subsidies, and increased pressures on multinationals were used to encourage exports, though without the supportive exchange-rate policy of minidevaluations adopted by Brazil.

72. See for example the influential work by Jose Ayala, José Blanco, Rolado Cordera, Guillermo Knohauer, and Armando Labra, "Económia y política en México," in Gonzalez Casanova and Enrique Florescano, eds., *México hoy* (Mexico City: Siglo XXI, 1969).

73. See Banco Nacional de Comercio Exterior, *México: La política del nuevo gobierno* (Mexico City: BNCE, 1971), pp. 117–22; Bela Balassa, "Foreign Trade and Industrial Policy in Mexico," in *Policy Reform in Developing Countries* (New York: Pergamon, 1977), pp. 31–49.

74. Rolando Cordera, "Los limites del reformismo," in Cordera, ed., *Desarrollo y crisis de la economía mexicana* (Mexico City: Fondo de Cultura Económica, 1981), pp. 368–421.

While seeking to maintain a populist image and "push out" exports, the government continued to expand its investment in capital-intensive industries including oil, petrochemicals, steel, railway stock, machine tools, and electrical machinery. This ambitious program was the heart of the government's industrial strategy. Given the government's other commitments and its limited ability to tax, the strategy implied a rupture with the financially conservative premises of "stabilizing growth." As in Brazil, the interests of political leaders combined with neostructuralist ideas to overthrow orthodoxy. The Ministry of Finance and the Central Bank, which had played central roles in economic policy making in the 1950s and 1960s, quickly lost power to the office of the president.[75] Inflation, it was now argued, could be contained through state investments aimed at breaking supply bottlenecks and through tax reform. Balance-of-payments constraints were downplayed.

The policy stance of the government triggered political conflicts that undermined coherent economic policy. On the one hand, efforts at tax reform were blocked by the private sector, which became increasingly alarmed by Echeverría's populism.[76] By 1973 the private sector and the government were in open conflict over policy issues. Private investment, both foreign and domestic, slowed, and capital flight increased. On the other hand, inflation activated labor demands, toward which Echeverría had expressed open sympathy. These problems were "solved" by increased borrowing from abroad. During the Echeverría *sexénio,* foreign debt increased from just under $6 billion to over $20 billion.[77] On August 31, 1976, in the last days of his administration, Echeverría devalued the peso, which had been fixed since the devaluation of 1954. Stabilizing growth had come to an end.

Echeverría's successor, José López Portillo, thus inherited an economy suffering from a weak currency, a large trade deficit, and rising external indebtedness. His initial strategy was to attempt to reconstruct the pre-Echeverría growth coalition.[78] A sophisticated medium-term adjustment proposal was signed with the IMF. The government drew on its traditional ties with the unions to impose wage restraint, seeking to restore private-sector confidence through an "Alliance for Production"

75. See Richard S. Weinert, "The State and Foreign Capital in Mexico," in Jose Luis Reyna and Richard S. Weinert, eds., *Authoritarianism in Mexico* (Philadelphia: Institute for the Study of Human Issues, 1977), p. 112.

76. Leopoldo Solís, *Economic Policy Reform in Mexico: A Case Study for Developing Countries* (New York: Pergamon, 1981), pp. 71–76.

77. For data on the accumulation of debt in Mexico and other countries see the World Bank, *World Debt Tables* (Washington, D.C., various issues).

78. The following draws on Stephan Haggard, "The Politics of Adjustment: Lessons from the IMF's Extended Fund Facility," *International Organization* 39 (Summer 1985): 525–29.

in which business promised renewed investment in return for increased fiscal and financial supports.

Oil appeared to promise deliverance from the political costs of stabilizing policies. In fact, however, the oil boom generated a variety of new political pressures on the government. First, the boom generated political forces, including the state-owned oil enterprise and its powerful unions, that pressed for expanded government commitments to the "oil complex" itself: exploration, drilling, and related industries such as petrochemicals. Second, the oil boom aggravated political and bureaucratic divisions within the government over the uses to which new-found oil money should be put.[79] The Ministry of Patrimony and Industrial Development favored increased state action to promote investment in capital goods, expanded support to industry, controls on banking and foreign exchange, and increased outlays for social expenditures and rural reforms. The Treasury and the Bank of Mexico, backed by the multilateral organizations and supported on some issues by the more liberal northern financial-industrial groups, called for a continuation of the stabilizing policies of the first two years of the López Portillo *sexenio*, a further rationalization of industry through phased import liberalization, a reduction of the state's role in production, an opening to foreign direct investment, and a realistic exchange-rate policy.

Increased external resources may have provided the means for launching liberalizing reforms, but they provided few incentives to do so. Borrowing and oil revenues allowed the government to push import substitution into new sectors, through increased financial and fiscal support for the largest private-sector groups, the major beneficiaries of López Portillo's Alliance for Production and of the oil boom itself. Public investment, though increasing, was concentrated in petroleum, electricity, steel, and infrastructure.

Broader political pressures also pushed in this direction. Leftist forces argued for a "national project" that would use oil revenues as an instrument for job creation, housing, health, education, and rural reforms.[80] Both the right-wing PAN and the left parties presented an electoral challenge as well. Neither came close to defeating the PRI, but both exploited political reforms to actively criticize the government.[81] The left sought to capture the symbols of the revolution for itself: democracy, development, anti-imperialism. Business groups initially supported the

79. The bureaucratic conflicts over oil and industrial policy are detailed in Judith A. Teichman, *Policymaking in Mexico: From Boom to Crisis* (Boston: Allen & Unwin, 1988), pp. 87–110.

80. Haggard, "Politics of Adjustment," p. 526.

81. An introduction to the political reforms is provided by Kevin J. Middlebrook, "Political Change in Mexico," in Susan Kaufman Purcell, ed., *Mexico–United States Relations* (New York: Academy of Political Science, 1981), pp. 55–66.

López Portillo strategy; as inflation increased after 1980, right-wing groups capitalized on growing middle-class and regional discontent over economic mismanagement and corruption.[82] High inflation and impending elections made pressures to offer wage concessions, extend food subsidies, and continue high levels of growth intense. In August 1982 the Ministry of Finance announced a new round of IMF-style reforms, marking a defeat for the expansionists within the cabinet. In a final political balancing act López Portillo reached out to the left by announcing the nationalization of the banking system in his last presidential address. In August 1982, with Mexico's announcement of its inability to service its debt, the debt crisis of the 1980s began.

THE END OF ISI?

Since the early 1980s, when external financing collapsed, Brazil and Mexico have experienced wrenching debt crises. The politics of the crisis are beyond the scope of this book; literature on the topic has grown rapidly.[83] If historical analysis offers any guide, we should expect the crisis of the 1980s to have a profound effect on development strategy. For the Latin American states, the debt crisis of the 1980s has surpassed the Depression in severity. The end of voluntary lending and the need to generate surpluses to service obligations have resulted in real devaluations and wage cuts, strengthening the export sector. Favored groups include not only domestic exporters of manufactures but export-oriented foreign investment, particularly in Mexico, and export-oriented agriculture. A continuation of external pressures on the Latin American NICs is likely to create new coalitional support for the outward-oriented policies championed by segments of the economic bureaucracy in both countries and greater efforts to lure foreign investors. A relief from external constraints would release resources for growth but could reinforce inward-looking tendencies.

As I have argued, though, how states respond to international constraints is a function of domestic political institutions and structures, as well as the constraints themselves. The point is clearly illustrated by the management of stabilization and balance-of-payments adjustment, the core policy challenge facing the two governments in the late 1980s. Brazil's strategy was more heterodox than Mexico's, in part because of its

---

82. On business influence see Maxfield and Montoya, eds., *Government and Private Sector in Contemporary Mexico.*

83. The following draws particularly on Robert R. Kaufman, *The Politics of Debt in Argentina, Brazil, and Mexico* (Berkeley: Institute of International Studies, University of California, 1988).

higher levels of inflation and the need to address the inertial component of inflation associated with widespread indexing through wage and price freezes. Yet the appeal of these ideas also had much to do with the fragility of the new democratic government of José Sarney that came to office in 1985 and the fact that the heterodox approach appeared to offer stabilization without the pain of traditional fiscal and monetary austerities and real wage cuts. This political explanation of heterodoxy is supported by the events of 1986 and 1987, when the experiment foundered on its failure to control fiscal and monetary policies. The democratic transition in Brazil provided the opportunity for long-standing popular-sector groups to reenter politics and established strong electoral constraints on economic policy. The rise of populist forces in the late 1980s suggests that Brazil will face strong political constraints as it tries to design an alternative to its long-standing emphasis on ISI.

Mexican policy exhibited several fluctuations during the *sexénio* of Miguel de la Madrid (1982–88), but the country's efforts to sustain IMF-like stabilization measures were unique among the major Latin American debtors. Pressures from a politically active private sector with strong ties to financial interests were important in sustaining orthodoxy. But so was the continuing ability of technocrats to count on the institutional capacities of the ruling party to contain pressures from labor and the left. Mexico has experienced a broadening of opposition forces and a more plural domestic politics; history has shown that the party is subject to electoral constraints on economic policy making. Yet the election of Carlos Salinas to the presidency in 1988, by however narrow a margin, shows within the Mexican political structure the growing power of the technocratic elite at the expense of the party apparat. Mexico has been far ahead of Brazil or Argentina in pursuing structural adjustments that orient Mexico in a more outward-looking direction; these adjustments include entry into the GATT and efforts at trade liberalization despite severe balance-of-payments difficulties. In comparative terms the development of state and society in Mexico has made the PRI more vulnerable to societal forces than the East Asian NICs, but institutional arrangements continue to provide Mexico with capacities that, compared with Brazil's fragile democracy, are unique.

Part III

CONTROVERSIES: DEPENDENCY, EQUITY, AND DEMOCRACY

CHAPTER EIGHT

Foreign Direct Investment
and the Question of Dependency

The publication of Peter Evans's influential study of multinational corporations in Brazil launched a "new wave" of dependency theorizing.[1] This new wave drew on theories of foreign investment emphasizing market imperfections and underlined the international constraints on governments in developing countries.[2] These theories hold that the costs of overseas investment deter firms from going abroad unless offset by oligopolistic advantages vis-à-vis local competitors. Access to finance and technology, marketing capabilities, managerial skills, and economies of scale give the multinational corporation bargaining leverage vis-à-vis host governments. Market power, rooted in market structure, translates into bargaining power.

While generating rich empirical work, this line of thinking deflected theoretical attention from analysis of the conditions under which governments in developing countries might successfully regulate the multi-

---

1. Peter Evans, *Dependent Development: The Alliance of Multinational, State, and Local Capital in Brazil* (Princeton: Princeton University Press, 1978); Gary Gereffi, *The Pharmaceutical Industry and Dependency in the Third World* (Princeton: Princeton University Press, 1983); Richard Newfarmer, *Transnational Conglomerates and the Economics of Dependent Development* (Greenwich, Conn.: JAI Press, 1980); Douglas C. Bennet and Kenneth E. Sharpe, *Transnational Corporations versus the State: The Political Economy of the Mexican Automobile Industry* (Princeton: Princeton University Press, 1985); Thomas Biersteker, *Multinationals, the State, and Control of the Nigerian Economy* (Princeton: Princeton University Press, 1987). The most sophisticated theoretical statement comes in Richard Newfarmer, ed., *Profits, Poverty, and Progress: Case Studies of International Industries in Latin America* (Notre Dame: Notre Dame University Press, 1985). For a critical review, see Stephan Haggard, "The Political Economy of Foreign Direct Investment in Latin America," *Latin American Research Review* 24, 1 (1989): 184–208.

2. See J. P. Agarwal, "Determinants of Foreign Direct Investment: A Survey," *Weltwirtschaftliches Archiv* 116, 4 (1980): 739–73.

nationals. As Richard Newfarmer put it succinctly, "neither the indus-trial organization analytic framework nor the bilateral monopoly ap-proach explains why the state assumes the 'political will' to bargain with TNCs or why it chooses to establish controls over [them]."[3] Bargaining outcomes frequently cut against the claim that multinationals dominate the "triple alliance" among state, foreign, and local capital, even in sectors such as computers where one would expect developing-country governments to be weakest.[4] The new dependency writing recognized the role of the state in mediating dependency relations, but the theory of public policy required to establish the links between politics, state inter-vention, and firm behavior was not developed.

The determinants of foreign direct investment are complex, and a complete account would consider macroeconomic variables as well as characteristics of the sector. This chapter argues, however, that phases of development and national policy help explain patterns of foreign direct investment over time and cross-nationally. I begin with a simple factor-endowments approach that stresses the relationship between comparative advantage and patterns of investment.[5] For a given endow-ment, three distinct levels of national policy can affect investment. The first concerns basic property rights. These have periodically been con-tested in Latin America, leading to nationalizations and corresponding uncertainty among investors. The second level is the structure of incen-tives that result from trade, exchange-rate, and pricing policies. Finally, within the context of a given structure of property rights and develop-ment strategy, governments develop discrete policies toward particular sectors and firms, such as tax incentives and various regulatory controls. Some regulations, such as restrictions on equity, may have the effect of severely limiting multinational activity.

If development strategy helps explain important aspects of firm be-havior, such as the propensity to export, and characteristics of the indus-trial structure, such as its concentration, it holds important implications for dependency thinking. First, it casts doubt on generalizations drawn from the import-substituting Latin American cases. Export-oriented manufacturing investment poses bargaining and regulatory problems

3. Richard Newfarmer, "An Introduction to the Issues," in Newfarmer, ed., *Profits, Poverty, and Progress*, p. 6.

4. See Theodore H. Moran, *Multinational Corporations and the Politics of Dependence: Copper in Chile* (Princeton: Princeton University Press, 1974). The argument is extended from raw materials to manufacturing by Joseph M. Grieco, *Dependency and Autonomy: India's Experience with the International Computer Industry* (Berkeley: University of California Press, 1984); also see Dennis Encarnation, *Dislodging Multinationals: India's Strategy in Comparative Perspective* (Ithaca: Cornell University Press, 1989).

5. See for example Kiyoshi Kojima, *Direct Foreign Investment: A Japanese Model of Multinational Business Operations* (New York: Praeger, 1978).

for host governments, but the problems differ from those in import-substituting manufacturing or extractive industries. Second, many of the outcomes that dependency literature traces to foreign direct investment should be seen rather as the result of resource endowments and policy incentives to which MNCs respond.[6] If foreign investment is affected by national strategies, "dependency" must be seen as effect as well as cause.

Here, as in previous chapters, I advance two sorts of arguments, one emphasizing similarities among countries that pursue similar strategies, a second differentiating within groups. Hong Kong was always open to foreign investors, but in Korea, Taiwan, and Singapore the shift to export-oriented policies was accompanied by new incentives to foreign direct investment. Import-substituting investment continued in the larger East Asian NICs, but export-oriented investment grew more rapidly. As governments adjusted through new industrial policies to changing comparative advantage, the composition of foreign investment followed suit.

The claim that foreign direct investment dominated the economic growth of the East Asian NICs is exaggerated.[7] In all cases except Singapore, export-led growth favored the development of local firms. Export-led growth in Korea and Taiwan was accompanied by a secular *decline* in dependence on total foreign savings, even though Korea borrowed heavily.

The Latin American NICs present a different pattern. Mexico has a long history of foreign direct investment in extractive industries, and both Brazil and Mexico were recipients of large portfolio investments before the Great Depression. In the 1930s manufacturing's share of foreign direct investment began to increase. Following the turn to a secondary phase of ISI in the mid-1950s, both countries allowed American firms to gain dominant positions in leading industries that were, because of scale, capital, and technology requirements, beyond the reach of local investors. ISI also created a bias against exports and contributed to chronic balance-of-payments difficulties that necessitated imports of foreign capital. By 1973 commercial loans surpassed foreign direct investment as the main source of foreign capital in Mexico and Brazil.

6. See for example Volker Bornschier, Christopher Chase-Dunn, and Richard Rubinson, "Crossnational Evidence of the Effects of Foreign Investment and Aid on Economic Growth and Inequality: A Summary of Findings and a Reanalysis," *American Journal of Sociology* 84, 3 (1978): 651–83.

7. Folker Froebel, Juergen Heinrichs, and Otto Kreye, *The New International Division of Labour: Structural Unemployment in Industrialized Countries and Industrialization in Developing Countries* (Cambridge: Cambridge University Press, 1981). See also Martin Landsberg, "Export-Led Industrialization in the Third World: Manufacturing Imperialism," *Review of Radical Political Economics* 11 (1979): 50–63.

Borrowing financed the development of national firms and contributed to a decline in the relative importance of foreign direct investment. The prolonged pursuit of ISI, despite the motivation of escaping dependence, resulted in a secular increase in aggregate dependence on foreign savings.

Development strategy does not account for everything. Variations in the role of foreign capital among countries pursuing similar strategies must be explained by the political and economic threats foreign firms pose, the level of development of local firms when MNCs enter, and the political links between the private sector and the government. National policy toward multinationals and their weight in the economy varies widely among the East Asian NICs. Singapore's industrialization has been dominated by foreign firms because of the political and economic weaknesses of the local manufacturing sector. Taiwan maintained a screening system for foreign investment and used its regulatory powers to achieve specific industrial objectives, whereas Hong Kong's investment rules were completely neutral as regards local and foreign firms. Both governments welcomed foreign investment, though. In Korea, by contrast, a closer alliance between business and the manufacturing sector combined with nationalist fears of Japan to keep policy toward foreign investment restrictive. Foreign direct investment constituted a smaller share of total capital inflows in Korea than in the other Asian NICs, and the absolute amounts of investment were also lower.

Brazil and Mexico also differ in their policies toward foreign investors. Following the 1964 coup in Brazil, the balance between local, foreign, and state capital tilted against the domestic private sector. The Brazilian military regime had fewer institutional links with the local private sector than did the PRI, and government policy in Mexico was somewhat more restrictive. Mexican attitudes were shaped by the country's proximity to the United States, a long history of investment disputes, and the fundamental struggles over property rights that characterized the Revolution and its aftermath. In the 1970s both countries gradually developed regulatory frameworks to control MNC behavior.

FOREIGN INVESTMENT IN THE EAST ASIAN NICS

The Japanese colonial administrations in Korea and Taiwan invested heavily in railroads, harbors, roads, communications, and power. Since the colonial authorities were interested in exploiting the colonies' agricultural potential, they seized untitled land and sold it to Japanese firms engaged in land development. Japanese investors held 20 to 25 percent of the total cultivated area in Taiwan before World War II, and between

12 and 20 percent in Korea.[8] In Taiwan sugar companies accounted for about two-thirds of Japanese-held land, and sugar refining was the major industry before the 1930s. Japanese interest in Korea centered on expanding rice exports to feed a growing—and restless—urban work force.

After the mid-1930s the colonial administration took steps to broaden the industrial bases of the two colonies, particularly Korea, to include manufacturing and raw-materials processing. State-chartered firms supported the development of Korea as a logistical base for Japan's thrust into China. Between 1925 and 1939 the share of mining and manufacturing in total output jumped from 19 percent to 45 percent. In Taiwan food processing continued to occupy a dominant position in manufacturing, but Japanese firms also invested in cement, chemicals, pulp and paper, fertilizer, and metalworking. In 1939, 46 percent of total Japanese investments in Taiwan were in private hands, and 54 percent of those were in industry.

The aggregate investment position of the two colonies, despite similarities in the composition of investment, differed sharply. Japanese investments in Taiwanese agriculture allowed the colony to run a trade surplus and to finance government investment and current expenditure out of revenue. By 1930 Taiwan was a net creditor to Japan. By contrast, Korea ran persistent deficits with the metropole, implying offsetting capital inflows in the form of government spending and private investment. Between 1916 and 1938 total capital formation in the two colonies was almost exactly the same. In Taiwan 18.2 percent was financed by long-term capital imports, whereas in Korea long-term capital imports equaled 128.1 percent of total capital formation.[9] Different returns in agriculture resulted in different degrees of dependence even within a single imperial system.

After the war Japanese properties in both countries fell into the hands of the new governments. Existing Japanese foreign investment was therefore eliminated. In the 1950s foreign investment played a greater role in Taiwan than in South Korea because of Syngman Rhee's unwillingness to normalize political relations with Japan. Foreign investment in Taiwan from 1952 to 1960 totaled $40 million, roughly 4 percent of U.S. aid flows for the period. Of eighty-six cases of direct foreign investment during the 1950s, fifty-eight were by overseas Chinese. These investments, like local investment, were concentrated in

8. Samuel Pao-San Ho, "Colonialism and Development: Korea, Taiwan, and Kwantung," in Ramon H. Myers and Mark R. Peattie, *The Japanese Colonial Empire, 1895–1945* (Princeton: Princeton University Press, 1984), p. 372.

9. Mizogushi Toshiyuki and Yamamoto Yuzo, "Capital Formation in Korea and Taiwan," in ibid.

light manufacturing, services, and real estate. Most took joint-venture form and were used to circumvent foreign-exchange controls and repatriate capital legally.[10] Korea and Taiwan were too small, too poor, and too politically fragile to attract any sustained interest from American companies.

The level of dependence on aid during the ISI period was extraordinarily high in both Korea and Taiwan.[11] Foreign capital inflows were equal to about 40 percent of gross domestic capital formation in Taiwan between 1952 and 1960. In Korea dependence on foreign aid increased following the Korean War. Between 1952 and 1960 foreign capital, virtually all of it aid, financed 70 percent of gross domestic capital formation. Both countries experienced a decline in dependence on foreign capital with the advent of export-led growth. By the second half of the 1960s only 5 percent of Taiwan's domestic capital formation was financed from abroad. With lower rates of domestic savings and booming investment, Korea, by contrast, remained a significant borrower.

Before World War II the entrepôts acted as intermediaries between the imperial powers and their own hinterlands, where foreign investment was extensive.[12] Early trading, shipping, and banking services began as British and Chinese investments but developed into firms with a local identity. Singapore's agency houses managed investments in plantation agriculture and mining in Malaya and the Netherlands East Indies, and they developed networks with Chinese merchants who became large landlords in the Malayan peninsula. Hong Kong–based trading firms were important in the China trade, and British banks in Hong Kong financed China's trade as well as the government's borrowing. As in Singapore, European investments in the hinterland—China in Hong Kong's case—dwarfed those in the entrepôt, but Hong Kong profited from its role as commercial and financial intermediary. Early postwar patterns of foreign investment in the two city-states differed in important ways. With the Chinese Revolution, flight capital moved into Hong Kong, accounting for perhaps as much as 40 percent of gross domestic capital formation between 1949 and 1965.[13] Anti-Chinese

10. On the characteristics of overseas Chinese investment in Taiwan see Thomas Gold, "Dependent Development in Taiwan" (Ph.D. diss., Harvard University, 1981), p. 170.

11. S. C. Tsiang and Rong-I Wu, "Foreign Trade and Investments as Boosters for Take-off: The Experiences of the Four Asian Newly Industrializing Countries," in Walter Galenson, ed., *Foreign Trade and Investment: Economic Development in the Newly Industrializing Asian Countries* (Madison: University of Wisconsin Press, 1985), p. 333.

12. On early foreign investment in Singapore and Hong Kong see Wong Lin Ken, "Singapore: Its Growth as an Entrepôt Port, 1819–1941," *Journal of Southeast Asian Studies* 9, 1 (1978): 50–84; Frank Leeming, "The Earlier Industrialization of Hong Kong," *Modern Asian Studies* 9, 3 (1975): 337–42.

13. Based on estimates drawn from Shou-eng Koo, "The Role of Export Expansion in Hong Kong's Economic Growth," *Asian Survey* 8 (August 1968): 499–515.

sentiment in Indonesia attracted some flight capital to Singapore in the late 1950s, but the amounts were smaller and were not carried by manufacturing entrepreneurs.

This review suggests some qualifications to the hypothesis that foreign investment conforms closely with stage of development. Though Japanese investment in agriculture and trade-related infrastructure was important in Korea and Taiwan, the Japanese did not view the colonies solely as agricultural appendages. As a result of a unique conception of empire, state-directed investment led, rather than followed, industrial development. Neither Korea nor Taiwan attracted much foreign investment during the ISI phase. Aid was the crucial form of external capital. Foreign investments in the entrepôts through the 1950s were overwhelmingly in commerce, transport, and finance, though in Hong Kong the Chinese Revolution resulted in an inflow of manufacturing investment as well.

Foreign Direct Investment and Export-Led Growth

The new emphasis on exports went hand in hand with an opening to foreign direct investment. Policy reform was spurred by balance-of-payments difficulties, which foreign investment could alleviate in two ways: directly through an inflow of capital, and indirectly by providing marketing channels for exports. The policy reforms associated with the shift in policy emphasis, such as devaluation and new tax incentives to business, encouraged foreign investment, as did more specific incentives such as the construction of export-processing zones.

Foreign direct investment entered under different regulatory auspices and political contexts, however. In Korea a Foreign Capital Inducement Law was passed in 1960 and revised under the military in 1961, though it provoked little response from investors. Control over foreign capital was centralized in the Economic Planning Board, providing the military government with a powerful tool for consolidating support from, as well as control over, the private sector. In 1962 the EPB gained the power to audit the activities of firms borrowing abroad. The Foreign Capital Deliberation Committee, located in the EPB, also had to approve all proposals for foreign direct investment and technology-transfer agreements. Screening of foreign investment was thus closely integrated with a centralized process for industrial planning.[14]

Korea, unlike the other East Asian NICs, experienced bitter political

14. For the history of the early efforts to induce foreign capital, see Stephan Haggard, Byung-kook Kim, and Chung-in Moon, "The Transition to Export-Led Growth in Korea, 1954–1966," unpublished ms., Harvard University, 1987.

conflicts over the role of foreign capital.[15] Park Chung Hee actively pursued a settlement of Korean property claims with Japan and in late 1962 reached an agreement that included a $300 million grant, $200 million in concessional government credits, and $100 million in commercial financing. The United States had long pushed for the agreement to help offset declining aid commitments, and Korean businessmen welcomed joint-venture prospects. The opposition portrayed the settlement as capitulation to a new Japanese East Asian Co-prosperity Sphere. Critics feared that funds would be used for political purposes. These fears were vindicated in 1965 when a series of scandals erupted over the allocation of foreign loans. Following the treaty crisis, the laws governing the entry of foreign capital were liberalized. As foreign direct investment began to flow in during the late 1960s, government policy became more restrictive. This restrictiveness and the preference for commercial borrowing can be explained by political and institutional factors: the desire to control the allocation of foreign borrowing and to limit the penetration of the Japanese, and the location of the screening mechanism in a dirigist planning bureaucracy.

In Taiwan a Statute for Investment by Foreign Nationals was promulgated in 1954 as a response to balance-of-payments problems, but it was not until the Statute for the Encouragement of Investment of 1960 that investors made any substantial response.[16] The statute, a central pillar of the transition toward export-led growth, differed from Korea's investment laws in that it applied equally to foreign and local investment. A separate Statute for Investment by Foreign Nationals created an Investment Commission in the Ministry of Economic Affairs that centralized and expedited foreign firms' dealings with the government and provided an instrument of control. Unlike the case in Korea, this Investment Commission was not tied to a strongly centralized and dirigist planning ministry but represented relatively liberal elements within the bureaucracy. Nor was the government constrained by domestic political resistance to foreign investment.

Investment commissions in developing countries generally wield great discretionary powers, so it is misleading to take legal statutes as a guide to government practice. Sector studies, the literature of foreign business associations (appropriately discounted), and the legislation itself suggest that, outside the export-processing zones, investment rules

---

15. Kwan Bong Kim, *The Korean-Japan Treaty Crisis and the Instability of the Korean Political System* (New York: Praeger, 1971).

16. On investment laws in Taiwan see Chi Huang, "The State and Foreign Capital: A Case Study of Taiwan" (Ph.D. diss., Indiana University, 1986), pp. 196–221; and Chung-yuan Huang, *Multinationals in the Republic of China: Laws and Policies* (Taipei: Asia and the World Forum, 1978).

were far from liberal. The relatively restrictive government stance can be seen in the rules governing the scope of foreign business activity, equity participation, and exports.[17]

Korea's Foreign Capital Inducement Law and Taiwan's Statute for the Encouragement of Investment were initially based on positive-list systems. Only listed activities were eligible for investment and the most lucrative incentives. This decision in itself created a restrictive bias compared to negative-list systems, but the presence of an industry on the list was still no guarantee that a proposal would be accepted. "Acceptable" projects were still required to specify, among other things, the technologies to be transferred, the royalties associated with those technologies, personnel policies, the extent of local procurement and sales, and the implications of the project for imports. All of these matters were subject to negotiation and were even used by the governments in negotiations with potential competitors. After 1973 the Korean government restricted the eligibility of projects that competed in overseas markets with local firms, that disrupted local demand and supply of raw materials and intermediates, or that had limited technological benefits.

In general, Taiwan was more moderate in its policies concerning local participation. The Investment Commission did not oppose 100 percent foreign ownership in principle, though on a case-by-case basis it encouraged joint ventures or divestment over time. From 1973 until the early 1980s, when investment laws were liberalized, Korea demanded joint ventures and gradual divestiture, though exceptions were made for a shifting list of desired industries.

Foreign investments located in the export-processing zones were required to export all of their output, but both countries made similar demands for investments outside the zones. Taiwan has had local-content requirements for a limited range of goods and urged foreign investors to source locally as part of their entry agreements. In the 1970s Korea made wide-ranging demands on foreign firms for local procurement of inputs, even in industries that were poorly developed. All of these rules suggest a willingness to limit competition between local and foreign firms in the domestic market and to forge linkages between foreign and local firms.

17. In addition to interviews with members of the Investment Commission in Taiwan and the Economic Planning Board in Korea, the following paragraph draws on Dong Sung Cho, "Incentives and Restraints: Government Regulation of Direct Investment between Korea and the United States," in Karl Moskowitz, ed., *From Patron to Partner* (Cambridge: Harvard University Press, 1985); T. Jefferson Coolidge, Jr., "The Realities of Korean Foreign Investment Policy," *Asian Affairs* 7 (July–August 1981): 370–85. For Taiwan, see Huang, "The State and Foreign Capital," pp. 196–221; Gold, "Dependent Development"; Dennis Simon, "Taiwan, Technology Transfer, and Transnationalism: The Political Management of Dependency" (Ph.D. diss., University of California, Berkeley, 1980).

Rules governing foreign direct investment in the city-states have been more liberal; in Singapore because MNCs were the centerpiece of the country's post-1967 growth strategy, in Hong Kong because of the strong tradition of laissez-faire. In Singapore balance-of-payments problems and sluggish investment were behind the Pioneer Industry Ordinances of 1959 that allowed 100 percent foreign ownership and full repatriation of profits. After the formation of the Economic Development Board in 1961, investment screening fell under a planning agency that exercised a high level of discretion in granting incentives. Conferral of "pioneer status" could exempt a firm from taxes on profits for up to ten years, depending on sector, size of investment, level of technology, and other criteria that changed with government priorities. In contrast to its Korean counterpart, however, the board had little private domestic manufacturing investment to orchestrate. In 1962 the board began its effort to lure foreign investors. In 1967 the government extended generous tax incentives to export-oriented investment, again under crisis conditions. These incentives, which strongly favored foreign firms, marked the turning point in Singapore's industrial strategy.

In contrast to the other NICs, Hong Kong has pursued a consistent policy toward foreign investment across the entire postwar period. Hong Kong makes no distinction between foreign and local investors, grants no special incentives to either, and has no restrictions on foreign ownership. Trade is free, and there are no exchange controls, capital gains taxes, sales taxes, or corporate capital taxes. Income taxes have historically been low. In 1966 the government formed a Trade and Development Council to promote investment and exports through the dissemination of information. The government maintained, and surveys confirmed, that the laissez-faire environment was the primary selling point for foreign firms.[18]

Once we recognize that Korea and Taiwan were less than fully open to foreign direct investment, it becomes difficult to sustain the view that the East Asian NICs were little more than multinational-dominated export platforms. Folker Froebel and his associates, for example, have argued that international subcontracting and offshore production were central to the industrial transformation that accompanied export-led growth.[19] Evaluating these claims demands a closer analysis of the role of export-

18. See Hong Kong Government, Industry Department, *Report on the Survey of Overseas Investment in Hong Kong's Manufacturing Industry 1984*. The top response among the factors considered favorable to investment in Hong Kong was "good international communication facilities." This was followed by "government's consistent economic policy of free trade and free enterprise," "free port," and "low tax rates."

19. Froebel, Heinrichs, and Kreye, *The New International Division of Labour;* Landsberg, "Export-Led Industrialization"; Andre Gunder Frank, "Asia's Exclusive Models," *Far Eastern Economic Review,* June 25, 1982, pp. 22–23.

processing zones (EPZs), subcontracting, and foreign investment in NIC trade.

EPZs are industrial estates where land, utilities, transport facilities, and even buildings are provided by the government, generally at subsidized rates. Labor also is frequently organized under government supervision and subjected to more stringent rules than those governing the work force as a whole. The zones offer additional incentives, such as complete tax holidays, unlimited profit repatriation, and duty-free entry of goods destined for reexport. The zones initially sought to attract 100 percent foreign-owned subsidiaries and even restricted entry to foreign firms. As a corollary, the EPZs had few linkages other than the wage bill with the domestic economy.

The position of the export-processing zones varies in larger and smaller East Asian NICs. The first East Asian EPZ was located in Taiwan and came into operation in 1965. Two additional zones were added in Taiwan in 1970, the same year that Korea's first zone was opened at Masan. Masan was followed by a proliferation of sector-specific Export Industrial Estates. Hong Kong and Singapore have retained most of the features of free ports, but Singapore has some Industrial Zones and, because of the high cost of land, the Hong Kong government developed industrial estates to attract land-intensive investments. In Hong Kong's typically reluctant fashion, this "intervention" did not occur until the late 1970s.

The EPZs were important in the early period of the export-oriented strategy in the larger NICs, but their importance should not be exaggerated. In both Taiwan and Korea the export take-off began before the construction of the zones. By 1975 Taiwan's zones accounted for about 9 percent of total exports. Between 1966 and 1970, 23 percent of foreign investment went into the zones, but this proportion declined to 19 percent between 1971 and 1975 and 16 percent between 1976 and 1980. By the late 1970s the benefits of locating in the zones had eroded as investment policies outside the zones became more liberal.[20] Exports from the Masan zone in Korea grew fairly steadily from its inception though, after 1975, at rates lower than the growth of exports from the country as a whole. The number of firms operating in the zone peaked in 1975, employment peaked in 1979, and new investment after 1974 was small and erratic.[21]

A better sense of the role of multinationals in the development of Korea and Taiwan can be gained by examining the MNCs' share of total

---

20. Data provided by the Export Processing Zone Administration.
21. See Peter Warr, "Korea's Masan Free Export Zone: Benefits and Costs," Australian National University Development Studies Centre, Occasional Paper 36 (Canberra, 1983).

Table 8.1. Sectoral shares of foreign direct investment in Korea, 1962–82 (percentages)

Sector	1962–66	1967–71	1972–76	1978	1980	1982	Total
Agriculture	—	1.2	1.3	0.8	0.4	1.0	1.2
Mining	0	—	—	—	—	—	0.2
Services	0	15.6	18.6	31.5	28.6	8.1	21.7
Manufacturing	99.0	83.1	79.9	67.6	71.0	90.4	76.9
Chemicals	21.5	13.0	9.9	29.5	50.0	31.6	20.5
Electrical and electronics	0	11.6	15.3	11.1	0	22.4	14.2
Textiles and apparel	3.8	13.9	21.0	0.2	0	3.1	10.4
Fertilizer and petrochemicals	70.5	19.4	7.7	8.5	0	0	8.2
Nonelectrical machinery	1.5	3.2	6.3	6.6	6.4	10.9	7.1
Metals	0	5.5	5.9	3.4	2.6	0.7	5.0
Transport equipment	0	0.3	6.3	4.8	0	5.1	4.1
Others	1.7	15.2	7.5	3.5	12.0	16.6	7.4
Total (US$ millions)	21.2	96.3	557.0	100.4	96.6	100.5	1,307

Note: A dash indicates a negligible percentage.
Source: Data provided by the Economic Planning Board.

exports and exports from different sectors.[22] Through 1974, when Korea turned toward a greater emphasis on heavy industry, MNCs accounted for 31.4 percent of Korea's total exports. MNCs accounted for less than 15 percent of Korea's total exports in two "leading sectors," textiles and apparel and the light manufacturing categorized as "other." In electronics, by contrast, almost all exports came from foreign firms. The story is similar for Taiwan. Foreign-invested firms accounted for just under 30 percent of exports in 1974, dropping gradually to under 20 percent by 1983. When exports are weighted by the share of foreign ownership, the role of foreign investment starts smaller and drops more sharply. As in Korea, local firms dominated Taiwan's leading export sectors, "other" manufactures and textiles. Only in the electronics sector did foreign firms contribute more than local firms to exports.

The sectoral composition of foreign direct investment confirms the expectation that changing comparative advantage and industrial policy will influence firm behavior. From 1962 to 1966 in Korea two projects, a fertilizer plant and a refinery, accounted for over 75 percent of total foreign investment. Following the reforms in 1964 and 1965, things

22. Data in this paragraph are drawn from Chung Lee, "U.S. and Japanese Investment in Korea: A Comparative Study," *Hitotsubashi Journal of Economics* 20 (1980): 26–41, and "United States and Japanese Direct Investment in Korea and the Extent of Their Dominance: Some Evidence from Korean Manufacturing Industries," mimeo, University of Hawaii, 1981; Eric Ramstetter, "The Impacts of Direct Foreign Investment on Host Country Trade and Output: A Study of Japanese and United States Investment in Korea, Taiwan, and Thailand" (Ph.D. diss., University of Colorado, 1986), p. 176; and data supplied by the Council on Economic Planning and Development, Taiwan.

Table 8.2. Sectoral shares of foreign direct investment in Taiwan, 1952–81 (percentages)

Sector	1952–70	1971–75	1976–81
Agriculture and food processing	3.7	0.9	2.6
Electronics and electrical machinery	39.4	26.4	28.7
Textiles	7.2	6.4	2.5
Chemicals	17.0	14.0	13.7
Metals	6.1	18.3	21.4
Machinery, equipment, and instruments	0	13.6	5.2
Transport	2.4	1.3	1.3
Banking	1.9	6.3	2.5
Services and construction	12.7	9.9	18.1
Others	8.7	2.0	3.1

Source: Republic of China, Council for Economic Planning and Development, *Taiwan Statistical Data Book*, various issues.

change. The decade from 1967 to 1976 was the heyday of investment in textiles, apparel, and electronics assembly (see Table 8.1). Investment in electronics continued through the 1970s, but the aggregate data conceal shifts away from component assembly toward consumer and industrial electronics. Textile and apparel investment dropped off to nothing, and investments in nonelectrical machinery, transport equipment, and chemicals—key sectors in the Heavy and Chemical Industry Plan—increased their share. Foreign firms in these sectors targeted for import-substitution had a much lower propensity to export. For example, 78 percent of total shipments by foreign firms in the textile sector were for export; the corresponding share in the transport equipment sector was 3 percent.[23] A similar shift in the sectoral composition of foreign investment took place in Taiwan (see Table 8.2). Electronics declined in relative importance, not only because of rising labor costs but also because of active government efforts to discourage investments in final-stage assembly, lure investment in new sectors (including metals, machinery and services), and upgrade electronics investment into new product lines.

Assessing the role of foreign-invested firms in Hong Kong demands some educated guessing, since the data are poor. A 1975 government survey, not repeated in the same form since, estimated that foreign-invested firms were responsible for about 9.7 percent and 10.6 percent of Hong Kong's so-called "domestic" or nonentrepôt exports in 1973 and 1974. These figures confirm the importance of local firms in the dramatic expansion of the colony's exports.[24] Foreign investment has

23. Republic of Korea, Economic Planning Board, "Foreign Direct Investment Special Survey 1979," mimeo, 1980.
24. Tzong-biau Lin and Victor Mok, "Trade, Foreign Investment, and Development in Hong Kong," in Walter Galenson, ed., *Foreign Trade and Investment: Economic Development in the Newly Industrializing Asian Countries* (Madison: University of Wisconsin Press, 1985).

Table 8.3. Sectoral shares of foreign direct investment in Hong Kong, selected years (percentages)

Sector	1970	1975	1979	1984
Electronics	40.9	34.7	23.0	35.5
Textiles	17.8	14.9	15.7	9.8
Watches and clocks	1.5	11.1	7.3	
Chemicals	2.5	5.7	13.2	7.0
Electrical products	1.6	5.7	9.0	8.0
Printing and publishing	4.0	3.6	6.7	
Food	1.0	3.5	5.3	7.2
Toys	4.7	3.4	2.9	
Construction	3.9	3.1	1.5	
Metal fabrication	2.0	2.8	2.5	
Metal products	2.0	2.8	4.5	
Others	17.9	8.5	8.4	24.9
Total	100	100	100	100

Sources: Kin-chok Mun and Suk-ching Ho, "Foreign Investment in Hong Kong," in Tzong-Biau Lin, Rance P. L. Lee, and Udo-Ernst Simonis, eds., *Hong Kong: Economic, Social, and Political Studies in Development* (White Plains, N.Y.: M. E. Sharpe, 1979); Hong Kong, Trade Industry and Customs Dept., *Overseas Investment in Hong Kong Manufacturing Industry: Industrial Survey Report* (1975); and Hong Kong Industry Dept., *Report on the Survey of Overseas Investment in Hong Kong Manufacturing Industry* (1984). Numbers may not add to 100 because of rounding and incomplete sectoral coverage.

been slight in the textile and garment industry, the sector that has led Hong Kong's manufacturing growth. Reexports must also be considered. Between 1960 and 1980 they accounted for between 20 percent and 30 percent of Hong Kong's total exports. Value-added on this trade is low, but it has sustained a commercial and shipping establishment largely in local hands. The sectoral composition of foreign investment in Hong Kong has shifted over time, though more subtly than in Korea and Taiwan where government exercised greater influence over foreign firms (see Table 8.3). Textiles and apparel and other light manufactures gave way to investments in clocks and watches and chemicals, though again the data probably conceal changes taking place within product categories, particularly in consumer electronics.[25]

In contrast to the other NICs, where the relative importance of foreign investment in exports and output declined over time, Singapore saw a sharp erosion in the relative position of national business after the switch to export-promoting policies. In 1959 foreign investment played a limited role in domestic production. Foreign firms established strong positions in several sectors, but domestic firms accounted for the lion's share of investment in the important food sector and in other light

25. See Hong Kong Productivity Centre, *Study of the Hong Kong Electronics Industry* (1982).

Table 8.4. Sectoral shares of foreign direct investment in Singapore, 1974–82 (total stocks, percentages)

Sector	1974	1978	1982
Food, beverages, and tobacco	3.7	3.4	3.8
Textiles, apparel, and footwear	7.2	4.9	1.8
Leather, rubber, wood, and cork products	6.2	4.0	1.8
Chemicals and plastics	6.0	5.0	7.7
Petroleum and petroleum products	43.7	44.0	40.6
Basic and fabricated metals	9.3	4.0	4.6
Nonelectrical machinery	0	9.3	9.6
Electrical and electronic machinery	10.3	11.8	19.0
Transport equipment	5.5	6.2	5.1
Precision equipment (photographic, optical, etc.)	3.8	4.0	2.5
Other	4.1	3.4	3.5

Source: Calculated from Singapore, Economic Development Board, *Annual Report 1983/4.*

industry. By 1973 the relative position of domestic firms had declined dramatically.[26] In 1970 foreign-invested firms accounted for 25 percent of all establishments but for 69 percent of output, 66 percent of value-added, 55 percent of employment, and an astounding 84 percent of exports. Moreover, this dominance went unchanged through the mid-1980s.[27]

As in the other NICs, so in Singapore the composition of foreign investment shifted in the 1970s in response to changing comparative advantage and the Second Industrial Revolution policy of speeding wage increases and providing incentives to selected "hi-tech" sectors (see Table 8.4). Investment in textiles, apparel, footwear and leather, rubber, and wood processing dropped off sharply over the decade. Fabricated metals, nonelectric machinery, but particularly electronics and electrical machinery show relative gains.

It could be argued that this account understates the importance of foreign firms in the growth of the East Asian NICs by ignoring the crucial role of buying groups and subcontracting. The one detailed study on the role of trading companies, commodity traders, buying offices, and marketing affiliates in the exports of the East Asian NICs found that they accounted for 10.8 percent of Korea's exports in 1980.[28]

26. On foreign direct investment in Singapore see Kunio Yoshihara, *Japanese Investment in Southeast Asia* (Honolulu: University Press of Hawaii, 1978); and Frederic Deyo, *Dependent Development and Industrial Order: An Asian Case Study* (New York: Praeger, 1981).

27. For data on foreign direct investment in Singapore, see Department of Statistics, *Report on the Census of Industrial Production* (various issues).

28. ESCAP/UNCTC Joint Unit on Transnational Corporations, Economic and Social Commission for Asia and the Pacific, *Transnational Trading Corporations in Selected Asian and Pacific Countries* (New York: United Nations, 1985).

Eighty-five percent of these exports were handled by Japanese trading companies. However, the companies handled only 6.5 percent of Korea's textile exports and 5.5 percent of "other" manufactured products, including machinery and electrical and electronic products. Given Korea's single-minded effort to develop its own trading companies over the 1970s, this figure is certainly much lower than it must have been for the 1960s, when orchestrating the entry of American buying groups was a major objective of AID's efforts to promote exports.[29] These groups were undoubtedly important in Taiwan in the early days of export-led growth and, given the failure of Taiwan to form domestic trading companies on the Korean model, probably remained high. The involvement of foreign trading companies is not inimical to the development of national firms, however; quite the opposite is the case. Without the knowledge of the market and the channels that buyers provided, local firms, and small ones in particular, would have been unable to export.

It is clear that changing comparative advantage and industrial policy affect the composition of foreign direct investment. Industrial strategy also affects the export behavior of firms. There is a debate on the export performance of Japanese as opposed to American multinationals.[30] Even if a difference does exist, and the evidence is inconclusive, overall export/sales ratios of MNCs in the East Asian NICs were still high in the 1970s, exceeding 50 percent in Taiwan, Singapore, and Hong Kong (see Table 8.5). They were lowest in Korea, which is consistent with the government's industrial strategy. Data available for Taiwan provide evidence of the changing trade behavior of firms over time.[31] Firms entering the country before 1960 exported only 18 percent of total output. For those established between 1961 and 1966, after the exchange-rate reforms and through one year of operation of the first EPZ, the proportion rose to 36.6 percent. Firms established between 1967 and 1971 exported 75 percent of production.

Given the emphasis placed on foreign direct investment in recent dependency and world-systems theorizing, it is worthwhile to put such investment in perspective by taking a more highly aggregated view of the role of foreign capital in the growth of the East Asian NICs. Foreign investment may have contributed to skill formation, technological de-

29. See Amicus Most, *Expanding Exports: A Case Study of the Korean Experience* (Washington, D.C.: U.S. Agency for International Development, 1969).

30. For recent reviews of this debate, see Kiyoshi Kojima, "A Model of Trade-Oriented Direct Investment," and Chung H. Lee, "Is There Anything Unique about Japanese Direct Foreign Investment?" in Seiji Naya, Vinyu Vichit-Vadakan, and Udom Kerdipibule, eds., *Direct Foreign Investment and Export Promotion: Policies and Experiences in Asia* (Honolulu: East-West Resource Systems Institute, 1987).

31. Chi Schive, "Direct Foreign Investment and Linkage Effects: A Case Study of Taiwan" (Ph.D. diss., Case Western Reserve University, 1978).

Table 8.5. Export/sales ratios for foreign manufacturing affiliates in the East Asian NICs, selected years

Country	1975	1977	1979	1981	1983
Korea	31.7	36.0			
Taiwan	56.1	61.8	55.1	55.1	50.9
Singapore	68.1	73.0	74.1	70.0	
Hong Kong		80.5			77.6

Sources: For Korea, Economic Planning Board surveys, cited in B. Y. Koo, "The Role of Direct Foreign Investment in Korea's Recent Economic Growth," in Walter Galenson, ed., *Foreign Trade and Investment: Economic Development in the Newly Industrializing Asian Countries* (Madison: University of Wisconsin Press, 1985). For Taiwan, Investment Commission, *A Survey of Overseas Chinese and Foreign Firms and Their Effects on National Economic Development* (in Chinese), various issues. For Singapore, Department of Statistics, *Report of the Census of Industrial Production,* various issues. For Hong Kong, data are for American affiliates only; for 1977, Department of Commerce, *U.S. Direct Investment Abroad, 1977* (1981); for 1983, Department of Commerce, *U.S. Direct Investment Abroad: Operations of U.S. Parent Companies and Their Foreign Affiliates: Revised 1983 Estimates* (1986).

velopment, and marketing know-how, but the importance of foreign direct investment in gross domestic capital formation has been relatively small for all of the NICs except Singapore (see Table 8.6).[32] Also noteworthy is a wide variation in the balance between foreign direct investment and other capital flows across the four Asian NICs. These differences are plausibly connected with policy choices. Foreign direct investment accounts for only a small share of foreign capital inflows into Korea. This fact is driven primarily by the country's heavy reliance on borrowing, but the country's restrictive posture regarding direct investment is undoubtedly important. The absolute amounts of foreign direct investment in Korea are substantially smaller than those in Taiwan, Hong Kong, and Singapore. The 1983–85 period, when Korea's debt burden was viewed by technocrats as excessive and foreign investment laws were liberalized, saw the share of direct foreign investment in total capital inflows shift upward, though only slightly. Foreign direct investment also plays a relatively small role in total capital formation in Taiwan, though unlike Korea, Taiwan has been a net *exporter* of capital since 1966 (with the exception of the period of the first oil shock). The role of foreign direct investment in the city-states is larger both in relation to gross domestic capital formation and in relation to total capital inflow, a fact no doubt influenced by their more liberal investment laws.

32. My thanks to Eric Ramstetter for constructing Table 8.6.

Table 8.6. Net direct foreign investment (DFI) as a share of gross domestic capital formation (GDCF) and net foreign capital inflows (FCAP) in the East Asian NICs, 1966–85

Country	1966–72	1973–75	1976–78	1979–82	1983–85
Korea					
DFI (US$ million)	28.2	90.5	87.7	53.5	137.2
% of GDCF	1.6	1.7	0.8	0.3	0.6
% of FCAP	4.3	5.6	10.9	1.1	7.4
Taiwan					
DFI	36.9	59.3	78.7	136.7	229.9
% of GDCF	2.9	1.4	1.2	1.1	2.0
% of FCAP	a	15.4	a	a	a
Singapore					
DFI	83.1b	532.0	423.9	1186.6	1158.9
% of GDCF	12.7b	26.4	17.3	21.7	14.5
% of FCAP	23.4b	78.1	107.6	104.0	281.3
Hong Kong					
DFI			183.6	613.9	641.9
% of GDCF			4.4	6.5	8.3
% of FCAP			64.1	50.0	54.5

anet capital outflow; calculation meaningless.
b1967–72.

Notes: For Korea, Taiwan, and Singapore, total DFI figures are taken from balance-of-payments data, which ideally include equity capital, reinvested earning, and other capital movements, though these often go unreported. FCAP = −(current account balance) + (unrequited transfers). For Hong Kong, total disbursement of DFI for OECD members only; FCAP = total financial flows by OECD, OPEC, and multilateral agencies. Some data for Hong Kong are not available.

Sources: For data on total DFI for Korea and Singapore, International Monetary Fund, *Balance of Payments Yearbook*, various issues; for data on GDCF for Korea and Singapore, IMF, *International Financial Statistics*, various issues; GDCF data for Hong Kong from Hong Kong Census and Statistics Department, *Monthly Bulletin of Statistics*, various issues, and *Estimates of Gross Domestic Product, 1966–1982* (1983); DFI data for Hong Kong from Organization for Economic Cooperation and Development, *Geographical Distribution of Financial Flows to Developing Countries*, various issues; DFI and GDCF data for Taiwan from Republic of China, Central Bank of China, *Balance of Payments, Taiwan District, Republic of China,* and *Financial Statistics, Taiwan District, Republic of China,* various issues.

FOREIGN INVESTMENT IN BRAZIL AND MEXICO

Latin America's import of foreign capital began to accelerate in the 1860s and, by World War I, accounted for about 20 percent of the world's total.[33] Most of this investment was in portfolio form and heavily concentrated in the railroads that were opening new land to cultivation. In 1920 Argentina, Brazil, and Mexico accounted for 82 percent of total

33. A review of portfolio investment in Latin America is provided by Barbara Stallings, *Banker to the Third World: U.S. Portfolio Investment in Latin America, 1900–1986* (Berkeley: University of California Press, 1987).

investment in Latin American railroads.[34] But these three large Latin American countries differed in the nature and extent of their dependence on foreign capital. In Mexico the commodity composition of exports was diversified, but foreign control was high. In Brazil and Argentina the product concentration of exports was high, but production of the main exports—coffee in Brazil, wheat and beef in Argentina—was in local hands, and foreign investment was largely in portfolio form.

Mexico has differed from the other NICs in experiencing profound social conflicts over the definition of property rights. Porfírio Díaz followed the ideas of his liberal advisers and actively welcomed foreign capital, which loomed extremely large in the Porfirian economy. Total foreign investment in Mexico in 1910 was about $1.7 billion, of which 85 percent was direct. In 1911 foreign investment controlled 98 percent of the mining sector, 100 percent of petroleum, 87 percent of electricity, and 94 percent of banking. Only 3.5 percent of total foreign investment was in manufacturing, but it accounted for 90 percent of total manufacturing investment.[35]

The Revolution and the 1917 Constitution reasserted the direct ownership of the nation over all subsoil resource rights.[36] However, a combination of government weakness, dependence on oil taxes, U.S. backing for the oil companies, and threat of military intervention initially made postrevolutionary Mexican governments unable to assert these property rights. By the 1930s the institutional capacity of the Mexican government had increased through the centralization of economic functions and the formation of a national oil company. These changes allowed a redefinition of the relationship with foreign capital, and in 1938 Cárdenas nationalized the oil industry. The intransigence of the oil companies redounded to Cárdenas's political advantage not only in Mexico, where his tough stance was wildly popular, but also in Washington, where the Roosevelt administration took a more lenient stance toward nationalization than its Republican predecessors. The combination of revolution, Depression, and Cárdenas's policy sharply reduced the overall position of foreign direct investment in the economy.[37]

34. Bill Albert, *South America and the World Economy from Independence to 1930* (London: Macmillan, 1983).

35. These estimates are from Fernando Rosenzweig et al., *História moderna de México; El Porfiriato: La vida economica* (Mexico City: Editorial Hermes, 1965). For a full discussion of these estimates and others, see David Glass, "The Politics of Economic Dependence: The Case of Mexico" (Ph.D. diss., University of California, Berkeley, 1984), chap. 3.

36. The classic account of the oil nationalization is Lorenzo Meyer, *Mexico and the United States in the Oil Controversy, 1917–1942* (Austin: University of Texas Press, 1977).

37. John Womack, "The Mexican Economy during the Revolution, 1910–1920: Historiography and Analysis," *Marxist Perspectives* 1 (Winter 1978): 80–123; Glass, "Politics of Economic Dependence."

Table 8.7. Sectoral shares of foreign direct investment in Mexico, 1911–80 (stocks, percentages)

Sector	1911	1940	1950	1960	1970	1980
Agriculture	6.7	1.9	0.7	1.8	1.1	0.1
Mining	28.2	23.9	19.8	15.6	5.5	5.0
Petroleum	3.6	0.3	2.1	2.0	0.9	
Manufacturing	4.5	7.1	26.1	55.7	73.8	
Electricity	—	24.2	1.4	0.1	0.1	
Commerce	4.2	3.5	12.4	18.1	15.5	
Transport and communications	38.9	31.6	13.3	2.8	0.3	
Public services	8.2	—	—	—	—	
Banks	5.7	—	—	—	—	
Other	—	0.2	1.4	2.5	2.8	
Commercial trade						8.9
Services						8.5
Industry						77.5

Note: Columns do not add to 100 percent due to rounding and incomplete sectoral coverage. Dashes indicate negligible percentages.

Sources: For 1911–70, David Glass, "The Politics of Economic Dependence: The Case of Mexico" (Ph.D. diss., University of California, Berkeley, 1985), Table 2-6. For 1980, Van R. Whiting, Jr., "Constraint on Choice: The Political Economy of Foreign Direct Investment in Mexico," unpublished ms., pp. 4–19.

The sectoral distribution of foreign direct investment changed over time, in line with national policy and stage of development (see Table 8.7). By the end of the Porfiriato over 70 percent of all foreign direct investment was in agriculture, mining, and transport and communications, particularly railroads. In the 1920s manufacturing's share of foreign investment increased as American firms entered to service the domestic market. Between 1940 and 1960, the period when ISI emerged as a strategy, manufacturing's share of total investment jumped dramatically, reaching a stable level in 1970.

The history of Mexican debt has also reflected changing national priorities and capabilities.[38] During the Porfiriato bonds were issued to finance government objectives, primarily the expansion of the railway system. From the beginning of the Revolution through the end of World War II, Mexico was continually involved in conflicts with its creditors. From 1914 until 1922 Mexico was unable to service its obligations. From 1922 through 1930 three separate agreements were reached in an effort to assuage both the American banks and the U.S. government. All proved unworkable and collapsed, and after the nationalization of the oil companies debt discussions broke off altogether. When talks resumed

38. For a history of Mexican debt, see Jan Bazant, *História de la deuda exterior de México* (Mexico City: El Collegio de México, 1968).

Table 8.8. Sectoral distribution of U.S. investment in Brazil, 1929–85 (percentages)

Sector	1929	1940	1952	1980	1985
Manufacturing	23.7	29.2	50.6	68.0	74.7
Petroleum (distribution)	11.9	12.9	17.1	4.7	3.0
Public utilities (incl. transport)	50.0	46.7	14.9	7.3	4.5
Trade	8.2	7.5	17.4		
Other	6.2	3.7		5.6	3.4
Banking and finance				12.5	11.4
Mining				1.9	—

Note: Dash indicates a negligible percentage.
Source: Werner Baer, *The Brazilian Economy,* 3d ed. (New York: Praeger, 1989), p. 216.

in 1942, the United States was at war, debt was discounted in the market, and Mexico received substantial relief from its creditors.

The data on foreign direct investment in Brazil before 1945 are sketchier than those for Mexico.[39] Changes in the sectoral composition of American investment over time are broadly similar to those for aggregate foreign direct investment in Mexico, though manufacturing became important earlier in Brazil (see Table 8.8). In 1929 exactly half of all American investment was in public utilities and transportation. Manufacturing's share increased in the 1930s and by 1952 already dominated the total. The postwar decades witnessed an increasing trend toward investment in manufacturing and services.

In prewar Brazil, to a greater extent than in Mexico, the story of foreign capital is a story of foreign debt. In 1927, 53 percent of British, American, and French investment was still in government bonds, and this figure was a decline from earlier periods.[40] Debt service was a continual problem for the governments of the First Republic. From 1890 through 1933 almost 75 percent of total trade surpluses went to meet debt repayment and service.[41] Falling coffee prices in 1898 and 1914 brought on debt crises and stringent rescheduling agreements. With the Depression commodity prices again fell, and new lending dried up. Brazil suspended payments in 1931. A repayment plan avoided the previous policy of contracting new debt in order to meet past obligations, but repayment was erratic until 1943 when Brazil, like Mexico,

39. On early patterns of direct foreign investment in Brazil see Eric Baklanoff, "External Factors in the Economic Development of Brazil's Heartland: The Center-South, 1850–1930," in Baklanoff, ed., *The Shaping of Modern Brazil* (Baton Rouge: Louisiana State University Press, 1969).
40. Albert, *South America and the World Economy,* p. 47.
41. For a history of Brazilian debt, see Annibal V. Villela and Wilson Suzigan, *Government Policy and the Economic Growth of Brazil, 1889–1945* (Rio de Janeiro: IPEA/INPES, 1977), appendix D.

exploited wartime conditions to unilaterally declare a plan unfavorable to bondholders.

Some comparisons are possible between patterns of investment in the East Asian and Latin American NICs through the end of World War II. Investment in infrastructure linked to the export of primary commodities was important in both regions, though with an increasing share going to industry over time. The key agents initiating these activities in Latin America were national governments working closely with foreign banks and investors. In the larger East Asian cases investment followed Japanese imperial design, which favored industry as well as agriculture. The end of empire left significant Japanese investment in the hands of new governments. The state's role in the economy expanded during the 1930s in both Brazil and Mexico, and national policy toward foreign capital became more aggressive. Nonetheless, there was a greater continuity of foreign presence in Latin America.

Foreign Direct Investment and Import Substitution

The literature on import-substituting direct investment in Brazil and Mexico is voluminous, and only a few points of comparative and theoretical relevance can be discussed here.[42] The first set of issues concerns the sectoral composition of foreign direct investment. The turn to secondary ISI in the mid-1950s was accompanied by new efforts to attract foreign investment in consumer durables and, later, intermediate and capital goods. Foreign direct investment was concentrated in rapidly growing industries such as transportation equipment, chemicals, electrical machinery, and metals, industries that were largely beyond the reach of national firms. MNCs played a central role in this new phase of Brazilian and Mexican growth, except in several capital-intensive intermediates, such as petrochemicals and steel, where the state preempted foreign participation by creating state-owned enterprises. The relative position of multinational corporations in the two countries peaked in the 1970s. Two factors help account for the relative decline in the role of direct foreign investment: the state's increased role in brokering the

---

42. On Mexico, Miguel Wionczek, *El nacionalismo y la inversion extranjera* (Mexico City: Siglo XXI, 1973); Fernando Fajnzylber and Trinidad Martinez Tarrago, *Las empresas transnacionales* (Mexico City: Fondo de Cultura Economica, 1976). On Brazil, Evans, *Dependent Development;* Carlos von Doellinger and Leonardo C. Cavalcanti, *Empresas multinacionais na indústria brasileira* (Rio de Janeiro: IPEA/INPES, 1979). See also Peter Evans and Gary Gereffi, "Foreign Investment and Dependent Development: Comparing Brazil and Mexico," in Sylvia Ann Hewlett and Richard S. Weinert, eds., *Brazil and Mexico: Patterns of Late Development* (Philadelphia: Institute for the Study of Human Issues, 1982); Rhys Jenkins, *Transnational Corporations and Industrial Transformation in Latin America* (New York: St. Martin's, 1984).

negotiation of joint ventures among state, foreign, and local firms; and the increase in foreign commercial borrowing that could be channeled to strengthen both private and state-owned national firms.

A second set of issues surrounds the behavior of firms. Multinationals operating in Latin America have been criticized for their propensity to import, transfer and monopoly pricing, capital intensity, and failure to generate employment. Plausible explanations could be developed for these behaviors as rational responses to government incentives, but I will elaborate the case for one aspect of MNC behavior that is of comparative interest: the propensity to export. The bias in ISI policies against exports naturally affected MNC operations. Efforts increased after the late 1960s to force MNCs to export, and in the 1970s and 1980s firms in some sectors, such as automobiles, turned to global sourcing strategies on their own account. In many cases, however, the trade behavior of foreign firms was dictated by their strategy on entry, and for firms outside the industrial parks on the U.S.-Mexican border this strategy centered on serving the domestic market. Exports accounted for a small portion of multinationals' sales in both countries, despite sometimes lavish incentives.

Before addressing these arguments in more detail, I outline briefly the trends in the rules governing foreign investment in the two countries. As with the East Asian cases, any such outline is necessarily schematic because of the complexity of the law, frequent changes, and the importance of discretion and negotiations in determining the precise terms of entry. Nonetheless, some broad trends are clear, and they follow political as well as economic objectives.

In Brazil the shift toward secondary ISI was manifest in new incentives that favored foreign over national firms. In 1955 the exchange-rate system was altered to give foreign investors in priority sectors favorable treatment in the remission of profits.[43] This gain came in addition to duty exemptions on imports of capital and intermediate goods and high levels of protection on final output. The liberal attitude toward foreign investment and profit remittance was reversed under the center-left governments of Jánio Quadros and João Goulart for both political and balance-of-payments reasons. What followed was a period of slowed growth of manufacturing investment.

Attracting foreign investment was an important component of the military's economic strategy. Restrictions on profit remittance were eased and efforts made to establish a favorable investment climate. From 1968 through 1976 foreign manufacturing investment grew extremely rap-

---

43. On the background to Instruction 113 see Nathaniel Leff, *Economic Policy-Making and Development in Brazil, 1947–1964* (New York: John Wiley, 1968), chap. 3.

idly. During the 1970s government policy moved to regulate various aspects of MNC behavior, including extent of local content, imports and exports, and degree of local participation. Particularly strict laws governed technology transfer and licensing agreements in sectors that the government sought to promote.[44]

In Mexico declared policy moved in an increasingly restrictive direction during the postwar period. In 1944 the government issued an emergency decree requiring that new foreign investment be limited to a minority position, though before 1960 the list of activities covered was small. In 1958 foreign interests were required to divest their holdings in communications, and in 1959 the government nationalized the foreign-owned power and light companies, but in a context in which it continued to encourage manufacturing investment. In 1962 a local-content scheme was imposed on foreign automobile manufacturers, and during the 1960s the Mexicanization requirement was extended to mining and petrochemicals.[45]

The Echeverría administration (1970–76) adopted a control-oriented posture toward foreign investment. In 1973 the government passed a Law to Promote Mexican Investment and Regulate Foreign Investment. This law codified sectoral restrictions on the scope of foreign investment and subjected all investment to a process of screening and registration. The law also included a Mexicanization provision limiting foreign investment to 49 percent of total capital. Nonetheless, a gap existed between announced policy and practice, and the newly created National Commission on Foreign Investment retained wide discretion; it could allow "exceptional" majority foreign ownership under a fairly flexible set of criteria. From the beginning of the López Portillo administration, only shortly after the law had been promulgated, the government relaxed restrictions in response to balance-of-payments difficulties, slowed growth, and the interest in promoting particular sectors. More important, continuities in the broader system of incentives, and the oil-related boom, pulled import-substituting foreign investment into Mexico; focusing on the rules governing foreign direct investment alone, as many studies do, is a misleading guide to the total policy environment facing foreign firms. With the turn to secondary ISI, foreign firms received duty exemptions for the import of capital goods, tax breaks, and levels of protection that were high, though not as restrictive as those in Brazil.

I have already shown the increasing share of manufacturing in total foreign investment over time (in Table 8.7). Demonstrating the role of

44. On the rules governing foreign direct investment in Mexico see Harry K. Wright, *Foreign Enterprise in Mexico: Laws and Policies* (Chapel Hill: University of North Carolina Press, 1971); Van R. Whiting, Jr., "Transnational Enterprises and the State in Mexico" (Ph.D. diss., Harvard University, 1981).

45. See Whiting, "Transnational Enterprises."

Table 8.9. Sectoral distribution of U.S. investment in Mexican manufacturing, 1950–70 (percentages)

Sector	1950	1960	1970
Food, beverages, and tobacco	25.9	10.4	14.2
Textiles and apparel	2.6	2.8	2.7
Paper	0.1	3.8	3.1
Rubber	10.1	8.6	4.1
Chemicals	24.8	35.4	29.7
Nonmetallic minerals[a]	4.7	5.9	3.9
Basic metals	5.4	5.2	3.7
Fabricated metals	3.0	3.9	6.0
Nonelectrical machinery	1.4	2.8	5.4
Electrical machinery	4.9	8.7	10.3
Transport equipment	12.8	6.1	10.2
Other[b]	4.1	6.4	6.8

[a]Except coal and oil.
[b]Includes statistical error.
Source: A. Sepulveda and A. Chumacero, *Inversion extranjera en México* (Mexico City: Fondo de Cultura Económico, 1973), Appendix Table 2.

industrial policy demands further sectoral disaggregation. Foreign investment in Mexico during the period of ISI was less concentrated sectorally than in Brazil and was attracted to traditional industries as well as manufacturing. Nonetheless, four industry groups—chemicals, machinery, food, and transport equipment—accounted for 65 percent of the total in 1970 (see Table 8.9). The substantial foreign investment in food is a function of Mexico's proximity to the American market. Agribusiness investment expanded rapidly in the 1970s and 1980s.[46] Within manufacturing, however, the presence of foreign firms was strongest in those industries "leading" the secondary phase of ISI. Foreign-invested firms accounted for more than 60 percent of manufacturing production in chemicals, machinery, and electrical machinery, the three fastest-growing sectors over the 1960s.[47] The sectoral composition of foreign investment helps account for the finding of high levels of concentration in the sectors in which multinationals play a role.[48]

Brazil, though data there are also subject to limitations, shows striking

46. See Steven Sanderson, *The Transformation of Mexican Agriculture: International Structure and the Politics of Rural Change* (Princeton: Princeton University Press, 1986).

47. A. Sepulveda and A. Chumacero, *Inversion extranjera en México* (Mexico City: Fondo de Cultura Económico, 1973), Appendix Table 2, pp. 389–90.

48. Richard Newfarmer and Willard Mueller, *Multinational Corporations in Brazil and Mexico: Structural Sources of Economic and Non-economic Power,* report to the U.S. Senate, Committee on Foreign Relations, Subcommittee on Multinational Corporations (Washington, D.C.: USGPO, 1975); Salvador Cordero, *Concentración y poder económica en México,* Cuadernos del Centro de Estúdios Sociológicos 18 (Mexico City: Collegio de México, 1977).

similarities to Mexico in the sectoral distribution and overall role of multinationals. In 1970, 75 percent of all net fixed assets held by reporting U.S. manufacturers in Brazil were concentrated in three industries: chemicals, transportation, and machinery. These three sectors were the top contributors to import substitution and among the top five fastest-growing sectors during the early phases of ISI in the 1950s.[49]

The MNCs' large share of total sales suggests their strong position in the domestic market, particularly in the sectors that led the secondary phase of ISI. In 1970 the share of sales of foreign firms (more than 25 percent foreign equity) was largest in autos (100 percent), electrical products (81 percent), appliances (73 percent), rubber manufacture (71 percent), and industrial machinery (67 percent), with strong representation in auto parts (63 percent) and chemicals (55 percent) as well.[50] Local sales were highest in sugar, lumber, cement, food processing, and textiles. The position of foreign firms appears to have eroded somewhat during the 1970s. A 1970 sample of 1,719 companies showed that state firms controlled 22 percent of equity, foreign firms 37 percent, and domestic firms 41 percent. In a 1980 sample of 4,002 firms, the state's share of total equity had increased to 27 percent, whereas foreign firms' share had dropped to 29 percent and domestic firms improved their position slightly to 44 percent of total equity.[51] There are increases, some quite dramatic, in the sales by national firms in several sectors once the preserve of foreign companies, including chemicals, industrial machinery, auto parts, plastics, and electrical products. Differences in sample size may account for some of this change, but it is plausible to argue that national firms benefited from learning and from increased finance available through foreign borrowing and from national policies that encouraged local development.

Data on the role of American MNCs in manufactured exports from Brazil and Mexico between 1960 and 1972 provide a stark contrast to the East Asian pattern and suggest the powerful influence of national strategy on firm behavior (see Table 8.10). Between 1966 and 1972 there was a sharp increase in the share of exports to total sales; it is during this period that both governments began to encourage multinationals to export. Nonetheless, the levels of exports to total sales remain substan-

49. Newfarmer and Mueller, *Multinational Corporations in Brazil and Mexico*, p. 105; Samuel A. Morley and Gordon W. Smith, "Import Substitution and Foreign Investment in Brazil," *Oxford Economic Papers* 23 (March 1971): 120–35.

50. "Quém e quém na economía brasiliera," *Visão*, August 1971 and August 1980, cited in Joseph Mooney and Richard Newfarmer, "State Enterprise and Private Sector Development in Brazil," unpublished ms. Mooney and Newfarmer correct the *Visão* sample to define a "foreign" firm as one with 25 percent foreign equity.

51. Ibid.

Table 8.10. Export/sales ratios and intracompany exports for U.S. MNCs, Mexico and Brazil, 1960–72 (percentages)

	Exports/local sales	Intracompany exports/total MNC exports
Mexico		
1960	1.3	56
1966	1.9	75
1972	5.1	82
Brazil		
1960	0.4	69
1966	1.4	62
1972	3.5	73

Source: Richard Newfarmer and Willard Mueller, *Multinational Corporations in Brazil and Mexico: Structural Sources of Economic and Non-economic Power,* report to the U.S. Senate, Committee on Foreign Relations, Subcommittee on Multinational Corporations (Washington, 1975).

tially lower than in the East Asia NICs. MNC exports were concentrated in ISI industries: transportation equipment, electrical and nonelectrical machinery, and chemicals. Export/sales ratios for these industries were similarly low in Korea. This finding sheds light on Peter Evans's and Gary Gereffi's conclusion that "TNC-led export promotion . . . is thus largely dependent on the willingness of the TNC parent to buy or allocate production from its Brazilian or Mexican subsidiary."[52] Where MNCs enter primarily to service the local market, conflicts will arise between the interests of firms and the balance-of-payments concerns of host governments; such conflicts have occurred in import-substituting sectors in East Asia as well. They are less acute there because balance-of-payments problems are generally less severe, but also because a greater share of foreign investment is export-oriented. The East Asian NICs are not, therefore, more dependent on foreign firms for exports; what few data exist suggest exactly the opposite (see Table 8.11).

Finally, an aggregate picture of the role of foreign savings and foreign direct investment in the Latin American NICs provides several interesting contrasts to the East Asian pattern. Though Taiwan differs from Korea in its higher level of domestic savings, both countries decreased their dependence on foreign savings after a forced weaning from American aid. The opposite trend is visible in Mexico and Brazil (see Table 8.12). Dependence on foreign savings dropped in both countries in the 1960s but increased during the heavy-industry push of the 1970s. Before the early 1970s a large proportion of total foreign capital was in the form of foreign direct investment. Thereafter borrowing increased and

52. Evans and Gereffi, "Foreign Investment," p. 147.

Table 8.11. Share of foreign-invested firms' exports in total NIC exports, selected years (percentages)

Year	Korea	Taiwan	Singapore	Hong Kong	Mexico	Brazil
1969						43.0
1970			83.5			
1974	31.4	28.6		10.0		
1977					37.0 (19.9)	
1978	18.3	29.1	91.8			
1982		25.1				
1983			89.7			
1984				17.8		

Sources: Korea, 1974: see Table 8.1; 1978: Korea Exchange Bank, *Monthly Review,* November 1980, p. 7. Taiwan, see Table 8.5. Singapore, see Table 8.4. Hong Kong, 1974: estimate in C. L. Hung, "Foreign Investments," in David Lethbridge, ed., *The Business Environment of Hong Kong* (Hong Kong: Oxford University Press, 1980); 1984: Hong Kong Industry Department, *Report on the Survey of Overseas Investment in Hong Kong's Manufacturing Industry, 1984* (Hong Kong: Industry Department, 1985). Mexico: World Bank, *Mexico: Manufacturing Sector: Situation, Prospects and Policies* (Washington, D.C.: World Bank, 1979), number in parentheses excludes investment in the border processing zones. Brazil: Deepak Nayyar, "Transnational Corporations and Manufactured Exports from Poor Countries," *Economic Journal* 88 (1978), p. 62.

Table 8.12. Foreign savings as a share of gross domestic investment (GDI) and foreign direct investment as a share of net foreign capital inflows in Mexico and Brazil, 1956–83

	Foreign savings/GDI	Foreign direct investment/net foreign capital
Mexico		
1956–60	14.4	
1961–65	10.0	41.8
1966–70	12.0	42.2
1971–75	15.2	23.0
1976–80	14.7	20.5
1981–83	11.1	17.2
Brazil		
1956–60	13.1	
1961–65	2.8	38.3
1966–70	4.1	39.6
1971–75	14.9	31.7
1976–80	23.7	25.4
1981–83	22.7	26.5

Source: Barbara Stallinga, "The Role of Foreign Capital in Economic Development: A Comparison of Latin America and East Asia," in Gary Gereffi and Don Wyman, eds., *Manufactured Miracles: Paths of Industrialization in East Asia and Latin America* (Princeton: Princeton University Press, 1990).

Table 8.13. Debt and debt-service ratios in Korea, Mexico, Brazil, and Argentina, 1970–85

	1970	1975	1980	1985
Korea				
Long-term debt ($ billions)	2.1	6.2	18.5	35.7
Debt-service ratio (%)	19.5	11.6	12.3	15.2
Mexico				
Long-term debt ($ billions)	5.9	15.6	41.2	89.0
Debt-service ratio (%)	23.6	24.9	32.1	36.9
Brazil				
Long-term debt ($ billions)	5.1	23.7	56.7	91.0
Debt-service ratio (%)	12.5	17.9	34.5	26.6
Argentina				
Long-term debt ($ billions)	5.1	6.5	16.7	40.1
Debt-service ratio (%)	21.6	22.0	17.7	41.7

Source: World Bank, *World Debt Tables 1986* (Washington, D.C.: World Bank, 1986), and previous issues. Long-term debt includes all public and private guaranteed and private nonguaranteed debt of more than one year maturity. The debt-service ratio is total debt service divided by total export earnings.

the relative share of foreign direct investment dropped, though compared to the East Asian NICs a comparatively large portion of total capital inflows remained in the form of foreign direct investment.

The increase in dependence on foreign savings was caused by the rapid expansion of foreign borrowing. An exploration of the causes and consequences of the debt crisis that ensued would go beyond the scope of this book and would have to include an analysis of the financial markets and lending practices of the banks as well as the unfavorable international conjuncture of the early 1980s—high interest rates, low commodity prices, and slowed world growth.[53] As I suggested in Chapter 8, no account of the crisis would be complete without attention to the domestic political economy of debt accumulation. In the short run, monetary and fiscal policies exacerbated the crisis. Over the longer run, however, the strategy of import substitution itself proved debt-intensive and resulted in biases against exports that contributed to debt-servicing problems. This result can be seen by comparing Korea's debt-service ratio with that of the larger Latin American borrowers (see Table 8.13). Korea's borrowing trajectory since 1970 is very similar to that of Argentina, but Korea's strong export performance allowed it to avoid ris-

53. See Miles Kahler, "Politics and International Debt: Explaining the Crisis," in Kahler, ed., *The Politics of International Debt* (Ithaca: Cornell University Press, 1986).

ing debt-service ratios that have plagued Latin America; Korea's debt-service ratio was lower in 1985 than it was in 1970.

POLICY, POLITICS, AND FOREIGN INVESTMENT

Several dependency claims, including those on denationalization and the distortions attributed to MNC operations, hinge critically on the sectoral composition of investment and the policy context. In Korea, Taiwan, and Hong Kong local firms were located in the economy's most dynamic growth sectors and could compete in an expanding world market without the threat of denationalization. In Brazil and Mexico the shift to a secondary phase of ISI depended to a greater extent on foreign capital and state-owned enterprises, squeezing the relative position of the domestic private sector, though the precise balance in the triple alliance still varies among countries pursuing ISI.[54] The comparison of the export behavior of MNCs across the two regions suggests a much stronger influence of national strategy, and the argument could easily be extended to other aspects of MNC behavior such as capital intensity, the appropriateness of MNC products and processes, and employment generation and equity—the subject of the next chapter.

I have not addressed the question of the bargaining power of the multinational corporations directly, but my analysis is germane to some of the central controversies on this subject as well. Both the "new wave" dependency theorists and their bargaining-school critics agree that the distribution of gains between firm and host is the result of negotiation; they differ primarily in their predictions on who prevails. Dependistas emphasize the daunting array of resources that multinationals command and the difficulties states face in regulating MNC behavior.[55] Bargaining theorists emphasize the organizational, economic, and political resources of the state and the role of tactics and learning over time.[56]

---

54. In a critique of the perspective offered here Dennis Encarnation has pointed out that the pattern of MNC dominance is not a necessary concomitant of ISI. Encarnation notes that the Indian government maintained a tight regulatory regime that limited MNC penetration while encouraging firms to pursue innovative strategies that allowed them to control domestic markets. Encarnation also notes that India paid dearly for this control-oriented approach and, more important, that this variance must be traced ultimately to domestic political factors, including the nationalist foreign economic policy of the Congress party, the country's control-oriented approach to development, and the close relationship between business and government. See Encarnation, *Dislodging Multinationals*, pp. 177, 193, 221–25.

55. A clear statement of this position is Thomas Biersteker, "The Illusion of State Power: Transnational Corporations and the Neutralization of Host-Country Legislation," *Journal of Peace Research* 17, 3 (1980): 207–21.

56. On the bargaining approach the classic statement remains Moran, *Copper and*

The analysis presented here suggests that different findings may reflect differences in type of foreign direct investment. The dynamics of host-firm bargaining, including the resources each party brings to bear and the bargaining agenda itself, varies among extractive, import-substituting, and export-oriented investment. The first wave of literature on foreign investment in the developing world focused on extractive industries.[57] Investments there had characteristics that weakened the bargaining power of the host at the point of entry. Investments were extremely large and demanded that the firm adopt a long time horizon, which allowed the investor to extract substantial guarantees and support for the project before committing resources. Once the investment was sunk, and host governments learned to manage relatively straightforward production processes, bargaining power shifted toward the host. Costly investments became relatively easy targets for regulation, rewriting of contract terms, and even nationalization. Bargains "obsolesced."

The host-firm relationship is quite different in import-substituting industries, the main focus of "new wave" dependistas. The ability of the state to control access to the local market allows for increased selectivity, at least in larger countries. If the industry is a new one, there is no established clientele; if the industry is already established, domestic firms will view foreign entrants as a competitive threat unless they can profit from joint-venture arrangements. For a range of smaller investments, the immediate impact on employment growth and government revenue is likely to be small. The point of entry may therefore be the moment at which the investor is *weakest*.

The bargaining relationship changes once firms are established.[58] Networks of suppliers, distributors, consumers, joint-venture partners, and labor provide a political base of support for the MNC. Product differentiation, dependence on external sources of technology, advertising, trademarks, and consumer loyalty enhance the bargaining power of import-substituting firms over time and reduce the credibility of nationalization as an alternative. The bargaining agenda is not as simple as dividing a rent or expanding national control over an indigenous re-

Dependency in Chile. See also Van R. Whiting, Jr., "Markets and Bargains: Foreign Investment and Development Strategies in Mexico," in Donald Wyman, ed., *Mexico's Economic Crisis: Challenges and Opportunities* (San Diego: Center for U.S.-Mexican Studies, University of California, San Diego, 1983).

57. See Moran, *Copper and Dependency in Chile;* Franklin Tugwell, *The Politics of Oil in Venezuela* (Stanford: Stanford University Press, 1975); Paul Sigmund, *Multinationals in Latin America: The Politics of Nationalization* (Madison: University of Wisconsin Press, 1980); Raymond Vernon, "Sovereignty at Bay: Ten Years After," *International Organization* 35 (Summer 1981): 517–39.

58. This point is made repeatedly in the case studies in Newfarmer, ed., *Profits, Poverty, and Progress.*

source; rather, it turns on complex regulatory issues such as the appropriateness of products and processes, the transfer of technology, linkages with local producers, and employment policies. Moreover, many of these regulatory efforts constitute attempts to offset distortions resulting from more basic policy choices. The effort to promote exports with high levels of protection and overvalued exchange rates is a prime example.

Export-oriented investments present a third type of foreign direct investment.[59] Offshore assembly operations are motivated primarily by labor costs and location. In general, one would predict that the bargaining power of developing countries over this type of investment will be weak across the investment cycle. Labor is abundant in the developing world, and the creation of employment is a continually pressing concern. Yet the most important issues on the bargaining agenda are likely to concern labor: the effect of assembly work on the health of women workers, the influence of assembly zones on internal migration, and the wage bill itself. The power of the multinational is further enhanced by the fact that export-oriented investments tend to be relatively small and are in mobile assets such as machinery.

On the other hand, some drawbacks attributed to offshore assembly per se are probably more manipulable than is commonly thought. The criticism that such investments result in few domestic linkages partly results from national policies that isolate the processing zone in order to protect the domestic market. Moreover, the calculations of benefit from this type of investment are likely to be relatively straightforward. Balance-of-payments effects and returns to labor are fairly easily weighed against the costs of infrastructural and administrative support.[60]

The full implications of the distinction among types of foreign investment can be explored only through comparative studies across different types, an effort beyond the scope of this book. One point bears reiterating, however. To the extent that national strategies influence the sectoral composition of investment, they will also help determine the overall bargaining setting in which state and firms operate.

---

59. See Joseph Grunwald and Kenneth Flamm, *The Global Factory: Foreign Assembly in International Trade* (Washington, D.C.: Brookings, 1985).

60. See Dennis J. Encarnation and Louis T. Wells, Jr., "Evaluating Foreign Investment," in Theodore H. Moran, ed., *Investing in Development: New Roles for Private Capital* (New Brunswick, N.J.: Transaction, 1986), pp. 61–86.

CHAPTER NINE

Industrial Strategy and Income Distribution

The previous chapter argued that government incentives had predictable effects on foreign direct investment, the behavior of multinationals, and dependency. This chapter applies a similar explanatory logic to the social structure by examining the effects of state intervention on income distribution. Not surprisingly, the most powerful effects result from policies that influence the distribution of basic assets. Land reforms, followed by relatively supportive agricultural policies, contributed to a comparatively egalitarian distribution of income in Korea and Taiwan. A sustained commitment to education also differentiates the East Asian NICs from Brazil and Mexico. The influence of industrial strategy is more difficult to isolate, but evidence suggests that it also affected income distribution. Export-oriented policies contributed to a more egalitarian distribution of income and a more rapid alleviation of poverty than did the pursuit of ISI.

The starting point for such analysis must be Simon Kuznets's well-known observation of an "inverted-U" pattern in the evolution of income distribution.[1] Because productivity and income can be expected to grow more rapidly in the modern sector than in agriculture, income disparities widen as the modern sector expands. Inequality increases in the early stages of growth. Once the rural labor surplus is exhausted, wages rise and a more egalitarian equilibrium is achieved.

Cross-sectional studies have shown that poorer countries do experience rising inequality in the early stages of growth, but the variance around the "Kuznets curve" (plotting income distribution against per

---

1. Simon Kuznets, "Economic Growth and Income Inequality," *American Economic Review* 45 (March 1955): 1–28.

capita GNP) is high and there are important exceptions to the pattern.[2] The East Asian NICs combined rapid growth with relatively equal, and even improving, income distribution. Mexico and Brazil, by contrast, exhibited rising inequality over long periods of time. These variations suggest that other factors can overturn, or accelerate, the hopeful prediction of an equity "turning point"; among these factors are the structure of property rights, demography, and technological change.

The effect of industrial policy on income distribution and poverty alleviation has also come in for close scrutiny.[3] Incentives to labor-intensive manufacturing, such as those adopted by the East Asian NICs, should produce a more favorable income distribution in labor-abundant economies than a strategy that favors capital intensity in production. Under relatively neutral incentives, firms in labor-rich countries will substitute labor for capital where feasible and pursue labor-absorbing investments. The transition from an employment structure dominated by lower-paying agricultural jobs to one dominated by higher-paying jobs in the modern sector will therefore be accelerated. The demand for labor increases more rapidly, and the turning point after which unemployment falls and real wages rose will be reached sooner. The distribution of income may even improve during the transition if income within the modern sector is less skewed than in agriculture. Incentives to use labor will also favor a more equitable distribution of capital, since labor-intensive manufacturing is characterized by lower entry barriers, lower capital requirements, and fewer economies of scale.

ISI policies, by contrast, encourage capital-intensive industrialization. This, in turn, produces segmentation in labor markets, since it requires more skilled and educated labor and is more likely to produce "wage spreading," or increasing differentials, between managerial and non-managerial ranks. ISI dampens employment growth and contributes to industrial concentration and to monopoly or oligopoly rents for owners of capital.[4] Such a strategy also concentrates workers and thus facilitates

2. For a review of the cross-national evidence on the Kuznets hypothesis, see Gary Fields, *Poverty, Inequality, and Development* (Cambridge: Cambridge University Press, 1980), pp. 59–124; Montek Ahluwalia, "Inequality, Poverty, and Development," *Journal of Development Economics* 3 (1976): 307–42.

3. On the debate about the effect of policy on income distribution see Irma Adelman and Cynthia Taft Morris, *Economic Growth and Social Equity in Developing Countries* (Stanford: Stanford University Press, 1973); Hollis Chenery, *Redistribution with Growth* (New York: Oxford University Press, 1974); Henry J. Bruton, "Industrialization Policy and Income Distribution," in Charles R. Frank and Richard C. Webb, eds., *Income Distribution and Growth in the Less-Developed Countries* (Washington, D.C.: Brookings, 1977).

4. See Richard Webb, "Wage Policy and Income Distribution in Developing Countries," in Frank and Webb, *Income Distribution and Growth;* Anne Krueger, "The Relationships between Trade, Employment, and Development," in Gustav Ranis and T. Paul Schultz, eds., *The State of Development Economics: Progress and Perspectives* (New York: Oxford University Press, 1988).

labor organization and the exercise of market power. Crucial for any assessment of the consequences of development strategies is sorting out the relative effects of three different factors on income distribution: labor power, market structure, and government policy.

Interestingly, the literature on the relationship between "dependent development" and inequality is also critical of ISI, though it reaches that criticism by a different causal route.[5] The political influence and production strategies of the multinationals are held accountable for policies and processes that skew the distribution of income in favor of capital, segment labor markets, and create "labor aristocracies."

The distribution of income has presented economists with thorny problems of theory, data, and method; the purpose of the following comparison is necessarily modest. First, I outline the cross-national differences between countries pursuing different growth strategies, using indicators of poverty alleviation and physical well-being as well as relative income distribution. I then assess the extent to which cross-national differences can be traced to government policy, including industrialization strategy.

INCOME DISTRIBUTION AND WELFARE IN THE EAST ASIAN NICS

Relative Income Distribution

The Gini coefficient is a measure of relative income distribution that theoretically can vary between zero (perfect equality of income) and one (all income accruing to one person or household). In reality Gini coefficients of o.3 or below reflect low levels of inequality, those above o.5 high inequality. Table 9.1 presents data on the Gini coefficients for household income in the NICs.

Strikingly, Korean income distribution was comparatively equitable *prior* to the transition to export-led growth.[6] Land reform is the most plausible explanation, though no doubt the destruction of the Korean War also had a powerful leveling effect. In the absence of significant scale economies in rice production, reform could occur without substantial disruption of production and could even enhance efficiency. Income

5. For summaries, see Volker Bornschier and Christopher Chase-Dunn, *Transnational Corporations and Underdevelopment* (New York: Praeger, 1985), and Thomas Biersteker, *Distortion or Development? Contending Perspectives on the Multinational Corporation* (Cambridge: MIT Press, 1978).

6. Serious shortcomings in the Korean data bias them in an egalitarian direction. See Edwin S. Mason et al., *The Economic and Social Modernization of the Republic of Korea* (Cambridge: Harvard University Press, 1980), chap. 12; V. V. Bhanoji Rao, "Income Distribution in East Asian Developing Countries," *Asian Pacific Economic Literature* 2 (March 1988): 29–30.

Table 9.1. Gini coefficients for household income in the NICs, 1950–85

Year	Korea	Taiwan	Singapore	Hong Kong	Brazil	Mexico
1950						0.526
1953		0.558				
1957				0.470		0.551
1960					0.53	
1961		0.440				
1963				0.462		0.555
1964		0.360				
1965	0.344					
1966		0.358	0.498	0.467		
1968		0.362				0.577
1970	0.332	0.321			0.59	
1971				0.409		
1972		0.318			0.61	
1974		0.319		0.398		
1975			0.448			0.579
1976	0.391	0.307		0.409	0.60	
1977						
1978		0.306			0.56	
1979			0.424	0.373		
1980		0.303			0.56	
1981			0.443	0.453		
1982	0.357	0.308	0.465			
1983					0.57	
1984		0.312	0.474			
1985		0.317				

Sources: Korea: Sang-mok Suh and David Williamson, "The Impact of Adjustment and Stabilization Policies on Social Welfare: The South Korean Experiences during 1978–1985," in Giovanni Andrea Cornia, Richard Jolly, and Frances Stewart, *Adjustment with a Human Face* (Oxford: Clarendon Press, 1988), p. 232. Taiwan: Shirley W. Y. Kuo, *The Taiwan Economy in Transition* (Boulder, Colo.: Westview, 1983), p. 96, and *Report on the Survey of Personal Income Distribution in Taiwan Area* (Taipei: Director General of Budget, Accounting and Statistics, 1986). Singapore: V. V. Bhanoji Rao, "Income Distribution in East Asian Developing Countries," *Asian-Pacific Economic Literature* 2 (March 1988): 28. Hong Kong: Tzong-biau Lin, "Growth, Equity, and Income Distribution in Hong Kong," *The Developing Economies* 23 (December 1985): 395. Brazil: Gary Fields, "Poverty, Inequality, and Economic Growth," in G. Psacharopoulos, ed., *Essays on Poverty, Equity and Growth* (forthcoming). Data for 1960–72 are Gini coefficients of monetary income among households; for 1976–83, for total gross personal income among households. Mexico: David Felix, "Income Distribution Levels in Mexico and the Kuznets Curve," in Sylvia Ann Hewlett and Richard S. Weinert, eds., *Brazil and Mexico: Patterns in Late Development* (Philadelphia: Institute for the Study of Human Issues, 1982), p. 267.

distribution improved somewhat during the initial period of export-led growth, as labor was drawn into a manufacturing sector in which the wage structure was relatively egalitarian. Distribution worsened over the 1970s, probably because of growing inequality in business income.[7] This result might be explained by biases favoring large firms during the

7. Mason et al., *Economic and Social Modernization*, pp. 429–33.

heavy-industry drive, though the rising inequality in business incomes began in the late 1960s. The "big push" did increase the demand for skilled labor and led to a widening of wage differentials by educational background. The female labor force participation rate also increased dramatically in the 1970s, and wage differentials by gender are notoriously large in Korea.[8] Income distribution improved in the early 1980s, but viewed over the long run the distribution of income as measured by the Gini coefficient has been surprisingly stable since the initiation of export-led growth.

Taiwan shows both similarities to and differences from the Korean pattern. The high Gini coefficient for 1953, though not wholly reliable, is suggestive of the concentration of income before the completion of the land reform. As in Korea, land reform explains why the distribution of income was relatively equal by the early 1960s. After the transition to export-led growth, income distribution continued to improve. The gap between urban and rural incomes widened but was offset by a sharp reduction of inequalities within the manufacturing sector. This reduction was the major cause of improvement, but income distribution within the farm sector also improved. Unlike in Korea, the government promoted a decentralized pattern of industrialization that provided opportunities for off-farm income. The KMT also invested heavily in agricultural modernization and generally avoided the lure of heavy industry that contributed to the worsening of income distribution in Korea in the 1970s.[9]

Cross-national comparisons of Gini coefficients for household income are risky because of differences in analytic techniques, family size, and income over the life cycle. The difference between Korea and Taiwan and the city-states in the mid-1960s is nonetheless quite striking. Singapore and Hong Kong appear to have had levels of inequality significantly higher than in the larger East Asian NICs. High inequality within large and diverse service sectors is one reason for this difference.[10] Inequality rose in Hong Kong during its early experience with export-led growth (1957–66) but fell in both city-states between 1966 and 1979. The lowest level of inequality achieved by Hong Kong and Singapore in the 1970s was still well above that in Taiwan, however.

The main factors contributing to the improvement of income dis-

8. See David L. Lindauer, *Labor Market Behavior in the Republic of Korea*, World Bank Staff Working Paper 641 (Washington, D.C., 1984).

9. See Shirley W. Y. Kuo, Gustav Ranis, and John C. H. Fei, *The Taiwan Success Story: Rapid Growth with Improved Income Distribution in the Republic of China, 1952–1979* (Boulder, Colo.: Westview, 1981), pp. 85–108.

10. Toshiyuki Mizoguchi, "Economic Development Policy and Income Distribution: The Experience of East and Southeast Asia," *The Developing Economies* 23 (December 1985): 312.

tribution in the city-states were similar to those in Korea and Taiwan: a decrease in unemployment, rising wages, and the shift of labor into the manufacturing sector, where earnings were relatively equal across occupation, skill level, and industry.[11] Demographic factors help explain periods of declining equality. Hong Kong experienced a wave of immigration from the mainland in the 1950s and again in 1979–80 before efforts were made to staunch the flow. Singapore also pursued a more open policy toward immigration and guest workers in the late 1970s to reduce wage pressures.

Changes in economic structure and the policies supporting them also help explain the reversal. Disaggregations of income distribution show that inequality is less in Hong Kong's manufacturing sector than in the service sector in which the colony increasingly specialized in the late 1970s.[12] Policy played a more direct role in Singapore. The high-wage policy associated with the restructuring effort of the Second Industrial Revolution and the new emphasis placed on services and specialized manufacturing niches widened wage differentials, particularly because of the policy of allowing greater numbers of immigrants to man low-paying jobs.[13] As a result of these reversals, Hong Kong and Singapore show only a marginal improvement in relative income distribution since 1966.

An indicator that more graphically captures the degree of social stratification is the share of income accruing to the poorest 20 and 40 percent of households (see Table 9.2). Such a snapshot does not say anything about social mobility, since the poorest 20 percent at one point in time are not necessarily the poorest later on. The comparison shows, however, that the poor have received a substantially larger share of national income in the East Asian NICs than in Brazil and Mexico, though the differences between Hong Kong and the Latin American NICs are less pronounced. Distributional trends in Taiwan again demonstrate that a comparatively equitable outcome cannot be traced to export-led growth alone. The share of income accruing to the poorest in Taiwan in 1953 was roughly comparable to Mexico's in the 1950s and Brazil's in 1960, but it jumped dramatically between 1953 and 1964. The timing and magnitude of the improvement suggest that the land reform of the

11. Rao, "Income Distribution," pp. 28–31; Tzong-biau Lin, "Growth, Equity, and Income Distribution Policies in Hong Kong," *The Developing Economies* 23 (December 1985): 391–413; Ronald Hsia and Laurence Chau, *Industrialization, Employment, and Income Distribution: A Case Study of Hong Kong* (London: Croom Helm, 1978); I. Islam and C. Kirkpatrick, "Export-Led Development, Labour-Market Conditions, and Distribution of Income: The Case of Singapore," *Cambridge Journal of Economics* 10 (June 1986): 113–27; V. V. Bhanoji Rao and M. K. Ramakrishnan, *Income Inequality in Singapore* (Singapore: Singapore University Press, 1980).
12. Tzong-biau Lin, "Growth, Equity . . . in Hong Kong."
13. Rao, "Income Distribution," pp. 30–31.

Table 9.2. Income share of the poorest in the NICs, selected years

	Bottom 20 percent	Bottom 40 percent
Korea		
1964	7.0	18.0
1970	7.0	18.0
1976	5.7	16.9
Taiwan		
1953	3.0	11.3
1964	7.7	20.3
1972	8.6	21.8
1980	8.8	22.7
Hong Kong		
1957	5.7	15.4
1966	4.7	13.1
1976	5.3	15.3
1981	3.7	12.5
Brazil		
1960	n.a.	8.0–11.5
1970	n.a.	6.8–9.9
1976	n.a.	6.8–9.9
Mexico		
1950	6.1–7.8	14.3–17.7
1957	4.4–6.0	11.3–15.5
1963	3.6	9.2–10.3
1968	2.8–3.6	7.9–10.8
1977	1.9–2.6	8.0–8.2

Sources: Korea 1964 and 1970: Irma Adelman and Sherman Robinson, *Income Distribution in Developing Countries: A Case Study of Korea* (New York: Oxford University Press, 1978), p. 46; Korea 1976: *World Development Report 1988* (Washington, D.C.: World Bank, 1988), Table 26, p. 273. Taiwan: Shirley W. Y. Kuo, *The Taiwan Economy in Transition* (Boulder, Colo.: Westview, 1983), pp. 96–97. Hong Kong: Tzongbiau Lin, "Growth, Equity, and Income Distribution in Hong Kong," *The Developing Economies* 23 (December 1985): 395. Brazil: Guy Pfefferman and Richard Webb, "Poverty and Income Distribution in Brazil," *Review of Income and Wealth* 29 (June 1983): 105. Mexico: David Felix, "Income Distribution Levels in Mexico and the Kuznets Curve," in Sylvia Ann Hewlett and Richard S. Weinert, eds., *Brazil and Mexico: Patterns in Late Development* (Philadelphia: Institute for the Study of Human Issues, 1982), p. 268. Ranges for Brazil and Mexico reflect different assumptions about the underreporting of income.

1950s had a more powerful effect than the turn to exports—not surprising when we consider the share of population in agriculture.

Absolute Welfare and Poverty Alleviation

To capture the welfare effects of economic growth, we need to examine measures of absolute, as well as relative, income and poverty; indeed, one could argue that these are the more important measures. Real wage

Table 9.3. Growth of real wages in manufacturing in the NICs (1970 = 100)

Year	Korea	Taiwan	Singapore	Hong Kong	Brazil	Mexico
1948				59.9		
1954		56.0				
1960		55.7	90.0	62.9		
1962	59.6					
1965	55.7	72.9		94.0		92.4
1968					94.6	
1970	100.0	100.0	100.0	100.0	100.0	100.0
1975	130.3	124.2		116.2	128.2	113.3
1980	192.7	192.1	120.0	151.5	155.3	115.4
1985	251.2	252.8			159.8	80.4

Sources: Korea: Economic Planning Board, *Major Statistics on the Korean Economy* (Seoul: EPB), various issues. Taiwan: *Statistical Yearbook of the Republic of China 1985* (Taipei: Director General of Budget, Accounting, and Statistics, 1985), and *Taiwan Statistical Data Book 1987* (Taipei: Council on Economic Planning and Development, 1987). Singapore and Hong Kong: calculated from Gary Fields, "Industrialization and Employment in Hong Kong, Korea, Singapore and Taiwan," in Walter Galenson, ed., *Foreign Trade and Investment: Economic Development in the Newly Industrializing Asian Countries* (Madison: University of Wisconsin Press, 1985), p. 353. Brazil and Mexico: Program Regional del Empleo en America Latina y el Caribe (PREALC), *Mercado de trabajo en cifras, 1950–1980* (Santiago: PREALC, 1982), pp. 149–50; *PREALC Newsletter* 14 (August 1987).

growth in the manufacturing sector has been extremely rapid in Korea and Taiwan under export-led growth policies, though much more sluggish in the city-states that periodically pull labor from their hinterlands. The divergence between the larger Asian NICs and Brazil and Mexico became particularly marked during the debt crisis of the 1980s, when real wages in Mexico fell below their level in the mid-1960s (see Table 9.3).

One interesting finding is that real wage growth was negative in both Korea and Taiwan at the time export-oriented policies were launched. Real wages in Hong Kong were also stagnant in the 1950s and did not take off until the 1960s. Singapore, with the least rapid growth in real wages of all the East Asian NICs, confirms this pattern. In 1960 wages in Singapore were the highest in Asia outside Japan. To counteract this disadvantage, the government used wage policy and control of labor to attract foreign direct investment. Unemployment, growing female participation in the labor force, and government control over the trade unions prevented real wages from rising in the 1960s. Between the turn to export-led growth and 1975, as Gary Fields notes, "average real monthly earnings per *worker* failed to grow . . . [but] due to a doubling of the female labor force participation rate, and the falling unemployment rate, real wages per *family* increased about 40 percent over the same time

Table 9.4. Physical quality of life index for the NICs, selected years

Year	Korea	Taiwan	Singapore	Hong Kong	Brazil	Mexico
1950		63			53	
1951						55
1957	58					
1959						65
1960		77		76	63	
1968	76					
1970		87	83		66	71
1971				86		
1980	85	88	86	92	74	78
1985	88	94	91	95	77	84

Sources: Morris David Morris, *Measuring the Condition of the World's Poor: The Physical Quality of Life Index* (New York: Pergamon, 1979), pp. 149–50; for 1980, Roger Hansen and contributors, *U.S. Foreign Policy and the Third World: Agenda 1982* (New York: Praeger, 1982), pp. 160–71; for 1985, John Sewell, Stuart Tucker, and contributors, *Growth, Exports and Jobs in a Changing World Economy: Agenda 1988* (New Brunswick, N.J.: Transaction, 1988), pp. 246–57.

period."[14] This outcome underscores the critical importance of examining employment growth before making any assessment of the welfare effects of different strategies, a topic taken up in detail below.

Income provides a measure of resources that can be applied to the satisfaction of needs; it does not directly measure living conditions. Morris David Morris has combined three indicators of physical well-being into a Physical Quality of Life Index (PQLI): infant mortality, life expectancy, and basic literacy.[15] Theoretically, the PQLI can vary between zero and one hundred; the range in 1970 was from 12 in Guinea-Bissau to 97 in Sweden. By the early 1970s the East Asian NICs already approached the levels of the advanced industrial states (see Table 9.4). The improvement in Brazil was much more modest. By the 1980s Mexico had approached Korea, which lagged somewhat behind the other East Asian NICs in improving the quality of life.

These data cannot be taken as firm evidence for the effect of industrialization strategy, since such indicators are responsive to other social policies. They are important, however, in confirming once again the significance of initial conditions. Living standards increased more rapidly in Korea and Taiwan during the period of export-led growth than they

14. Gary Fields, "Industrialization and Employment in Hong Kong, Korea, Singapore, and Taiwan," in Walter Galenson, ed., *Foreign Trade and Investment: Economic Development in the Newly Industrializing Asian Countries* (Madison: University of Wisconsin Press, 1985), p. 349.
15. Morris David Morris, *Measuring the Condition of the World's Poor: The Physical Quality of Life Index* (New York: Pergamon, 1979).

did under import substitution in Mexico and Brazil, but Taiwan and Hong Kong had *already* achieved quality-of-life standards that surpassed those in Mexico and Brazil in the 1950s, and Korea's were roughly comparable despite substantially lower levels of per capita income.

Export-Led Growth, Income Distribution, and Poverty Alleviation

With the exception of Hong Kong, the East Asian NICs all improved their relative income distributions immediately following the transition to export-led growth. Widening income disparities between traditional and modern sectors were offset by narrowing wage differentials within the manufacturing sector. This observation, in turn, can plausibly be attributed to a development strategy that provided incentives to the use of unskilled and semiskilled labor. Real wages were stagnant at the time export-led growth policies were launched, but incomes rose quickly thereafter.

As the East Asian NICs moved into a secondary phase of export-led growth, the economic structure became increasingly differentiated and income inequality increased. Though research remains to be done, it is likely that business income became more concentrated as firms grew in size and that this was a crucial factor in widening inequality, particularly in Korea. Booming financial, equity, and real-estate markets also provided new opportunities for capital gains for the wealthy, particularly after the currency appreciations of the late 1980s. In Korea, Singapore, and Hong Kong, Gini coefficients in the 1980s were above or near their levels of the mid-1960s, and Taiwan witnessed some deterioration as well. If Kuznets's expectation of worsening income distribution is taken as a baseline, however, then the maintenance of a relatively egalitarian distribution of income during a period of rapid growth must be seen as an accomplishment.

Viewed comparatively, the initial distribution of assets seems more important than industrial strategy in determining income distribution.[16] Because of the land reforms of the 1950s, levels of inequality in Korea and Taiwan before the transition to export-led growth were well below those in Brazil and Mexico. Government strategy mattered, but not industrial strategy alone. Taiwan's record, the best among the Asian NICs, suggests the importance of improving the distribution of income *within* the agricultural sector. Korea also avoided greater increases in inequality in the 1970s because of its agricultural pricing policies.

16. On the critical importance of considering initial conditions see Surjit S. Bhalla and Paul Glewwe, "Growth and Equity in Developing Countries: A Reinterpretation of the Sri Lankan Experience," *World Bank Economic Observer* 1 (September 1986): 35–64.

But we still face a puzzle: Why didn't income distribution worsen with rapid industrial growth? One reason is highly flexible labor markets. The simplest hypothesis explaining this flexibility is in underlying labor-market conditions. Labor was weak precisely because it was abundant. Moreover, import substitution in Korea and Taiwan was relatively brief, and manufacturing accounted for a small share of GNP at the time of the transition. None of the East Asian NICs faced the networks of urban forces tied to the ISI process which have been an important feature of Latin American politics.

Institutional and political factors that have influenced wage setting in other developing countries were also absent in the East Asian NICs.[17] Unions were directly controlled or penetrated by the government in Korea, Taiwan, and Singapore. Union weakness was evident not only in the private sector but among public-sector workers as well; they have not played the significant role they have in Latin America. Nor was there any political space for labor-based political parties, because of the ability of both governments to manipulate external threats to curtail the activities of the left. The most important populist challenges came in Korea in the immediate postwar period and in Singapore in the 1950s. Both were decisively defeated. In Hong Kong migration and a politically divided and sectorally fragmented union structure limited labor's power. Industrial-structural characteristics of export-led growth further contributed to labor weakness, as Fred Deyo has argued.[18] Low skill levels, instability of employment, vulnerability to external fluctuations, relatively small firm size, and high female participation rates, particularly among younger women, all inhibited the development of the stable working-class communities that provide the social foundation for effective labor organization.

Labor's political exclusion in all of the East Asian NICs gave state elites and the private sector a substantial degree of freedom. Minimum wage laws, protective labor legislation, social security, and welfare expenditures have been limited. Governments retained substantial power to settle disputes, and managers retained autonomy and discretion on the shop floor.[19] Given labor-market conditions, even strong unions might not have been able to secure a premium over the wages that prevailed in their absence. This argument suggests that repressive and exclusionary policies were by no means necessary for export-led growth. But it is plausible that political coalitions that included labor would have influ-

---

17. This is a central theme of Frederic C. Deyo, *Beneath the Miracle: Labor Subordination in the New Asian Industrialism* (Berkeley: University of California Press, 1989). See also Gary Fields, "Employment, Income Distribution, and Economic Growth in Seven Small Open Economies," *Economic Journal* 94 (March 1984): 74–83.

18. See Deyo, *Beneath the Miracle*, pp. 51–87.

19. On East Asian industrial relations at the firm level see ibid., pp. 152–66.

enced the overall direction of policy and reduced the flexibility of both the private sector and the state.

Income Distribution in Brazil and Mexico

The size distribution of income has been consistently more unequal in Brazil and Mexico than in the East Asian NICs (see Table 9.1), the poorest 40 percent of the population has received a lower share of national income than in Korea, Taiwan, and Hong Kong (Table 9.2), and that share has decreased over time. Wage increases and social improvements came at a slower pace than in East Asia, and overall levels of physical well-being have been lower (see Tables 9.3 and 9.4).

There is little dispute about the poor equity performance of the Latin American NICs, but charged debates have raged over changes in the distribution of income over time, particularly in Brazil. In 1972 Albert Fishlow published an analysis of Brazilian income distribution in which he argued that income distribution deteriorated between 1960 and 1970. This deterioration, moreover, was in line with the priorities of the post-1964 military government: "Destruction of the urban proletariat as a political threat, and reestablishment of an economic order geared to private capital accumulation."[20] The policies of the new government included the restructuring of wage-setting institutions to increase the government's say, elimination of the right to strike, mandatory wage guidelines, and adjustments of the minimum wage that underestimated inflation. Government guidelines were not wholly successful in containing wage drft, but they did have measurable effects.[21] The military launched other reforms that favored the wealthy, including investment tax credits, changes in financial markets, and the expansion of higher education. The very success of the "miracle," with its emphasis on consumer durables, was partly due to the prior concentration of income that created an upper-middle-class market.[22]

Fishlow's study was followed by a flood of literature. By the early 1980s income distribution in Brazil had probably received more attention than in any other developing country.[23] Most studies upheld Fish-

20. Albert Fishlow, "Brazilian Size Distribution of Income," *American Economic Review* 62 (May 1972): 400.
21. Edmar Bacha and Lance Taylor, "Brazilian Income Distribution in the 1960s: 'Facts,' Model Results, and the Controversy," *Journal of Development Studies* 14 (April 1978): 286–90.
22. This was a component of the structuralist critique of ISI. See, for example, Celso Furtado, *Obstacles to Development in Latin America* (Garden City, N.Y.: Anchor, 1970), pp. 163–72.
23. A defense of the Brazilian record in the 1960s is contained in Carlos Langoni, *Distribuição de rendas e desenvolvimento económico do Brasil* (Rio de Janeiro: Editora Expressão e Cultura). See also John Wells, "The Diffusion of Durables in Brazil and Its Implications

low's analysis of the trend in the *relative* distribution of income in the 1960s. Debate centered on the causes of the deterioration, whether the relative distribution of income was a relevant measure of welfare, and whether Fishlow's pessimistic projections for the 1970s had proved warranted. Those arguing that relative income distribution was irrelevant used data on wage trends, employment, the diffusion of durables, social indicators, and evidence of social mobility to argue that the rapid growth of the 1970s helped alleviate poverty.[24] The living standards of the poor increased at roughly the same rate as national per capita income and the "middle-income" strata of better-off farmers, skilled workers, and small business owners grew, even though a large number of families continued to live in poverty.

Evidence on trends in the relative distribution of income in the 1970s was more ambiguous. Income inequality among regions, among sectors, and between rural and urban incomes all fell, but these improvements were offset by steeply rising income inequality within the agricultural sector.[25] The overall distribution of income in Brazil probably changed little during the 1970s and is roughly the same today as it was in the early postwar period.[26]

The Gini coefficients for Mexico show a rising trend of inequality from 1950 through the mid-1970s.[27] The big relative gainers were the 80th to 95th percentiles, and the chief relative losers the bottom 40 percent (see Table 9.2). The Mexican economy grew rapidly over most of this period, and so did the average real incomes of most income brackets, including those of the poorest. The number of households living below a fixed poverty line decreased between 1963 and 1977, and indicators of physical quality of life also improved.

What factors help explain the differences in income distribution in the East Asian and Latin American NICs over the long run? One major

for Recent Controversies concerning Brazilian Development," *Cambridge Journal of Economics* 1, 3 (1977): 259–79; Guy Pfefferman and Richard Webb, "Poverty and Income Distribution in Brazil," *Review of Income and Wealth* 29 (June 1983): 101–24; M. Louise Fox, "Income Distribution in Post–1964 Brazil: New Results," *Journal of Economic History* 43 (March 1983): 261–71; Samuel A. Morley, *Labor Markets and Inequitable Growth* (New York: Cambridge University Press, 1982).

24. This is the basic argument in Pfefferman and Webb, "Poverty and Income Distribution"; Morley, *Labor Markets;* and Jose Pastore, *Inequality and Social Mobility in Brazil* (Madison: University of Wisconsin Press, 1982).

25. David Denslow and William G. Tyler, *Perspectives on Poverty and Income Inequality in Brazil*, World Bank Staff Working Paper 601 (Washington, D.C., 1983), pp. 18–29.

26. For a discussion, see Denslow and Tyler, *Perspectives.*

27. On income distribution in Mexico see Wouter van Ginneken, *Socio-economic Groups and Income Distribution in Mexico* (New York: St. Martin's, 1980); Pedro Aspe and Paul Sigmund, *The Political Economy of Income Distribution in Mexico* (New York: Holmes & Meier, 1984); David Felix, "Income Distribution Trends in Mexico and the Kuznets Curve," in Sylvia Ann Hewlett and Richard S. Weinert, eds., *Brazil and Mexico: Patterns in Late Development* (Philadelphia: Institute for the Study of Human Issues, 1982).

factor is the persistence in Brazil and Mexico of high levels of inequality and extensive poverty in the countryside and high inequality between rural and urban areas. In Mexico in 1975, 52 percent of poor families were in the rural sector. Approximately two-thirds of these were small landowners and workers on communal lands called *ejidos,* the other third landless workers. In that year these families included 76 percent of *all* families in agriculture in Mexico.[28] Rural inequality has increased in the postwar period as a result of policies favoring larger, commercial enterprises, though the modernization of agriculture has contributed to a reduction in underemployment and rising absolute incomes in the rural sector.

The story is even more pronounced in Brazil, which has been less successful than Mexico in increasing agricultural employment. In 1975, 61 percent of the poor were rural.[29] One-half were located in the northeast, where agricultural productivity is substantially lower than in the southern states and the opportunities for off-farm income are smaller. In the 1970s rural income inequality soared as a result of subsidies that favored landowners over landless workers and larger over smaller farmers, though, as in Mexico, there is evidence of rising absolute incomes in both the modern and the traditional agricultural sectors.[30]

The causes of the persistence of rural inequality and poverty in Brazil and Mexico are numerous and complex: slow growth in the demand for rural labor; pricing policies and government supports that favor large landholders and more capital-intensive techniques; sharp regional inequalities in the distribution of infrastructure, irrigation, and new technologies; and a secular decline in the share of public investment and finance going to the rural sector. The skewed distribution of income has been worsened by three additional factors, each providing contrasts with East Asia: highly concentrated land ownership, poor access to education, and industrialization strategy.[31]

EAST ASIA AND LATIN AMERICA COMPARED

Patterns of Landholding

The distribution of landholdings has been substantially more equal in Korea and Taiwan than in Mexico and Brazil (see Table 9.5). Between

28. Joel Bergsman, "Income Distribution and Poverty in Mexico," unpublished ms., World Bank, September 1982, p. 11.
29. Pfefferman and Webb, "Poverty and Income Distribution," p. 103.
30. Denslow and Tyler, *Perspectives,* p. 24.
31. See John Sheahan, *Patterns of Development in Latin America: Poverty, Repression, and Economic Strategy* (Princeton: Princeton University Press, 1987), chap. 2; Morley, *Labor Markets,* pp. 266–76; and Irma Adelman, "A Poverty-Focused Approach to Development Policy," in John P. Lewis and Valeriana Kallab, eds., *Development Strategies Reconsidered* (New Brunswick, N.J.: Transaction, 1986).

Table 9.5. Landholding patterns in the NICs, selected years

Size of holdings (unit)	Percentage of holdings	Percentage of area	Percentage of holdings	Percentage of area
Korea (*tanbo*)	1960		1970	
1–5	34.3	13.0	31.9	10.6
5–10	36.0	31.6	24.6	27.9
10–20	24.2	32.3	26.8	33.3
20–30	4.1	10.7	5.1	13.6
30+	0.8	3.8	1.6	7.3
Taiwan (distribution of owner-cultivator households) (*chia*)	1952		1960	
0–0.5	47.3	9.9	20.7	5.2
0.5–1	23.3	15.1	45.9	30.5
1–2	16.9	21.1	15.3	19.3
2–3	5.7	12.3	14.8	30.3
3–5	3.9	13.2	2.7	10.2
5+	3.4	28.4	0.6	4.6
Brazil (hectares)	1970		1975	
0–5	36.6	1.3	38.6	1.2
5–20	30.2	5.5	28.4	4.7
20–100	23.6	16.7	23.3	15.5
100–1,000	8.5	36.9	8.8	35.9
1,000+	0.7	39.6	0.9	42.7
Mexico (hectares)	1960		1970	
0–5	65.9	0.8	61.0	1.2
5–25	16.6	1.6	20.4	3.5
25–100	9.4	5.5	11.0	8.5
100–1,000	6.4	15.2	6.6	27.1
1,000+	1.7	78.4	1.0	59.7

Sources: For Korea: Sung Hwan Ban, Pal Yong Moon, and Dwight H. Perkins, *Rural Development* (Cambridge: Harvard University Press, 1980), Table 139, pp. 360–61. Taiwan: John C. H. Fei, Gustav Ranis, and Shirley W. Y. Kuo, *Growth with Equity: The Taiwan Case* (New York: Oxford University Press, 1979), p. 42. Brazil and Mexico: Merilee S. Grindle, *State and Countryside: Development Policy and Agrarian Politics in Latin America* (Baltimore: Johns Hopkins University Press, 1986), Table 5–13, pp. 96–97. Figures may not add to 100 because of rounding and unreported property.

1952 and 1960 in Taiwan, land reforms increased the households owning medium-sized plots (0.5–3.0 *chia*) from 46 percent to 76 percent of all holdings. The distributional gains from the Mexican revolution and Cárdenas's reforms, by contrast, were partly reversed in the postwar period by the inadequate size of redistributed holdings and the emergence of a new class of commercial farmers backed by an array of state supports.[32] Land reform continued in the postwar period under sporadic peasant pressure, but the regularization of title has been slow and the problem of small, low-output, sub-subsistence units persists. Those changes in the distribution of land which have taken place do not appear to have favored smallholders. Brazil never had a substantial land reform of any sort; a 1964 law was aborted by the military takeover. Brazil's landholding pattern remains highly dualistic, with huge latifundia or *fazendas* coexisting side by side with minifundia and a large population of landless laborers.

Redistributing landholding will not necessarily increase incomes if efficiency is reduced or if agricultural policies are not supportive. One could also argue that rural poverty is a function less of land ownership than of insufficient employment alternatives. Yet both observations serve only to underscore the importance of state interventions specifically targeted to increasing the welfare of the rural poor. Politically, one of the most important brakes on such policies is precisely the power of large landholders. The difference in landownership between the two regions is striking, the timing in the improvement of income distribution in East Asia appears to confirm the importance of land reform, and, theoretically, the association between concentrated assets and income is not only plausible but nearly tautological.[33] It appears incontrovertible that rural social structure and the basic distribution of assets weigh heavily on the current distribution of income in Brazil and Mexico.

Education and Equity

Comparisons between East Asian and Latin American NICs reveal striking differences in the commitment to education (see Table 9.6). In 1960 the East Asian NICs had achieved levels of primary-school enrollment that equaled or surpassed those in Mexico and Brazil, despite significantly lower levels of per capita income. At the time of the turn to export-led growth firms could count on relatively well-educated workers, even from a pool that included recent migrants to the cities.

Though none of the East Asian NICs is representative, Korea exemplifies the interplay between culture, history, and policy in determining educational outcomes.[34] Historically, education has been highly val-

32. On postwar agricultural policies in Mexico and Brazil see Merilee S. Grindle, *State and Countryside: Development Policy and Agrarian Politics in Latin America* (Baltimore: Johns Hopkins University Press, 1986), pp. 99–104, 107–11.

33. For an effort to explore the general relationship, see Nguyen T. Quan and Anthony Y. C. Koo, "Concentration of Land Holdings: An Empirical Exploration of Kuznets' Conjecture," *Journal of Development Economics* 18, 1 (1985): 101–17.

34. Irma Adelman and Sherman Robinson, *Income Distribution Policy in Developing Countries: A Case Study of Korea* (New York: Oxford University Press, 1978), p. 41.

Table 9.6. School enrollments in the NICs as a percentage of age cohort,[a] 1960–85

	Primary	Secondary	Tertiary
Korea			
1960	94%	27%	4.6%
1970	103	42	8.0
1975			9.8
1980	109	76	
1985	96	94	32.0
Taiwan			
1960	95		
1970	98		
1980	100		
1985	100		
Singapore			
1960	112	32	6.4
1970	105	46	6.7
1980	108	58	
1984	115	71	
1985			12.0
Hong Kong			
1960	91	24	4.4
1970	117	36	7.3
1980	107	64	
1984	105	69	
1985			13.0
Brazil			
1960	95	11	1.6
1970	82	26	7.3
1980	99	34	
1983	103	35	
1985			11.0
Mexico			
1960	80	11	2.6
1970	104	22	6.1
1980	120	47	
1985	115	55	16.0

[a]Generally, the primary level refers to students aged 6–11; secondary, 11–17; and tertiary, 20–24. Totals can exceed 100 percent when students younger and older than the cohort are enrolled.

Sources: For 1960, United Nations, *Compendium of Social Statistics 1977* (New York: United Nations, 1980); other dates, World Bank, *World Tables 1988* (Washington, D.C.: World Bank, 1988), and *World Development Report 1988* (New York: Oxford University Press, 1988), pp. 280–81. For Taiwan: school-aged children enrolled in primary school, Council for Economic Planning and Development, *Taiwan Statistical Data Book* (Taipei: CEPD, 1988).

ued in Korean society. The Japanese reshaped the Korean educational system to serve their own cultural and political interests, but they also expanded primary education. Between 1953 and 1963—prior to the turn to export-led growth—Korea's literacy rate rose from 30 percent to 80 percent, implying an effective commitment to rural as well as urban education. By 1965 Korea's investment in human resource development exceeded the norm for countries with three times its per capita GNP.

Studies that have disaggregated the sources of income distribution in Brazil and Mexico consistently find education to be among the more important factors accounting for income inequalities among workers.[35] In Brazil primary-school enrollment as a share of the school-aged cohort dropped between 1960 and 1970, full enrollment in primary schools was not achieved until 1980, and the quality of primary education was highly suspect.[36] University enrollments, a preserve of the elite, increased dramatically in both Mexico and Brazil in the 1960s.

The most telling differences, though, are at the secondary level. The expansion of secondary education can initially increase inequality, since it permits some students to attain higher income levels. As more gain access, however, secondary education lowers wage differentials among skill levels. By 1960 Korea, Singapore, and Hong Kong had achieved levels of secondary-school enrollment between two and three times those in Mexico and Brazil. When Brazil expanded secondary education most aggressively, in the 1960s, primary-school enrollments were falling. In East Asia secondary enrollments expanded steadily only after universal primary schooling had been achieved.

The assumed correlation between expansion of formal education and improved income distribution has been viewed with increasing skepticism in recent years.[37] Changing the education system will not overcome such barriers to equity in the economic and social structure as slow employment growth, an entrenched status hierarchy, or weak meritocratic norms. Yet expanded access to education does equalize human capital resources, narrows wage differentials, and improves the ability of individuals to respond to their environment. And as with access to land, differences in access to education across the two regions are striking.

Employment and Wages

We turn finally to the relationship between development strategy and income distribution. A standard criticism of countries pursuing import-

35. See, for example, Fishlow, "Brazilian Size Distribution"; van Ginneken, *Socioeconomic Groups.*

36. On the issue of educational quality see Peter T. Knight, "Brazilian Socioeconomic Development: Issues for the Eighties," *World Development* 9 (November–December 1981): 1068.

37. See for example Frederick H Harbison, "The Education-Income Connection," in Frank and Webb, *Income Distribution.*

substituting policies holds that they have failed to generate adequate employment in the manufacturing sector because of biases against labor use.[38] Large differentials between wages in agriculture and manufacturing accelerate rural-to-urban migration, and slow employment growth produces segmented labor markets in the cities. A small, relatively highly paid, modern work force, or "labor aristocracy," coexists with swollen tertiary and informal sectors dominated by low-paying and undesirable jobs such as petty commerce and domestic service. This labor-market structure contributes to overall inequality.

The record on employment growth provides a first cut at assessing this argument (see Table 9.7). Korea, Taiwan, and Singapore have seen extremely high growth in manufacturing employment, traceable directly to the rapid expansion of labor-absorbing, export-oriented industries.[39] Overall employment grew faster than population in all of the East Asian NICs except Hong Kong. Though overall employment growth has been roughly the same in Brazil and Mexico, the growth of more desirable manufacturing employment has been lower than in Korea, Taiwan, or Singapore. These figures still do not capture the whole story, however; the demographic backdrop must also be considered. In Latin America population growth places a much greater strain on labor markets than in East Asia. Annual average population growth from 1965 to 1980, for example, was 2.4 percent in Brazil and 3.1 percent in Mexico, compared with 2.1 percent in Hong Kong, 1.9 percent in Korea, and only 1.6 percent in Singapore.[40]

The choice of import-substituting policies bears some responsibility for this record. The 1950s saw high output growth in Brazil, but slow growth in manufacturing employment because of the capital-intensive nature of development during that decade. Workers were absorbed into low-productivity, low-wage jobs in the tertiary sector.[41] The 1960s and 1970s, and particularly the period of the miracle, were more buoyant as manufacturing replaced services as the sector with the most rapid growth in employment. This growth was partly due to changes in incentives toward the expansion of exports under the military, but on the whole industrial growth in the 1960s was more labor-saving than it had been in the 1950s.[42] The difference was in the extremely rapid growth of output. The importance of aggregate growth for employment creation is particularly clear when the miracle is compared with the period of

38. See for example Anne Krueger, *Trade and Employment in Developing Countries: Synthesis and Conclusions* (Chicago: University of Chicago Press, 1983).

39. Fields, "Industrialization and Employment."

40. World Bank, *World Development Report 1988* (New York: Oxford University Press, 1988), p. 275.

41. Morley, *Labor Markets*, p. 27.

42. Ibid.

Table 9.7. Annual average employment growth in the
NICs, selected years (percentages)

	Manufacturing	Overall
Korea		
1954–60		1.3
1965–70	11.1	2.5
1970–85	10.4	3.7
Taiwan		
1952–60	5.2	2.3
1960–70	8.6	3.6
1970–85	10.6	4.2
Singapore		
1970–84	8.3	5.4
Hong Kong[a]		
1961–71	4.2	3.0
1971–81	3.6	5.5
Brazil		
1950–60	2.2	2.8
1960–70	4.9	2.7
1968–73	5.9	3.1
1973–76	4.9	
Mexico[b]		
1940–50	5.7	3.6
1950–60	3.6	2.0
1960–69	5.4	2.7
1970–80	4.8	4.0

[a]Growth of working population.
[b]Manufacturing figures are for manufacturing,
mining, and electricity.
Sources: Korea, *Korea Statistical Yearbook* (Seoul: Economic Planning Board, various issues). Taiwan, *Taiwan Statistical Data Book 1988* (Taipei: Council on Economic Planning and Development, 1988), p. 13.
Singapore, *Yearbook of Statistics 1986* (Singapore: Department of Statistics), p. 55. Hong Kong, *Hong Kong
1981 Census: Main Report,* vol. 1: *Analysis* (Hong Kong:
Census and Statistics Department, 1982), p. 138. Brazil: Samuel Morley, *Labor Markets and Inequitable
Growth* (New York: Cambridge University Press,
1983), pp. 26, 28–29. Mexico: Peter Gregory, *The Myth
of Market Failure* (Baltimore: Johns Hopkins University
Press, 1986), pp. 28–29.

stabilization following the military coup, which had sharply negative consequences for both employment and wage growth.

During the 1940s Mexico experienced far-reaching structural change.[43] Real wages fell, and the manufacturing labor force expanded rapidly. Employment growth in industry slowed sharply in the 1950s and rebounded in the 1960s, though overall employment growth under secondary ISI was slow. Manufacturing had been the "leading sector" in employment creation in the 1940s, 1950s, and 1960s, but in the 1970s employment in construction, commerce, finance, and services all grew faster than in industry.

In both Brazil and Mexico formal urban employment has exceeded the growth of the economically active population in the long run (1950–80). Nonetheless, manufacturing employment grew much more slowly than in the East Asian NICs, even when we adjust for differences in the growth of output. By 1980 manufacturing accounted for a larger share of the work force in the East Asian NICs than in Brazil and Mexico, where the productive absorption of labor has been an ongoing policy problem.

This difference is reflected in the growth of the urban informal sector, defined as self-employed workers, unpaid family workers, and domestics. The informal sector has expanded at the same rate as the formal sector in both Brazil and Mexico, and in 1980 it accounted for 17 percent of the urban work force in Brazil and 22 percent in Mexico. Micro-level studies in Latin America have uncovered symbiotic links between the "formal" and "informal" sectors, and the informal sector has recently been heralded as a dynamic and creative response to the myriad of legal and institutional barriers to the operation of small business.[44] Surprisingly, occupational data on the East Asian NICs suggest large numbers of workers in categories that overlap the "informal sector" in Latin America. In Korea in 1985, for example, 25.1 percent of nonfarm household workers were self-employed, 7.0 percent were family workers, and 10.6 percent were day laborers. Unfortunately, we do not yet have the comparative research that would explain differences in the nature of the informal sector across regions. Given the relatively slow growth of manufacturing employment in Latin America, however, we can suggest that the informal sector is more likely to reflect the lim-

---

43. See Peter Gregory, *The Myth of Market Failure: Employment and the Labor Market in Mexico* (Baltimore: Johns Hopkins University Press, 1986), pp. 14–33.

44. See Alejandro Portes and Lauren Benton, "Industrial Development and Labor Absorption: A Reinterpretation," *Population and Development Review* 10 (December 1984): 589–612; Alejandro Portes, "Latin American Class Structures," *Latin American Research Review* 20, 3 (1985): 7–39; Hernando de Soto, *The Other Path* (New York: Basic Books, 1988).

ited opportunities in higher-productivity formal employment than the higher returns to small entrepreneurship.

An alternative measure of labor-market dualism involves looking at wage differentials between the manufacturing sector and the rest of the economy, and within the manufacturing sector. One simple measure of the overall position of the manufacturing sector is the ratio of average wages in manufacturing to per capita GNP (see Table 9.8).[45] Lower ratios indicate more equal distribution of income between manufacturing and other sectors; increases in this ratio imply a redistribution in favor of manufacturing-sector wages. Differences in the firm and sectoral coverage of industrial censuses mean that cross-national comparisons should be approached with caution, but rough orders of magnitude and changes over time are instructive. The comparatively high ratios for Korea probably reflect the omission of small firms from the industrial census. More disaggregated comparisons show that wages are low in manufacturing compared to other urban employment and that differentials between rural and urban incomes have been comparatively narrow.[46] The pattern over time conforms roughly with policy changes, however: a drop in the ratio following the turn to export-led growth, a slight increase during the "big push," and a subsequent reversal following the return to more market-oriented policies in the 1980s. Taiwan also shows a low ratio of manufacturing wages to per capita GNP, though trends do not follow policy changes as they do in Korea. Manufacturing appears to be a particularly low-paying sector in the city-states.

By this measure the distribution of income across broad sectors widened in Brazil during the ISI period of the 1950s but narrowed thereafter. After 1968 this narrowing in differentials could be attributed to a combination of government controls on minimum wages and growing demand for agricultural labor resulting from an export boom.[47] Trends in Mexico cannot be charted with any confidence until the 1960s. Even if the aberrant observation for 1965 is dismissed, there is a widening of differentials across broad sectors under secondary ISI in the 1960s, though, as in Brazil, there is a steady decline thereafter, suggesting that both countries might have reached a turning point in the contribution of rural-urban differentials to overall inequality.

45. I thank David Lindauer for advice on constructing these indicators. See also Richard Webb, "Wage Policy and Income Distribution," and Peter Gregory, "The Impact of Institutional Factors on Urban Labor Markets," World Bank Studies in Employment and Rural Development 27, July 1975 (mimeo).

46. See Lindauer, *Labor Market Behavior*, p. 14; Mason et al., *Economic and Social Modernization*, pp. 425–28.

47. Morley, *Labor Markets*, p. 191.

Table 9.8. Ratio of average wage in manufacturing to GNP per capita, 1949–85

Year	Korea	Taiwan	Singapore	Hong Kong[a]	Brazil	Mexico
1949					2.6	
1955		1.5				
1958	2.7					
1959					3.6	
1960		1.3				2.2
1965	2.5	1.2			3.1	4.3
1970	2.0	1.3	1.2.			3.2
1971					2.4	
1973				1.0		
1975	1.6	1.1	1.1			2.8
1976					1.7	
1980	2.2	1.2	0.9	0.8	1.3	2.3
1984	1.7					
1985		1.2	1.0	0.8		

[a]GDP per capita

Sources: Calculated from United Nations, *The Growth of World Industry, 1953–1965: National Tables* (New York: United Nations, 1967); United Nations, *The Growth of World Industry*, various issues; United Nations, *Yearbook of Industrial Statistics*, various issues; International Monetary Fund, *International Financial Statistics*, various issues; *Statistical Yearbook of the Republic of China 1985* (Taipei: Director General of Budget, Accounting, and Statistics, n.d.); *Taiwan Statistical Databook 1987* (Taipei: Council on Economic Planning and Development, n.d.).

Relatively equality of wages within the manufacturing sector is, as I have already argued, an important factor contributing to equity in the East Asian NICs. Wages were presumably more equal across sectors in the East Asian NICs because of greater exposure to international market forces: through free-trade policies in Hong Kong and Singapore, and through competitive pressures associated with dependence on exports in Korea and Taiwan. Import substitution fosters the development of high-wage enclaves, though both Taiwan and Korea combined export-oriented policies with import substitution in the 1960s and 1970s.

A simple measure of the degree of dualism within manufacturing is the ratio of the average wage in the highest-paid sector to the average wage in the lowest-paid sector (see Table 9.9). The data provide some confirmation for the hypothesis of greater wage dispersion across sectors in Latin America than in East Asia. There is a narrowing of these differentials in Taiwan after the transition to export-led growth and in Singapore after 1970, though Korea, the most protectionist of the East Asian NICs, shows the same differentials across the 1960s. More disaggregated studies show that the relatively low-wage sectors within manufacturing are precisely those in which the NICs established their comparative advantage: textiles, apparel, footwear, and electronics.

Table 9.9. Ratio of average wage in highest-wage sector to lowest-wage sector in manufacturing, 1949–85

Year	Korea	Taiwan	Singapore	Hong Kong	Brazil	Mexico
1949					2.5	
1955		3.5				
1959			2.6		2.6	
1960		3.2				2.2
1963	2.6					
1965		2.7	3.4		3.1	2.9
1970	2.6	2.4	3.3		3.0	3.0
1971						
1973				2.0		
1975	2.5	2.1	2.5			2.6
1976					2.4	
1980	2.3	1.8	3.1	2.7	3.3	2.6
1984						
1985	2.1		3.5	1.8		3.0

Sources: Calculated from United Nations, *The Growth of World Industry, 1963–1965: National Tables* (New York: United Nations, 1967); United Nations, *The Growth of World Industry,* various issues; United Nations, *Yearbook of Industrial Statistics,* various issues; *Statistical Yearbook of the Republic of China 1985* (Taipei: Director General of Budget, Accounting, and Statistics).

Higher-wage sectors included nonelectrical machinery, transport equipment, industrial chemicals, and steel, the targets of import-substitution efforts in Korea and Taiwan.[48] Differentials between "light" and "heavy" industry also exist in Singapore, even though it is a free port.

Differentials across sectors within manufacturing widened during the Second Industrial Revolution in Singapore but not during the big push in Korea, perhaps reflecting Korea's greater emphasis on the market in determining wages. Sectoral differentials widened in both Brazil and Mexico during secondary ISI—in Mexico in the early 1960s, and in Brazil from 1950 through the mid-1960s. In both countries these differentials fell then rose again by the end of the 1970s. We can treat trends over time with greater confidence than cross-national comparisons, but the differentials across industries in Brazil and Mexico in 1980 are substantially larger than in Taiwan, Korea, or Hong Kong.

IMPORT SUBSTITUTION, WELFARE, AND INCOME DISTRIBUTION

Employment growth in the manufacturing sector in Korea, Taiwan, and Singapore during the period of export-led growth was higher than

48. Deyo, *Beneath the Miracle,* p. 176.

in Mexico and Brazil during successive phases of ISI. Evidence from the occupational structure and employment status (self-employed, family workers, permanent employees) of workers suggests greater dualism in the Latin American cases, though the precise character of the "informal" sector in East Asia remains underresearched. There is some evidence of a higher "manufacturing sector premium" in Brazil and Mexico during the initial period of ISI, though the premium has diminished over time. The Latin American NICs also show somewhat greater wage dispersion across sectors within manufacturing. All of these factors contribute to income inequality, even before we consider the additional consequences that stem from the concentration of business income associated with ISI.

This picture is consistent with at least three different explanations, however; I will call them the welfare argument, the structure argument, and the policy argument. The welfare argument emphasizes the trade-off in the development process between employment creation and "premature" growth in real wages.[49] "Institutional factors" are used to explain why modern-sector wages remain high, even in the presence of surplus labor. These factors are of two sorts. First, governments intervene in labor markets to protect worker welfare. Such interventions include minimum-wage laws, social insurance provisions, legal provisions establishing various conditions of employment, and mandated obligations to provide employees with fringe benefits such as housing and medical care. Second, unions exercise power through collective bargaining and the threat to strike.

Some share of East Asia's success in creating employment might be attributed to limited labor legislation, social security and welfare, and weak unions, though I have placed equal emphasis on a political argument that underlines the authoritarian underpinning to export-led growth. In either case institutions broadly conceived did limit labor's power. As a result, real-wage growth was controlled at the outset of industrialization, and when wages rose, they did so in response to market signals.

Governments in Brazil and Mexico have intervened in labor markets much more extensively than their counterparts in any of the East Asian countries, with the exception of Singapore, apparently giving some plausibility to the welfare argument. But when these interventions aimed at enhancing worker welfare, they had little effect, and they have more frequently been turned to the purpose of controlling labor demands.

---

49. A. D. Smith, *Wage Policy Issues in Economic Development* (New York: St. Martin's, 1969); Fields, "Employment, Income Distribution"; Bruce Scott, "National Strategies: Key to International Competition," in Scott and George C. Lodge, *U.S. Competitiveness in the World Economy* (Boston: Harvard Business School Press, 1985).

Brazil's system of industrial relations remains a legacy of the Vargas era.[50] Getúlio Vargas shaped a complex corporatist system that included state-mandated employer and employee syndicates and regional labor offices, and courts to mediate between them. A social welfare system was also put in place, though it was chronically underfunded. With the return to democracy, the corporatist structure became the locus of clientelistic and patronage politics. By the early 1960s labor leaders were using the strike weapon, alliances with populist politicians, and an independent labor confederation to advance labor interests in a more militant fashion. After the coup of 1964 the institutional structure and sheer coercion were used to repress labor demands. Strikes were effectively banned, the government intervened in the internal organization of unions, and various instruments were used to control wage growth, though high demand for labor permitted scope for some industry-specific actions during the period of the miracle. With the *abertura* of the late 1970s, labor activism increased, and major strikes spread through the São Paulo region in 1978. Workers in import-substituting industries, including chemicals, metalworking, and autos, were a major force in the resurgence of militant unionism.[51]

The political relationship between state and organized labor has been much closer in Mexico than in Brazil. The Constitution of 1917, the close political ties between organized labor and political leaders in the 1920s, and the formal relationship established between ruling party and unions under Cárdenas in the 1930s all held out the promise of an activist state committed to worker welfare. The state-labor nexus was turned to the purpose of control under presidents Manuel Ávila Camacho and Miguel Alemán, however, with the dominant position of the Confederación de Trabajadores de México (CTM) as the key organizational instrument. Strike activity has varied with the political proclivities of the president, increasing, for example, during the presidencies of Adolfo López Mateos (1958–64) and Luís Echeverria (1970–76), when an independent union movement emerged.[52] These patterns may have contributed to the rising manufacturing-sector differential during the early 1960s but cannot explain the decline over the early 1970s. Over the long term, as two observers note, "the government has effectively pre-

50. The following draws on Kenneth Paul Erickson and Kevin J. Middlebrook, "The State and Organized Labor in Brazil and Mexico," in Hewlett and Weinert, *Brazil and Mexico*.

51. See Margaret Keck, "The New Unionism in the Brazilian Transition," in Alfred Stepan, ed., *Democratizing Brazil* (New York: Oxford University Press, 1989), pp. 261–64.

52. See Ian Roxborough, *Unions and Politics in Mexico: The Case of the Automobile Industry* (New York: Cambridge University Press, 1984).

vented or restricted strikes in the important economic sectors that are subject to federal jurisdiction."[53] Minimum-wage policies, supposedly one of the major instruments of government intervention in support of labor, have not had a substantial effect on worker earnings over the long run.[54]

In sum, there are periods of Brazil's history when workers were more closely integrated into the political process than in any of the East Asian NICs. In Brazil some of organized labor's gains in the 1950s and 1960s, and after 1978, might be attributed to institutional factors and the position of labor in the broader political system. The Mexican political leadership could never wholly ignore the interests of the urban working class, which continues to be a critical pillar of PRI support. In both countries the position of labor played into broad industrial-strategic decisions in the 1950s which favored urban workers in leading ISI sectors.

On the other hand, labor's ties with government in Brazil and Mexico have often proved a two-edged sword. The change in regime in 1964 in Brazil ushered in a period of wage repression. In Mexico clear boundaries have been drawn around labor demands, and institutional structures continue to circumscribe the range of autonomous labor action. In the 1980s labor's close relationship with the PRI proved a tremendous disadvantage, as the government used its ties with the official union movement to contain real-wage growth as one component of its strategy of adjusting to its burden of external debt.

Critics of the welfare argument claim that the focus on wage-setting institutions and state intervention has the tail wagging the dog: labor power and the possibilities of organization and political pressure are themselves a function of capital intensity in production. Capital intensity provides opportunities for labor organization because of high productivity, inelastic demand for skilled labor, and the existence of various rents, including those resulting from government favors.

Yet where exactly should the emphasis be placed? An argument consistent with the Kuznets hypothesis, which I call the "structure argument," is that modern-sector wage pressures are created by features inherent in modern-sector technology and market structure, particularly capital and skill intensity.[55] High wages are the result not of labor-market distortions but of market dynamics, including choice of technique within sectors, higher productivity, market demand for scarce

53. Erickson and Middlebrook, "The State and Organized Labor," p. 241.
54. Gregory, *The Myth of Market Failure*, p. 253.
55. Webb, "Wage Policy and Income Distribution," p. 234.

skills, and structural constraints on their supply. The historical timing of industrialization also comes into play.[56] Modern industry, it is argued, requires a relatively high and increasing input of resources per worker when compared with earlier industrialization. Technological change has led to an inexorable increase in the minimum efficient size of plant, and the range of economically viable possibilities for substituting labor for capital has narrowed. There is evidence for this claim in Brazil. In his detailed study of the Brazilian labor market during the miracle period, Samuel Morley finds that the skill-intensive pattern of growth can be attributed to a rapid growth of the skill intensity of the tertiary sector and to technical changes *within* sectors favoring white-collar over blue-collar workers.[57]

Morley's arguments are important in helping explain the widening of income differentials during the period of the miracle, but they take the industrial structure as given. The "policy argument" underscores the fact that the state plays a powerful role in determining product and technology choice. Protection, subsidies, and tax incentives increase capital and skill intensity over the long run. Possibilities for factor substitution may be lower in automobiles and pharmaceuticals, but the development of such industries is itself partly the result of government policy.

The "policy argument" sheds light on the debate about dependency and inequality. Evidence from both Korea and Singapore suggests that governments were sensitive to concerns about multinationals in designing exclusive labor regimes. But multinationals in the East Asian NICs have not been an institutional factor for higher wages as they have been in other developing countries. The reason has to do with the incentives MNCs faced. In East Asia foreign investors exploited labor-cost advantages in producing for export. In the Latin American cases, by contrast, MNCs operated in protected, oligopolistic markets. Future debate on the role of multinationals in income distribution in Latin America must begin by considering the effect of various policy interventions by the state.

The welfare, structure, dependency, and policy arguments are difficult to disentangle. Government intervention in labor markets has been prevalent in Mexico and Brazil and has sometimes favored the organized urban working class. But state intervention has just as frequently aimed at controlling labor. The structure, dependency, and policy argu-

56. See, for example, the special issue of *CEPAL Review* 24 (December 1984) on employment problems; David Felix, "The Technological Factor in Socio-economic Dualism: Toward an Economy-of-Scale Paradigm for Development Theory," *Economic Development and Cultural Change* 25 supplement (January 1977): 181–211.

57. Morley, *Labor Markets*, pp. 200–222.

ments are in fact complementary, but as I have argued in Part Two and in this chapter, industrial structure and dependency must both be placed within the context of government strategy.

THE EFFECTS OF THE CRISIS OF THE 1980S

When the debt crisis broke in the early 1980s, there was a presumption that adjustment could be achieved fairly quickly. It proved mistaken. External shocks—the cutoff in lending, the rise in interest rates, and the fall in commodity prices—were much more severe than originally predicted. The policy changes required were more far-reaching and complex than had been foreseen, extending beyond short-term stabilization and balance-of-payments adjustment to structural measures that reshaped basic relationships between state and economy and between national and international economies.

As the crisis stumbled through its first decade, the distributional consequences of stabilization and structural adjustment received greater attention. There were at least two reasons for this focus, the first being humanitarian. In the poorest countries, the crisis threatened to push the most vulnerable and disadvantaged to utter destitution and malnutrition.[58] Concern about distribution also stemmed from the growing political constraints on the adjustment process. Fiscal austerity, restrictive monetary policies, high inflation, and efforts at structural reform such as trade liberalization and the reform of pricing policies all triggered intense distributional conflicts.[59]

An analysis of the distributional consequences of the debt crisis is beyond my scope and will have to await new research. I need only underline that the fates of the Latin American and the East Asian NICs diverged more sharply in the 1980s than in any previous postwar decade. While experiencing severe depressions and falling living standards, Latin American countries were also forced to undergo severe fiscal retrenchment. Social services and investment were cut dramatically. Real wages collapsed as policies shifted the burden of adjustment onto organized labor, particularly in Mexico, which adopted the most orthodox policy stance of any of the large Latin American debtors.[60]

---

58. Giovanni Andrea Cornia, Richard Jolly, and Frances Stewart, eds., *Adjustment with a Human Face: Protecting the Vulnerable and Promotion Growth* (Oxford: Clarendon Press, 1987).

59. See Joan Nelson et al., *Fragile Coalitions: The Politics of Adjustment* (New Brunswick, N.J.: Transaction, 1989).

60. See Robert Kaufman, "Economic Orthodoxy and Political Change in Mexico: The Stabilization and Adjustment Policies of the de la Madrid Administration," in Barbara

Equally detrimental for the distribution of income were the opportunities for holders of liquid assets to protect themselves from the effects of the crisis through capital flight.[61]

Adjustment in the 1980s differed across the East Asian NICs, and it is too early to gauge the distributional implications of the political and economic changes taking place. The most important fact for comparative purposes, though, was the continuation of relatively robust growth rates, with its implication of rising living standards.

Over the longer run, however, the distributional implications of the crisis in Latin America may be more positive than is frequently thought.[62] The groups hurt most by the debt crisis are urban groups linked to the ISI process and the gradual expansion of the state, government employees among them. These groups were the primary beneficiaries of social services and the various rents associated with a protectionist industrial policy, overvalued exchange rate, and government subsidies. By contrast, the forced adjustments may well benefit the rural poor who are net sellers of tradable agricultural products or workers in the agro-export sector. In urban areas the informal sector is less affected by reduced subsidies and protection, and it may in fact flourish from the change in incentives. In absolute terms, there is little doubt, the debt crisis has had a devastating impact on the region, and even small changes in welfare can push the poorest into destitution. Yet some of the adjustments currently under way may result in improved distribution and even a political strengthening of previously excluded groups.

STATE STRATEGY AND SOCIAL OUTCOMES

The lessons to be learned from the East Asian NICs concerning equity have been read very selectively. Strategy may matter in determining income equality across regions, but not only the strategy of letting the market work. Active state policies to guarantee an equitable distribution of basic assets were key. Land reforms and high-quality, egalitarian educational systems contribute more than industrial strategy to explaining differences in the distribution of income.

Stallings and Robert Kaufman, *Debt and Democracy in Latin America* (Boulder, Colo.: Westview, 1989).

61. Jeffry Frieden, "Winners and Losers in the Latin America Debt Crisis: The Political Implications," in ibid.

62. The following paragraph draws on Alain de Janvry and Elisabeth Sadoulet, "Rural Development in Latin America: Relinking Poverty Reduction to Growth," paper prepared for the conference on poverty research, International Food Policy Research Institute and the World Bank, Airlie House, Virginia, October 25–28, 1989.

Even when we take these other differences into account, however, industrial strategy unquestionably plays a role in explaining distributional outcomes across the two regions. The incentives to use labor in the East Asian NICs and the flexibility of labor markets increased the demand for labor and led quickly to elimination of the labor surplus and to growth in real wages. In the aggregate the Asian NICs did better in providing employment, improving absolute income, and reducing poverty than their Latin American counterparts. Industrial strategy not only improved absolute income but contributed to a relatively equal distribution of income as well. The market determination of wages may have tilted the functional distribution of income toward profits, but there is no reason to think it did so to a greater extent than under import-substituting policies. The export-oriented strategy resulted in greater creation of employment and greater equality of wage income both between the manufacturing and other sectors and within the manufacturing sector itself.

These observations about the distributional consequences of export-led growth bring us to a second misreading of the East Asian cases. To the extent that labor markets responded flexibly to the laws of supply and demand, they did so because of a particular political structure that limited the ability of workers to "interfere" in the determination of wages. The labor market worked efficiently precisely because the political market was narrowly circumscribed. The "successful" strategy of the East Asian NICs cannot be separated from labor regimes that systematically reduced labor's political and shopfloor voice. This crucial irony—equity without democracy—must be faced by both critics and defenders of the East Asian model.

This observation raises an important puzzle. Why did the authoritarian regimes of East Asia pursue egalitarian, growth-oriented policies whereas those in Latin America failed to do so? The question returns us to the relationship between industrialization and the nature of the political system.

CHAPTER TEN

Authoritarianism and Democracy: Political Institutions and Economic Growth Revisited

A central theme of this book is the relationship between economic growth and political institutions. Though international pressures weigh heavily on developing countries, the ability of such countries to formulate coherent responses is contingent on institutional arrangements and capabilities, among them the nature of economic decision-making structures and the policy instruments available to political elites. What defines a country's political system, however, is how interests are represented, and in particular whether the regime is democratic or authoritarian.[1]

We may explore the links between regime type and economic development from two directions. The first involves asking whether level of development or economic growth of a particular sort helps account for differences in regime type. The causal connection between growth strategy and political regime may be made in either strong or weak form. The strong argument holds that there are political prerequisites for the

1. Democratic regimes are those in which free speech and organization are guaranteed, leaders are chosen in competitive elections, election results are honored, and governments are not systematically subject to the veto or control of nonelected individuals or outside institutions such as the military, monarchy, or bureaucracy. Authoritarian regimes, by contrast, truncate civil liberties, restrict open political competition, and limit opposition and interest group activity. See Juan Linz, "Totalitarian and Authoritarian Regimes," in Fred Greenstein and Nelson Polsby, eds., *Handbook of Political Science*, vol. 3; *Macropolitical Theory* (Reading, Mass.: Addison Wesley, 1975), and Myron Weiner, "Empirical Democratic Theory," in Weiner and Ergun Ozbudan, eds., *Competitive Elections in Developing Countries* (Durham: Duke University Press, 1987). The emphasis on regime type is distinct from two other lines of inquiry into the relationship between economic growth and political development. On the trade-off between human rights and growth see Jack Donnelly, "Human Rights and Development: Complementary or Competing Concerns," *World Politics* 36 (January 1984): 255–83. On the relationship between economic growth and political participation see Samuel P. Huntington and Joan M. Nelson, *No Easy Choice* (Cambridge: Harvard University Press, 1976).

pursuit of a particular growth strategy. Political elites and their coalition partners are aware of these institutional requirements and restructure or maintain the political system to attain their economic policy goals. The weak form of the argument holds that authoritarian politics are "functional" for a particular strategy, even if economic objectives are not sufficient in themselves to explain changes of regime.

Like income distribution, basic political structures have numerous determinants. Thus it would be surprising to find a simple correlation between development strategy and regime type. Yet too many studies begin and end with this simple expectation, sidestepping both theory and the more indirect relationships that come into play. Since development strategies affect the composition of interest groups, it is plausible to argue that they also influence the coalitions that support or oppose particular political arrangements.

In fact, the association between industrial strategy and authoritarian rule in Latin America appears to be weak. There is no strong theoretical reason to link ISI with authoritarian rule. ISI occurred under a variety of different political arrangements and, if anything, mobilized new social groups into political life. Economic conditions did have consequences for politics in Latin America, but the salient conditions were macroeconomic and the relevant policies involved stabilization rather than industrial objectives. The cases of Brazil, Argentina, Chile, and Uruguay all suggest that high inflation contributes to popular-sector mobilization and political polarization—conditions under which militaries are more likely to intervene. Orthodox stabilization measures can draw political elites toward authoritarian controls.

The link between industrial strategy and authoritarian politics is more plausible in the East Asian NICs. By focusing policy attention on the role of labor in maintaining competitiveness, export-led growth inclined political and economic elites toward the control and/or political exclusion of the working class. This inclination narrowed the coalitional base of support for democratic politics and thus contributed to the maintenance of authoritarian or closed political systems. Not until the expansion of the middle class, a by-product of rapid economic development, did new social pressures for democratic rule emerge.

The functional form of the argument linking development strategy with regime type leads directly to the second broad question: Are certain political systems better than others at promoting growth? Do authoritarian regimes, given the particular economic and social conditions in the developing world, outperform their democratic counterparts? Is there an inevitable trade-off between democracy and development?

If a link does exist between authoritarianism and economic development, it should operate through the ability of authoritarian governments to pursue growth-promoting policies that would not be possible under democratic auspices. Crucial policy reforms in the NICs have historically been associated with authoritarian rule; any assessment of the NICs must weigh this high cost of "success." Nonetheless, important caveats, qualifications, and objections must be addressed. There are no theoretical reasons to think that authoritarian regimes are *uniquely* capable of solving the collective-action problems associated with development. This absence provides hope that newly democratizing countries will develop institutions conducive to both political liberty and economic growth.

ECONOMIC GROWTH AND REGIME TYPE

Sociological interpretations of politics have, at least since de Tocqueville, linked successful democratic experiments with features of the social structure. A small step connected the social structure to economic development, producing an economic theory of democracy. Democratic institutions, it was argued, rested on such preconditions as literacy, mass communication, income equality, and political stability that could be met only at a certain level of development.[2] Both an adequate level of economic development and sufficient growth rates were required to sustain the legitimacy of democratic institutions. Cross-national statistical studies have found significant correlations between level of development and democratic rule, even when tested against other hypotheses.[3]

Drawing on a stylized version of Western European experience, this "preconditions" approach to democratization assigned a pivotal role to the middle classes. Historically, the middle class opposed the status hierarchies associated with traditional forms of rule, sought to check the growth of arbitrary state power through law, and supported ideologies that drew parallels between the benefits of economic and political competition. As Barrington Moore argued succinctly, "No bourgeoisie, no democracy."[4]

These theories fell on hard times in the late 1960s. Only a cursory examination of the historical record is required to show that the rise of

2. The most influential statement is Seymour Martin Lipset, "Some Social Requisites of Democracy: Economic Development and Political Legitimacy," *American Political Science Review* 53 (March 1959): 69–105. See also Robert Dahl, *Polyarchy* (New Haven: Yale University Press, 1971).

3. See for example the comprehensive effort of Kenneth A. Bollen and Robert W. Jackman, "Economic and Non-Economic Determinants of Political Democracy in the 1960s," *Research in Political Sociology*, vol. 1 (Greenwich, Conn.: JAI Press, 1985).

4. Barrington Moore, *Social Origins of Dictatorship and Democracy* (Boston: Beacon, 1966), p. 418.

capitalism in Western Europe was not uniformly associated with liberal politics; much depended on the particular form capitalism took and the coalitional structures in which it was embedded.[5] A wave of bureaucratic-authoritarian installations in the developing world in the 1960s and 1970s also cast doubt on a simple correlation between level of development and democracy.[6] This "new authoritarianism" afflicted not the poorest developing countries but relatively advanced ones in which growth was rapid and the level of industrialization relatively high.

A theoretical quest ensued for the particular economic conditions that inhibited the "normal" process of political development. Peter Evans argued that a common interest in rapid accumulation among members of the triple alliance of state, local, and foreign capital demanded the exclusion and repression of the urban popular sector during the secondary phase of ISI: "In the context of dependent development, the need for repression is great while the need for democracy is small."[7] Fernando Henrique Cardoso argued similarly that the accumulation processes of associated-dependent development "required that the instruments of pressure and defense available to the popular classes be dismantled."[8] Guillermo O'Donnell awarded a more central role to political variables, including popular-sector mobilization, the growth of technocratic roles, and the military's perception of threat, but his central hypothesis took the same functionalist form: authoritarianism was linked to the deepening phase of ISI.[9]

Three distinct strands to these arguments centered on the political position of labor and the left. The first argument concerned the economic requirements of secondary import substitution.[10] To maintain forward momentum in the production of consumer durables, income had to be concentrated in order to create an adequate market. Wage controls were also necessary to meet the increasing demand for investible resources. As economic propositions, these claims have been sub-

5. See Karl de Schweinitz's overlooked study *Industrialization and Democracy* (New York: Free Press, 1964), pp. 158–86.

6. David Collier, ed., *The New Authoritarianism in Latin America* (Princeton: Princeton University Press, 1979).

7. Peter Evans, *Dependent Development: The Alliance of Multinational, State, and Local Capital in Brazil* (Princeton: Princeton University Press, 1979), p. 35.

8. Fernando Henrique Cardoso, "Associated-Dependent Development: Theoretical and Practical Implications," in Alfred Stepan, ed., *Authoritarian Brazil* (New Haven: Yale University Press, 1973), p. 147.

9. Guillermo O'Donnell, *Modernization and Bureaucratic Authoritarianism: Studies in South American Politics* (Berkeley: Institute for International Studies, University of California, 1973).

10. This is the focus of Evans, *Dependent Development;* O'Donnell, *Modernization;* Fred Deyo, *Beneath the Miracle: Labor Subordination in the New Asian Industrialism* (Berkeley: University of California Press, 1989).

jected to close scrutiny and wide criticism.[11] Nor is it likely that militaries knew about or accepted such arguments, and it is even less likely that they were a primary motivation for political intervention.

Other critics have noted that the timing of industrialization also cut against the deepening hypothesis.[12] In Mexico the single-party dominant system was in place prior to the deepening phase of the mid-1950s. There is no evidence of increasing repression or a tightening of authoritarian rule as a result of the new strategy. Secondary ISI in Brazil began before the military intervention of 1964 and, if anything, was reversed in the period immediately following the coup.

A second line of argument common in the dependency tradition links ISI to authoritarianism through the need to attract foreign capital. Multinationals, banks, and such multilateral institutions as the IMF and the World Bank are more likely to invest where labor and the left are controlled. To the extent that this argument implicitly relies on the dictates of ISI, it suffers the same weakness as the deepening hypothesis. Manufacturing multinationals were not attracted to Latin America by low wages; their main interest was in the domestic market.

It is plausible, however, that MNCs (and local investors, for that matter) might increase investment following authoritarian installations in countries previously characterized by strong pressures from labor and the left. Certainly support for democracy eroded in the private sector in Brazil under João Goulart, for example, which might have played some role in the calculations of coup leaders.[13] However, it is important to be precise about the relationship between economic strategy and the interests of the private sector. Business may be attracted to authoritarian solutions in countries where they see strong threats from labor or the left to their economic viability or basic property rights. Yet they may also accept or even support democratic forces where the threat from the left has been ameliorated, where continued authoritarian rule is itself the cause of political instability and uncertainty, or where democracy would allow greater business access to decision making and limit unwanted state intervention.[14] This instrumental approach to politics is visible in Brazil in the late 1970s when São Paulo industrialists openly broke with the military and advocated political liberalization. It also helps explain

11. See Youseff Cohen's articulate review "Democracy from Above: The Political Origins of Dictatorship in Brazil," *World Politics* 40 (October 1987): 30–54.

12. José Serra, "Three Mistaken Theses regarding the Connection between Industrialization and Authoritarian Regimes," in Collier, *The New Authoritarianism*.

13. This is the theme of Rene Armand Dreifuss, *A conquista do estado: Ação política, poder, e golpe de clase* (Petrópolis: Vozes, 1981).

14. See, for example, David Becker, *The New Bourgeoisie and the Limits of Dependency: Mining, Class, and Power in "Revolutionary" Peru* (Princeton: Princeton University Press, 1983).

the growing appeal of the opposition Partido de Acción Nacional (PAN) in Mexico. The PAN, a conservative party with business support in the north, has strongly protested the PRI's monopoly of political power.

These qualifications suggest a third and more plausible political-economic explanation not only of bureaucratic-authoritarian installations but of the policy actions that follow such coups. The explanation focuses on the contribution of economic crises to broader political and class conflicts rather than the "requirements" of a particular industrial strategy or the need to mollify foreign investors.[15] Military intervention usually comes in response to political crises in which contending forces are sharply polarized over such basic issues as property rights and the distribution of income. Recession and inflation will exacerbate such distributive struggles, providing incentives for groups to mobilize to protect their income shares. Economic conditions, even if they do not appear to be the immediate cause of authoritarian installations, contribute to the level of political conflict and polarization.

This pattern is visible not only in Brazil but in Argentina (1966 and 1976), Turkey (1971 and 1980), Chile (1973), and Uruguay (1973). Sometimes, as in Chile, economic crises can be attributed to the expansionist macroeconomic policies of populist governments, though in Brazil inflation and balance-of-payments problems are more accurately seen as a by-product of developmentalism.[16] Whatever their cause—and there is no reason to believe causes would necessarily be common across countries—these inflation-stabilization crises play an important role in postcoup politics. Once militaries intervene, economic crisis provides a rationale for imposing "discipline" on the economic system by limiting the demands of labor and the left.

This broader political explanation of bureaucratic-authoritarian installations has the advantage that it can be extended beyond countries pursuing ISI. It appears to fit Korea in 1961, 1971–72, and 1980 and the consolidation of PAP rule in Singapore in the early 1960s. Yet if similar outcomes are visible across countries pursuing different development strategies, such a finding would undermine the link between a particular *industrial* strategy, such as export-led growth, and authoritarianism. The evidence from the East Asian cases does not permit an outright rejection of the hypothesis, though, particularly if we pay closer attention to the political agenda of the opposition, the coalitional bases

---

15. Michael Wallerstein, "The Collapse of Democracy in Brazil: Its Economic Determinants," *Latin American Research Review* 15, 3 (1980): 3–40; Cohen, "Democracy from Above."

16. On the macroeconomics of populism see Jeffrey D. Sachs, "Social Conflict and Populist Policies in Latin America," National Bureau of Economic Research Working Paper 2897 (Cambridge, Mass., March 1989).

of support for authoritarian rule, and the policy objectives of the government in the postcoup period.

The political systems of Taiwan and Hong Kong are the legacy of peculiar historical events and cannot be traced to the dictates of any particular economic strategy, though the centralization of KMT power in Taiwan in the early 1950s did have an economic rationale. Unlike in Brazil and Mexico, however, the private sector has played little role in the democratic opening in either country. The evidence of business skepticism regarding a more open politics is particularly clear in Hong Kong. In consultations with the Chinese over the drafting of the Basic Law, business representatives made clear their preference for a continuation of functional representation and indirect elections over constitutional solutions that would move politics in a more competitive and partisan direction.

Korea provides three cases of authoritarian intervention. The major justification for the military's seizure of power in Korea in 1961 was to increase the effectiveness of government in promoting growth. The coup was a response not only to short-term political instability but to the underlying economic strategy that spawned it. The military's initial economic objectives were oriented toward planning and a rationalized program of import substitution, however; export-led growth came only later. The promulgation of the Yusin Constitution in 1973 and the coup d'état of 1980 are more plausibly interpreted as efforts to reestablish the political conditions for export-oriented growth, even if Park Chung Hee did change industrial policy in a more inward-oriented direction in the mid-1970s. In both cases labor and populist political forces specifically challenged the authoritarian political premises of the country's development strategy. In both cases technocratic allies of the military linked eroding international competitiveness to rising wages and labor activism. It is also revealing that the major business associations played no role in the struggle for democracy in the mid-1980s and even opposed political liberalization.

Singapore appears to provide the clearest evidence of a connection between strategy and political organization, though some important qualifications are required even there. The imposition of new controls on labor was quite consciously linked to the effort to attract export-oriented foreign investment. The organizational infrastructure for controlling labor was set in place during the conflict with the left in the early 1960s, and changes in the labor laws came after a sweeping parliamentary victory in 1967. The new restrictions thus did not constitute a change of regime but rather a further step in the consolidation of single-party corporatist rule. There can be little doubt, though, that single-party rule was justified by economic objectives and performance.

In sum, the hypothesized link between the deepening phase of ISI and authoritarianism is not convincing. A more plausible explanation of bureaucratic authoritarianism combines increased labor and populist political mobilization with inflationary pressures and a general loss of economic confidence. These conditions weaken middle-class and business support for democratic institutions. In such settings militaries intervene primarily to restore order, but they have generally used their new-found authoritarian powers to pursue economic objectives by controlling demands from labor and the left.

Similar settings provided the context for authoritarian political changes in Korea and Singapore. Nonetheless, for both opposition and government, the political underpinnings of export-led growth were explicitly at issue both before and after the consolidation of authoritarian rule. The dependence of export-led growth on the labor regime also shaped the political preferences of business and thus contributed to an authoritarian equilibrium. Cross-class alliances linking organized labor with portions of the private sector have been wholly absent in the East Asian NICs, limiting the base of support for democratic politics.

AUTHORITARIANISM, DEMOCRACY, AND ECONOMIC GROWTH

This discussion has focused on self-conscious links between political institutions and economic strategy: whether political and economic elites change or maintain institutions with the explicit objective of realizing economic aims. The claim may also be made in a weaker, functional form. Are authoritarian institutions functional for economic growth, even if their original determinants are not primarily economic?[17]

One way of linking political institutions to economic performance is to examine how institutions reconcile individual and collective rationality. A central tenet of the theory of collective action states that groups will organize not to advance collective welfare but to guarantee a disproportionate share of societal income for themselves. Decision making that is responsive to particularistic group interests can lead to outcomes that are suboptimal for society as a whole.[18] Among the policy reforms that might be modeled as collective-action problems are stabilization, devaluation, trade liberalization, the opening to foreign direct investment,

17. The following draws on Stephan Haggard and Chung-in Moon, "Institutions and Economic Growth: Theory and a Korean Case Study," *World Politics* 42 (January 1990): 210–37.
18. Mancur Olson, *The Rise and Decline of Nations* (New Haven: Yale University Press, 1982); Robert Bates, *Markets and States in Tropical Africa: The Political Bases of Agricultural Policies* (Berkeley: University of California Press, 1981).

the rationalization of fiscal incentives, tax reform, financial-market reform, and shifts in the composition of government spending. In various combinations such policy reforms were central to export-led growth and to certain phases of ISI in Brazil and Mexico as well.

Institutions can overcome these collective-action dilemmas by restraining the self-interested behavior of groups through sanctions; collective-action problems can be resolved by command. Since authoritarian political arrangements give political elites autonomy from distributionist pressures, they increase the government's ability to extract resources, provide public goods, and impose the short-term costs associated with efficient economic adjustment. Weak legislatures that limit the representative role of parties, the corporatist organization of interest groups, and recourse to coercion in the face of resistance should all expand governments' freedom to maneuver on economic policy.

As we have already made this argument empirically in the country studies, I review the evidence only briefly. Korea provides a particularly stark contrast between performance under democratic and under non-democratic rule. The governments of Syngman Rhee and Chang Myon were completely unable to formulate and implement clear development priorities. The military instituted wide-ranging reforms of the bureaucracy and of state-society relations, permitting a more coherent economic policy. Crucial economic reforms were launched under nominally democratic auspices in 1964 and 1965, but Park retained emergency powers and the opposition was disadvantaged in ways that suggest a far from fully democratic system. Singapore also shows stark contrasts in economic performance between the intense party conflict in the late 1950s and the period following the consolidation of PAP power when a coherent economic strategy emerged.

Taiwan appears to present the clearest case of the capacities of authoritarian regimes, particularly in the sweeping land reform of the early 1950s. Taiwan also raises a puzzle, though, since the KMT had been authoritarian and ineffective on the mainland; I return to this problem below. Finally, Hong Kong's political institutions show surprising similarities to those of the other East Asian countries. The granting of complete power to the financial secretary and the limits on effective representation foreclosed the opportunities for rent seeking and redistributive politics. Laissez-faire and an administrative state were by no means in conflict.

Brazil and Mexico at different points also provide supporting evidence for this institutionalist argument. The PRI's ability to weather the 1954 devaluation and to maintain a stable macroeconomic policy through the late 1960s might be attributed to the peculiar political capacities of the party. Since policy becomes much more incoherent thereafter, Mexico raises a puzzle similar to Taiwan: Why do similar regimes perform so differently at different points in their history? The wide-ranging economic reforms that followed the military coup in 1964 in Brazil also seem to confirm the contention that authoritarianism permits political leaders a wide leeway, though, as in Mexico, the Brazilian military became more responsive to demands from interest groups over time.

A series of important objections can be raised against this line of analysis, however. First, it is not clear why the policies that emanate from "strong" states should be optimal or efficient. As Douglass North has argued, the state can raise the costs of transacting and can specify and enforce property rights to capture the resulting gains for itself.[19] Indeed, authoritarian states should be even more effective than democratic ones in this predatory behavior. An institutional argument focuses attention on the capacity to formulate and implement policy; it must be coupled to an argument about why politicians have an incentive to promote economic efficiency. For this reason I have placed particular weight on external shocks in explaining policy change. In Korea and Taiwan economic policy regimes embodying a variety of growth-inhibiting distortions were reformed in a quest to alleviate pressing balance-of-payments problems and increase national autonomy.

A second problem concerns whether the authoritarian-democratic distinction is adequate to capture the most salient institutional variations across countries. One reason why the cross-national evidence on the relationship between regime type and economic performance is weak and contradictory is that the "authoritarian" category is so diverse.[20] The authoritarian label covers not only technocratic autocracies but also patrimonial states such as Zaire and Haiti, which have proved incapable of pursuing any coherent policy at all. Focusing on the East Asian

19. Douglass C. North, "Government and the Cost of Exchange in History," *Journal of Economic History* 44 (June 1984): 260; North, *Structure and Change in Economic History* (New York: Norton, 1981); Robert H. Bates, "Contra Contractarianism: Some Reflections on the New Institutionalism," *Politics and Society* 16 (September 1988): 387–401.

20. Conflicting evidence on the relationship between regime type and economic performance can be found in Thomas E. Skidmore, "The Politics of Economic Stabilization in Postwar Latin America," in James M. Malloy, ed., *Authoritarianism and Corporatism in Latin America* (Pittsburgh: University of Pittsburgh Press, 1977); John Sheahan, "Market-Oriented Economic Policies and Political Repression in Latin America," *Economic Development and Cultural Change* 28 (January 1980): 267–91; Robert Marsh, "Does Democracy Hinder Economic Development in the Latecomer Developing Nations?" *Comparative Social Research* 2 (1979): 215–49; William G. Dick, "Authoritarian versus Nonauthoritarian Approaches to Economic Development," *Journal of Political Economy* 82, 4 (1974): 817–27; Erich Weede, "The Impact of Democracy on Economic Growth: Some Evidence of Cross-national Analysis," *Kyklos* 36, 1 (1983): 21–40; Karen Remmer, "The Politics of Stabilization: IMF Standby Programs in Latin America, 1954–1984," *Comparative Politics* 19 (October 1986): 1–25; Stephan Haggard and Robert Kaufman, "The Politics of Stabilization and Structural Adjustment," in Jeffrey Sachs, ed., *Developing Country Debt and Economic Performance*, vol. 1: *The International Financial System* (Chicago: University of Chicago Press, 1989).

success cases, it could be argued, introduces a serious selection bias and thus limits the power of any generalizations concerning regime type.

One way to circumvent this problem is to go beyond regime type to other institutional factors that have affected the NICs' performance and could thus differentiate "strong" from "weak" authoritarian regimes. I have attempted to show how other institutional features of the state, including the organization of interest groups, the centralization of decision-making authority, and the instruments available to government officials, also affected ability to formulate and implement coherent policy. Yet as the case studies have also shown, many of these institutional characteristics were themselves a by-product of the consolidation of authoritarian political power. Thus while there are good reasons to disaggregate the state, disaggregation does not reduce the analytic utility of beginning with the authoritarian-democratic distinction.

It could be argued that this distinction, though useful for broad cross-national comparisons, cannot explain variations in state capacity across issue areas or vis-à-vis different social groups within the same country.[21] In particular, if the state is "autonomous" only from the working class, peasants, or marginal groups, we would have little way of differentiating an institutionalist perspective from societal theories of public policy. Policy could be parsimoniously explained by the preferences of the dominant coalition.[22] A critical test of the institutionalist perspective is whether state structures can insulate political elites from the demands of the powerful. This is what happened in some crucial reform episodes, including the transition to export-led growth in Korea, Taiwan, and Singapore. Many "reforms," such as those pursued by the Brazilian military after 1964, appear to have benefited the politically powerful at the expense of the weak. Yet this distributional outcome is not, in itself, sufficient to discount a statist approach to public policy change. The restructuring of incentives may occur despite business protest, even if the private sector, or portions of it, ultimately benefit.

BRINGING POLITICS BACK IN

A fourth objection to an institutionalist approach to economic policy concerns the relationship between politics and policy. One advantage of

21. See Herbert Kitschelt, "Four Theories of Public Policy Making and Fast Breeder Reactor Development," *International Organization* 40 (Winter 1986): 65–104.

22. This critique is made by Nora Hamilton, *The Limits of State Autonomy: Post-Revolutionary Mexico* (Princeton: Princeton University Press, 1982), and Michael Shafer, "States, Sectors, and Social Forces: Korea and Zambia Confront Economic Restructuring," *Comparative Politics,* forthcoming 1990. A critical reflection on the relationship between Marxism and rational choice models is Adam Przeworski, "Marxism and Rational Choice," *Politics and Society* 10, 2 (1985): 125–53.

focusing on overall institutional arrangements is to emphasize recurrent patterns and relatively enduring constraints on policy making. This is also a weakness, though, since it can lead to an overemphasis on the state as organizational structure at the expense of government as a creature of political exigencies. Coalitional calculations clearly constrain authoritarian leaders. As I showed in Chapter 6, the East Asian NICs were constrained by domestic politics to a much greater extent in the 1980s than they had been in the 1950s and 1960s, even before transitions to democratic rule. State elites in both Brazil and Mexico also faced difficult political calculations in the 1970s, despite authoritarian or semiauthoritarian political structures. Why?

In the early stages of military rule new authoritarian governments exploit their coercive capabilities and the disorganization of the opposition to carry through an agenda of political and economic transformation, including the forging of new ruling coalitions. As politics is routinized, however, military governments necessarily strike compromises with existing social groups. Accommodations to societal pressures may be particularly generous in the late phases of authoritarian rule, as militaries seek to engineer political transitions to a more open politics while maintaining control over the process. This pattern is clearest in Brazil.

If authoritarianism contributed to economic growth in the NICs, will the transition to democracy necessarily result in a worsening of economic performance? The question is no longer of merely academic interest. At the start of the 1990s, all of the NICs except Singapore were moving in a more liberal and democratic direction. Korea and Brazil have both formally returned to democratic rule. Taiwan and Mexico face somewhat greater difficulties in transforming dominant parties that have become closely intertwined with the state, but politics has been substantially liberalized in both countries. The preparation for the transfer of Hong Kong to China in 1997 unleashed a wave of new political activity, particularly following the crushing of the democracy movement in China in 1989.

It is premature to judge the performance of the newly democratic NICs, but history and theory both suggest that democratization will place new constraints on economic policy. There are at least three reasons.[23] First, political transitions typically reflect an increased level of political mobilization and conflict; it is usually because such conflict cannot be overcome through repression that authoritarian regimes give way to constitutional ones. Because political mobilization generally in-

---

23. The following draws on Stephan Haggard and Robert Kaufman, "Economic Adjustment in New Democracies," in Joan Nelson, ed., *Fragile Coalitions: The Politics of Economic Adjustment* (New Brunswick, N.J.: Transaction, 1989), pp. 59–60.

creases in the late phases of authoritarian rule, new democratic leaders confront previously repressed demands and strong pressures to reward supporters and incoming groups. Particularly where development has been highly inequitable, as in Brazil, or repressive, as in Korea, social expectations will be high.

Pressures from below are coupled with tenure insecurity within the new leadership. In the immediate posttransition period the possibility often exists that authoritarian political forces will reenter politics. Not only will economic policy choices have coalitional consequences, therefore; they may also affect the very survival of the new regime. These uncertainties shorten the time horizons over which politicians calculate the costs of policy choice.

Finally, democratization is likely to involve substantial turnover in technical personnel and changes in decision-making institutions. With increased social demands, the uncertainties facing new political leaders, and the technocrats' own interest in supporting the democratic experiment, incoming economic policy teams are more likely to pursue programs that meet expectations and reduce social conflict in the short run.

Like authoritarian regimes, however, the new democracies exhibit wide variation. Two factors can be expected to affect economic policy: the nature of the transition, and the degree of continuity between the old order and the new. Of the NICs, Brazil clearly had the greatest difficulty sustaining coherent economic policies during the transition, even though many of its problems were clearly inherited. Brazil's transition in the mid-1980s involved substantial popular mobilization, and the José Sarney government sought to appease a broad array of newly mobilized social forces through expansionist policies. This political strategy contributed to the breakdown of several heterodox stabilization efforts, pushing Brazil to near-hyperinflation in 1989. One reason that Mexican economic policy began to lose coherence in the 1970s was the PRI's effort to respond to a variety of new political challenges brought on by its own liberalizing measures. Yet in contrast to Brazil, the government in Mexico retained a substantial array of political instruments of control and was capable of imposing relatively orthodox economic policies and liberalizing reforms.

As in Brazil, Korea's transition also involved substantial political mobilization. In 1988 and 1989 business faced unprecedented pressures from organized labor, and the executive confronted a rebellious legislature. Yet the conservative government also showed important continuities with the past, particularly in the strong role of the bureaucracy in formulating economic policy. Though the KMT faces new economic claimants, it operates in a less polarized political setting than does the ruling party in Korea; like the PRI in Mexico, moreover, it continues to hold strong political cards. In both cases economic performance remained strong, and thus for economic as well as political reasons neither is likely to undergo marked shifts in policy under democratic auspices.

A look beyond the NICs suggests there are no *unique* institutional solutions for reducing the political constraints on economic policy. Authoritarian rule may have facilitated reform in the past, but a variety of institutions may be functionally equivalent in their ability to induce restraint from competing social groups. The literature on Western European corporatism suggests that peak associations with a secure place in the political process and clear access to decision making can guarantee mutual restraint and efficient decision making in a democratic setting.[24] Democratic corporatist structures can mitigate the collective-action dilemmas that characterize state-labor and labor-management relations by institutionalizing bargaining and changing the rate at which labor discounts future advantages from sustained cooperation.[25]

Features of a more routinized democratic politics may also alleviate some of the pressures that are likely to operate during democratic transitions.[26] Electoral cycles are less likely to be characterized by extensive mobilization, and conflicts are less likely to be posed in stark, zero-sum terms. Political leaders will of course be concerned with public support, but they will not be subject to fundamental uncertainties regarding their tenure. Since time horizons will be longer, political leaders can capitalize on "honeymoon" periods to undertake reform initiatives with short-term costs that can be expected to yield longer-term gains. Finally, there is likely to be greater continuity in fundamental decision-making processes.

Smoothly functioning democratic structures cannot be simply willed into existence. The very political weakness and the history of working-class exclusion in the NICs are important impediments to democratic development. Yet given the emphasis the export-led growth model places on labor and human capital, and the need in Latin America for a new social consensus on economic priorities, the very existence and economic success of social democratic models holds out at least the promise of an efficient yet more humane growth path.

---

24. Peter Katzenstein, *Small States in World Markets: Industrial Policy in Europe* (Ithaca: Cornell University Press, 1985).

25. Peter Lange, "Unions, Workers, and Wage Regulation: The Rational Bases of Consent," in John H. Goldthorpe, ed., *Order and Conflict in Contemporary Capitalism* (Oxford: Clarendon Press, 1984).

26. The following draws on Haggard and Kaufman, "Economic Adjustment in New Democracies," p. 60.

PATHWAYS FROM THE PERIPHERY

It is now possible to locate the institutional argument of this chapter within a larger explanatory framework. The most important debate in development studies over the last two decades has concerned the appropriateness of market-oriented policies for solving the problems of backwardness. The four East Asian NICs are frequently contrasted with the large Latin American NICs as proof of the benefits of liberalization. Their experience raises two questions. It is clear the East Asian NICs are more outward-oriented than their Latin American counterparts, but to what extent have they been liberal? I have argued that Korea, Taiwan, and Singapore all combined elements of the market with strong state guidance, though in different mixes. State institutions played a critical role in easing entry into international markets by providing information, support, and guidance. Hong Kong succeeded through laissez-faire, but only because of peculiar circumstances, among them the influx of entrepreneurial capital from China and the existence of private commercial and financial groups that performed functions similar to the state in the other NICs.

The second question is more central to this book's purposes: Why do countries adopt the particular development strategies they do? Is it possible for an aggressive, export-oriented strategy to be replicated elsewhere? More generally, under what conditions are governments likely to undertake fundamental reforms in their development strategies?

Basic changes in development orientation are likely to be triggered by external pressures that affect the entire range of a country's economic activities. The origins of industrialization in Brazil and Mexico can be traced to the late nineteenth century, but the adoption of import-substituting policies was driven by external constraints, particularly depression and war. Given the opportunities provided by size, these decisions were reinforced by changes in the terms of trade and periodic balance-of-payments crises—crises that were partly attributable to ISI itself.

In Korea and Taiwan import substitution was a response to constraints similar to, if not more binding than, those in Latin America. In neither case did ISI last longer than ten years, however. The reason for this relatively short duration must also be sought in international political and economic relationships. American aid financed ISI; its threatened withdrawal made ISI less plausible. International shocks also played an important role in the development trajectories of the city-states. Singapore's outward-oriented strategy followed its breakup with Malaya and the withdrawal of British military bases. Even laissez-faire Hong Kong supports the generalization: policy did not change following the United Nations embargo of China, but manufacturers, many transplanted from the mainland, were forced to find new markets abroad.

A second set of arguments about policy choice concerns the role of societal coalitions. Once a particular development route was "chosen," it acquired a domestic political logic of its own. Import-substituting policies created new political forces in Brazil and Mexico. The continuing pursuit of ISI broadened the array of interests tied to the import-substituting process, creating constraints on the freedom of state maneuver. The basic premises of ISI came under serious scrutiny only after a new round of external shocks associated with the debt crisis of the early 1980s.

The transition to export-led growth also spawned new firms, but they were firms with strong ties to international markets. East Asian governments faced new international pressures in the 1970s from protection, slowed growth in advanced-country markets, and the entry of new competitors, but their response was to upgrade and diversify rather than to withdraw. Even in Korea, where the questioning of export-led growth went farthest, exports continued to play a central role in the economy.

Instrumental coalitional arguments focus on the manifest political influence of key social groups and are useful in explaining the state's freedom of maneuver. Just as the emergence of import-substituting and export-oriented firms constrained state action, so the relative decline or weakness of other groups created opportunities for state initiative. In all of the NICs the weakening of agricultural elites provided opportunities to pursue an industrializing project. In the East Asian cases the weakness of organized labor and the absence of leftist and populist political parties resulted in a degree of policy freedom not found in Latin America. These factors contributed to the ability to launch export-oriented policies.

Such arguments have a fundamental limitation, though. By relying solely on the configuration of social groups to explain state action, they tend to ignore or downplay the independent interests and organizational capabilities of state elites. Of course, no state, not even the most highly organized and penetrating one, can escape constraints stemming from basic resource endowment, level of development, and performance of the economy; to think of state autonomy as the total absence of constraint would be nonsensical. But it is equally important not to lose sight of the organizational bases of political power. Political elites sit astride coercive state machineries. Where states control the channels of access to decision making, are coherently organized to assess information and make decisions, and have the instruments available to implement those decisions, political elites become independent actors.

Because state officials manage the crucial nexus between the domestic

269

and the international political economies, they are naturally responsive to external pressures, particularly those operating through the balance of payments. Yet the response to shocks depends on the political strategies of politicians, domestic institutional arrangements, and available economic ideas. In East Asia insulated, developmentalist states forged new alliances with business around an aggressive strategy of exports. Rather than policy initiatives reflecting coalitional interests, policy created new coalitional configurations—and even restructured society through changes in basic incentives to different lines of economic activity. Such initiatives were not limited to the export-oriented cases. The early stages of both primary and secondary ISI in the Latin American countries also reflected political strategies and institutional capabilities of states that were, by the standards of developing countries, relatively advanced.

Despite the tremendous growth of economic interdependence, states remain the central actors shaping the international political economy. They do so not simply through diplomacy and international agreements—the classical province of international relations theory—but through the control they exercise over the linkages between the international and domestic economies. Interdependence has a social and a political foundation. Yet states do not respond uniformly to the challenges they face. External pressures, even the most powerfully constraining ones, are filtered through the prism of domestic political life. The challenge for the developing world now is to find modes of integration with the world economy that exploit the gains from interdependence but do not violate the domestic quest for political freedom and equity.

Index

Taiwan Relations Act, 139
Triple alliance, 17, 22, 151, 220, 257. *See
also* Dependency theory

United Nations Economic Commission
on Latin America (ECLA), 162, 177.
See also Ideas, role in policy
United States Agency for International
Development (AID), 68, 69, 70, 92,
206
United States policy advice, 98–99

and Brazil, 167, 174
and Korea, 68–71, 98
and Mexico, 168
and Taiwan, 84–88, 92–93, 98

Vargas, Getúlio, 165–67, 171–74, 248

Winsemius Report, 108–9
World Bank, 108, 177, 258
World-systems theory, 3, 206

Cornell Studies in Political Economy

EDITED BY PETER J. KATZENSTEIN

Library of Congress Cataloging-in-Publication Data

Haggard, Stephan.
  Pathways from the periphery: the politics of growth in the newly
industrializing countries / Stephan Haggard.
      p. cm.—(Cornell studies in political economy)
    ISBN 0-8014-2499-2 (alk. paper)
    ISBN 0-8014-9750-7 (pbk.: alk. paper)
    1. Developing countries—Economic policy. 2. Developing countries—
Industries. 3. Economic development. I. Title.
II. Series.
HC59.7.H275 1990
338.9′009172′4—dc20   90-32300